Text Book Of

HYDRAULICS AND PNEUMATICS

(Subject Code 17522)

For
Semester - V
Third Year Diploma Course in Automobile Engineering Group

As Per MSBTE's 'G' Scheme Syllabus

C. P. Murgudkar

B.E. (Mech.) FIV, MIE, DBE, Master of Valuation,
Industrial / Project Consultant
Kolhapur

N3220

Hydraulics and Pneumatics　　　　　　　　　　　　　　　　**ISBN 978-93-5164-760-7**

First Edition : July 2015
© : Author

The text of this publication, or any part thereof, should not be reproduced or transmitted in any form or stored in any computer storage system or device for distribution including photocopy, recording, taping or information retrieval system or reproduced on any disc, tape, perforated media or other information storage device etc., without the written permission of Author with whom the rights are reserved. Breach of this condition is liable for legal action.

Every effort has been made to avoid errors or omissions in this publication. In spite of this, errors may have crept in. Any mistake, error or discrepancy so noted and shall be brought to our notice shall be taken care of in the next edition. It is notified that neither the publisher nor the author or seller shall be responsible for any damage or loss of action to any one, of any kind, in any manner, therefrom.

Published By :　　　　　　　　　　　　　　　　　　　　　　　　　**Printed By :**
NIRALI PRAKASHAN　　　　　　　　　　　　　　　　　　　**Repro Knowledgecast Limited**
Abhyudaya Pragati, 1312, Shivaji Nagar　　　　　　　　　　　　　　　　　　　　　　　　　**Thane**
Off J.M. Road, PUNE – 411005
Tel - (020) 25512336/37/39, Fax - (020) 25511379
Email : niralipune@pragationline.com

✦ DISTRIBUTION CENTRES

PUNE
Nirali Prakashan : 119, Budhwar Peth, Jogeshwari Mandir Lane, Pune 411002, Maharashtra
Tel : (020) 2445 2044, 66022708, Fax : (020) 2445 1538
Email : bookorder@pragationline.com, niralilocal@pragationline.com

Nirali Prakashan : S. No. 28/27, Dhyari, Near Pari Company, Pune 411041
Tel : (020) 24690204 Fax : (020) 24690316
Email : dhyari@pragationline.com, bookorder@pragationline.com

MUMBAI
Nirali Prakashan : 385, S.V.P. Road, Rasdhara Co-op. Hsg. Society Ltd.,
Girgaum, Mumbai 400004, Maharashtra
Tel : (022) 2385 6339 / 2386 9976, Fax : (022) 2386 9976
Email : niralimumbai@pragationline.com

✦ DISTRIBUTION BRANCHES

JALGAON
Nirali Prakashan : 34, V. V. Golani Market, Navi Peth, Jalgaon 425001,
Maharashtra, Tel : (0257) 222 0395, Mob : 94234 91860

KOLHAPUR
Nirali Prakashan : New Mahadvar Road, Kedar Plaza, 1st Floor Opp. IDBI Bank
Kolhapur 416 012, Maharashtra. Mob : 9850046155

NAGPUR
Pratibha Book Distributors : Above Maratha Mandir, Shop No. 3, First Floor,
Rani Jhanshi Square, Sitabuldi, Nagpur 440012, Maharashtra
Tel : (0712) 254 7129

DELHI
Nirali Prakashan : 4593/21, Basement, Aggarwal Lane 15, Ansari Road, Daryaganj
Near Times of India Building, New Delhi 110002
Mob : 08505972553

BENGALURU
Pragati Book House : House No. 1, Sanjeevappa Lane, Avenue Road Cross,
Opp. Rice Church, Bengaluru – 560002.
Tel : (080) 64513344, 64513355,Mob : 9880582331, 9845021552
Email:bharatsavla@yahoo.com

CHENNAI
Pragati Books : 9/1, Montieth Road, Behind Taas Mahal, Egmore,
Chennai 600008 Tamil Nadu, Tel : (044) 6518 3535,
Mob : 94440 01782 / 98450 21552 / 98805 82331,
Email : bharatsavla@yahoo.com

niralipune@pragationline.com | www.pragationline.com
Also find us on www.facebook.com/niralibooks

Dedication ...

Dedicated
    To
        My Beloved Parents

C. P. Murgudkar

Preface ...

This book is written for 5th Semester (3rd Year) Diploma Students studying in Automobile Engineering. The topics in the book cover entire syllabus of the subject Hydraulics and Pneumatics prescribed by MSBTE - G Scheme.

In the main, then, this book deals with the hydraulic and pneumatic systems which are widely used in automobiles as well as in manufacturing and automobile servicing stations. An Automobile Diploma Engineers are required to work with these systems, its components and trouble shooting.

The first 3 topics basically deal with 'Fluid Mechanics' and remaining 3 topics are concerning hydraulics and pneumatics. As far as Hydraulic and Pneumatic Circuits are concerned, the Normal Position and Actuated Position of circuit as well as valves are shown in this book.

Great care has been taken to avoid errors in calculations and illustrated figures. However, if reader finds any error in this book, the suggestions/ changes/corrections from those readers are always welcome.

While writing this book, the author have referred good number of literature and titles written on Hydraulics and Pneumatics of renowned authors and publications. The author of this book takes this opportunity to acknowledge the direct and indirect contribution in shaping this book.

The author thanks Shri. Jigneshbhai Furia, Publisher of Nirali Prakashan and Marketing Staff and Other Staff of Nirali Prakashan especially Mr. Akbar Shaikh, Mr. Kiran Velankar and Ms. Chaitali Takle for making completion of this book.

C. P. Murgudkar

Syllabus...

1. **Overview of Fluid Mechanics** [10 Hrs., 22 Marks]
   1.1 Fluid Fundamentals [08 Marks]
   - Classification of Fluid, Properties of Fluids like Specific Weight, Specific Gravity, Surface Tension, Capillarity, Viscosity. Specifications of Hydraulic Oil.
   - Pascal's law.
   - Types of fluid flow- Steady, Unsteady, Rotational, Irrotational, Laminar, Turbulent, One, Two and Three Dimensional Flow, Uniform and Non-Uniform Flow. (Definitions and Applications only), Pressure Measurement.
   - Concept of Atmospheric Pressure, Gauge Pressure, Vacuum Pressure, Absolute Pressure.
   - Pressure Gauges - Piezometer Tube, Simple and Differential Manometer, Micro – Manometer. (Theoretical Treatment only, No Analytical treatment / Problems on Manometers), Bourdon Tube Pressure Gauge.

   1.2 Hydrodynamics [14 Marks]
   - Basic Principles of Fluid Flow
   - Law of Continuity and its applications.
   - Energy possessed by the Liquid in Motion.
   - Bernoulli's Theorem and its applications such as Venturimeter, Orificemeter and Pitot Tube. (Analytical treatment with derivation for measurement of discharge is expected) Hydraulic coefficients.
   - Concept of Vena Contracta.
   - Coefficient of Contraction, Coefficient of velocity, Coefficient of discharge, Coefficient of resistance, Relation between the hydraulic coefficients.

2. **Hydraulic Devices** [08 Hrs., 16 Marks]
   2.1 Centrifugal Pumps. [08 Marks]
   - Types, Construction and Working of Centrifugal Pump.
   - Types of Casing.
   - Need of priming.
   - Heads, Losses and Efficiencies of Centrifugal Pump. (No Analytical Treatment.)
   - Net positive suction head
   - Fault findings and remedies.
   - Pump selection.

   2.2 Reciprocating Pumps [08 Marks]
   - Construction and Working of Single and Double Acting Reciprocating pump.
   - Positive and Negative slip.
   - Air vessels - their functions and advantages.
   - Power and Efficiencies of Reciprocation Pump. (No Analytical Treatment)
   - Reasons of Cavitations and Separation.
   - Comparison between Reciprocating and Centrifugal Pump.

3. **Miscellaneous Fluid Machines** [06 Hrs., 12 Marks]
   3.1 Simple Hydraulic Devices
   - Working Principles, Construction and Applications of Hydraulic Jack, Hydraulic Ram, Hydraulic Lift, Hydraulic Press.

   3.2 Other Pumping Devices
   - Gear Pumps used in Hydraulic Circuits, Vane Type, Swash Plate Type Pump. Comparison of above Pumps for various characteristics and their applications.

4. **Basic Components of Hydraulic and Pneumatic Systems** [08 Hrs., 18 Marks]
   4.1 Hydraulic and Pneumatic Actuators. [10 Marks]
   - Hydraulic Actuators - Hydraulic cylinders (Single, Double Acting and Telescopic) – Construction and Working, Hydraulic Motors (Gear and Piston Type) – Construction and Working.
   - Pneumatic Actuators - Pneumatic Cylinders (Single and Double Acting) - Construction and Working, Air motors (Gear and Piston Type) - Construction and Working.

   4.2 Valves for Hydraulic and Pneumatic Systems [08 Marks]
   - Classifications of Valves, Poppet, Ball, Needle, Throttle, Pressure Control Directional Control, Sequencing, Synchronizing, Rotary Spool, Sliding Spool Two Position, Multi position. Non-return valves. Proportionating valve.
   - Construction and Operation of above valves.

5. **Accessories of Hydraulic and Pneumatic Systems** [06 Hrs., 12 Marks]
   5.1 Filters
   - Hydraulic Filters and Strainers – Full Flow and Proportional Types, Function and Working, Difference Between Filters and Strainers.
   - Pneumatic Filters – Screen type and Mechanical type, Function and Working, FRL Unit

   5.2 Hoses and Connectors for Hydraulic and Pneumatic Systems - Types, Construction and Applications.

   5.3 Seals and Gaskets for Hydraulic and Pneumatic Systems - Types, Function, Construction, Commonly used Seals and Gasket Materials.

6. **Hydraulic and Pneumatic Circuits** [10 Hrs., 20 Marks]
   6.1 Hydraulic Circuits [10 Marks]
   - Hydraulic Symbols
   - Meter in, Meter Out. Bleed off, Sequencing.
   - Introduction to Electro-Hydraulics – Concept, Principles and Applications
   - Applications of Hydraulic Circuits – Hydraulic Power Steering, Hydraulic Brakes, Milling Machine, Hydraulic Press

   6.2 Simple Pneumatic Circuits [10 Marks]
   - Pneumatic Symbols
   - Speed Control Circuit (Meter in, Meter out), Sequencing.
   - Applications of Pneumatic Circuits – Air Brake, Low Cost Automation in Industries, Pneumatic Power Tools (Drill, Hammer and Grinder).
   - Comparison of Hydraulic and Pneumatic Circuits.

Contents...

1. **Overview of Fluid Mechanics** — 1.1 – 1.42

2. **Hydrodynamics** — 2.1 – 2.20

3. **Hydraulic Devices** — 3.1 – 3.28

4. **Simple Hydraulic Devices** — 4.1 – 4.28

5. **Basic Components of Hydraulic and Pneumatic Systems** — 5.1 – 5.66

6. **Accessories of Hydraulic and Pneumatic Systems** — 6.1 – 6.22

7. **Hydro-Pneumatic Systems and Circuits** — 7.1 – 7.40

    Appendix A — A.1 – A.4

    Appendix B — B.1 – B.10

    Appendix C — C.1 – C.4

    MSBTE Question Paper Solutions — P.1 – P.5

Chapter 1

OVERVIEW OF FLUID MECHANICS

Weightage of Marks = 08, Teaching Hours = 05

Learning Objectives
1. Know the types of Fluids used and their Properties.
2. Understand types of Fluid Flows.
3. Know Fluid Pressure Measurement and Measuring Gauges.
4. Understand Principle used in hydrodynamics.

Contents

Fluid Fundamentals
- Classification of Fluid, Properties of Fluids like Specific Weight, Specific Gravity, Surface Tension, Capillarity, Viscosity. Specifications of Hydraulic Oil.
- Pascal's law.
- Types of Fluid Flow - Steady, Unsteady, Rotational, Irrotational, Laminar, Turbulent, One, Two and Three Dimensional Flow, Uniform and Non Uniform Flow. (Definitions and Applications only) Pressure Measurement.
- Concept of Atmospheric Pressure, Gauge Pressure, Vacuum Pressure, Absolute Pressure.
- Pressure Gauges - Piezometer Tube, Simple and Differential Manometer, Micro – Manometer. (Theoretical Treatment only, No Analytical treatment / Problems on Manometers.) Bourdon Tube Pressure Gauge.

1.0 INTRODUCTION

What is Fluid Mechanics?
- It is a branch of science that deals with the behaviour of fluids (either liquids or gases) at rest as well as in motion.
- When fluid is at rest i.e. when it is not moving e.g. when it is stored in tank, container, bottle, drum etc. then the study of fluid is called **'Fluid Statics'**.
- When fluid is in motion i.e. when it is moving e.g. when it is running through pipes, channels, rivers, canals etc. then that study of fluid in motion is called **'Fluid Kinematics'**. In this study, the forces on fluid are not considered.
- When fluid in motion is studied with various forces acting on it then that study is called **'Fluid Dynamics'** or **'Hydrodynamics'**.

1.1 OVERVIEW OF FLUID PROPERTIES AND CLASSIFICATION

Fluids are classified in three categories:

(a) **Liquids:** Oil, water etc. are liquids and liquids are incompressible (cannot be compressed).

(b) **Gases:** Hydrogen, oxygen, nitrogen etc. are gases and gases are compressible. When compressed their volume reduces.

(c) **Vapours:** When liquid is heated beyond particular value, the liquid starts converting into vapour. Vapours are compressible similar to gases.

Liquid withstands a slight amount of tension due to the molecular attraction between the particles which causes an apparent shear resistance between two adjacent layers.

Coefficient of expansion of liquids are small:
- No liquid can exist as 'liquid' at zero pressure.
- In fact all known liquids vaporize at various pressures above zero, depending on the temperature.
- In liquid there are dissolved gases. If pressure falls below certain value for that liquid then dissolved gases come out and form bubbles which create many problems.

1.1.1 Ideal and Real Fluids

Ideal fluid: A fluid which is incompressible and having no viscosity is called Ideal fluid. It is imaginary fluid. Because every fluid is having viscosity.

Real fluid: A fluid which possesses viscosity is called real fluid. All fluids are real fluids.

Some important properties of fluid:

To know fluid mechanics we have to start with the study of main and important properties of fluid.

1.1.2 Density (ρ)

This property is also known as Mass Density or Specific Mass. It is denoted by a letter ρ (Rho).

Definition of Density: *It is the ratio of the mass of fluid to its volume.*

So,
$$\rho = \frac{\text{Mass of fluid}}{\text{Volume of fluid}}$$

Measure of mass is in kg

Measure of volume is in cu. mt.

The density of water is 1000 kg/m^3 in SI system.

The density of mercury is 13000 kg/m^3 in SI system.

It may be noted that the density of mercury is more than water, so mercury cannot float on water. On the other hand, oil of density say 900 kg/m³ will floaton water, because its density is less than water.

1.1.3 Specific Gravity (S) [S-15]

This property is concerned with the above property i.e. Density. It is a comparison.

Definition of specific gravity: *It is defined as a ratio of density of fluid to density of standard fluid.*

So, Specific Gravity (S) = $\dfrac{\text{Density of fluid}}{\text{Density of standard fluid}}$

$(S) = \dfrac{\text{Density of fluid}}{\text{Density of water}}$

Specific gravity is a dimensionless quantity. It is just a number, because in numerator and denominator, we are taking densities (kg/m³).

Density of water = 1000 kg/m³

∴ $S = \dfrac{\text{Density of fluid}}{1000}$

1.1.4 Specific Weight (w) [W-14]

This property is also known as weight density.

Definition of specific weight: *It is a ratio between the weight of fluid to its volume.*

So, $w = \dfrac{\text{Weight of fluid}}{\text{Volume of fluid}}$

$= \dfrac{(\text{Mass of fluid}) \times (\text{Acceleration due to gravity})}{\text{Volume of fluid}}$

$= \left(\dfrac{\text{Mass of fluid}}{\text{Volume of fluid}}\right) \times \text{Acceleration due to gravity}$

$\boxed{w = \rho \times g}$ ... because Density $\rho = \dfrac{\text{Mass}}{\text{Volume}}$

It may be noted that the specific weight of water is ...

Sp. wt. of water = Density of water × g

$(w)_{water} = 1000 \times 9.81$ Newton / m³

1.1.5 Specific Volume

This property is also related to density of fluid (ρ).

Definition of specific volume: *It is the volume of fluid occupied by unit mass.*

So, Specific volume $= \dfrac{\text{Volume of fluid}}{\text{Mass of fluid}}$

$= \dfrac{1}{\frac{\text{Mass of fluid}}{\text{Volume of fluid}}}$

$= \dfrac{1}{\rho} \ldots \dfrac{\text{Mass}}{\text{Volume}} = \rho$

Hence specific volume is reciprocal of density, it is expressed in m^3/kg. This property is commonly applied to gases.

1.1.6 Viscosity [W-14, S-15]

It is also known as 'Dynamic viscosity'. (The word dynamic is arrived because this property is related to moving liquid or flowing liquid).

Definition of Viscosity: *It is defined as a property of a fluid which offers resistance to the movement of one layer of fluid over another adjacent layer of the fluid.*

Consider 2 layers of liquid:

Layer (A) is moving with velocity u.

Layer (B) is slightly faster. It is moving with velocity u + du. The distance between two layers is 'y'. The layer (A) causes shear stress over layer (B). This shear stress is proportional to the rate of change of velocity of layers; with respect to distance 'y' between the layers.

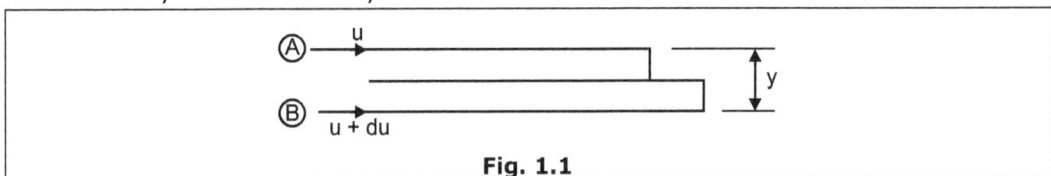

Fig. 1.1

So, Shear stress $\tau \propto \dfrac{du}{dy}$

∴ $\tau = \mu \dfrac{du}{dy}$

μ (mu) is called 'Constant of Proportionality' and is nothing but a 'Dynamic Viscosity' or simply 'Viscosity'.

- The viscosity of water is high.
- The viscosity of coconut oil is low.
- The practical significance of viscosity is that, how liquid flows on the surface. If liquid moves fastly then it is high viscosity fluid. If liquid moves slowly (as in case of oil) then liquid is having low viscosity.

- The viscosity is of most importance for printing ink. Before printing, the viscosity of printing ink needs to be checked very accurately. If viscosity of ink is not as per requirement then printing will not be proper.
- The unit of viscosity is $\dfrac{\text{Newton - second}}{\text{meter}^2} = \dfrac{\text{N-s}}{\text{m}^2}$

1.1.7 Kinematic Viscosity (ν)

It is defined as the ratio between the viscosity (also known as dynamic viscosity) and density of fluid. It is denoted by a letter 'ν' (nu).

So, Kinematic viscosity $= \dfrac{\text{Viscosity}}{\text{Density}}$

$$\nu = \dfrac{\mu}{\rho}$$

The unit of kinematic viscosity is m^2/sec.

1.1.8 Surface Tension (λ)

Definition of Surface Tension: *It is a tensile force acting on the surface of liquid in contact with air (or gas), such that this surface behaves like 'Elastic Membrane' under tension.*

- When water is in contact with air, on the water free surface, there is thin tensile film of water. This is surface tension.
- Due to surface tension only we can float ships on water.
- When rod or nail is kept on the water surface, the thin film (under tension) on the water surface is *punctured* and nail dips into the water.
- When shaving razor blade is kept gently on the water surface, it will float on water. This is due to surface tension. When we push the blade from top, it will dip into water, because the film is punctured.
- The SI unit of surface (denoted by letter 'λ' – lambda) tension is N/meter.
- The surface tension of water is 0.0728 N/mt.
- The surface tension of kerosene is 0.0277 N/mt.
- The surface tension of mercury is 0.5140 N/mt.

Now we will see:

1.1.9 Surface Tension of Liquid Droplet

The water falls from tap or pipe, we can see the 'droplet' formed in the shape of sphere. The surface tension plays a major role in forming the shape of sphere to droplet of water.

So let us calculate the surface tension on the outside surface of droplet. The droplet of water is full of water, hence called as 'Solid Droplet'.

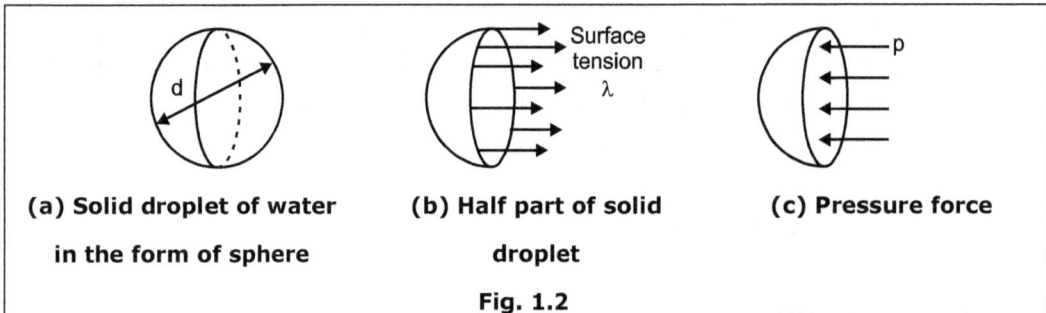

(a) Solid droplet of water in the form of sphere (b) Half part of solid droplet (c) Pressure force

Fig. 1.2

Let λ = Surface tension in N/mt
 p = Pressure intensity inside the droplet
 d = Diameter of droplet

- First of all cut the droplet in two halves.
- Let us find forces acting on half part.

    (a) Tensile force due to surface tension λ

$$F_1 = \lambda \times \text{circumference of sphere}$$
$$F_1 = \lambda \times \pi d$$

    (b) Pressure force on cross-sectional area of droplet. If p is pressure intensity then,

$$p = \frac{\text{Pressure force}}{\text{Cross-sectional area}}$$
$$p = \frac{F_2}{\frac{\pi}{4} d^2}$$

∴ $$F_2 = \frac{\pi}{4} d^2 \times p$$

- When solid droplet is fully filled and is stable then it is a state of equilibrium. Under this state,

$$F_1 = F_2$$

∴ $$\lambda \times \pi d = \frac{\pi}{4} d^2 \times p$$

∴ $$\boxed{\lambda = \frac{p \times d}{4}}$$

- From above equation it is clear that surface tension is directly proportional to diameter of droplet and pressure intensity inside the droplet.

1.1.10 Surface Tension on Liquid Jet

- When liquid flows out of nozzle, a jet is formed.

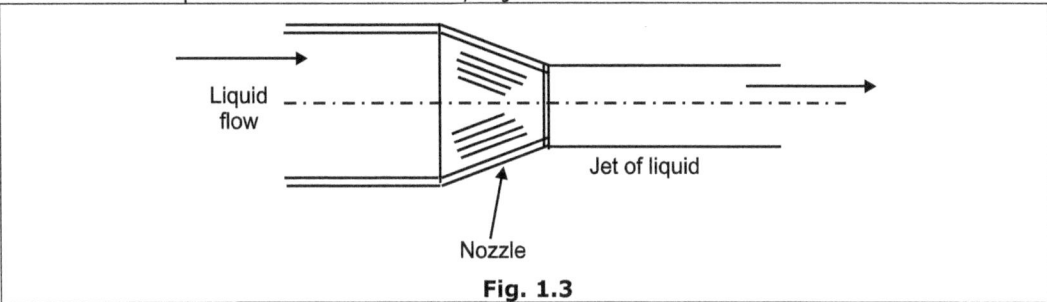

Fig. 1.3

- This jet is having shape of cylinder.
- The jet is full of liquid.

Consider a jet of diameter 'd' and length 'L'.

(a) Solid jet fully filled with water

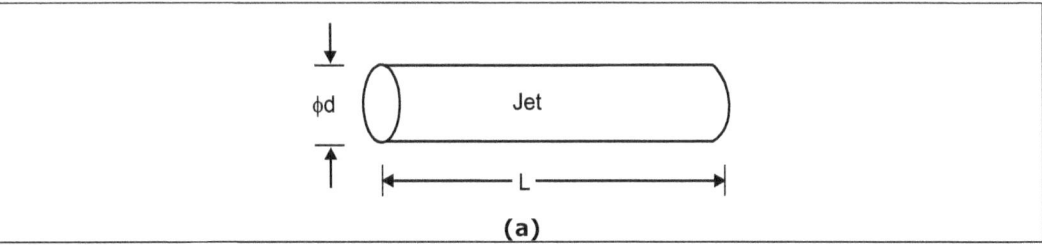

Let us cut the jet in two halves.

(b) Half part of jet on which λ is acting

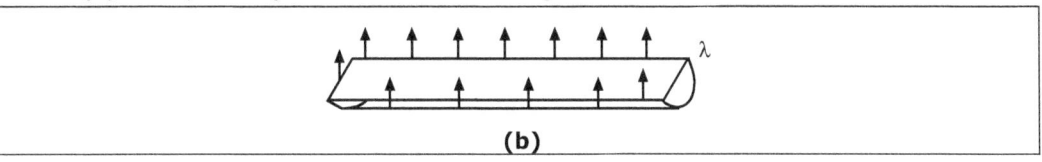

(c) Pressure intensity acting

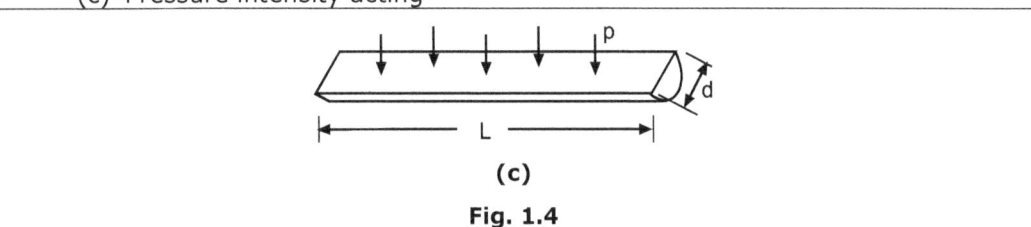

Fig. 1.4

- Let us find forces acting on half part (similar to spherical droplet).

    (a) Tensile force due to surface tension λ.

    $$F_1 = \lambda \times 2L$$

(b) Pressure force acting inside the jet.

$$p = \frac{\text{Pressure force}}{\text{Cross-sectional area}}$$

$$p = \frac{F_2}{L \times d}$$

∴ $F_2 = p \times L \times d$

- When jet is stable and fully filled, then it is a state of equilibrium.

Under this state,

$$F_1 = F_2$$

∴ $\lambda \times 2L = p \times L \times d$

∴ $$\boxed{\lambda = \frac{p \times d}{2}}$$

1.1.11 Surface Tension on Hollow Bubble

- Soap bubble is Hollow Bubble.
- When we destroy the bubble we can understand that there is only 'air' inside the bubble.
- Hence soap bubble is hollow from inside. It is filled with air.
- We can easily imagine that the soap bubble is formed due to heavy surface tension from outside and inside of bubble. Hence in soap bubble the surface tension is double.

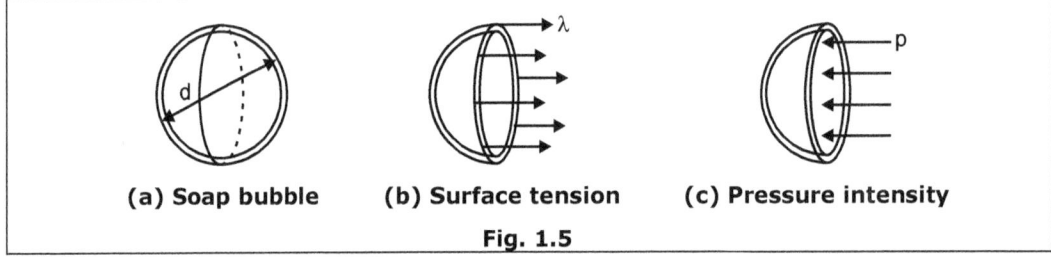

(a) Soap bubble   (b) Surface tension   (c) Pressure intensity

Fig. 1.5

- First of all cut the bubble in two halves.
- Let us find forces acting on half part.

   (a) **Tensile force:** Due to surface tension λ.

   $$F_1 = 2 \, (\lambda \times \text{Circumference})$$
   $$= 2\lambda \pi d$$

(b) Pressure force: On cross-sectional area of bubble, if p is the pressure intensity then

$$p = \frac{\text{Pressure force}}{\text{Cross-sectional area}}$$

$$p = \frac{F_2}{\frac{\pi}{4} d^2}$$

$$\therefore \quad F_2 = \frac{\pi}{4} d^2 p$$

- When bubble is stable, it is the state of equilibrium. Under this state,

$$F_1 = F_2$$

$$2\lambda \pi d = \frac{\pi}{4} d^2 p$$

$$\therefore \quad \boxed{\lambda = \frac{p \times d}{8}}$$

- Summary of surface tension values in above three cases:

Case	Tensile Force (F$_1$)	Pressure Force (F$_2$)	At Equilibrium	Value of λ (N/m)
Solid droplet	$\lambda \times \pi d$	$\frac{\pi}{4} d^2 p$	$F_1 = F_2$	$\lambda = \frac{p \times d}{4}$
Liquid jet	$\lambda \times 2L$	$L \times d \times p$	$F_1 = F_2$	$\lambda = \frac{p \times d}{2}$
Soap bubble	$2(\lambda \times \pi d)$	$\frac{\pi}{4} d^2 p$	$F_1 = F_2$	$\lambda = \frac{p \times d}{8}$

1.1.12 Capillarity

Let us first understand this property.

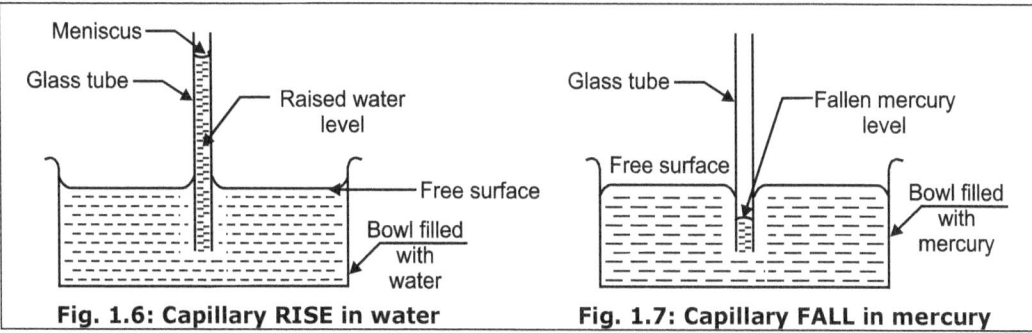

Fig. 1.6: Capillary RISE in water   Fig. 1.7: Capillary FALL in mercury

- Refer Fig. 1.6: When glass tube of small diameter (5 mm/4 mm or so) open at both ends is dipped into water or filled with water and inverted in water bowl then we can observe that, the water level in the tube stabilizes at higher level, than free surface level of water in bowl. This is 'RISE' of liquid level and this phenomenon is known as capillary rise and this property of water is known as capillarity.

- Refer Fig. 1.7: Similar small diameter tube open at both ends is filled with mercury (Hg) and inverted in mercury bowl, then we can observe that the level of mercury stabilizes at lower level than the free surface level of mercury in bowl. This is 'FALL' of liquid level and this phenomenon is known as 'Capillary Fall' and this property of mercury is known as 'capillarity'.
- The surface of liquid in capillary tube is known as 'Meniscus'.
- If tube diameter is 5 mm then capillary rise of water is 5.9 mm above the surface of water in bowl.
- If tube diameter is 5 mm then capillary fall of mercury is 1.9 mm below the surface of mercury in bowl.
- Let us calculate mathematical formula for capillary rise / fall.

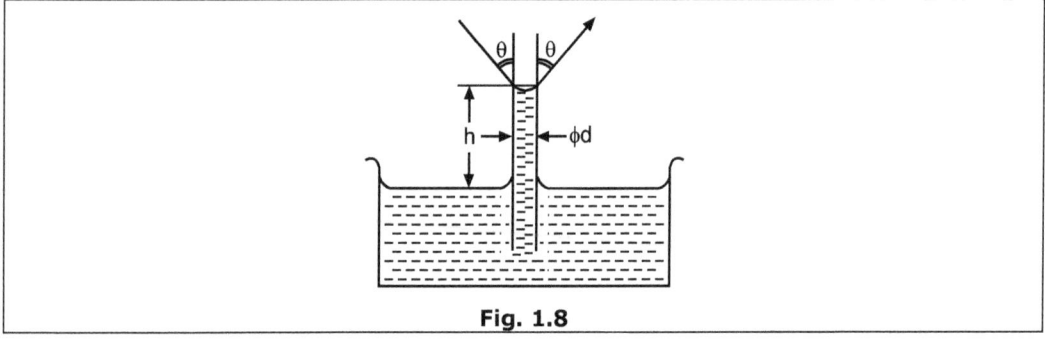

Fig. 1.8

If h is capillary rise or fall, then

$$h = \frac{4 \lambda \cos \theta}{\rho \times g \times d}$$

where,
λ = Surface tension
ρ = Density of liquid
g = Gravitational constant
d = Diameter of glass tube
θ = Angle of contact

- When liquid is water then θ = almost 0, therefore $\cos \theta$ = 1, hence there will be capillary RISE because 'h' works out positive.
- When liquid is mercury then θ = 128°, therefore $\cos \theta$ = – 0.615, hence there will be capillary FALL because 'h' works out negative.

1.1.13 Vapour Pressure

- **Definition:** It is a specific value of pressure for each liquid. It is the pressure at which liquid starts boiling (without heat) and vapour bubble of the liquid starts forming. This pressure is known as vapour pressure.
- The pressure of water at mean sea level is 10.3 mt of water. If we took this water and filled it in closed cylinder and if we reduce the pressure of water to 2.5 mt then water automatically starts boiling and vapour bubbles will start forming.
- These vapour bubbles are dangerous in case of reciprocating pump. Bubbles cause separation and cavitation in reciprocating pump.
- Vapour pressure for each liquid is different.

1.1.14 Compressibility [S-15]

- Compressibility of fluid is a measure of change in volume when pressure on the liquid increases or changes.

$$\text{Compressibility} = \frac{\text{Volumetric change}}{\text{Change in pressure}}$$

- Let us understand this property: (Refer Fig. 1.9)

  (a) Fluid is in cylinder which is under pressure P_1 and the volume of fluid is V_1.

  (b) Now, let us move the piston towards left [from (1) to (2)]. This movement will increase the pressure on fluid. And new increased pressure is say P_2.

  Due to this increase in pressure the volume of fluid will reduce. Let the reduced volume be V_2.

- Change in pressure = $dp = P_2 - P_1$
- Volumetric strain = $\dfrac{\text{Change in volume}}{\text{Original volume}}$

Let
$$dv = \text{Change in volume} = V_1 - V_2$$

$$\text{Volumetric strain} = \frac{dv}{V_1}$$

Hence
$$\boxed{\text{Compressibility} = \frac{dv/V_1}{dp}}$$

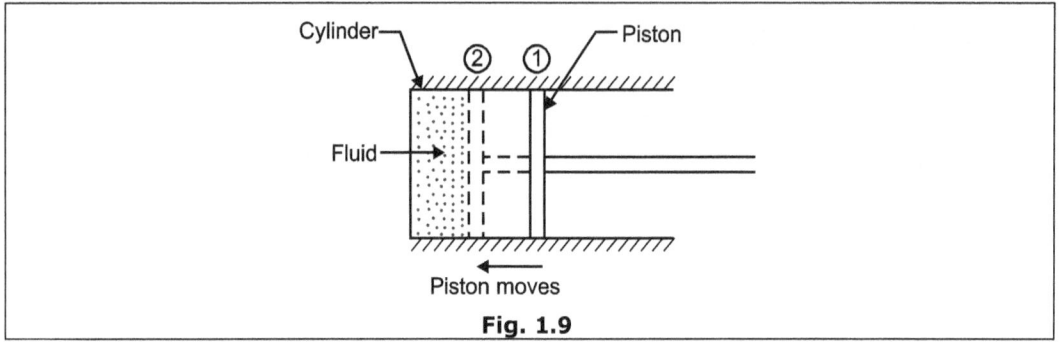

Fig. 1.9

1.1.15 Specifications and Standards of Hydraulic Oil

- In hydraulic system we are pressurising the fluid (i.e. oil) by pump. This oil conveys (carry) energy and produces required force at actuators to obtain useful mechanical work.

- In the beginning of hydraulic system development era, the design engineers used water as a medium. (In fact the word 'Hydraulic' means 'Water'). But water has following disadvantages:

  (a) It freezes at 0°C, hence cannot be used in low temperature zones.
  (b) It is corrosive.
  (c) Its lubrication properties are poor.
  (d) Water cannot be used at temperature higher than 100°C because it starts boiling and converting into steam.

- In view of these disadvantages, modern fluids were specifically developed to suit Hydraulic systems.

- A satisfactory hydraulic oil must have following properties:

  (i) **Good lubrication property:** In hydraulic system DC valve, actuators, pressure relief valves etc. are the components in which one surface moves/rotates with respect to other. The hydraulic fluid must separate and lubricate such surfaces, so that the life of components increases.

  (ii) **Good chemical stability:** The oil when pressurises, its temperature increases, when it moves in circuit its temperature further increases. Oil also is in constant contact with rubber seals, filter materials. In such instances, there is possibility of chemical reaction between oil and contact materials. This results in formation of sludges, carbon separation or precipitation. These contamination result into jamming of system and create major problems. So a good hydraulic oil must be chemically stable and must be least responsive to chemical reactions under heat.

(iii) **Non-corrosive:** A good hydraulic oil must be non-corrosive to metal surfaces in contact.

(iv) **High flash point:** Flash point is a temperature at which liquid catches fire automatically when heated. The flash point of good hydraulic oil must be as high as possible so that fire possibility is nullified.

(v) **System compatibility:** We have already notified the concept of compatibility while studying IC engines. Diesel engine is compatible to Diesel as a fuel only. If we use petrol in Diesel engine, the engine will not run. Similarly if major changes/modifications in the hydraulic system are done, then also the original oil must perform its functions well. It must be compatible.

(vi) **Minimum toxicity:** A good hydraulic oil must be minimum toxic to human beings working with them. Some fire resistant hydraulic oils are highly toxic which can cause occupational diseases.

(vii) **Good heat dissipation:** Heat dissipation means, discharging the heat and becoming cool. When fluid is moving/pressurising, its temperature increases. The good oil must have property to fast dissipation of heat to atmosphere or cooler. That clearly means that oil must have high thermal conductivity.

(viii) **Low foaming tendency:** When oil returns to receiver, it comes in contact with air above the liquid surface. The oil has tendency to absorb air or gas and which results in foam formation. A good hydraulic oil must release the air/gas very quickly so that it does not form foam.

(ix) **Fire resistant:** Hot oil can catch fire. A good oil must be fire resistant to avoid accidents.

(x) **Low coefficient of expansion:** A good hydraulic oil must have very low coefficient of expansion for minimum volume of oil required at operating temperature.

(xi) **Low specific gravity:** If the specific gravity of oil is low then overall weight of hydraulic system will be minimum.

(xii) **Cost and Availability:** The cost of oil must be affordable. And at the same time it must be available in bulk.

1.1.16 Hydraulic Fluids Available

(A) Petroleum Based Hydraulic Oils: Most widely used (similar to Engine/Gear oil).

(B) Water Based Hydraulic Fluids
  (a) Water-in-oil emulsion
  (b) Oil-in-water emulsion
  (c) Water + Glycol mix

(C) Synthetic Hydraulic Fluids: Phosphate Esters:

(A) Petroleum Based Hydraulic Oils:

These are thick oils (Maroon coloured/Chocolate coloured) similar to engine oils used in automobiles. These oils are most popular and used in major hydraulic circuits.

Special additives are added to these oil so that its foaming tendency reduces, its lubrication property improves and becomes user friendly.

Advantages of Petroleum based oils:
  (i) Good lubricating property.
  (ii) Good rust preventive.
  (iii) Good heat dissipation tendency.
  (iv) Easy to keep clean.
  (v) Available with ease.

Disadvantages of Petroleum based oils:
  (i) The oils are having tendency to ignite. So in hazardous places, these oils are having last choice.
  (ii) These oils make the ground surface slippery which is due to leakages. The slipper ground can result into accidents.

(B) Water Based Hydraulic Fluids:

These fluids are water based i.e. water is base in which other liquids are mixed.

  (i) Water in oil emulsion: This is a mixture of water (40%) and oil (60%).
  (ii) Oil in water emulsion: This is a mixture of oil in water.
  Advantages and Disadvantages of Water based Hydraulic Fluids: These fluids are fire resistant. If water content reduces then the viscosity of these fluid reduces.
  (iii) Water + Glycol: In this mixture, water and polyglycols are mixed in 50%/50%.

(C) Synthetic Hydraulic Fluids (Phosphate Esters):

These are synthetic fluids, non-flammable and can be used at high temperature upto 150°C. In fact these fluids cannot work at lower temperatures. These are most expensive fluids and rarely used.

1.1.17 General Characteristics and Specifications / Standards of Petroleum Based Hydraulic Fluids

Type	Specification	Appearance	Flash Point	Viscosity Index	Pour Point
Turbine oil with additives	JISK 2213	Brown	200°C and above	95	– 7.5°C
Hydraulic working fluid	ASTM D 6158	Clear and Colourless	185°C or above	90	– 15°C
Antiwear working fluid	ASTM D 6158	Clear and Colourless	185°C or above	90	– 12°C

1.1.18 Types of Flows

Let us see the types of flows.

There are six types of flows:

1. Steady and unsteady flow.
2. Uniform and Non-uniform flow.
3. Laminar and Turbulent flow.
4. Compressible and Incompressible flow.
5. Rotational and Non-rotational flow.
6. One, Two and Three-dimensional flow.

We will see the flows one by one.

1.1.18.1 Steady and Unsteady Flow

Fluid is flowing in pipe. Consider point P in flow.

At this point, let

$$p_p = \text{density of fluid}$$
$$p_v = \text{velocity of fluid}$$
$$p_p = \text{pressure of fluid}$$

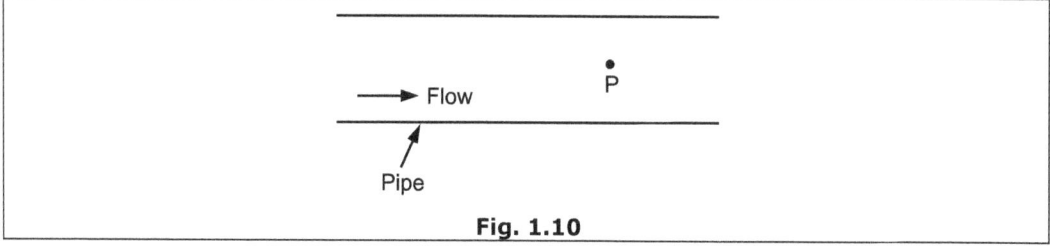

Fig. 1.10

If these three quantities remain same over a passage of time then flow is called steady flow.

If say velocity at point P is v, then if

$$\left(\frac{\partial v}{\partial t}\right) = 0 \text{ the follow is steady}$$

If $\left(\frac{\partial v}{\partial t}\right) \neq 0$ the flow is unsteady

In unsteady flow at particular point P, the velocity, pressure and density do not remain same over passage of time.

1.1.18.2 Uniform and Non-Uniform Flow

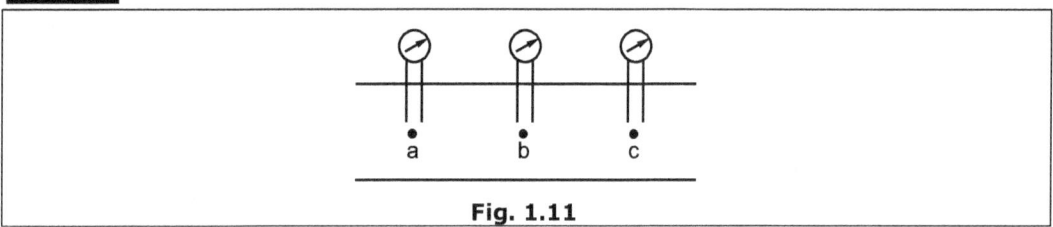

Fig. 1.11

'Uniform flow' is defined as that type of flow in which the velocity at any given time does not change with respect to length of direction of flow. At points a, b and c, velocity must be same at given time i.e.

$$\left(\frac{\partial v}{\partial s}\right)_{t1} = 0$$

'Non-Uniform flow' is that type of flow in which the velocity at any given time changes with respect to length of direction of flow.

$$\left(\frac{\partial v}{\partial s}\right)_{t1} \neq 0$$

Important: If cross-section of pipe is uniform over entire length of pipe then velocity of flow will also be uniform. But if the cross-section of pipe is different at different sections obviously the velocity will not be uniform over the entire length.

1.1.18.3 Laminar and Turbulent Flow [W-14]

Laminar flow is the flow in which the fluid particles move along well defined path or stream line and all the streamlines are straight and parallel. A, B and C are three layers moving in a parallel way and smoothly one over the other. This is laminar or streamline or viscous flow.

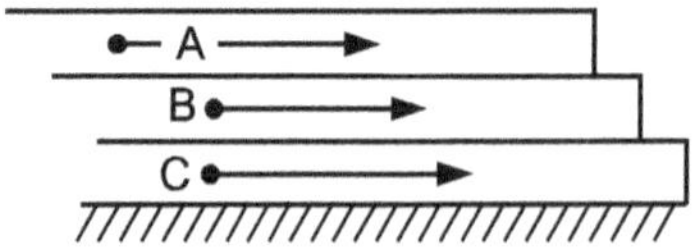

Fig. 1.12

Turbulent flow: This is the most common type of flows occurring in nature e.g. water falls.

Turbulent flow is a flow in which fluid particles move in a zig-zag path. They do not follow definite path, they collide with each other and move in any direction. In this flow, we can see eddy currents. The velocity of flow changes from point to point and time to time.

Important: The velocity at which laminar flow changes to turbulent flow in a pipe is called 'critical velocity' of flow.

1.1.18.4 Compressible and Incompressible Flow

Compressible flow is the flow in which the density of fluid changes from point to point.

Incompressible flow is the flow in which density (ρ) of fluid **does not** change throughout the flow.

Important: The gases are compressible.

The liquids are incompressible.

1.1.18.5 Rotational and Non-Rotational Flow

Rotational flow is the flow in which fluid particles, while flowing along the streamlines also **rotate** about their own axis.

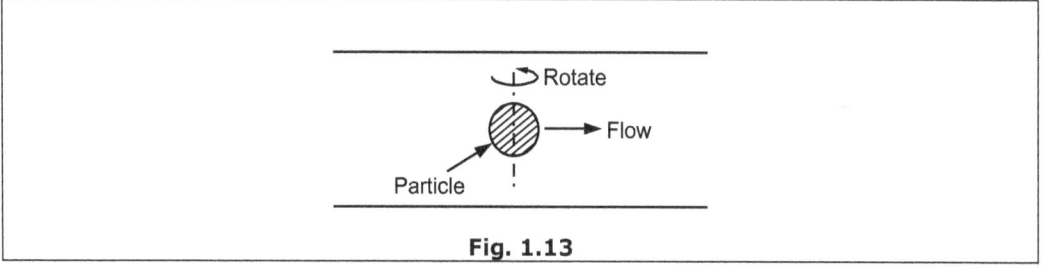

Fig. 1.13

Non-rotational or Irrotational flow is the flow in which fluid particles while flowing along the streamline **does not rotate** about its own axis.

1.1.18.6 One, Two and Three Dimensional Flow

This is another method of describing fluid motion.

- Consider point 'R' in a space. We can describe this point as → R (x, y, z).

  Then at any given time, the velocity of point R is given by

  $$V = f(x, y, z)$$

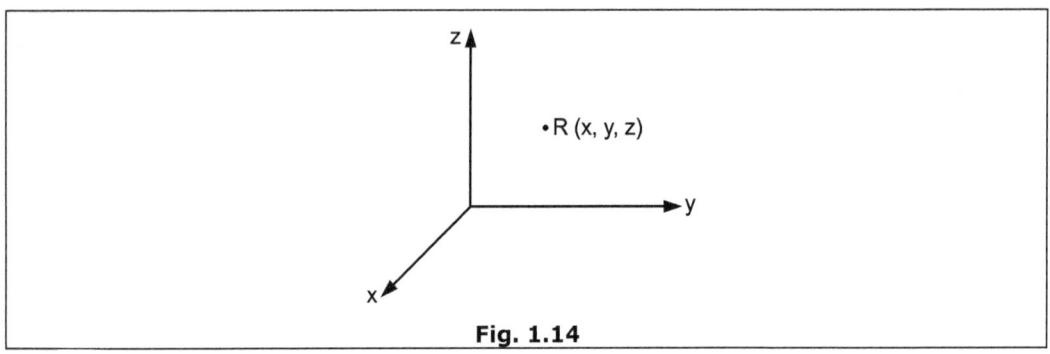

Fig. 1.14

i.e. velocity is a function of x, y, z.

- **Three Dimensional flow:** It is that type of flow in which velocity of fluid at any given point (having three dimensions) is a function of time and three mutually perpendicular directions.

- **Two Dimensional flow:** Sometimes, the flow condition may be such that velocity at any given point at given time depends on only two space coordinates, say x and y or y and z etc. Then that flow is called two dimensional flow.

$$V = f(x, y)$$

- **One Dimensional flow:** It is that type of flow in which flow parameter i.e. velocity is a function of time and only one space coordinate, say x or y or z.

∴ $$V = f(x)$$

1.1.19 Pascal's Law

- Pascal was a French Scientist who discovered the law in 17th century.

- **Pascal's law:** It states that pressure applied on confined fluid is transmitted undiminished in all directions and acts with equal force on equal areas and at right angle to them.

- A static fluid in a closed vessel has following characteristics:

   (a) Pressure works on a plane at right angle.

   (b) Pressure is transmitted equally in all directions.

   (c) Pressure applied on part of fluid is transmitted throughout the fluid equally.

- To understand Pascal's law we know what is pressure intensity (for details please refer chapter 2).

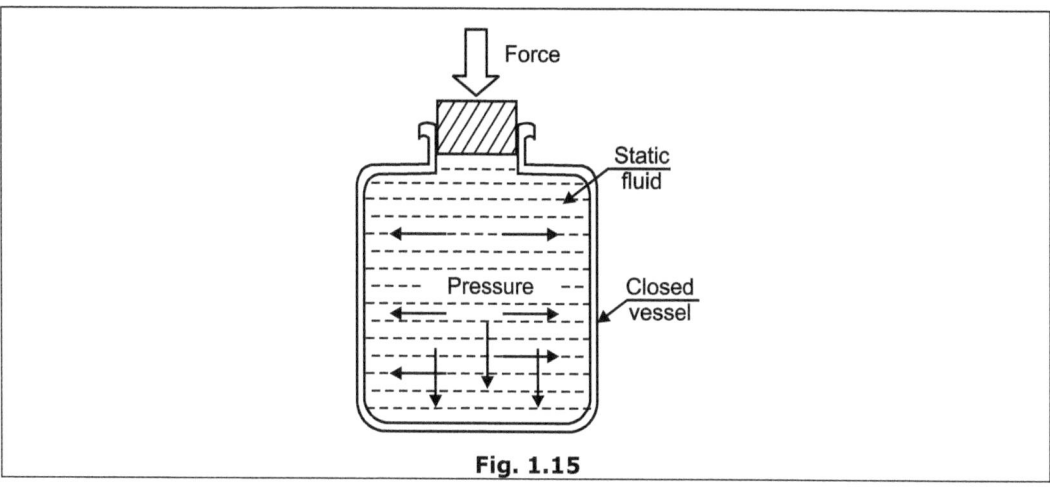

Fig. 1.15

- **Pressure Intensity (p):** It is the normal force exerted by a fluid at a point per unit area of surface.

$$p = \frac{dP}{dA}$$ ... p = Pressure intensity at any point at elemental area dA

dP = Force exerted in normal direction

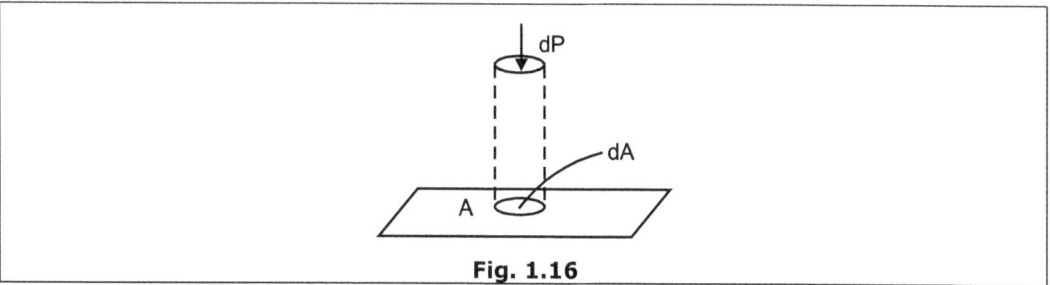

Fig. 1.16

- Intensity of pressure (p) is measured in Newton/meter² or Pascal.
- Pascal's law can also be stated as: The intensity of pressure at a point in a fluid at rest is the same in all the directions.

Proof of Pascal's Law:

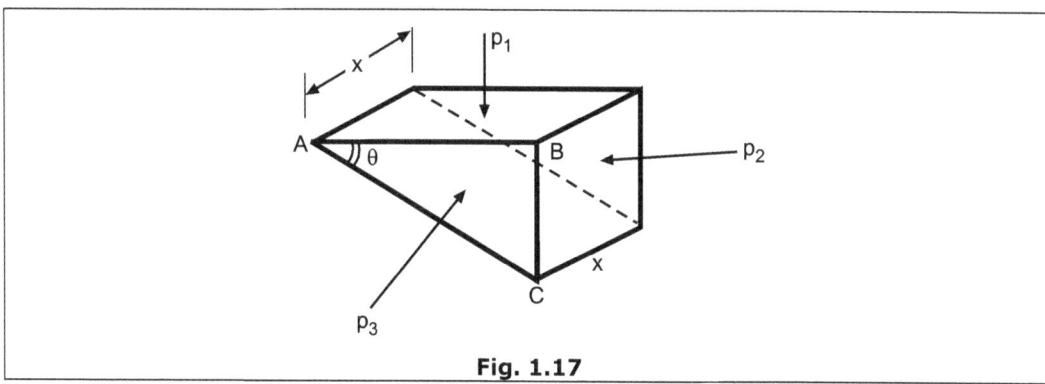

Fig. 1.17

Consider an elemental prism ABC of the fluid in fluid mass. Let x be the width of the prism. Let p_1, p_2 and p_3 be the pressure intensities on the faces A, B and C respectively.

It is clear that face AB is horizontal, face BC is vertical and face AC is at an angle θ with horizontal.

Hence the forces on these faces are:

$$\text{Force on face AB} = p_1 \times l(AB) \times x \quad \ldots\ldots\ldots\ldots\ldots\ldots p_1 = \frac{\text{Force}}{\text{c/s Area}}$$

$$\text{Force on face BC} = p_2 \times l(BC) \times x$$

$$\text{Force on face AC} = p_3 \times l(AC) \times x$$

The above forces act at right angle to the faces AB, BC and AC respectively.

Now, we know that, weight of prism is very small and prism is in existence, hence all the forces must be in the system of equilibrium.

- Resolving vertically,

$$p_1 \times l(AB) \times x = p_3 \times l(AC) \times x \times \cos\theta$$

But $\quad l(AC) \times \cos\theta = AB$

$\therefore \quad p_1 = p_3$

- Resolving horizontally,

$$p_2 \times l(BC) \times x = p_3 \times l(AC) \times x \times \sin\theta$$

But $\quad l(AC) \sin\theta = BC$

$\therefore \quad p_2 = p_3$

$\therefore \quad p_1 = p_2 = p_3 \quad$ ... Thus, pressure intensity at any point is same in all directions.

1.2 MEASUREMENT OF PRESSURE

- We are well aware that any fluid (liquid or gas) needs a container/tank to store it.
- This stored fluid will exert a force on the supporting surface of container.
- This exerted force by fluid is normal (perpendicular) to the surface.

Fluid Pressure

The force exerted by fluid per unit area is known as 'Intensity of Pressure' or 'Fluid Pressure'.

In simple words,

$$\text{Pressure} = \frac{\text{Force (N)}}{\text{Area on which it is acting (meter}^2)}$$

$\therefore \quad \boxed{P = \frac{F}{A} \text{ N/mt}^2}$

$\therefore \quad 1 \text{ N/mt}^2 = 1 \text{ Pascal}$

$\therefore \quad 1 \text{ Bar} = 1 \text{ N/mm}^2 \ldots$ in SI system

Pressure Head

Consider a tank with horizontal bottom. Tank is partly filled with a liquid having density 'ρ' and specific weight 'w'.

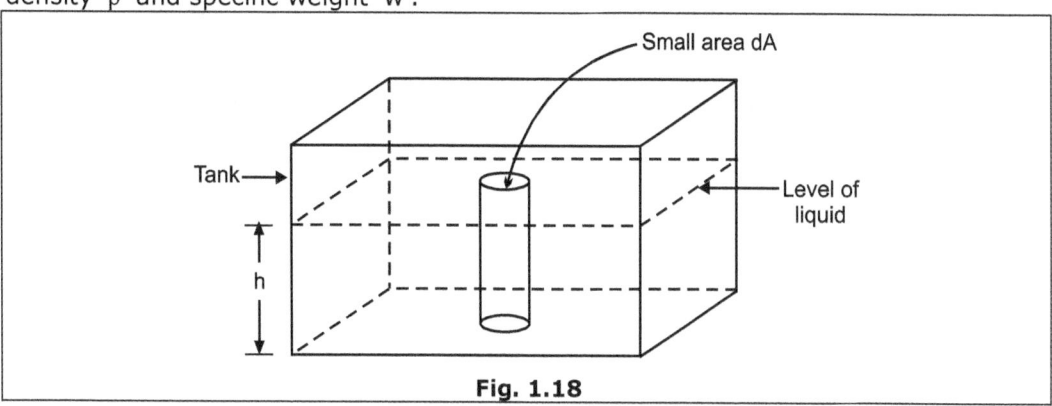

Fig. 1.18

The height of small area is 'h' (height of liquid)

So pressure force exerted by column (in cylinder shape) on area dA is

F = Weight of cylinder of liquid of area dA having height 'h'.

= Sp. wt. × (Volume of cylinder)

= w × (dA × h)

So intensity of pressure on elemental area dA is

$$p = \frac{\text{Force}}{\text{Area}} = \frac{w \times dA \times h}{dA} = wh$$

but $\quad w = \rho \cdot g$

∴ $\quad \boxed{p = h \cdot \rho \cdot g}$ ... (1)

- From above equation it is clear that if we know the height of liquid column and density of liquid, we can calculate the pressure intensity.
- From equation (1),

$$h = \frac{p}{\rho \cdot g}$$

h is called PRESSURE HEAD.

Most Important

'h' is a linear quantity. Hence we mention 'pressure head' then we must mention the name of liquid/fluid.

- If in Fig. 1.18 if h = 4 mt, and fluid stored in tank is water then we must mention that, 'pressure head is 4 mt of water'. That means pressure is:

$$p = wh = \rho \cdot g \cdot h = (1000 \times 9.81 \times 4) \text{ N/m}^2$$

$$p = 39240 \text{ N/m}^2$$

- Note that pressure at any point in the liquid will depend on the weight of liquid above that point.

1.2.1 Atmospheric Pressure [S-15]

- A huge layer of atmosphere (mixture of air, gases, dust etc.) surrounds the earth.
- The earth is moving into orbit of Sun with its huge atmosphere layer.

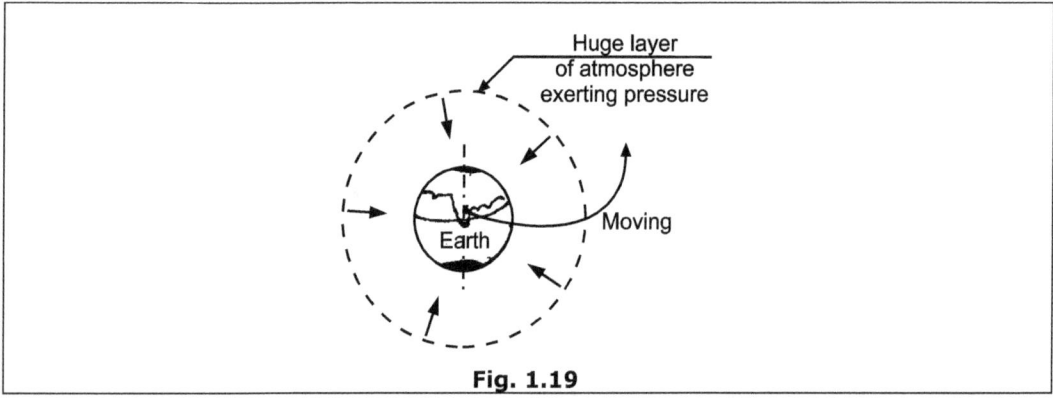

Fig. 1.19

- This layer of atmosphere exerts a pressure on earth.
- The said pressure caused by Atmosphere is called ATMOSPHERIC PRESSURE.
- Atmospheric pressure can be expressed in terms of
   Pressure Intensity $\Rightarrow$ 101300 N/m^2
- Atmospheric pressure can be expressed in terms of
   Head $\Rightarrow$ 10.3 mt of Water
   $\Rightarrow$ 760 mm of Mercury
- We are so accustom with this atmospheric pressure that we do not feel it. Actually it is acting on our body.
- Atmospheric pressure varies with altitude (height from earth surface).
- This pressure is also known as barometric pressure.
- The device adopted to measure the pressure at any point is called 'pressure gauge'.
- The pressure gauge records the pressure above atmospheric pressure. Hence, it is called 'gauge pressure'.
- Consider point 'A' at 7 mt. below the water level. The atmosphere will exert atmospheric pressure on the entire surface of water. This pressure will be transmitted to all points in water. If atmospheric pressure is 10 mt of water then total pressure head at point A is 10 + 7 = 17 mt of water.

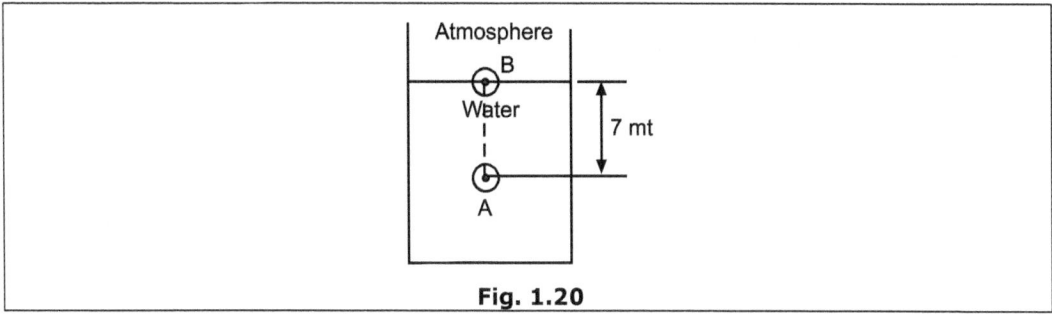

Fig. 1.20

- This pressure head inclusive of the atmospheric pressure head is called 'Absolute Pressure Head'.
- Hence we may express the pressure head at point 'A' in two ways:
  (i) Pressure head at point A ⇒ 7 mt. of water (gauge)
  (ii) Pressure head at point A ⇒ 17 mt. (abs.) of water
- Consider point 'B' on the surface of water. Then
  (i) Pressure head at point B ⇒ 0 mt. of water (gauge)
  (ii) Pressure head at point B ⇒ 10 mt. (abs.) of water.

1.2.2 Vacuum Pressure [S-15]

- **Definition:** If at a point the pressure if, is less than atmospheric pressure then it is called Vacuum Pressure or only Vacuum or Negative Pressure.
- Suppose the atmospheric pressure head is 10 mt. of water. If pressure head at point (B) is 6 mt. of water less than the atmospheric pressure head, then, (Refer Fig. 1.22)
  (i) Pressure head at point (B) ⇒ – 6 mt. or 6 mt. vacuum of water.
  (ii) Pressure head at point (B) ⇒ 10 – 6 = 4 mt. (abs) of water.
- For measurement of vacuum, vacuum gauge is used which is same as like pressure gauge.
- Vacuum creation: When piston of reciprocating pump is moving from left to right, the vacuum is created in the cylinder.

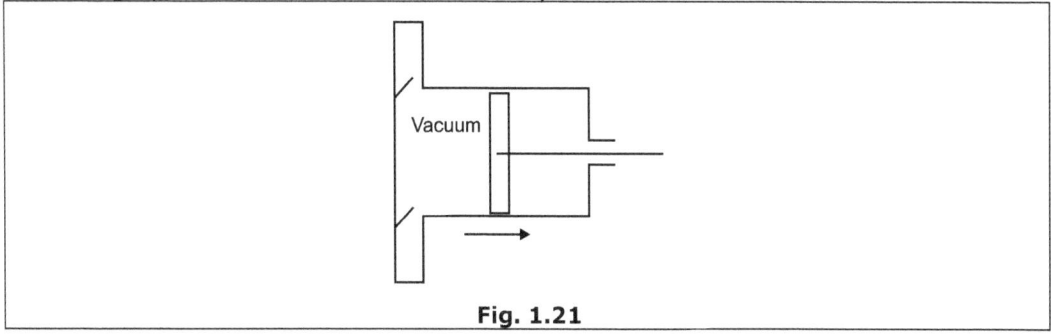

Fig. 1.21

1.2.3 Absolute Pressure

- **Definition:** It is defined *as the pressure which is measured with reference to Absolute vacuum.*
- Absolute vacuum is also known as absolute zero level or complete vacuum.
- Absolute Pressure = Atmospheric Pressure + Gauge Pressure

1.2.4 Gauge Pressure

- **Definition:** It is defined as *the pressure which is measured with the help of Pressure Measuring Devices.*
- The most used pressure measuring device is 'BOURDON'S PRESSURE GAUGE'.
- When we go to air filling station for filling the air in tyre-tube of our vehicle, then we can come across one Round Dialed Gauge. The air pressure is checked on this gauge. This is nothing but a Bourdon's Pressure Gauge.
- Manometer is also a pressure measuring device.

1.2.5 Various Pressures Expressed Graphically

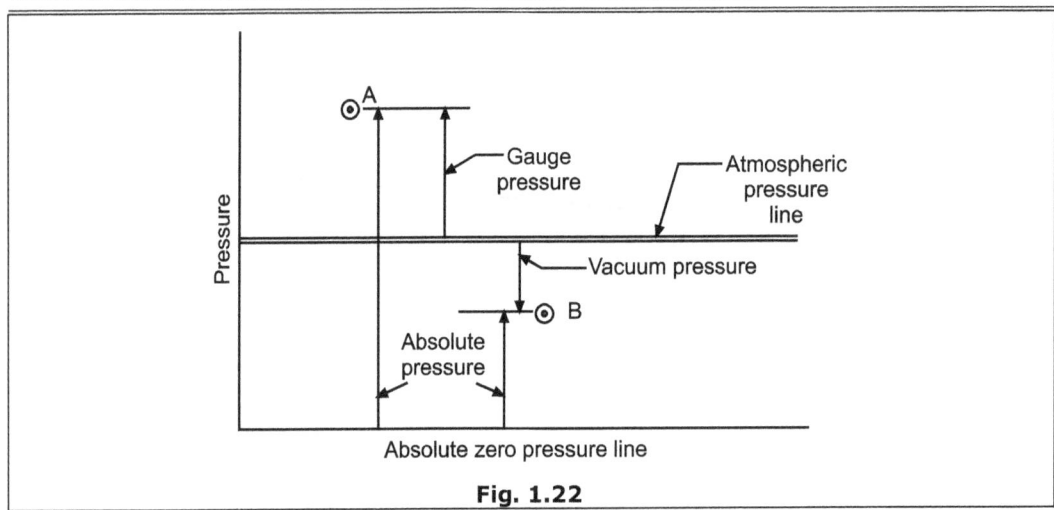

Fig. 1.22

1.2.6 Pressure Measurement

- Pressure of a fluid is measured by following devices:
  1. Manometers
  2. Mechanical gauges

Manometers

These are devices used for measuring a pressure at a point in a fluid by balancing the column of fluid by the same fluid or column of another fluid.

Types of Manometers

(i) Simple manometers

(ii) Differential manometers

Types of Simple Manometers

(a) Piezometer tube

(b) U-Tube manometer

(c) Micromanometer (or single column manometer or sensitive manometer)

Types of Differential Manometers

(a) U-Tube Differential Manometers

(b) Inverted-U-Tube Differential Manometers

Mechanical Gauges

These are the devices used for measuring the pressure by balancing the fluid column by using special types of tubes or springs.

Types of Mechanical Gauges

(a) Bourdon Pressure Gauge

(b) Diaphragm Pressure Gauge.

Manometers

Let us study various manometers.

1.2.7 Piezometer Tube

- It is the simplest instrument used for measuring pressure head.
- It is just a small diameter glass tube attached to pipe through liquid/fluid is flowing. The other end of tube is open to the atmosphere.

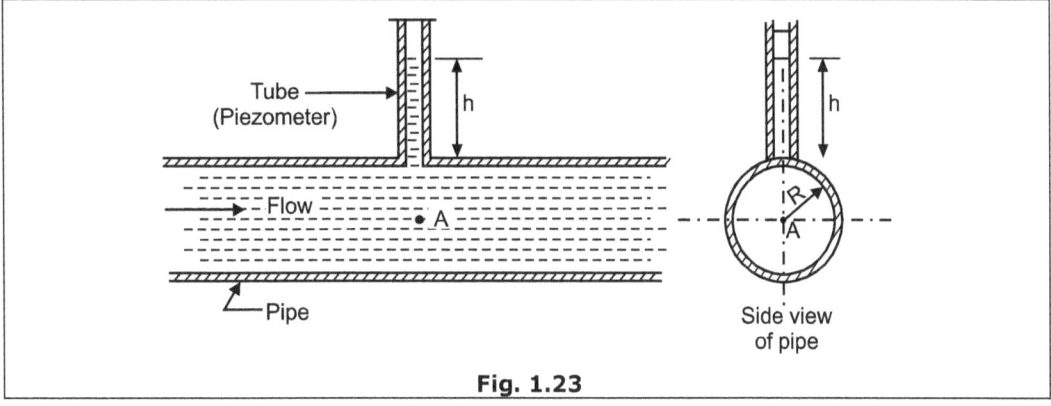

Fig. 1.23

- When water flows in pipe in shown direction, the water will rush in glass tube called PIEZOMETER TUBE and will attain height 'h' in Glass tube.

- The pressure head at point 'A' will be

    Pressure at point A → P_A = h + Radius of pipe R

    $$P_A = h + R$$

- To know the pressure at point A, every time we must take into account radius of pipe. To avoid this difficulty, the piezometer tube is modified as under.

    So now,

    $$p_A = h \text{ mt. of water}$$
    $$= \rho \times g \times h \text{ N/m}^2$$

- When pressure in pipe reduces, 'h' will come down.
- When pressure in pipe increases, 'h' will rise.

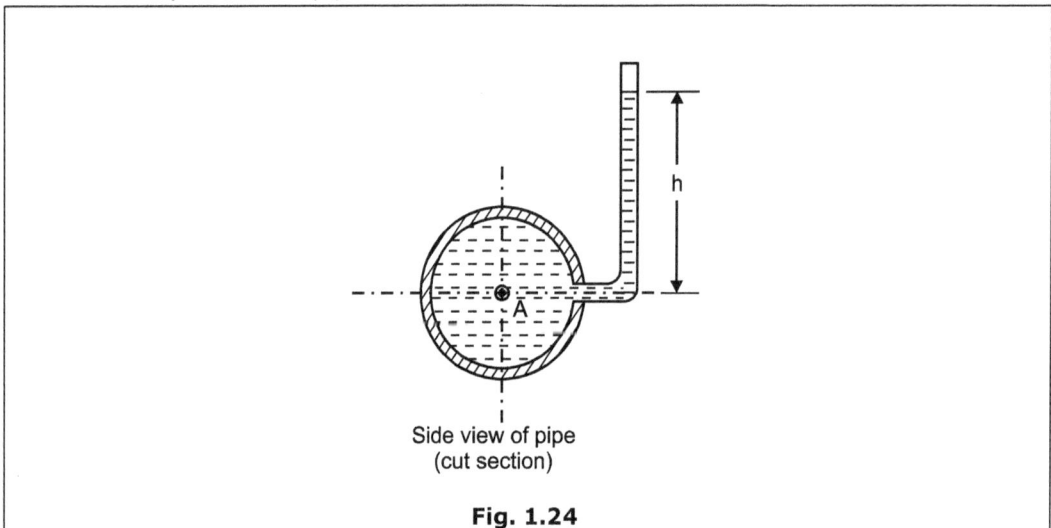

Side view of pipe (cut section)

Fig. 1.24

1.2.8 U-Tube Manometer

It consists of glass tube bent in 'U' shape.

- One end of tube is connected to the pipe.
- Other end is open to the atmosphere.
- Heavy liquid whose density is more than the density of flowing liquid (called light liquid) is used to take reading. This heavy liquid should be selected in such a way that it should not be mixed with flowing liquid. Generally, mercury (Hg) is used as a heavy liquid.

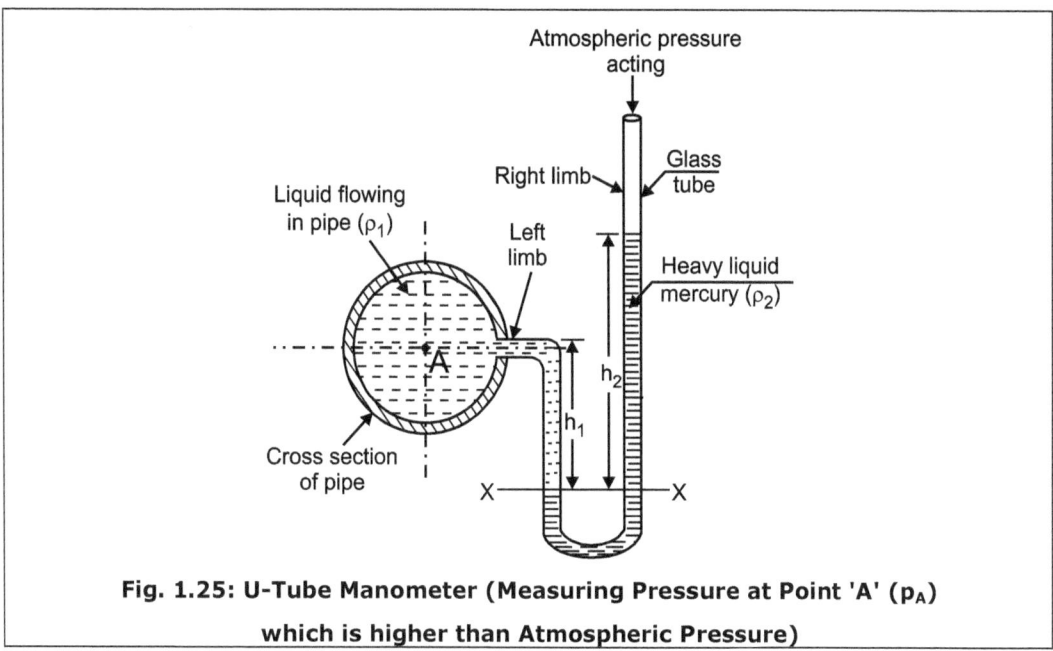

Fig. 1.25: U-Tube Manometer (Measuring Pressure at Point 'A' (p_A) which is higher than Atmospheric Pressure)

- We have to measure the pressure head at point 'A' i.e. p_A.
- When liquid is flowing through pipe, small quantity of water rushes to U-tube manometer and will press down the heavy liquid in left limb (column).
- When pressure at point 'A' will increase, more water comes in left limb. It will push down the heavy liquid, and as a result of it the level of heavy liquid in right limb will rise.
- When pressure at point 'A' will reduce, less quantity of water will come in left limb. Now heavy liquid will push the flowing liquid up in left column and so naturally, level of heavy liquid in right limb will come down.
- Finding the pressure p_A (Refer Fig. 1.25)

    Consider a datum line X-X.

    Let p_A = Pressure at point A

    h_1 = Height of light liquid above X-X

    h_2 = Height of heavy liquid (Hg) above X-X

    ρ_1 = Density of lighter liquid (flowing liquid)

    ρ_2 = Density of heavy liquid (Hg)

    Above line X-X pressure in left limb = Pressure in right limb

- So Pressure above X-X in left limb = $p_A + \rho_1 \times g \times h_1$

    Pressure above X-X in right limb = $\rho_2 \times g \times h_2$

Equating above two pressures,

$$p_A + \rho_1 g h_1 = \rho_2 g h_2$$

∴ $$\boxed{p_A = \rho_2 g h_2 - \rho_1 g h_1}$$

Finding the pressure p_A when it is below atmospheric pressure (Vacuum Pressure)

- The pressure at point 'A' is below atmospheric pressure.
- Hence level of Hg will go down in right limb whereas level of Hg in left limb will rise.

Finding pressure p_A:

Above line XX:

Pressure in left limb = Pressure in right limb

So,

Pressure above XX in right limb = 0

Pressure above XX in left limb = $p_A + \rho_1 g h_1 + \rho_2 g h_2$

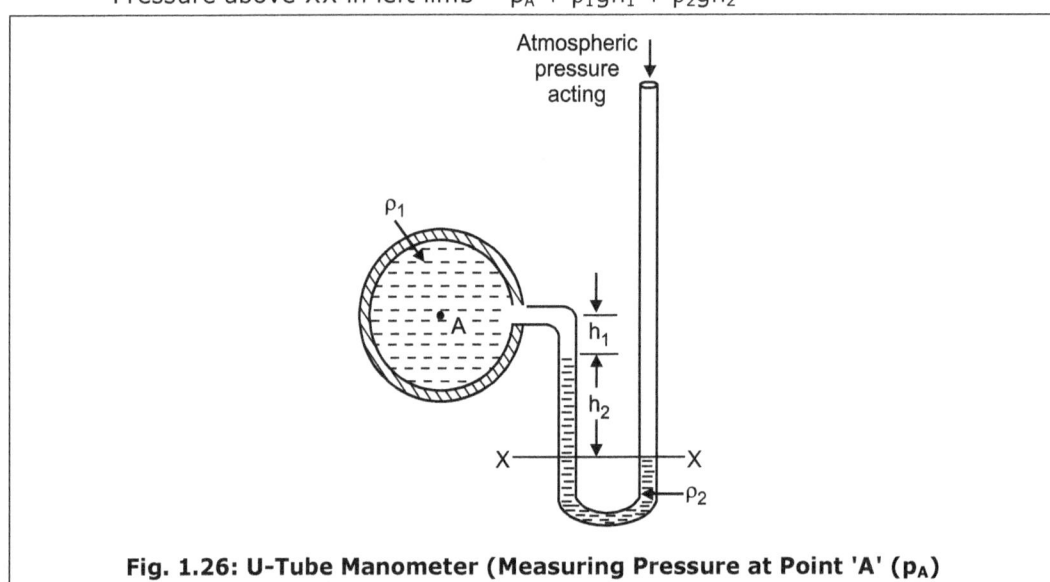

Fig. 1.26: U-Tube Manometer (Measuring Pressure at Point 'A' (p_A) which is lower than Atmospheric Pressure)

Equating above two pressures,

$$0 = p_A + \rho_1 g h_1 + \rho_2 g h_2$$

∴ $$p_A = -(\rho_1 g h_1 + \rho_2 g h_2)$$

– ve sign shows that p_A is vacuum pressure.

1.2.9 Micromanometer (Single Column Manometer) (Sensitive Manometer)

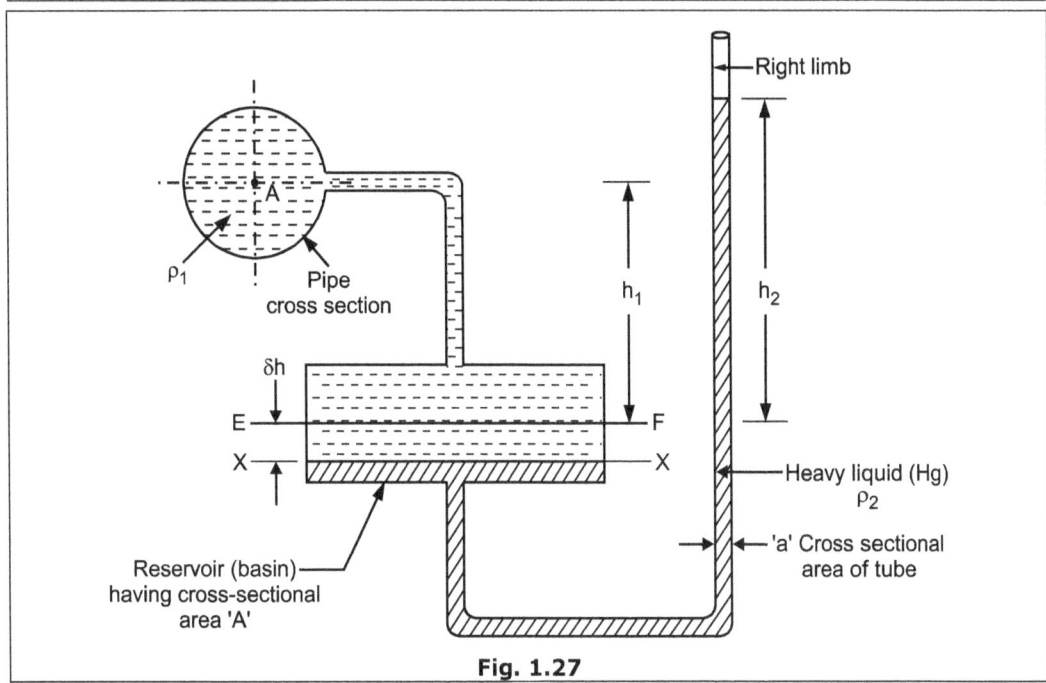

Fig. 1.27

- Micromanometer or sensitive manometer is a modified version of U tube manometer.
- It is used for precise measurement of pressure.
- With simple steel rule we can measure the dimension roughly. But with micrometer we can measure the dimensions in microns. Similarly with micro manometer we can measure slight changes of pressure in pipe. These slight changes are difficult to measure with the help of ordinary U-tube manometer.
- **Construction:** It is similar to U-tube manometer. The only difference is that a large area reservoir (Basin) is filled on left limb. The cross-sectional area of basin (reservoir) is 100 times more than cross-sectional area of tube i.e.

$$\frac{A}{a} = 100$$

∴ $A = 100\,a$

The left limb is either vertical or inclined.

Calculation of Pressure (+ve pressure) at point 'A' i.e. p_A

- The high pressure liquid in pipe will push the heavy liquid in basin downward.
- The original level of heavy liquid is EF.
- It will attain new level X-X and displacement will be 'δh' due to slight increase in pressure of liquid in pipe.

- This δh is very small and can be neglected because it will be difficult to measure it also.
- But this displacement in left limb will cause considerable rise in heavy liquid in right limb.
- That means we can magnify the slight pressure difference at point 'A', which can be easily measured by right limb.

$$\delta h = \frac{a \times h_2}{A}$$

- Similar to ordinary U tube manometer,
  Pressure above line XX in left limb = Pressure above line X-X in right limb
- Pressure above line XX in left limb = $p_A + \rho_1 g (\delta h + h_1)$
- Pressure above line XX in right limb = $\rho_2 g (\delta h + h_2)$
- Equating above two

$$p_A + \rho_1 g (\delta h + h_1) = \rho_2 g (\delta h + h_2)$$

$$\therefore \quad p_A = \rho_2 g (\delta h + h_2) - \rho_1 g (\delta h + h_1)$$

By putting value of $\delta h = \frac{a \times h_2}{A}$ and solving, we get

$$\boxed{p_A = \frac{a \times h_2}{A} [\rho_2 g - \rho_1 g] + [h_2 \rho_2 g - h_1 \rho_1 g]}$$

As the area 'A' is very large, $\frac{a}{A} \Rightarrow 0$

$$\therefore \quad p_A = h_2 \rho_2 g - h_1 \rho_1 g$$

...equation for ordinary U tube manometer

Calculation of p_A when right limb is inclined:
(Inclined Single Column Manometer / Inclined Micromanometer)

$$p_A = L \sin \theta \times \rho_2 g - h_1 \rho_1 g$$

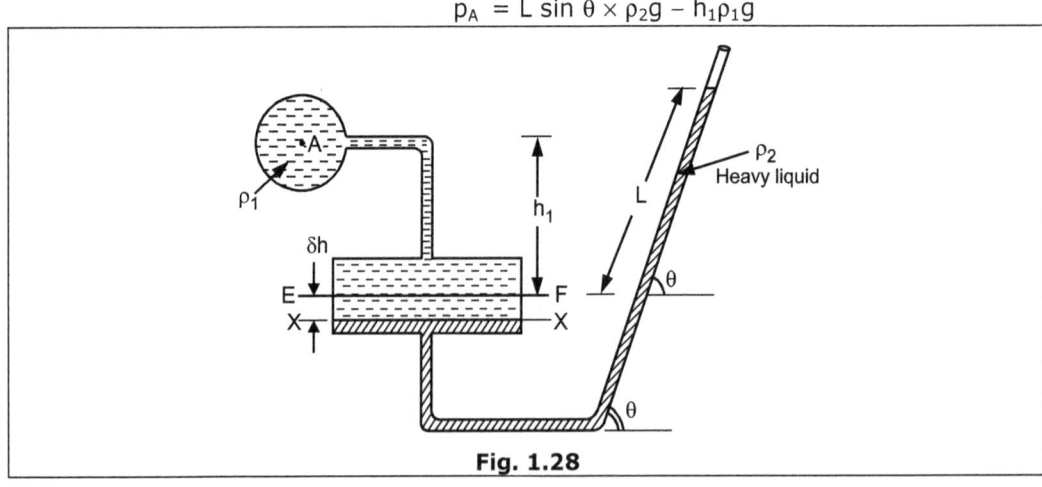

Fig. 1.28

1.2.10 Differential Manometers

- Differential manometers are the devices for measuring the difference of pressure between two points in a single pipe ($p_A - p_B$).

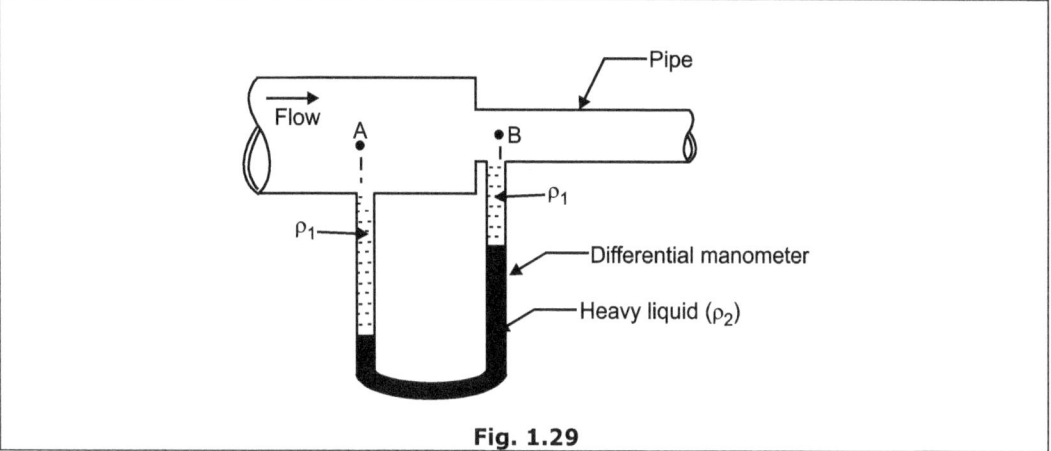

Fig. 1.29

- They are also used to measure pressure differences between two different pipes ($p_A - p_B$).

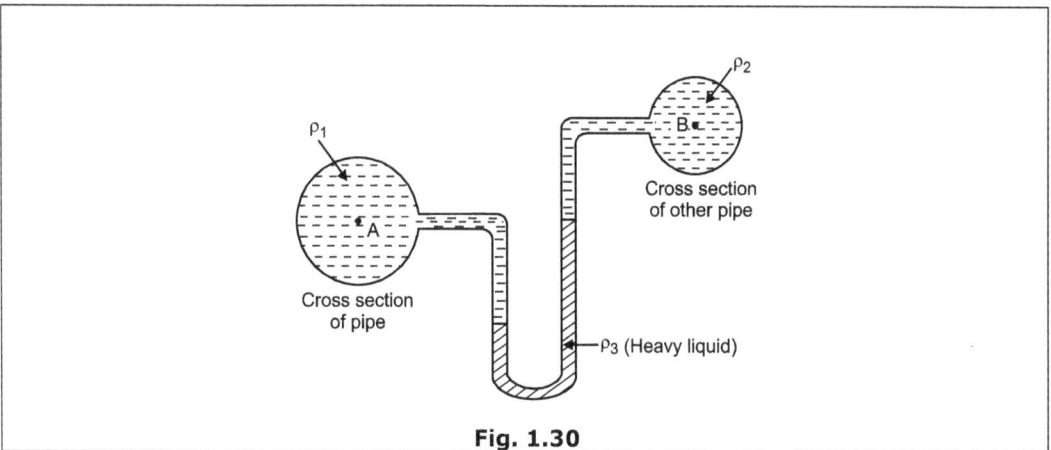

Fig. 1.30

- Hence differential manometers are used only for measuring the pressure difference. It cannot tell us the pressure (as in case of U tube manometer).

1.2.11 U-Tube Differential Manometer

These are of two types:

(i) U-Tube Differential Manometers when pipes are at different level.

(ii) U-Tube Differential Manometers when pipes are at same level.

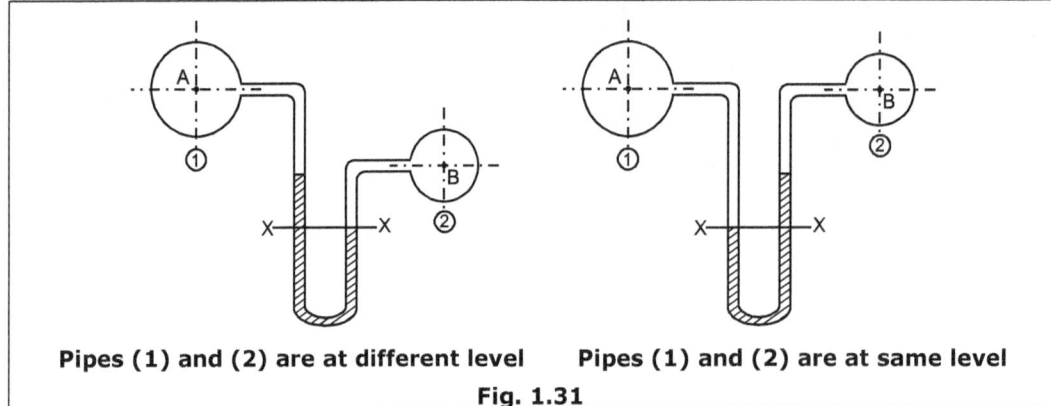

Pipes (1) and (2) are at different level   Pipes (1) and (2) are at same level

Fig. 1.31

1.2.12 U-Tube Differential Manometer when pipes are at different level – Finding the pressure difference ($p_A - p_B$)

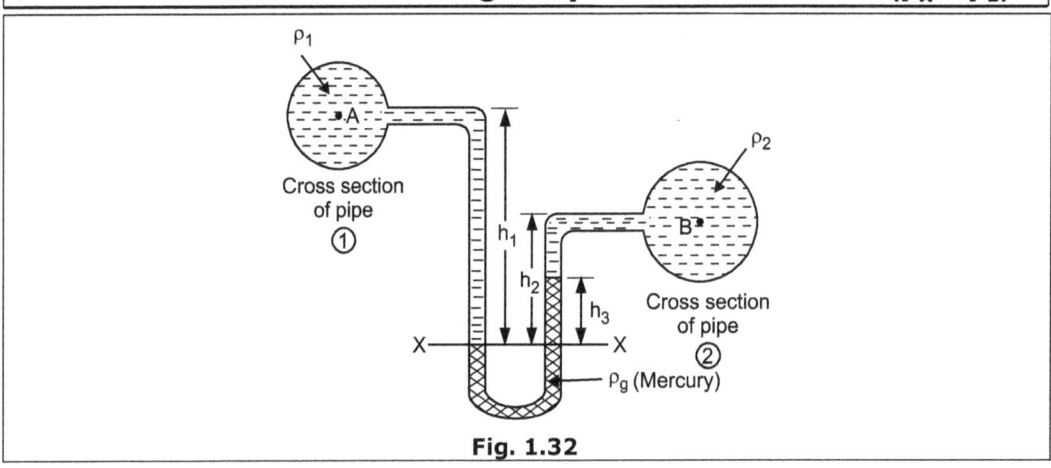

Fig. 1.32

Let ρ_1 = density of fluid flowing in pipe (1)

ρ_2 = density of fluid flowing in pipe (2)

ρ_g = density of mercury in heavy liquid in manometer

Then

$$\frac{\text{Pressure above datum line}}{\text{XX in left limb}} = \frac{\text{Pressure above datum line}}{\text{XX in right limb}}$$

- Pressure above XX in left limb = $p_A + \rho_1 g h_1$
- Pressure above XX in right limb = $p_B + \rho_2 g h_2 + \rho_g g h_3$

Equating we get

$$p_A + \rho_1 g h_1 = p_B + \rho_2 g h_2 + \rho_g g h_3$$

∴ $p_A - p_B = \rho_2 g h_2 + \rho_g g h_3 - \rho_1 g h_1$

$$\boxed{p_A - p_B = g(\rho_2 h_2 + \rho_g h_3 - \rho_1 h_1)}$$

1.2.13 U-Tube Differential Manometer when pipes are at same level – Finding the pressure difference ($p_A - p_B$)

Let ρ_1, ρ_2 and ρ_g be densities of three liquids.

Then

$$\text{Pressure above XX in left limb} = \text{Pressure above XX in right limb}$$

$$p_A + \rho_1 (x + h) = p_B + \rho_2 g x + \rho_g g h$$

$\therefore \quad p_A - p_B = \rho_2 gx + \rho_g g h - \rho_1 (x + h)$

$\therefore \quad \boxed{p_A - p_B = g(\rho_2 x + \rho_g h - \rho_1 [x + h])}$

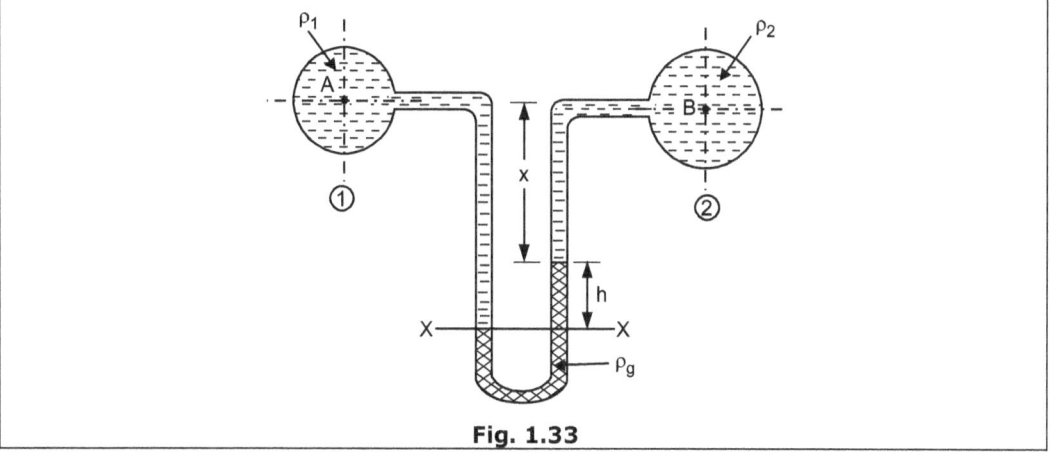

Fig. 1.33

1.2.14 Inverted U-Tube Differential Manometer

- Sometimes the piping network is complex. And in that case sometimes there is no space for regular U-tube differential manometer to hang.
- In such cases, inverted U-tube manometer is adopted.
- This is similar to regular U-type differential manometer, but the only difference is that instead of mercury i.e. heavy liquid here we have to use lighter liquid because we have work against gravity. This lighter liquid should have density lower than the two liquids flowing in the pipe.
- If we use mercury in inverted manometer, it will come down in inverted tube and will enter into a pipe due to its high density.

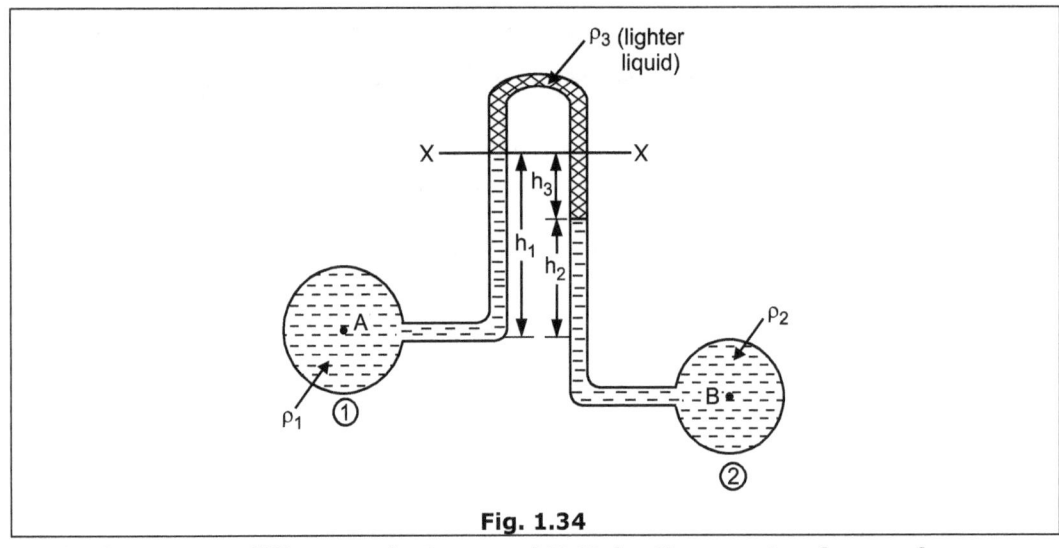

Fig. 1.34

To find pressure difference in Inverted U-Tube Manometer ($p_A - p_B$)

Let
ρ_1 = density of liquid flowing in pipe (1)
ρ_2 = density of liquid flowing in pipe (2)
ρ_3 = density of lighter liquid in manometer

Then

Pressure below line XX in left limb = Pressure below line XX in right limb

$$p_A - \rho_1 g h_1 = p_B - \rho_2 g h_2 - \rho_3 g h_3$$

∴ $$p_A - p_B = \rho_1 g h_1 - \rho_2 g h_2 - \rho_3 g h_3$$

$$\boxed{p_A - p_B = g(\rho_1 h_1 - \rho_2 h_2 - \rho_3 h_3)}$$

1.2.15 Difference Between Simple U-Tube Manometer and Differential U-Tube Manometer

Simple U-Tube Manometer	Differential U-tube Manometer
1. 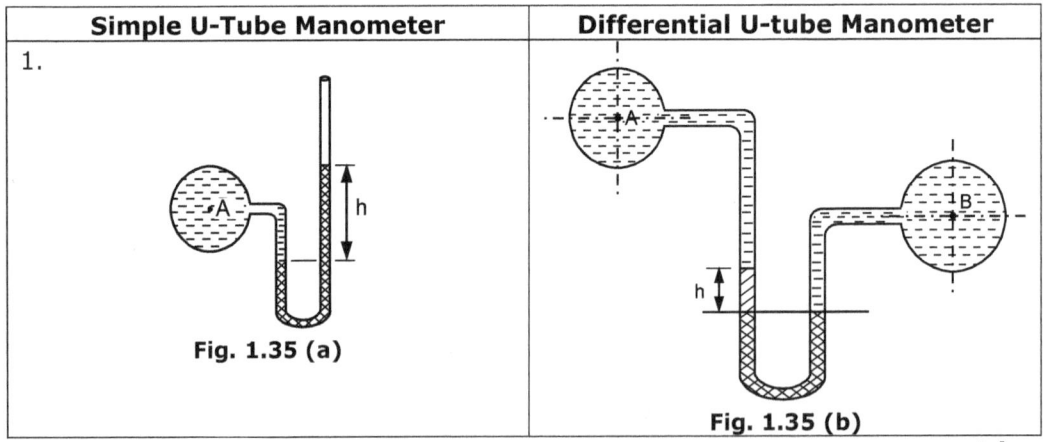 Fig. 1.35 (a)	Fig. 1.35 (b)

contd. ...

2. One end of tube is connected to pipe and other end is open to atmosphere.	2. Both ends of tube are attached to the tubes.
3. The manometer reading h gives pressure at point A i.e. p_A.	3. Manometer reading h gives pressure difference between points A and B i.e. $p_A - p_B$.
4. The heavy liquid is mercury.	4. The heavy liquid is mercury. But for inverted U-tube differential manometer, it uses lighter liquids.
5. It cannot be inverted.	5. It can be inverted.
6. We can modify this manometer into sensitive or micromanometer by attaching basin on left limb.	6. We cannot make such modifications.

1.2.16 Bourdon's Pressure Gauge [W-14]

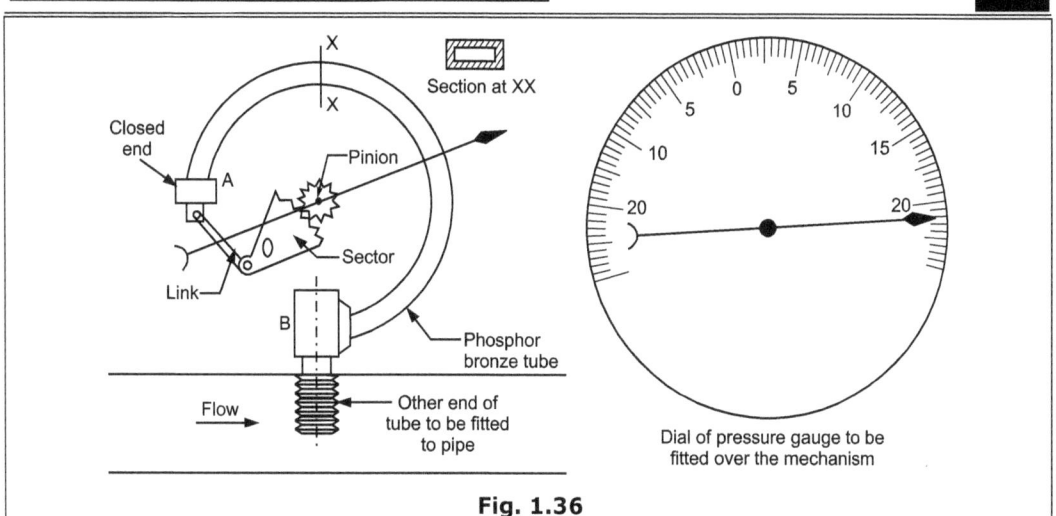

Fig. 1.36

- For measurement of 'Gauge Pressure', Bourdon's Pressure Gauge is used.

Construction: The device consists of a metallic tube of cross-section shown at XX (the cross-section of pipe is elliptical also) and is closed at one end. The other end is fitted to pipe where the pressure is to be measured. The dial and pointer are fitted over the mechanism.

Working: As the flowing fluid under pressure enters the tube, the tube tends to be straighten. If the cross-section of the tube is elliptical, it will try to become circular. As a result of this the closed end will try to move outward. This will operate 'pinion-sector' mechanism because it is connected to closed end through link 'OA'. When pinion rotates, the pointer will move on calibrated scale so that we will get reading of pressure.

Uses:

- For measuring high pressures e.g. in steam boilers, compressors etc.
- For measuring negative pressures i.e. pressure below atmosphere i.e. vacuum pressures.

Compound Gauge: The pressure gauge which measures +ve and –ve pressures is called compound gauge.

SOLVED PROBLEMS

Problem 1: *The right limb of simple U-tube manometer containing mercury is open to atmosphere while left limb is connected to pipe in which fluid of specific gravity 0.90 is flowing. The centre of pipe is 12 mt. below the level of mercury in the right limb. Find the pressure of fluid in the pipe if the manometer reading is 20 cm.*

Solution: Given data:

$$\rho_{oil} = S_{oil} \times \rho_{water}$$
$$= 0.8 \times 1000$$
$$= 800 \text{ kg/m}^3$$
$$\rho_m = S_m \times \rho_{water}$$
$$= 13.6 \times 1000$$
$$= 13600 \text{ kg/m}^3$$
$$h_{oil} = 20 - 12$$
$$= 8 \text{ cm}$$
$$= 0.08 \text{ mt}$$
$$h_m = 20 \text{ cm}$$
$$= 0.2 \text{ mt.}$$

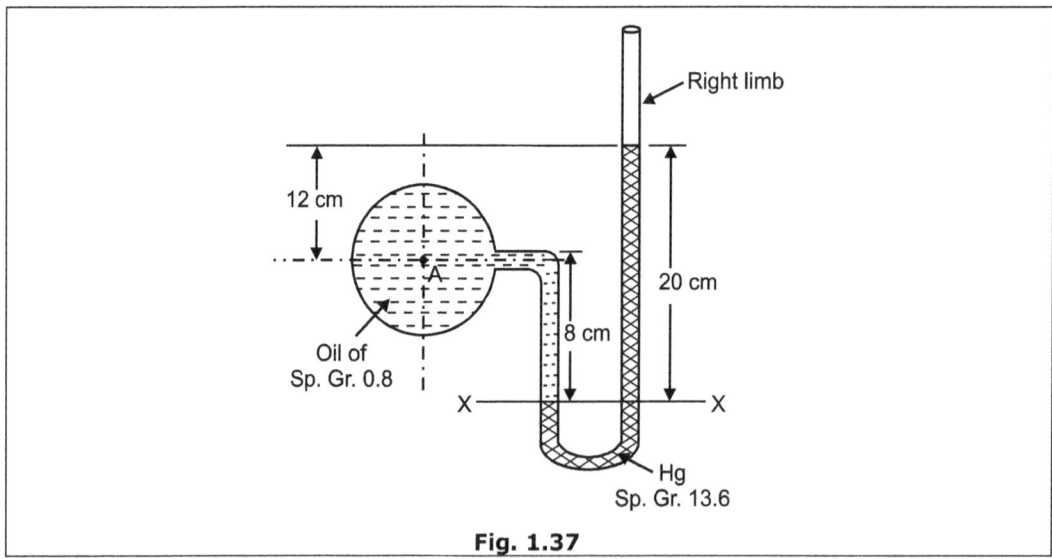

Fig. 1.37

We will solve this problem by taking pressure intensities above datum line X-X.

- Pressure above XX in left limb = $p_A + \rho_{oil} \times g \times h_{oil}$
  = $p_A + 800 \times 9.81 \times 0.08$
  = $p_A + 627.84$ ...(1)
- Pressure above XX in right limb = $\rho_m \times g \times h_m$
  = $13600 \times 9.81 \times 0.2$
  = $26{,}683.2$ ... (2)

But above line XX,

Pressure in left limb = Pressure in right limb

$p_A + 627.84 = 26{,}683.2$

∴ $\boxed{p_A = 25977 \text{ N/m}^2}$

Problem 2: *Find the pressure intensity at point A, if flowing liquid is water and heavy liquid is mercury (Refer Fig. 1.38) if h = 80 mm.*

Solution: We know

$\rho_1 = \rho_{water} = 1000 \text{ kg/m}^3$
$\rho_2 = \rho_m = 13600 \text{ kg/m}^3$
$h = 80 \text{ mm} = 0.08 \text{ mt}$

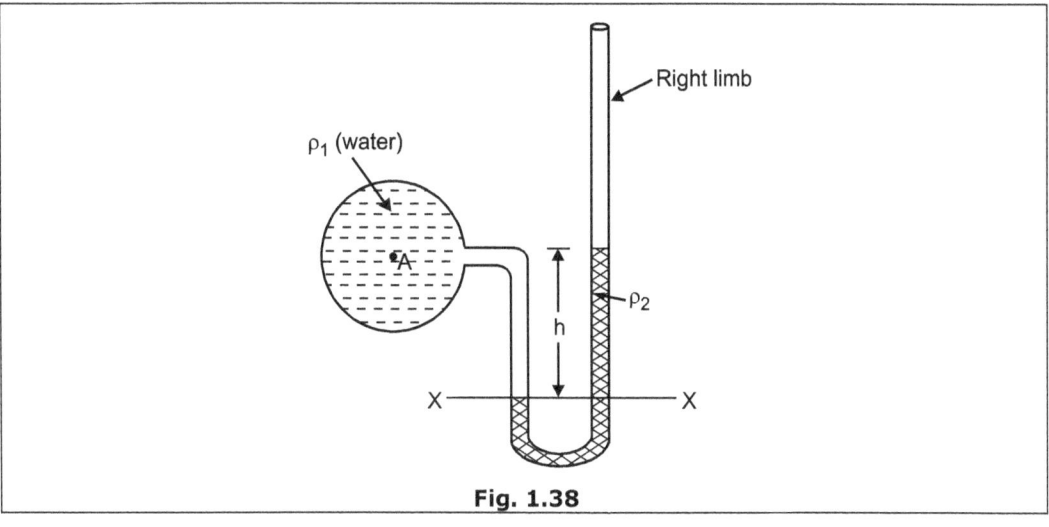

Fig. 1.38

Pressure above XX in left limb = Pressure above XX in right limb

$p_A + \rho_1 g h = \rho_m g h$

∴ $p_A = \rho_m g h - \rho_1 g h$
= $g h (\rho_m - \rho_1)$
= $9.81 \times 0.08 (13600 - 1000)$

$\boxed{p_A = 9888.48 \text{ N/m}^2}$

Problem 3: *A single column manometer is connected to a pipe containing liquid of specific gravity 0.9 as shown in Fig. 1.39. Find the pressure in pipe if the area of reservoir is 100 times the area of tube of manometer. The heavy liquid is mercury.*

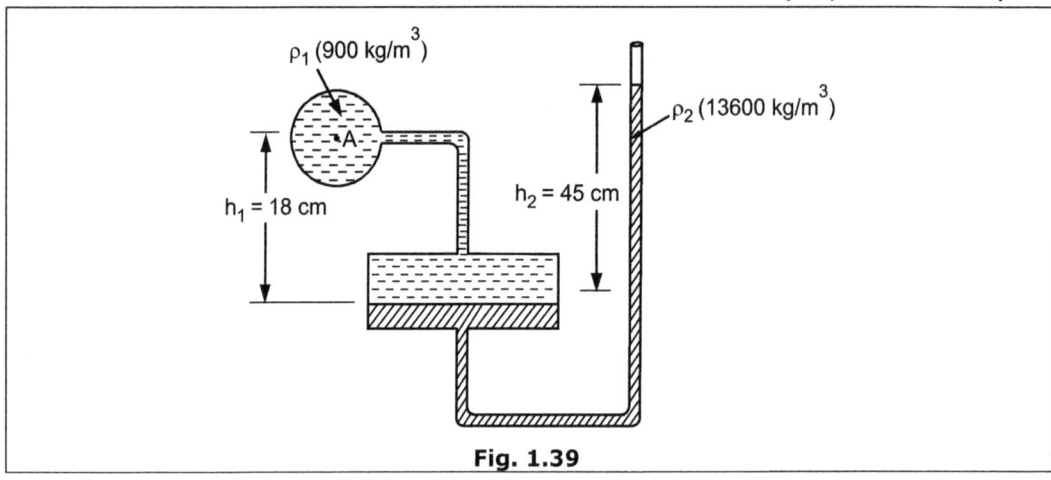

Fig. 1.39

Solution:
$$\rho_1 = 0.9 \times 1000 = 900 \text{ kg/m}^3$$
$$\rho_2 = 13.6 \times 1000 = 13600 \text{ kg/m}^3$$
$$h_1 = 18 \text{ cm} = 0.18 \text{ mt}$$
$$h_2 = 45 \text{ cm} = 0.45 \text{ mt}$$
$$A = \text{Area of tank}$$
$$= 100 \times a$$

∴ $\dfrac{A}{a} = 100$ ∴ $\dfrac{a}{A} = \dfrac{1}{100} = 0.01$

- Single column manometer means micromanometer or sensitive manometer.

We will solve this problem by following equation:

$$p_A = \frac{a \times h_2}{A}[\rho_2 \, g - \rho_1 \, g] + [h_2 \, \rho_2 \, g - h_1 \, \rho_1 \, g]$$

∴ $p_A = 0.01 \times 0.45 \, [13600 \times 9.18 - 900 \times 9.81]$
  $+ [0.45 \times 13600 \times 9.81 - 0.18 \times 900 \times 9.81]$
  $= 0.01 \times 0.45 \times 9.81 \, [13600 - 900] + [6120 - 162]$
  $= 0.044 \, [12700] + [5958]$

$$\boxed{p_A = 820.95 \text{ N/m}^2}$$

Problem 4: *A differential manometer is connected to two pipes as shown. $p_A = 1$ kgf/cm² and $p_B = 2$ kgf/cm². Find manometer reading if the liquid flowing through the pipe A is having specific gravity of 0.8.*

Solution: Given Data:

$$\rho_1 = 1.8 \times 1000 = 1800 \text{ kg/m}^3$$
$$\rho_2 = 0.8 \times 1000 = 800 \text{ kg/m}^3$$
$$p_A = 1 \text{ kgf/cm}^2$$
$$= 10000 \text{ kgf/m}^3$$
$$= 10000 \times 9.81 \text{ N/m}^2 = 98100 \text{ N/m}^2$$
$$p_B = 2 \text{ kgf/cm}^2$$
$$= 20{,}000 \times 9.81 \text{ N/m}^2$$
$$= 196200 \text{ N/m}^2$$
$$(1 \text{ kgf} = 9.81 \text{ N})$$

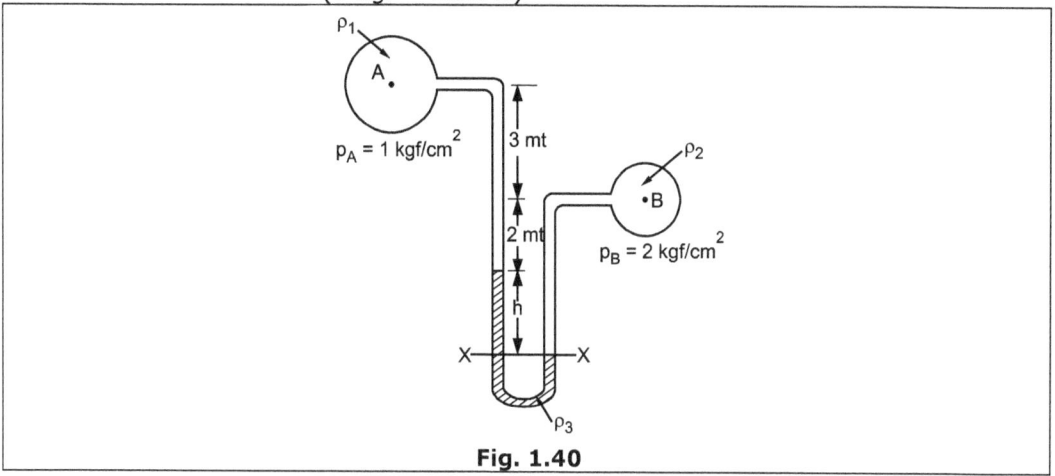

Fig. 1.40

Now refer line XX.

Pressure above XX in left limb = Pressure above XX in right limb

$$p_A + \rho_1 g h_1 + \rho_3 g h = p_B + \rho_2 g h_2$$

Now,
$$h_1 = 3 + 2 = 5 \text{ mt}$$
$$h = \text{We have to find out (manometer reading)}$$
$$h_2 = 2 + h$$
$$\rho_3 = 13.6 \times 1000 = 13600 \text{ kg/m}^3$$

∴ $[98100 + 1800 \times 9.81 \times 5$
$\quad + 13600 \times 9.81 \text{ h}] = 196200 + 800 \times 9.81 \times (2 + h)$

∴ $\quad 98100 + 88290 + 133416 \text{ (h)} = 196200 + 7848 \text{ (2h)}$
$\quad\quad 186390 + 133416 \text{ h} = 196200 + 15696 \text{ h}$
$\quad\quad\quad\quad 117720 \text{ h} = 196200 - 186390$
$\quad\quad\quad\quad 117720 \text{ h} = 9810$

∴ $\quad\quad\quad\quad h = \dfrac{9810}{117720} = 0.0833 \text{ mt.}$

$$\boxed{h = 83.3 \text{ mm}}$$

Problem 5: *Water is flowing through two different pipes to which inverted 'U' tube manometer is attached. The light liquid is having specific gravity 0.9. The pressure head of pipe A is 2 mt of water. Find the pressure in pipe B. (Refer Fig. 1.41).*

Solution: Refer line XX.

Pressure below line XX in left limb = Pressure below line XX in right limb

$$p_A - \rho_1 g h_1 = p_B - \rho_1 g h_2 - \rho_2 g h_3 \qquad \ldots (A)$$

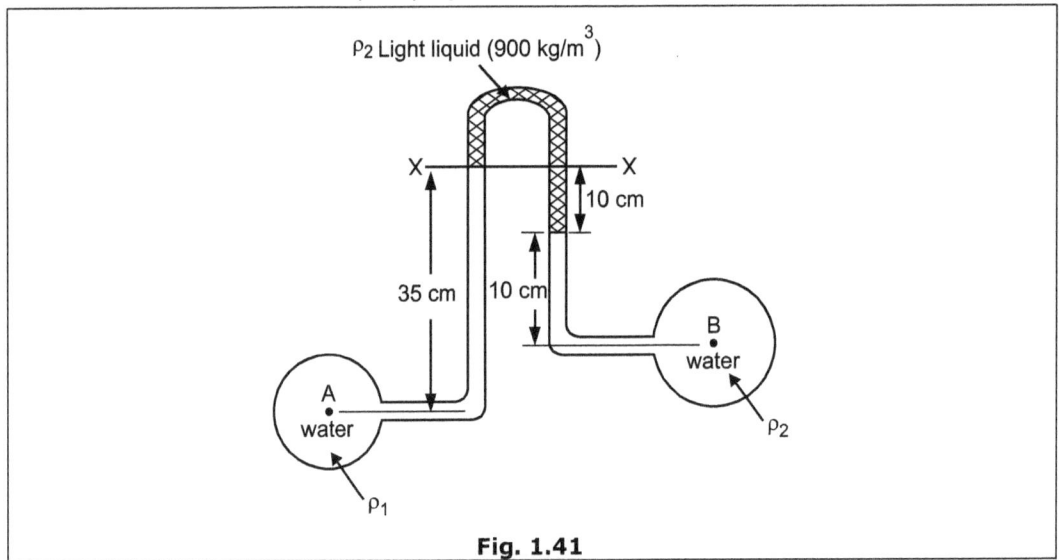

Fig. 1.41

Now given data is

$$\rho_1 = 1000 \text{ kg/m}^3$$
$$h_1 = 35 \text{ cm}$$
$$= 0.35 \text{ mt.}$$
$$p_A = 2 \text{ mt of water}$$
$$= \rho g h \text{ N/m}^2$$
$$= 1000 \times 9.81 \times 2$$
$$= 19620 \text{ N/m}^2$$
$$h_2 = 10 \text{ cm} = 0.1 \text{ mt.}$$
$$\rho_2 = 900 \text{ kg/m}^3$$
$$h_3 = 10 \text{ cm} = 0.1 \text{ mt.}$$

From equation (A),

$$19620 - 1000 \times 9.81 \times 0.35 = p_B - 1000 \times 9.81 \times 0.1 - 900 \times 9.81 \times 0.1$$
$$19620 - 3433.5 = p_B - 981 - 882.9$$

∴ $p_B = 19620 - 3433.5 + 9.81 + 882.9$

$$\boxed{p_B = 24917.4 \text{ N/m}^2}$$

Important points

- **Ideal fluid:** A fluid which is incompressible and having no viscosity is called Ideal fluid. It is imaginary fluid. Because every fluid is having viscosity.
- **Real fluid:** A fluid which possesses viscosity is called real fluid. All fluids are real fluids.
- **Specific gravity:** It is defined as a ratio of density of fluid to density of standard fluid.
- **Specific weight:** It is a ratio between the weight of fluid to its volume.
- **Specific volume:** It is the volume of fluid occupied by unit mass.
- **Viscosity:** It is defined as a property of a fluid which offers resistance to the movement of one layer of fluid over another adjacent layer of the fluid.
- **Kinematic Viscosity:** It is defined as the ratio between the viscosity (also known as dynamic viscosity) and density of fluid.
- **Surface Tension:** It is a tensile force acting on the surface of liquid in contact with air (or gas), such that this surface behaves like 'Elastic Membrane' under tension.
- **Vapour pressure:** It is a specific value of pressure for each liquid. It is the pressure at which liquid starts boiling (without heat) and vapour bubble of the liquid starts forming. This pressure is known as vapour pressure.
- **Compressibility:** Compressibility of fluid is a measure of change in volume when pressure on the liquid increases or changes.
- **Laminar flow** is the flow in which the fluid particles move along well defined path or stream line and all the streamlines are straight and parallel.
- **Turbulent flow** is a flow in which fluid particles move in a zig-zag path.
- **Compressible flow** is the flow in which the density of fluid changes from point to point.
- **Incompressible flow** is the flow in which density (ρ) of fluid **does not** change throughout the flow.
- **Rotational flow** is the flow in which fluid particles, while flowing along the streamlines also **rotate** about their own axis.
- **Non-rotational or Irrotational flow** is the flow in which fluid particles while flowing along the streamline **does not rotate** about its own axis.
- **Pascal's law:** It states that pressure applied on confined fluid is transmitted undiminished in all directions and acts with equal force on equal areas and at right angle to them.
- **Fluid Pressure:** The force exerted by fluid per unit area is known as 'Intensity of Pressure' or 'Fluid Pressure'.
- **Vacuum pressure:** If at a point the pressure if, is less than atmospheric pressure then it is called Vacuum Pressure or only Vacuum or Negative Pressure.

- **Absolute pressure:** It is defined as the pressure which is measured with reference to Absolute vacuum.
- **Gauge pressure:** It is defined as the pressure which is measured with the help of Pressure Measuring Devices.
- **Manometers:** These are devices used for measuring a pressure at a point in a fluid by balancing the column of fluid by the same fluid or column of another fluid.
- **Piezometer tube:** It is the simplest instrument used for measuring pressure head.
- **Differential manometers:** Differential manometers are the devices for measuring the difference of pressure between two points in a single pipe ($p_A - p_B$).

Practice Questions

1. What are three types of fluids? Enumerate.
2. Define: (i) Real fluid (ii) Ideal fluid
3. What is density? Explain.
4. What is the relation between specific weight and density? Explain.
5. Define viscosity. What is its unit in SI units system?
6. Define Surface Tension. Write formula for surface tension (λ) in a hollow liquid droplet (Bubble).
7. Define compressibility and explain its meaning.
8. Enumerate any four good or favourable properties of hydraulic fluid.
9. Write types of hydraulic fluids available.
10. Write Pascal's law and explain its details?
11. What is pressure intensity? Explain.
12. Write the proof of Pascal's law.
13. What is pressure head? Explain with neat sketch. Write its formula.
14. What is the difference between gauge pressure and absolute pressure?
15. Represent graphically various pressures and explain.
16. Write all types of Manometers.
17. What is piezometer? Explain how pressure is measured by piezometer.
18. What is micromanometer? Explain with neat sketch.
19. Compare simple U-tube manometer and Differential U-tube manometer (any four aspects).
20. What is Bourdon's Pressure Gauge? Explain it with neat sketch.
21. Why inverted U-tube manometer is used?
22. Draw figure of differential 'U' tube manometer when pipes are at different level and derive the formula for pressure difference.
23. What is steady and unsteady flow? Explain.
24. Enumerate types of flows.

Chapter 2

HYDRODYNAMICS

Weightage of Marks = 14, Teaching Hours = 05

Learning Objectives
⊃ Understand Principle used in Hydrodynamics.

Contents
Hydrodynamics
- Basic Principles of Fluid Flow
- Law of Continuity and its Applications.
- Energy possessed by the Liquid in Motion.
- Bernoulli's Theorem and its Applications such as Venturimeter, Orifice Meter and Pitot Tube. (Analytical treatment with derivation for measurement of discharge is expected). Hydraulic coefficients
- Concept of Vena Contracta.
- Coefficient of Contraction, Coefficient of Velocity, Coefficient of Discharge, Coefficient of Resistance, Relation between the Hydraulic Coefficients.

2.1 INTRODUCTION

We have already seen in Chapter 1, the definition of 'Hydrodynamics' or 'Fluid dynamics'. Once again we will review it.

Fluid dynamics / Hydrodynamics

It is the study of fluid in motion with the forces causing the flow; when the fluid is assumed incompressible.
- Dynamic behaviour of fluid is analysed by Newton's second law of motion.
- To understand the behaviour of flowing fluid, we must know what is 'Discharge' and 'Equation of Continuity'.

2.1.1 Rate of Flow or Discharges (Q)-Basic Principles of Fluid Flow

Rate of flow is defined as quantity of fluid flowing per second through a section of pipe or channel.

Important:

(i) When the fluid is incompressible (i.e. say water, oil etc.) then discharge is VOLUME of fluid flowing per second through a section of pipe or channel.

(ii) When fluid flowing is compressible (Air or Gas) then discharge is expressed in terms of WEIGHT of fluid flowing across a section of pipe.

- In this subject we are studying liquids, those are generally incompressible. Hence, consider a pipe as shown.

A = Cross-sectional area of pipe at section (m²) ①①

V = Average velocity of flow in pipe (m/sec)

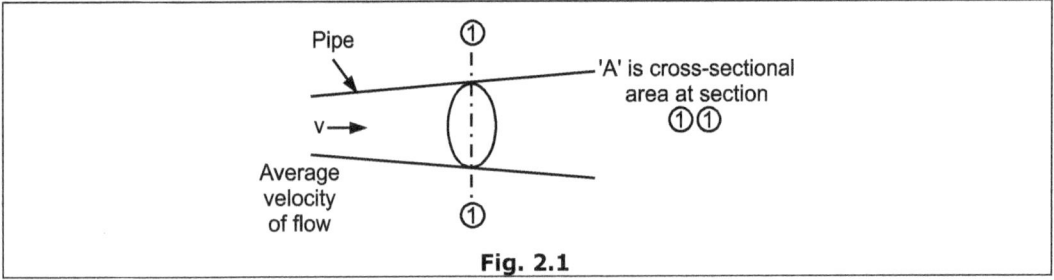

Fig. 2.1

Then discharge through section ① – ① is given by

$$Q = \text{C/s area of pipe at Section ① – ①} \times \text{Average velocity of flow in pipe}$$

$\boxed{Q = A \times V}$ m³/sec or litres/sec.

2.1.2 Equation of Continuity

- This equation is on the basis of 'Law of Conservation of Energy' (Law – Energy cannot be created nor be destroyed, it can only be converted into other form).

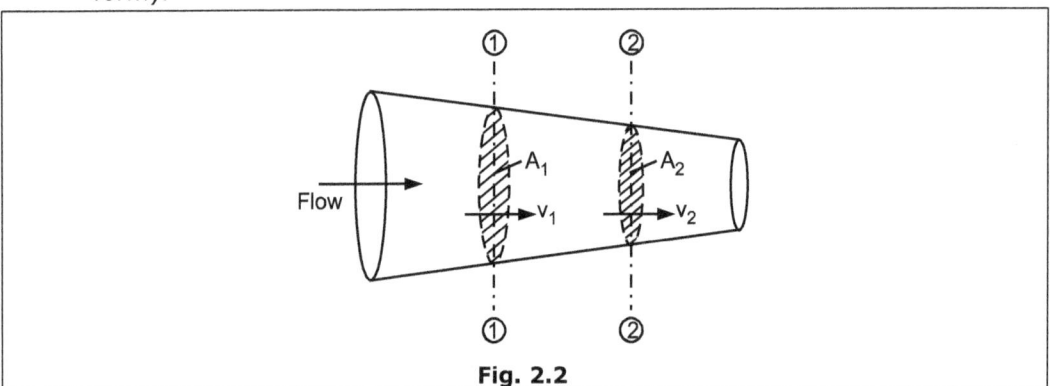

Fig. 2.2

- Consider a pipe (stream tube) having tapered shape. There is full of liquid in a pipe. The quantity entering per unit time is equal to quantity of fluid discharging per unit time.

Let v_1 = the velocity of fluid at Section ① ①
A_1 = the area of Section ① ①
v_2 = the velocity of fluid at Section ② ②
A_2 = the area of cross-section at Section ② ②

Then discharge at Section ① ① = $A_1 v_1$
discharge at Section ② ② = $A_2 v_2$

- The continuity equation tells us that

$$A_1 v_1 = A_2 v_2 = \ldots = A_n v_n = Q$$

2.1.3 Application of Continuity Equation

BRANCHING OF PIPE

- In water supply schemes, many a times to divert the flow of water, we have to make 'Branches' of pipes similar to branches of tree.

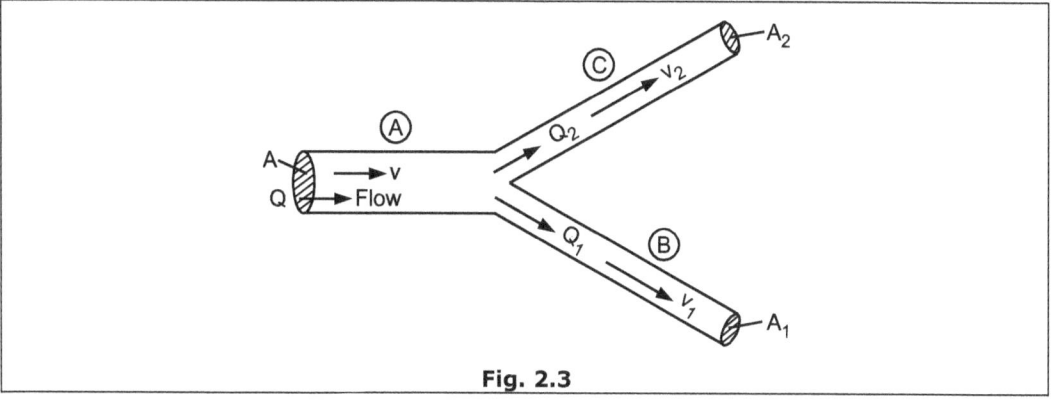

Fig. 2.3

- As shown in Fig. 2.3, a big size pipe having cross-sectional area A is branched in two pipes having smaller cross-section as A_1 and A_2. Then, it is obvious that

$$Q = Q_1 + Q_2$$
$$Av = A_1 v_1 + A_2 v_2$$

where v = Velocity of flow in pipe A
v_1 = Velocity of flow in pipe B
v_2 = Velocity of flow in pipe C

2.2 BERNOULLI'S THEOREM [W-14, S-15]

Theorem: In steady continuous flow of a frictionless incompressible fluid, the sum total of potential head, pressure head and kinetic head is same at all points in flow.

Primary Explanation of Theorem:

Consider a pipe as shown and consider points (1) and (2) in flow. Then as per Bernoulli's theorem,

$$\left(\begin{array}{c}\text{Potential}\\\text{head}\end{array} + \begin{array}{c}\text{Pressure}\\\text{head}\end{array} + \begin{array}{c}\text{Kinetic}\\\text{head}\end{array}\right)_{\text{point (1)}} = \left(\begin{array}{c}\text{Potential}\\\text{head}\end{array} + \begin{array}{c}\text{Pressure}\\\text{head}\end{array} + \begin{array}{c}\text{Kinetic}\\\text{head}\end{array}\right)_{\text{point (2)}}$$

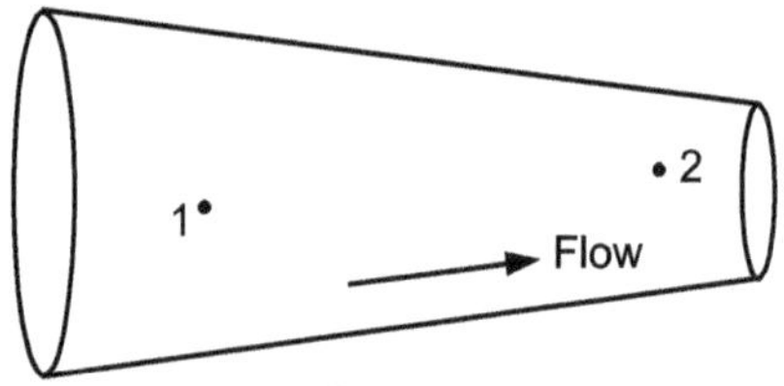

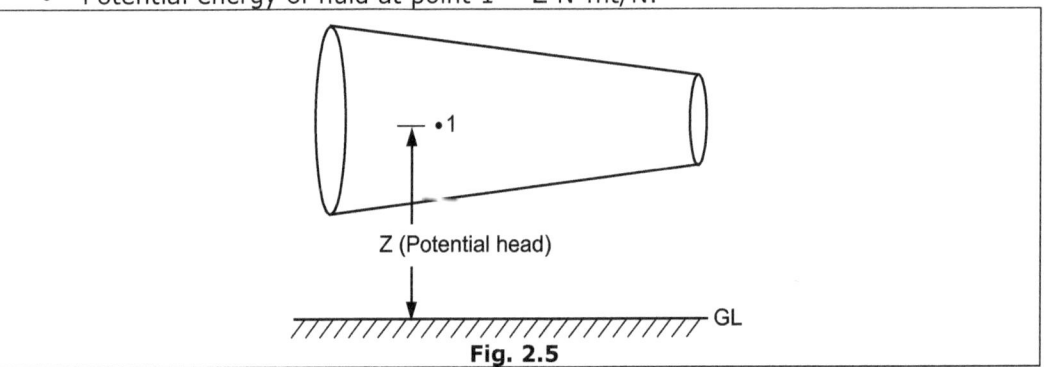

Fig. 2.4

- To understand the theorem clearly, let us study what is potential head, what is pressure head and what is kinetic head.
- **Potential head (Potential Energy):** The energy possessed by a fluid by virtue of its position or location in space.
  If point 1 in fluid is at Z mt height above Ground Level (GL). The potential head at point 1 is Z mt.
- So Potential head = Z mt, and
- Potential energy of fluid at point 1 = Z N-mt/N.

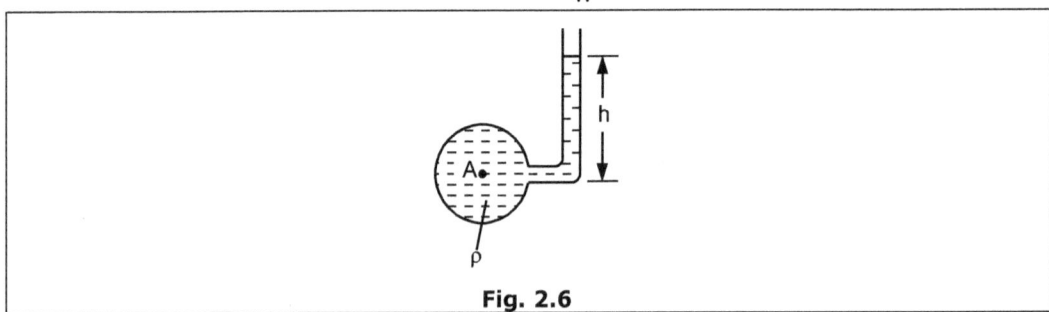

Fig. 2.5

- **Pressure Head (Pressure Energy):** Pressure energy is the energy possessed by a fluid by virtue of the pressure at which it is maintained.
- The pressure energy at point A = W·h Newton meter or joule.
- The pressure energy head at point A = $\frac{p}{w}$ meters ... p = ρgh.

Fig. 2.6

- **Kinetic Head (Kinetic Energy):** Kinetic energy is the energy possessed by a fluid by virtue of its motion.

    Consider point 1 in fluid, moving with velocity v m/sec. Then
- Kinetic energy of fluid = $\dfrac{v^2}{2g}$ N-m/N
- Kinetic head = $\dfrac{v^2}{2g}$ mt.

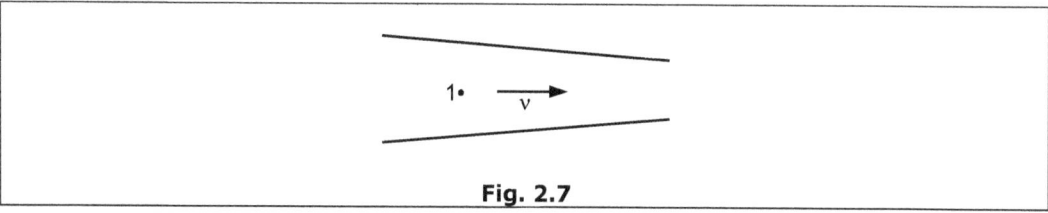

Fig. 2.7

- **Now, Total Energy possessed by a fluid:**

    Consider a particle or point (1) in flowing fluid.

    Let v = Velocity of flow at point (1 m/sec.)

    Z_1 = Height of point (1) from ground level

    $\dfrac{p_1}{w}$ = Pressure head at point (1)

    Then total energy possessed by fluid is

    = Potential head + Pressure head + Kinetic head

    $$= Z_1 + \dfrac{p_1}{w} + \dfrac{v_1^2}{2g}$$

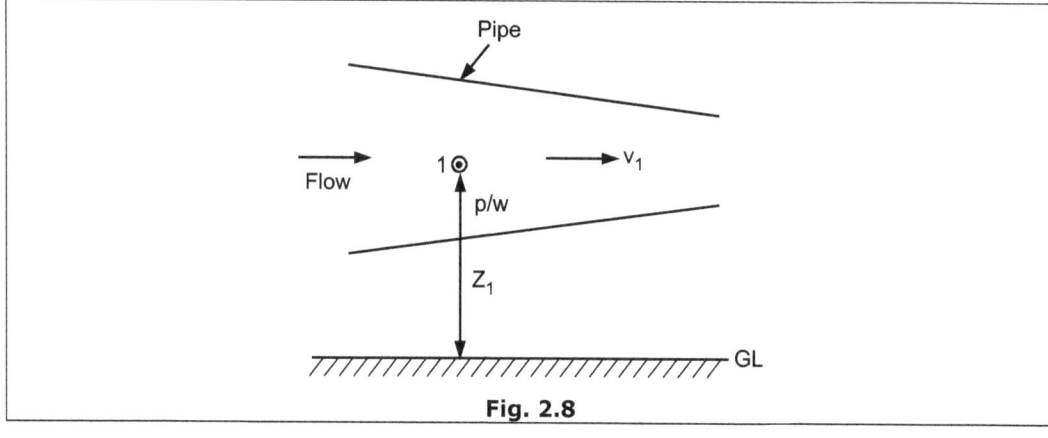

Fig. 2.8

Bernoulli's Theorem:

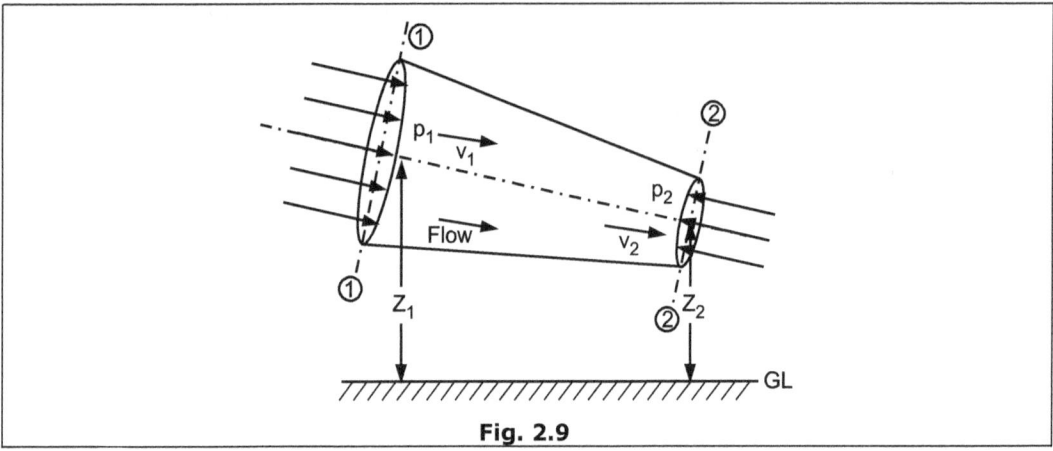

Fig. 2.9

As stated earlier, the Bernoulli's theorem states that at the sum total of energies is same at all points. Consider sections (1) (1) and (2) (2) in variable cross-section pipe. Then as per theorem,

(Total of energy)$_{Section\ 1-1}$ = (Total of energy)$_{Section\ 2-2}$

$$Z_1 + \frac{p_1}{w} + \frac{v_1^2}{2g} = Z_2 + \frac{p_2}{w} + \frac{v_2^2}{2g}$$

2.2.1 Applications of Bernoulli's Theorem [S-15]

- Bernoulli's theorem is applied in all problems of incompressible fluid where energy considerations are involved.
- We shall consider its application to the following measuring devices:
  1. Venturimeter: To measure flow (Q, m³/sec or lit./sec.)
  2. Orifice meter: To measure flow (Q, m³/sec or lit./sec.)
  3. Pitot tube: To measure velocity of flow (v, m/sec.)

2.2.2 Venturimeter

Venturimeter is a device used for measuring the rate of flow of fluid flowing through pipe.

It is a flow measuring device.

Construction: In its simplest form the device consists of:

(a) A short converging section

(b) Throat

(c) A long diverging section

The entrance and exit diameters will be same as that of pipe to which it is fitted. A U tube differential manometer is attached to the venturimeter, having mercury as heavy liquid.

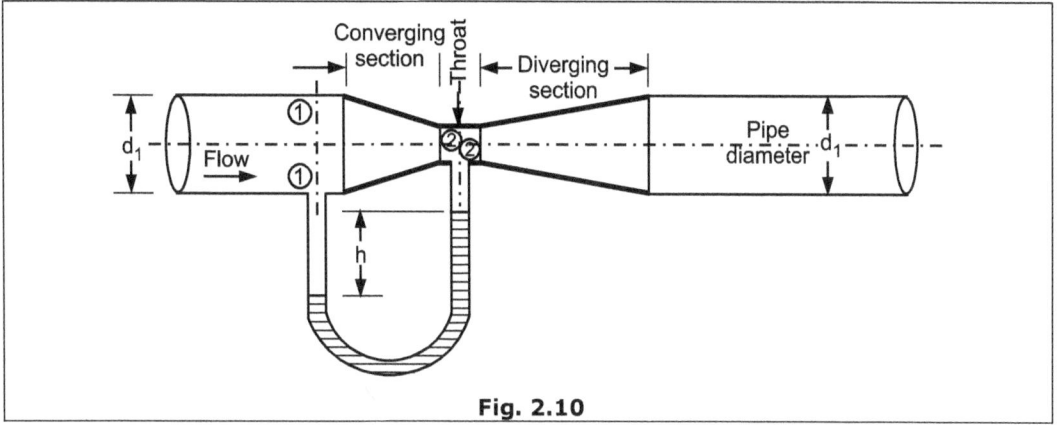

Fig. 2.10

Derivation of Discharge through Venturimeter:

- We know that venturimeter is used to measure discharge through a pipe. The discharge (Q) is given in meter³/sec. or lit./sec.
- The discharge is required to know. Because by knowing the quantity of water flowing through pipe per second, we can calculate the total time required to fill the overhead RCC tank, which supplies water to a nearby city/town/village.

Consider Fig. 2.10: Which shows a venturmeter. The diameter of pipe is d_1. Consider sections (1) (1) and (2) (2) at inlet of venturimeter and at throat section of venturimeter respectively.

Let
d_1 = pipe diameter at section (1) (1)
a_1 = c/s area of pipe at section (1) (1)
$= \frac{\pi}{4} d_1^2$
p_1 = pressure at section (1) (1)
v_1 = velocity of fluid at section (1) (1)

Similarly d_2, a_2, p_2 and v_2 are respective quantities at section (2) (2) i.e. at throat.

By applying Bernoulli's theorem at sections (1) (1) and (2) (2).

$$\begin{pmatrix} \text{Potential head +} \\ \text{Pressure head +} \\ \text{Kinetic head} \end{pmatrix}_{(1)-(1)} = \begin{pmatrix} \text{Potential head +} \\ \text{Pressure head +} \\ \text{Kinetic head} \end{pmatrix}_{(2)-(2)}$$

$$Z_1 + \frac{p_1}{w} + \frac{v_1^2}{2g} = Z_2 + \frac{p_2}{w} + \frac{v_2^2}{2g}$$

but $Z_1 = Z_2$ ... since pipe is parallel to GL

$$\therefore \quad \frac{p_1}{w} + \frac{v_1^2}{2g} = \frac{p_2}{w} + \frac{v_2^2}{2g}$$

$$\therefore \quad \frac{p_1}{\rho g} + \frac{v_1^2}{2g} = \frac{p_2}{\rho g} + \frac{v_2^2}{2g} \quad \because w = \rho g$$

$$\therefore \quad \frac{p_1 - p_2}{\rho g} = \frac{v_2^2 - v_1^2}{2g} \qquad \ldots (A)$$

But from manometer reading h, it is clear that

$$p_1 - p_2 = \text{Pressure difference between (1) (1) and (2) (2)}$$

$$= \rho g h$$

$$\therefore \quad h = \frac{p_1 - p_2}{\rho g}$$

$\therefore$ From equation (A),

$$\frac{v_2^2 - v_1^2}{2g} = h$$

$$\therefore \quad v_2^2 - v_1^2 = 2gh \qquad \ldots (B)$$

As per equation of continuity applied between sections (1) (1) and (2) (2),

$$a_1 v_1 = a_2 v_2 = Q$$

$$v_1 = \frac{a_2}{a_1} v_2$$

Putting value of v_1 in equation (B),

$$v_2^2 - \left(\frac{a_2}{a_1} v_2\right)^2 = 2gh$$

$$\therefore \quad v_2^2 \left(1 - \frac{a_2^2}{a_1^2}\right) = 2gh$$

$$\therefore \quad v_2^2 \left(\frac{a_1^2 - a_2^2}{a_1^2}\right) = 2gh$$

$$\therefore \quad v_2^2 = \frac{a_1^2 \, 2gh}{a_1^2 - a_2^2}$$

$$\therefore \quad v_2 = \sqrt{\frac{a_1^2 \, 2gh}{\left(a_1^2 - a_2^2\right)}}$$

$$\therefore \quad v_2 = \frac{a_1}{\sqrt{a_1^2 - a_2^2}} \sqrt{2gh}$$

But
$$Q = a_2 v_2$$
$$= a_2 \left[\frac{a_1}{\sqrt{a_1^2 - a_2^2}} \sqrt{2gh} \right]$$
$$\boxed{Q = \frac{a_1 \cdot a_2}{\sqrt{a_1^2 - a_2^2}} \sqrt{2gh}} \qquad \ldots (C)$$

Coefficient of Discharge

The discharge calculated by equation (C) is 'Theoretical Discharge' (Q_{TH}). Because it is calculated by knowing the dimensions of venturimeter and manometer reading.

'Actual Discharge' (Q_{act}) is slightly less than theoretical discharge, because of losses.

Hence, Coefficient of discharge (C_d) = $\dfrac{Q_{act}}{Q_{th}}$

C_d is always less than 1.

Actual Discharge of Venturimeter

$$Q_{actual} = C_d \times Q_{Th}$$

$$\boxed{Q_{act} = C_d \times \frac{a_1 a_2}{\sqrt{a_1^2 - a_2^2}} \sqrt{2gh}}$$

Recommended Dimensions for Venturimeter

(Design of venturimeter on the basis of diameter of pipe to which it is attached.)

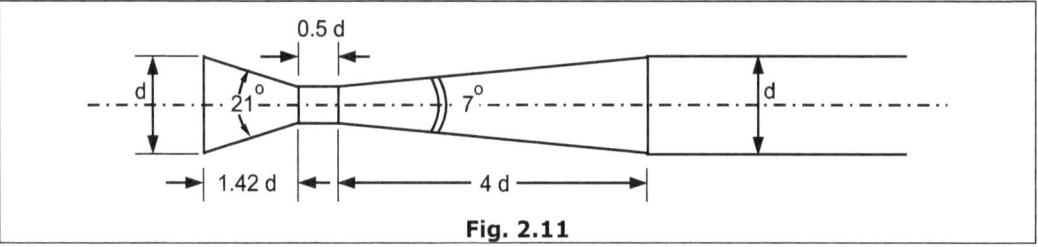

Fig. 2.11

By knowing the diameter of pipe (d), we can design the standard venturimeter by calculating various dimensions.

2.2.3 Orifice Meter [W-14, S-15]

- Similar to venturimeter, this is another device to measure the rate of flow of a liquid through a pipe.

It means discharge Q in m³/sec or lit./sec.

Construction: In its simplest form it consists of a flat circular plate which is having a circular sharp edged hole called ORIFICE which is concentric with the pipe.

The $\boxed{\text{diameter of orifice } (d_o) = \dfrac{1}{2} \text{ of diameter of pipe}}$.

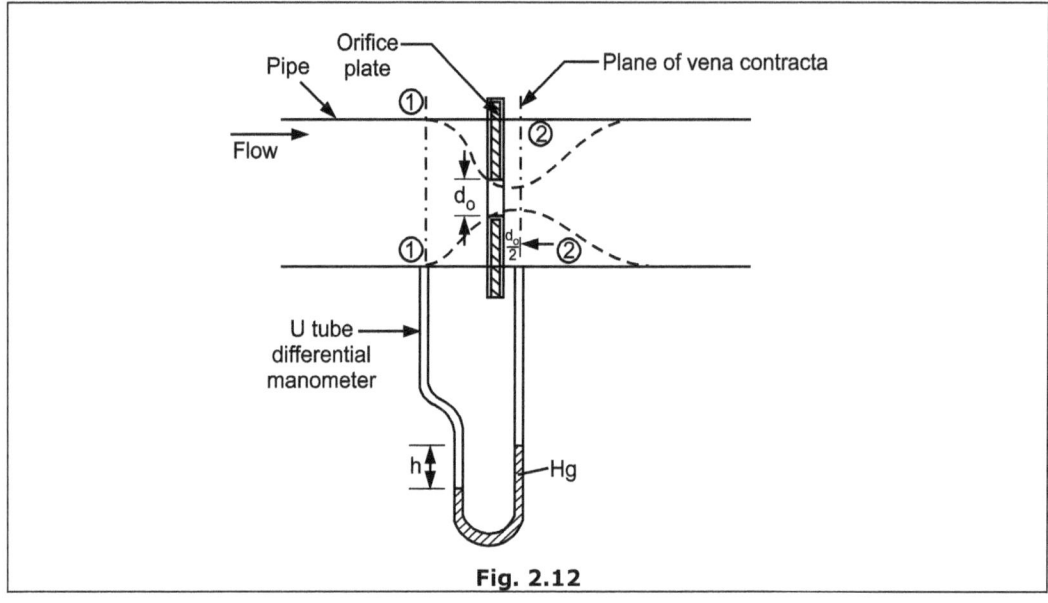

Fig. 2.12

Derivation of discharge through orifice meter

- In Fig. 2.12, an orifice plate having central hole i.e. orifice having diameter 'd_o' and hence cross-sectional area $\boxed{a_o = \frac{\pi}{4} d_o^2}$.
- A manometer is attached to sections (1) (1) and (2) (2) having heavy liquid as mercury.
- When flow of fluid enters an orifice, there would be a certain amount of frictional resistance at the sides of orifice. To reduce this resistance, the orifice is sharp edged.
- The jet of liquid in passing though an orifice, will contract in the beginning and then again will touch the walls of pipe and flow becomes parallel to pipe.
- The velocity of flow is destroyed on reaching the orifice, this causes lateral force on jet coming out of orifice and hence the area of jet reduces and then becomes parallel to pipe.

2.3 CONCEPT OF VENA CONTRACTA

The section of jet where contraction takes place and then jet becomes parallel is called VENA-CONTRACTA.

- The cross-sectional area of vena contracta is less than cross-sectional area of orifice.
- If area of orifice = a_o.
- If area of vena contracta = a_c.

- Then coefficient of contraction

$$\boxed{C_c = \frac{a_c}{a_o}}$$

- C_c is always less than 1.
- The plane of vena contracta is at a distance of $\frac{d_o}{2}$ from orifice plate.
- Refer Fig. 2.13.

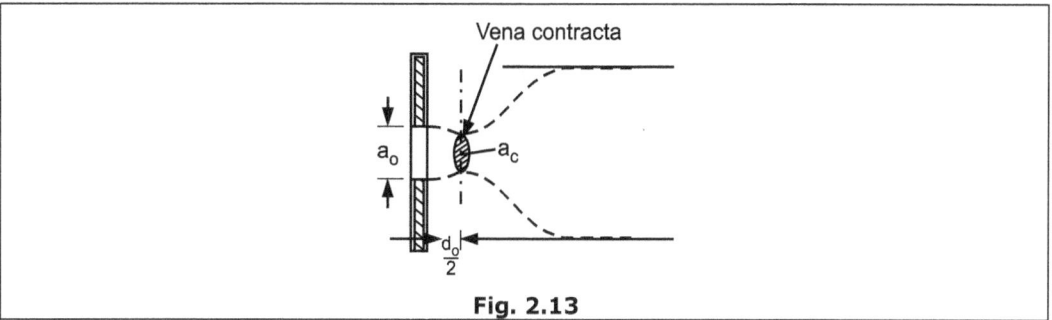

Fig. 2.13

Apply Bernoulli's theorem at sections (1) (1) and (2) (2).

$$\begin{pmatrix}\text{Potential head +}\\ \text{Pressure head +}\\ \text{Kinetic head}\end{pmatrix}_{(1)-(1)} = \begin{pmatrix}\text{Potential head +}\\ \text{Pressure head +}\\ \text{Kinetic head}\end{pmatrix}_{(2)-(2)}$$

$$Z_1 + \frac{p_1}{w} + \frac{v_1^2}{2g} = Z_2 + \frac{p_2}{w} + \frac{v_2^2}{2g}$$

where, v_1 = velocity of flow at section (1) (1)

v_2 = velocity of flow at section (2) (2)

But $Z_1 = Z_2 \rightarrow$ because arrangement is parallel to GL

∴ $\frac{p_1}{\rho g} + \frac{v_1^2}{2g} = \frac{p_2}{\rho g} + \frac{v_2^2}{2g}$ .... $w = \rho g$

∴ $\frac{p_1 - p_2}{\rho g} = \frac{v_2^2 - v_1^2}{2g}$ ... (A)

But as per venturimeter derivation, $\frac{p_1 - p_2}{\rho g} = h$ = manometer reading.

∴ $\frac{v_2^2 - v_1^2}{2g} = h$

∴ $v_2^2 - v_1^2 = 2gh$ ...(B)

But C_c = Coefficient of contraction

$= \frac{a_2}{a_o}$ ... section (2) (2) is at vena contracta

∴ $a_2 = a_o \times C_c$ ... (C)

where a_o = Cross-sectional area of orifice

But when we apply equation of continuity at sections (1) (1) and (2) (2), we get

$$Q = a_1 v_1 = a_2 v_2$$

$$\therefore \quad v_1 = \frac{a_2}{a_1} v_2$$

By putting value of a_2 from equation (C),

$$v_1 = \frac{a_0 \times C_c}{a_1} \cdot v_2$$

Now putting value of v_1 in equation (B) and solving, we get

$$\boxed{Q_{Th} = \frac{a_0 \, a_1 \sqrt{2gh}}{\sqrt{a_1^2 - a_0^2}}}$$

But the actual discharge Q_{act} will be less than theoretical discharge.

$$\therefore \quad C_d = \frac{\text{Coefficient of}}{\text{discharge}} = \frac{Q_{Act}}{Q_{Th}} < 1$$

$$\boxed{\begin{aligned} Q_{Act} &= C_d \times Q_{Th} \\ &= C_d \left[\frac{a_0 \, a_1 \sqrt{2gh}}{\sqrt{a_1^2 - a_0^2}} \right] \end{aligned}}$$

2.3.1 Pitot Tube

- **Pitot Tube** is a very simple instrument by which velocity head or velocity of a flowing fluid can be measured.

Construction: In its simplest form it is just like a glass tube with the lower end bent through 90°. It is placed in moving liquid with the lower end or opening facing the direction of motion of flow.

Working: The liquid flows up the tube until its kinetic energy is converted into potential energy. The velocity of flow, then can be calculated by taking height of liquid column stabilized in pitot tube.

Use: Pitot tube is used to measure velocity of flow in rivers.

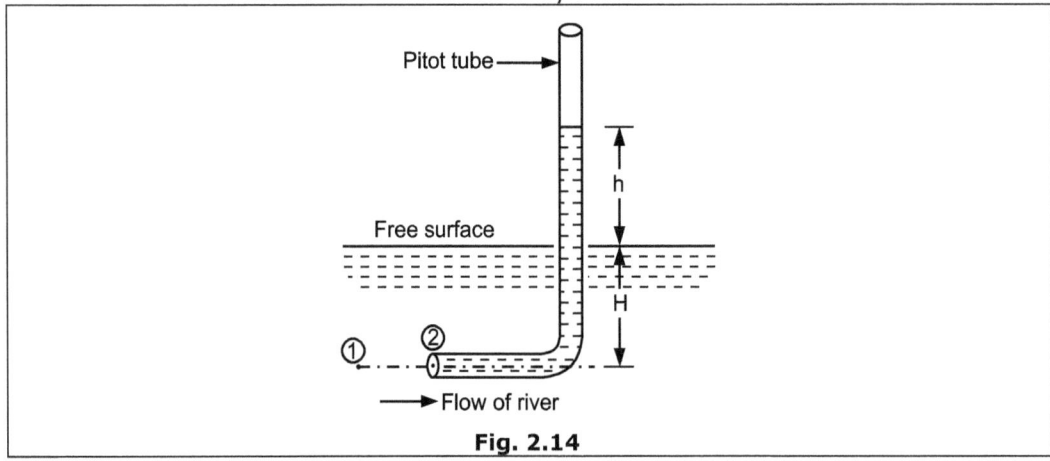

Fig. 2.14

Derivation of formula for calculation of velocity of flow:

- In Fig. 2.14, consider points (1) and (2) at the same level.
- Point (2) is just at the inlet of pitot tube.
- Point (1) is far away from the tube.

Let
- p_1 = Intensity of pressure at point (1)
- v_1 = Velocity of flow at point (1)
- p_2 = Intensity of pressure at point (2)
- v_2 = Velocity of flow at point (2)
- H = Depth of tube in flowing liquid
- h = Rise of liquid in tube above free surface

Applying Bernoulli's theorem at points (1) and (2),

$$Z_1 + \frac{p_1}{\rho g} + \frac{v_1^2}{2g} = Z_2 + \frac{p_2}{\rho g} + \frac{v_2^2}{2g} \quad \ldots w = \rho g \qquad \ldots(A)$$

But $\quad Z_1 = Z_2 \ldots$ since points (1) and (2) are at same level

and
$\quad p_1 = H \rho g \ldots$ at point (1)
$\quad p_2 = (H + h) \rho g \ldots$ at point (2)

∴ $\quad \dfrac{p_1}{\rho g} = H \ldots$ at point (1)

$\quad \dfrac{p_2}{\rho g} = (H + h) \ldots$ at point (2)

Putting above values in equation (A),

$$H + \frac{v_1^2}{2g} = (H + h) + \frac{v_2^2}{2g}$$

∴ $\quad \dfrac{v_1^2 - v_2^2}{2g} = h$

But at the entry of pitot tube, velocity of flow = 0

∴ $\quad v_2 = 0$

∴ $\quad v_1^2 - 0 = 2gh$

∴ $\quad \boxed{v_1 = \sqrt{2gh}}$

This velocity is theoretical velocity. $(v_1)_{actual}$ is slightly less than $(v_1)_{Th}$ because of some losses in pipe.

So, Coefficient of velocity $(C_v) = \dfrac{\text{Actual velocity}}{\text{Theoretical velocity}}$

∴ $\quad C_v = \dfrac{v_{Act}}{v_{Th}}$

∴ $\quad (v_1)_{Act} = C_v \times (v_1)_{Th}$

∴ $\quad \boxed{(v_1)_{Act} = C_v\sqrt{2gh}}$

Hence velocity at any point in flow is

$\quad \boxed{v = \sqrt{2gh}} \ldots$equation of pitot tube

SOLVED PROBLEMS

Problem 1: *A horizontal venturimeter with inlet and throat diameter as 40 cm and 20 cm respectively is used to measure flow of water. The differential manometer reading connected to venturimeter is 20 cm of mercury. Determine actual discharge. Take $C_d = 0.95$.*

Sol. Given Data: d_1 = diameter of inlet = 40 cm = 0.4 mt

$$\therefore \quad a_1 = \frac{\pi}{4} d_1^2$$

$$= 0.125 \text{ m}^2$$

d_2 = diameter at throat = 20 cm = 0.2 mt

$\therefore \quad a_2 = 0.0314 \text{ m}^2$

Manometer reading = 20 cm of Hg

$C_d = 0.95$

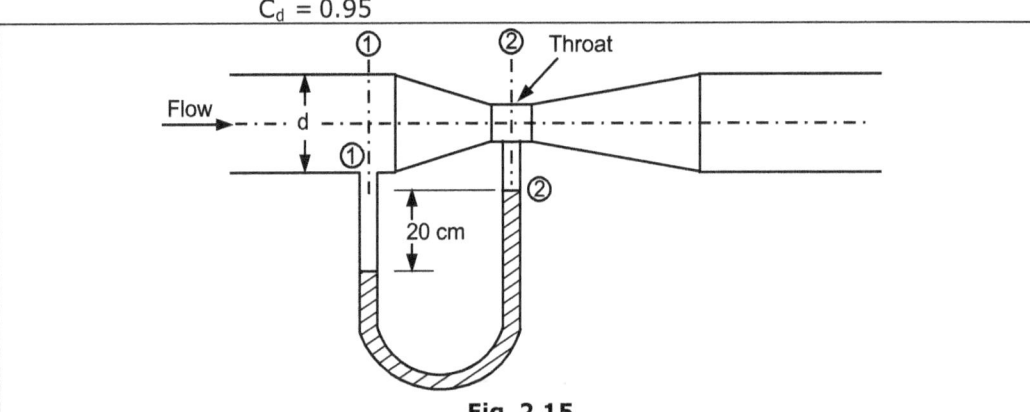

Fig. 2.15

Solution: We know the formula for actual discharge (Q) through venturimeter

$$Q_{Act} = C_d \cdot \frac{a_1 \, a_2}{\sqrt{a_1^2 - a_2^2}} \sqrt{2gh}$$

- We know C_d, a_1 and a_2.
- Now we have to find h i.e. manometer reading in terms of meters of water. The manometer reading given in problem is in terms of head of Hg.
- To convert head of Hg in equivalent head of water, use the following formula:

$$h = x \left[\frac{S_m}{S_w} - 1 \right]$$

where,   h = manometer reading in terms of meters of water

x = manometer reading in terms of meters of Hg = 0.2 mt

S_m = Sp. Gr. of Hg = 13.6

S_w = Sp. Gr. of Water = 1.0

$$\therefore \quad h = 0.2 \left[\frac{13.6}{1} - 1 \right] = 2.52 \text{ mt. of water}$$

$$\therefore \quad Q_{act} = 0.95 \times \frac{0.125 \times 0.0314}{\sqrt{0.125^2 - 0.0314^2}} \times \sqrt{2 \times 9.81 \times 2.52}$$

$$Q_{act} = 0.2183 \text{ m}^3/\text{sec.}$$

Problem 2: *A 30 cm × 15 cm venturimeter is provided in a vertical pipe line carrying water and flow being upward. The difference in elevation of throat and entrance of the venturi is 30 cm. The manometer reading is 25 cm. Find the pressure difference between entrance section and throat section. The heavy liquid is mercury.*

Solution: What is asked in problem: The pressure difference between sections (1) (1) and (2) (2). It may be noted that the pressure at section (1) (1) is more than at (2) (2). This problem can be solved by applying Bernoulli's theorem at sections (1) (2) and (2) (2).

$$\begin{pmatrix}\text{Pressure energy +}\\ \text{Kinetic energy +}\\ \text{Potential energy}\end{pmatrix}_{(1)-(1)} = \begin{pmatrix}\text{Pressure energy +}\\ \text{Kinetic energy +}\\ \text{Potential energy}\end{pmatrix}_{(2)-(2)}$$

$$\frac{p_1}{\rho g} + \frac{v_1^2}{2g} + Z_1 = \frac{p_2}{\rho g} + \frac{v_2^2}{2g} + Z_2$$

∴ $$\frac{p_1 - p_2}{\rho g} + (Z_1 - Z_2) = \frac{v_1^2 - v_2^2}{2g}$$

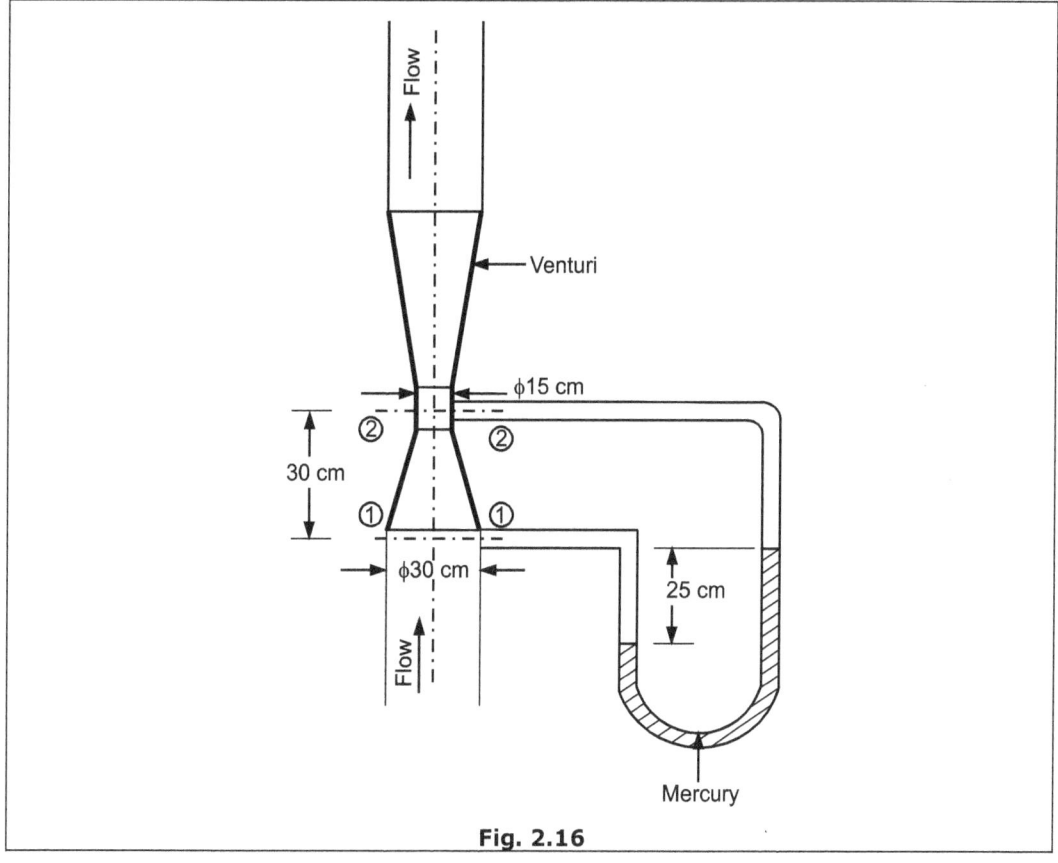

Fig. 2.16

We have to find out $p_1 - p_2$ and we know that $\dfrac{v_1^2 - v_2^2}{2g} = h$ ... (Refer derivation of discharge for venturimeter)

$\therefore \quad \dfrac{p_1 - p_2}{\rho g} + (Z_1 - Z_2) = h$

h = head in terms of water $= x\left[\dfrac{13.6}{1} - 1\right]$

$= 0.25\,[12.6]$

$= 3.15$ mt. of water

$Z_1 - Z_2 = 30$ cm from above figure $= 0.3$ mt.

$\therefore \quad \dfrac{p_1 - p_2}{\rho g} + 0.3 = 3.15$

$\therefore \quad p_1 - p_2 = (3.15 - 0.3) \times \rho g$

$= 2.85 \times 1000 \times 9.81 = \dfrac{27958.5}{10^4}$ N/cm²

$\therefore \quad p_1 - p_2 = 2.79$ N/cm²

Problem 3: *54 litres per second of oil with specific gravity 0.8 flow through a horizontal venturimeter 20 cm × 10 cm. Calculate the deflection of an oil by mercury differential gauge. Take $C_d = 0.98$.*

Solution: Note that:
- Venturimeter size 20 cm × 20 cm means:
  - Pipe diameter = 20 cm
  - Throat diameter = 10 cm
- Mercury differential gauge means U tube differential manometer.

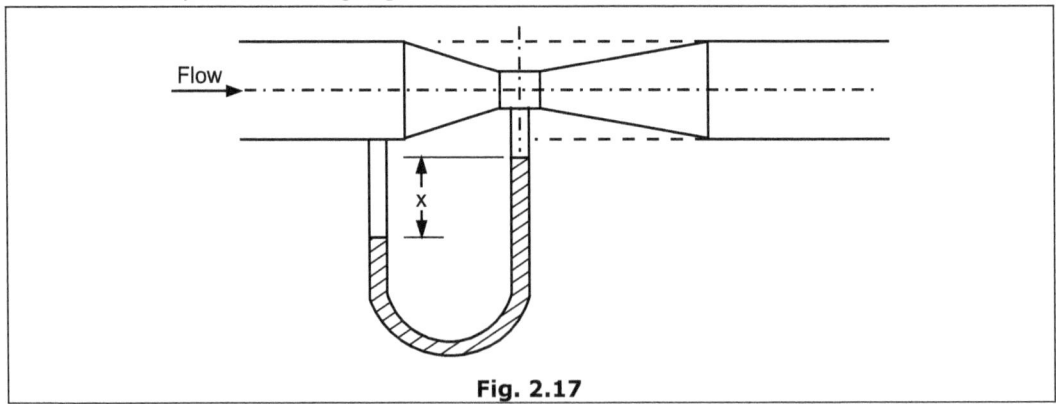

Fig. 2.17

What is asked in problem: Manometer reading of mercury i.e. x cm.

Given Data:

d_1 = pipe diameter = 20 cm

$$a_1 = \frac{\pi}{4}d^2 = \frac{\pi}{4} 20^2 = 314.16 \text{ cm}^2$$

$$d_2 = \text{throat diameter} = 10 \text{ cm}$$

$$a_2 = \frac{\pi}{4}d^2 = \frac{\pi}{4} 10^2 = 78.54 \text{ cm}^2$$

$$C_d = 0.98$$

Discharge i.e. $Q_{act} = 54$ lit./sec.

$$= 54 \times 1000 \text{ cm}^3/\text{sec.}$$

Now,
$$Q_{act} = C_d \cdot \frac{a_1 a_2}{\sqrt{a_1^2 - a_2^2}} \sqrt{2gh}$$

$$54 \times 1000 = 0.98 \times \frac{314.16 \times 78.54}{\sqrt{314.16^2 - 78.54^2}} \times \sqrt{2 \times 9.81 \times h}$$

$$54000 = 79.48 \sqrt{1962 \, h}$$

∴ $\quad 680 = \sqrt{1962 \, h}$

∴ $\quad h = \frac{680^2}{1962}$ ...... squaring both sides

$$h = 235.67 \text{ cm of oil}$$

but $\quad h = x\left[\dfrac{S_m}{S_{oil}} - 1\right]$

$$235.67 = x\left[\frac{13.6}{0.8} - 1\right]$$

$$235.67 = x\,[16]$$

∴ $\quad \boxed{x = 14.72 \text{ cm of Hg}}$

Problem 4: *An orifice meter with orifice diameter 100 mm is inserted in a pipe of 300 mm diameter. The manometer using mercury as a indicating liquid is giving reading of 400 mm.*

Find the rate of flow of oil having specific gravity 0.8 and $C_d = 0.64$.

Solution: We will solve this problem by following formula of actual discharge through orifice meter.

$$Q_{act} = C_d \cdot \frac{a_o \, a_1}{\sqrt{a_1^2 - a_o^2}} \times \sqrt{2gh}$$

where, $\quad a_1$ = Cross-sectional area of pipe

a_o = Cross-sectional area of orifce

h = Manometer reading in terms of oil

C_d = Coefficient of discharge

To find:	Given data:
$a_1 = \dfrac{\pi}{4} d_1^2$	d_1 = diameter of pipe
$= \dfrac{\pi}{4} \times 0.3^2$	= 300 mm
$= 0.0706 \text{ m}^2$	= 0.3 mt.
$a_o = \dfrac{\pi}{4} d_o^2$	d_o = diameter of orifice
$= \dfrac{\pi}{4} \times 0.1^2$	= 100 mm
$= 0.00785 \text{ m}^2$	= 0.1 mt.
$h = x \left[\dfrac{S_m}{S_{oil}} - 1 \right]$	x = manometer reading of mercury
$= 0.4 \left[\dfrac{13.6}{0.8} - 1 \right]$	= 400 mm = 0.4 mt
= 6.4 mt of oil	$C_d = 0.64$

$$\therefore Q_{act} = 0.64 \, \dfrac{(0.00785 \times 0.0706)}{\sqrt{(0.0706^2 - 0.00785)^2}} \times \sqrt{2 \times 9.81 \times 6.4}$$

$$\boxed{Q_{act} = 0.0566 \text{ m}^3/\text{sec}}$$

Problem 5: *A pitot tube is placed in the centre of 350 mm diameter water pipe line. Find the velocity of flow in pipe and discharge if pitot tube reading is 50 cm. Take coefficient of velocity at 0.98.*

Solution:
- Pilot tube is used to measure velocity of flow.
$$V = C_v \sqrt{2gh}$$
- The discharge is found out by continuity equation
$$Q = AV$$

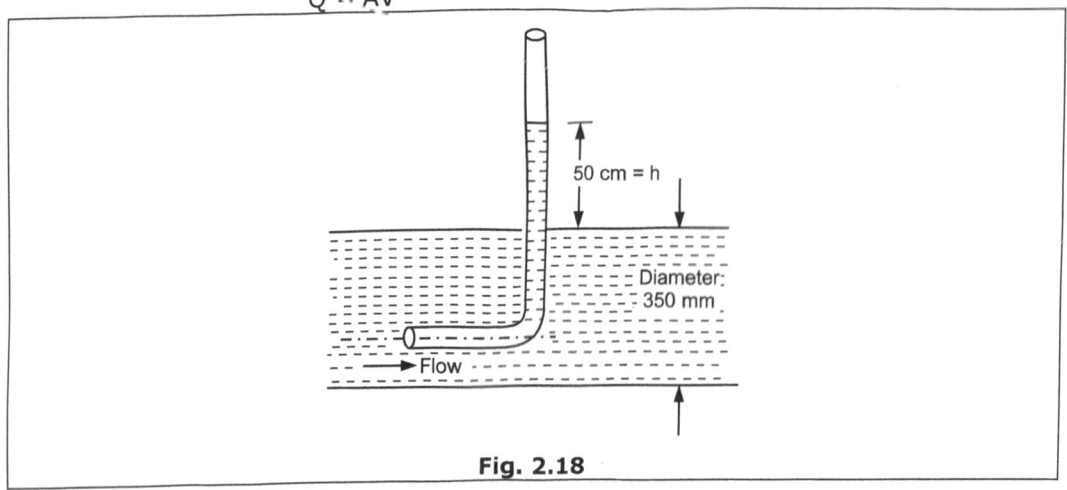

Fig. 2.18

Finding velocity:

$$V = C_v \sqrt{2gh} = 0.98 \sqrt{2 \times 9.81 \times 0.5}$$
$$V = 3.03 \text{ mt./sec.}$$

Finding discharge:

$$Q = \text{Area of pipe} \times \text{Velocity} = \frac{\pi}{4} \times 0.35^2 \times 3.03$$

$$Q = 0.29 \text{ m}^3/\text{sec.}$$

2.3.2 Relation between Hydraulic Coefficients [W-14]

While studying venturimeter, orifice meter, pitot tube, we have already came across with

(a) Coefficient of Discharge $(C_d) = \dfrac{\text{Actual Discharge}}{\text{Theoretical Discharge}}$

(b) Coefficient of Velocity $(C_v) = \dfrac{\text{Actual Velocity}}{\text{Theoretical Velocity}}$

(c) Coefficient of Contraction $(C_c) = \dfrac{\text{Area of jet at Vena Contracta}}{\text{Area of orifice}}$

Now, we will derive the equation which relates these three coefficients.

We know that

$$C_d = \frac{\text{Actual Discharge}}{\text{Theoretical Discharge}} = \frac{Q_{act}}{Q_{th}}$$

but $\quad Q = \text{Area} \times \text{Velocity} \ldots\text{continuity equation}$

Hence,

$$C_d = \frac{\text{Actual Area} \times \text{Actual Velocity}}{\text{Theoretical Area} \times \text{Theoretical Velocity}}$$

$$= \left(\frac{\text{Actual Area}}{\text{Theoretical Area}}\right) \times \left(\frac{\text{Actual Velocity}}{\text{Theoretical Velocity}}\right)$$

$$\boxed{C_d = C_c \times C_v}$$

Value of …..

- C_d varies from 0.61 to 0.65 for general purpose take $C_d = 0.62$ (if not given in problem).
- C_v is taken at 0.98 (if not given in problem)
- C_c is taken at 0.64 (if not given in problem)

Important Points

- **Rate of flow** is defined as quantity of fluid flowing per second through a section of pipe or channel.
- **Bernoulli's theorem:** In steady continuous flow of a frictionless incompressible fluid, the sum total of potential head, pressure head and kinetic head is same at all points in flow.

- **Potential head (Potential Energy):** The energy possessed by a fluid by virtue of its position or location in space.
- **Pressure head (Pressure Energy):** Pressure energy is the energy possessed by a fluid by virtue of the pressure at which it is maintained.
- **Kinetic head (Kinetic Energy):** Kinetic energy is the energy possessed by a fluid by virtue of its motion.
- **Venturimeter:** Venturimeter is a device used for measuring the rate of flow of fluid flowing through pipe. It is a flow measuring device.
- **Orifice meter:** Similar to venturimeter, this is another device to measure the rate of flow of a liquid through a pipe.
- **Concept of Vena Contracta:** The section of jet where contraction takes place and then jet becomes parallel is called VENA-CONTRACTA.
- **Pitot Tube:** It is a very simple instrument by which velocity head or velocity of a flowing fluid can be measured.

Practice Questions

1. Define rate of flow or discharge. What is the equation by which we can find out discharge?
2. State law of continuity. How this equation is applicable to find out rate of flow in branching of pipes?
3. What is potential head? Explain.
4. What is kinetic head? Explain.
5. State Bernoulli's theorem and explain with neat sketch.
6. Write applications of Bernoulli's theorem.
7. Define the discharge through venturimeter by using Bernoulli's theorem.
8. What is coefficient of discharge? Write its formula. What is its significance?
9. Design venturimeter for pipe diameter of 100 mm. Draw neat figure of venturimeter using half scale. Show all the sections of venturi.
10. What is vena-contracta? Explain.
11. Why orifice meter is used? Write formula for discharge through orifice meter.
12. What is C_d, C_v and C_c? Explain each term.
13. Derive relation between C_d, C_v and C_c.
14. What is pitot tube? Why it is used?

■■■

Chapter 3

HYDRAULIC DEVICES

Weightage of Marks = 16, Teaching Hours = 08

Learning Objectives

➲ Know working of pumps

➲ Select proper pumping devices

➲ Find faults in pumps

➲ Understand use of air vessel

Contents

Centrifugal Pumps

- Types, Construction and Working of Centrifugal Pump
- Types of Casing
- Need of priming
- Heads, Losses and Efficiencies of Centrifugal Pump. (No Analytical Treatment)
- Net Positive Suction Head
- Fault findings and remedies
- Pump selection

Reciprocating Pumps

- Construction and Working of Single and Double Acting Reciprocating pump
- Positive and Negative slip
- Air Vessels - their function and advantage
- Power and Efficiencies of Reciprocation Pump (No Analytical Treatment)
- Reasons of Cavitations and Separation
- Comparison between Reciprocating and Centrifugal Pump

3.1 CENTRIFUGAL PUMP

- Pump is a device which converts mechanical energy into hydraulic energy.

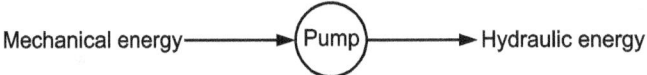

- The mechanical energy given to pump is in the form of – Electrical Energy (Motor) or Heat Energy (IC Engine), Steam Energy (Steam Turbine).
- Hydraulic energy created is in the form of pressure energy.
- Centrifugal pump works on the principle of forced vortex flow.
- **Forced vortex flow:** When a certain mass of liquid is rotated by an external torque, the rise in the pressure head of the rotating liquid takes place. The rise in pressure head at any point of the rotating liquid is proportional to the square of tangential velocity of the liquid at that point.
- Centrifugal pump is one of the Outward Flow Type.
- When heavy or huge quantity of fluid is to be handled and pressure is not important criteria then centrifugal pumps are used.
- **Applications of centrifugal pump:**
    (a) For transferring huge water quantity from main water reservoir to subwater reservoirs in city and towns.
    (b) For transferring milk from one station to other stations in milk processing plants (Dairies). These pumps are made of stainless steel.
    (c) For transferring water from ground level tank to overhead tank in apartment buildings.
    (d) It is used in handling sugarcane juice in sugar factories.
    (e) Centrifugal pumps (single stage / multistage) are having wide applications in oil handling plants / chemical plants.
    (f) Centrifugal pumps made up of special material are used in handling concentrated acids in chemical plants. These are called submerged centrifugal pumps.
    (g) Boiler water feed pumps, water softening plant pumps are centrifugal pumps.

Now, we will study the detail working of centrifugal pump.

3.1.1 Construction and Principle of Working of Centrifugal Pump

[S-15]

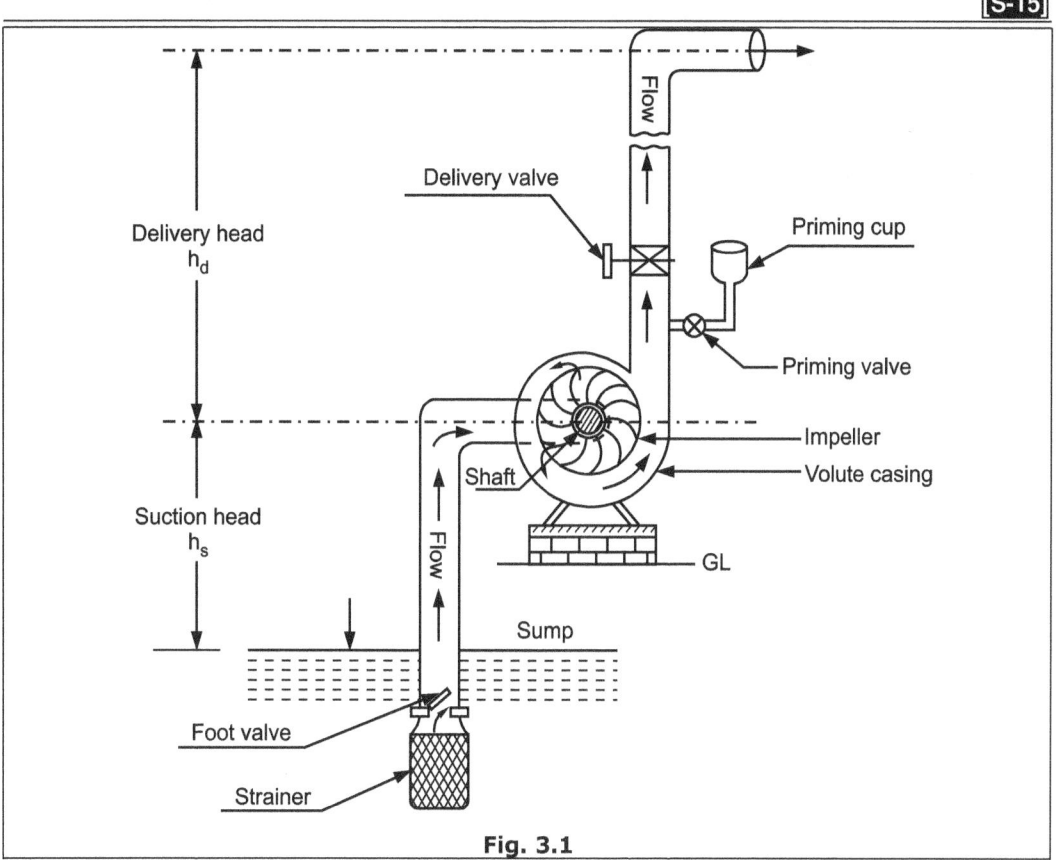

Fig. 3.1

Working Principle of Centrifugal Pump: The centrifugal pump works on the principle of forced vortex flow.

- When liquid is rotated by external torque, rise in the pressure head of rotating liquid takes place. This is called 'forced vortex flow'.
- It may be noted that, the rise of pressure head at any point in rotating liquid is proportional to the square of tangential velocity of the liquid at that point.

Construction of pump: Centrifugal pump is having following main parts:
1. Impeller
2. Casing
3. Suction pipe with foot valve and strainer
4. Priming cup and delivery pipe with delivery valve
5. Prime mover (electric motor or engine) to drive the pump.

Impeller is a rotating part of pump. It consists of series of backward vanes. Impeller is encased in casing. On one side of casing, suction pipe is attached at the centre. On the other side, the shaft on which impeller is 'keyed' (fixed by using key) comes out. This shaft is coupled to electric motor shaft which is a prime mover. The upper 'mouth' of casing is attached to delivery pipe. There is priming cup through which liquid to be lifted (say water) can be poured. There is delivery valve on this pipe. At the end of suction pipe which is dipped in sump, there is a strainer (mesh to arrest the foreign particles in water sump) and foot valve. This is a typical unidirectional valve which allows the flow in one direction (shown in Fig. 3.1) only. The reverse flow is not possible.

Working of pump: The stepwise working of pump is as under (Note that liquid being handled by pump is water).

(a) Pour the water through priming cup. Suction pipe, casing and part of delivery pipe will be completely filled by water. Close the priming valve.

(b) Start the electric motor of pump and open the delivery valve.

(c) The motor will rotate impeller with same speed of motor (standard speed of AC induction motor is 960 r.p.m. or 1440 r.p.m.). This rotation results into rotation of water i.e. centrifuged head is imparted on water. Due to vortex flow, pressure of water increases and water leaves the outer circumference of impeller with velocity and pressure. A partial vacuum is then formed at the centre of rotating water. The water from sump rushes into suction pipe through stainer and foot valve. The water leaving the impeller goes to scroll casing in which pressure of water further increases because of special shape of casing. This pressurised water flows out through delivery pipe by overcoming delivery head (h_d).

3.1.2 Types of Casings of Centrifugal Pump

- Casing plays a vital role in working of pump.
- Casing is an air-tight passage surrounding the impeller.
- Casings are generally made up of Graded cast iron. Casings are also known as chamber.
- Casing is designed in such a way that, the kinetic energy of water discharged at the outlet of impeller is converted into pressure energy before water leaves the casing and enters into delivery pipe.
- It is important to note that, before starting the pump, we must ensure that casing is full of water. If casing is partly filled with water, then there will not be lifting of water. Impeller will only go on running without doing any work.

There are three types of casings used for pump:

3.1.3 Volute Casing (Volute Chamber)

It is a spiral type casing in which the area between impeller and casing goes on increasing. The water leaving the impeller flows over the circumference of the impeller. The velocity of this water decreases with increasing area of flow. When water reaches the delivery pipe, its velocity is considerably reduced but its pressure will be high.

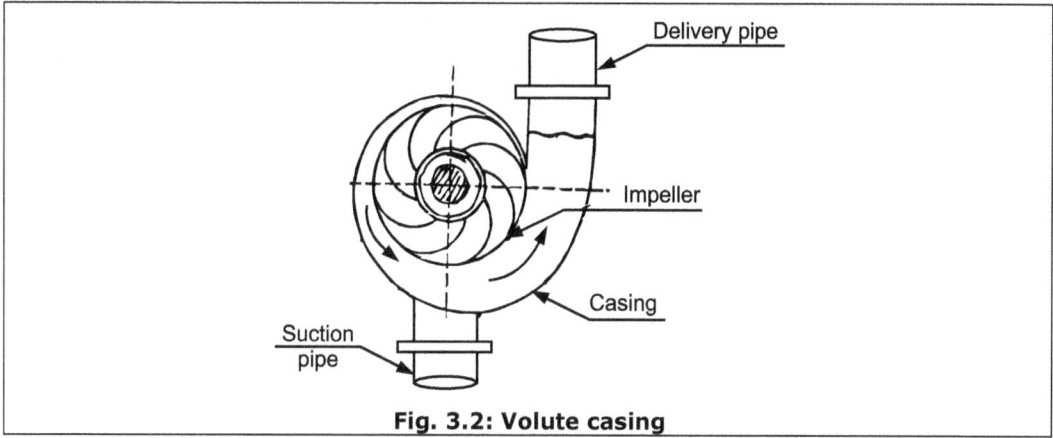

Fig. 3.2: Volute casing

Main disadvantage of this casing is that, eddy currents of water (Eddy current – Non-useful flow of water in certain regions) are formed which reduces its efficiency.

3.1.4 Vortex Casing (Vortex Chamber) (Whirlpool Chamber)

This is a modification of volute casing. In this casing, a circular chamber is provided in between impeller and spiral casing. Water flows from impeller through circular chamber into casing. Circular chamber reduces the eddy currents and efficiency increases.

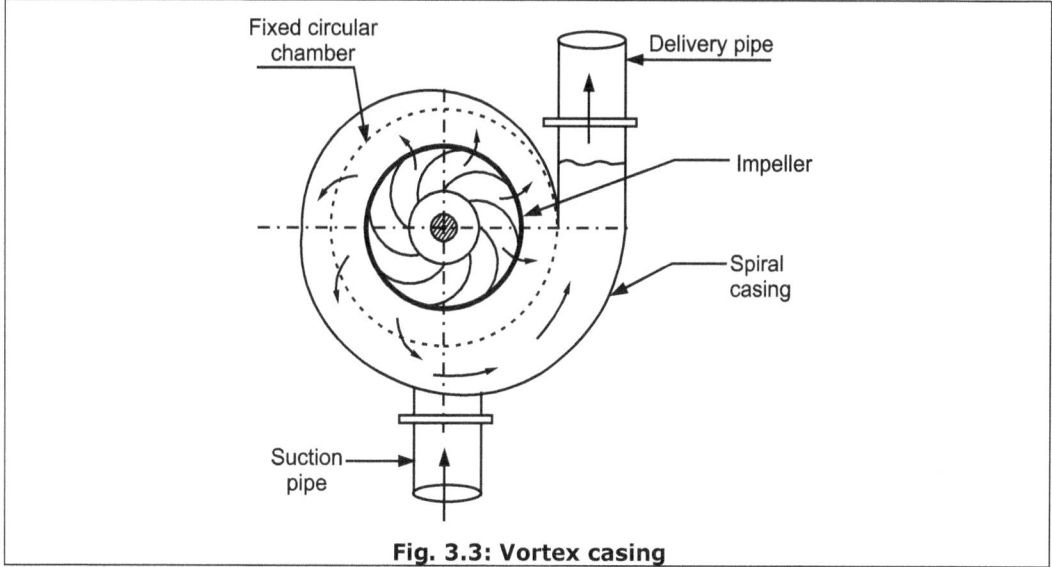

Fig. 3.3: Vortex casing

3.1.5 Casing with Guide Blades

To increase the pump efficiency still further this casing is used. In this casing, impeller is surrounded by guide blades mounted on ring called 'diffuser ring'. The guide blades are placed at such an angle that the water enters without shock. Due to guide vanes, area between impeller and casing decreases which helps in increase in pressure of water. In this casing, the eddy current percentage is almost reduced. Pump fitted with guide blades is called 'Turbine Pump'.

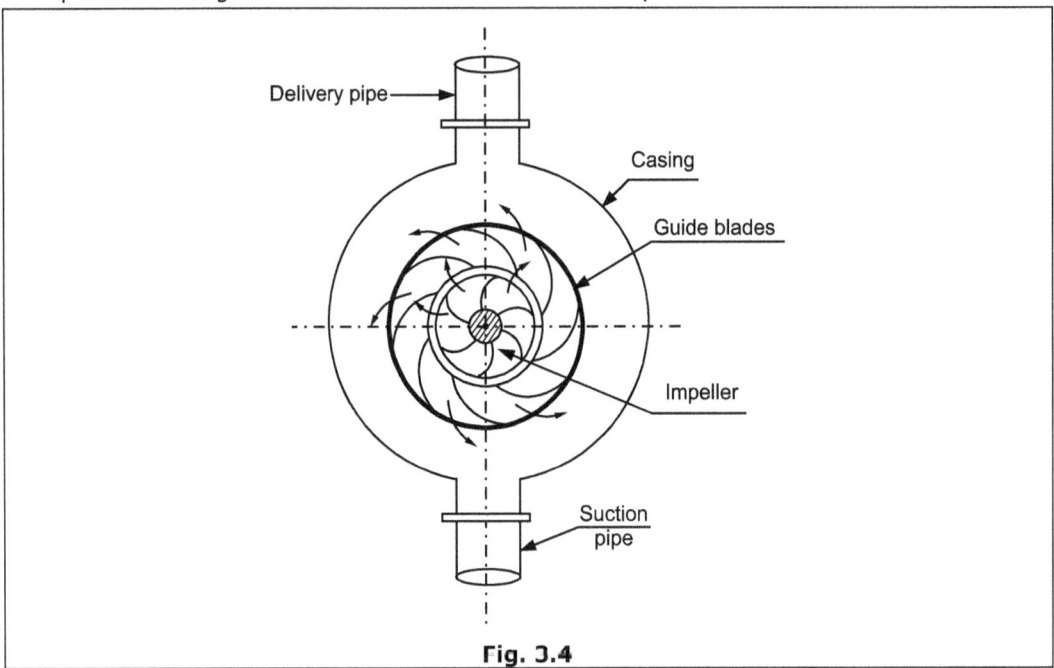

Fig. 3.4

3.1.6 Type of Impellers Used in Centrifugal Pump

- Impeller is a heart of pump.
- It is the impeller which imparts torque on water by its rotation and due to this force, vortex flow is created and pump starts lifting the water.
- Impellers are made from steel, gun metal, cast iron and stainless steel. The selection of material depends on liquid to be handled by pump.

  (a) Water and other non-corrosive liquids – cast iron.

  (b) Acids handling in chemical industry – stainless steel or gun metal (Acids are corrosive)

  (c) Hot water handling – cast steel.

  (d) Milk handling in dairies – stainless steel.

Following are the types of impellers:

(a) Closed-type impeller: The vanes of this impeller are covered by Disks (Plates) called 'shouds on both sides'. Due to disks, water is guided on vanes in better manner. This impeller can be used for clean liquids only. If liquid is not clean then there is a possibility of clogging.

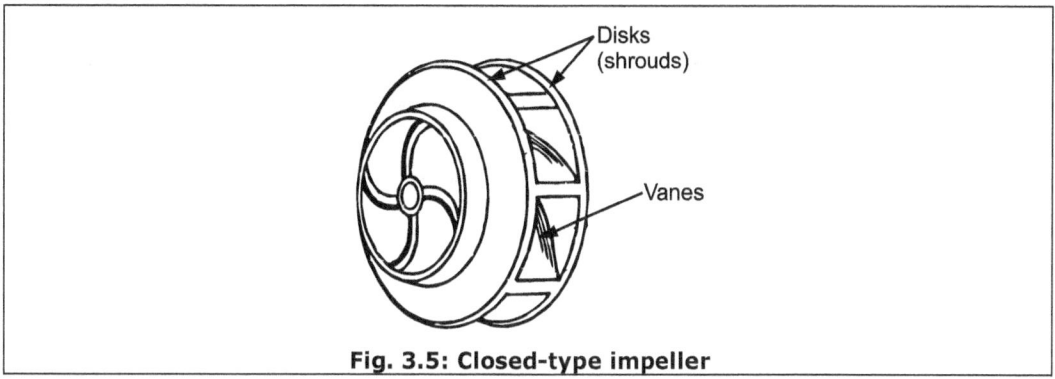

Fig. 3.5: Closed-type impeller

(b) Semi-open type impeller: In this type, the vanes are covered on one side only. Vanes are open on other side. Due to this arrangement, this impeller can handle semi-solid liquids like paper pump or sewage water (drainage water); or water containing salt, clay or sand etc.

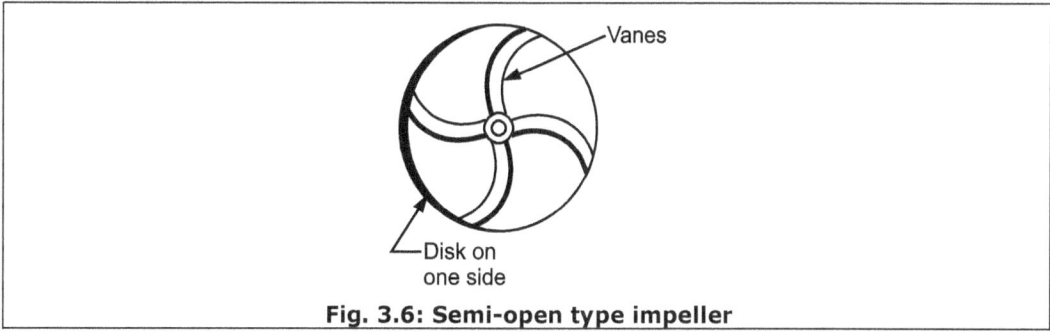

Fig. 3.6: Semi-open type impeller

(c) Open-type impeller: In this impeller, there are no plates on either side. There are only vanes attached to boss of impeller. This impeller is used for handling of dirty water, thick liquids etc.

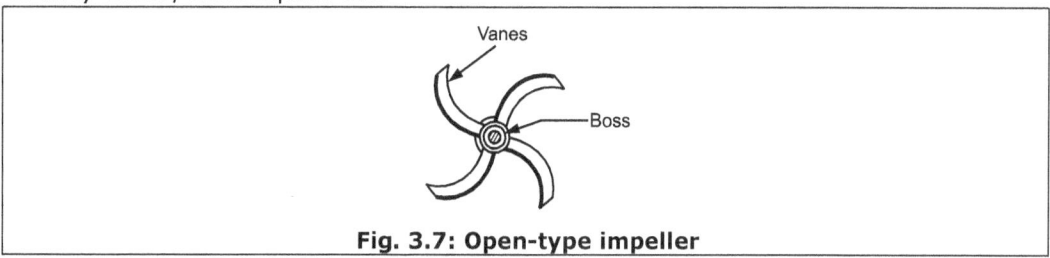

Fig. 3.7: Open-type impeller

3.1.7 Multistaging of Centrifugal Pump

- As compared to reciprocating pump, the delivery head developed by centrifugal pump is lower. To increase the pressure of liquid and to transfer the liquid at high height, multistaging is done. This multistaging is called 'multistaging for high heads' or 'pumps in series'.

- To increase the discharge (Q) of pump, 2-3 pumps are arranged in parallel, and there is common delivery pipe to all these pumps. Discharge of each pump is added, and aggregate high discharge will be available at the end of common delivery pipe. This is another type of multistaging and it is called 'multistaging for high discharge' or 'pumps in parallel'.
- Now let us see these both types.

(A) Multistaging for high pressure (pumps in series):

In this multistaging, two impellers with casing are mounted on common shaft:

- Water enters at atmospheric pressure in impeller (1).
- Outlet of impeller No. (1) is high pressure water.
- This outlet is given to inlet of impeller No. (2).
- Naturally, the outlet of impeller No. (2) is still higher pressure water.
- If more impellers are mounted on the same shaft, we can obtain still higher pressure water.

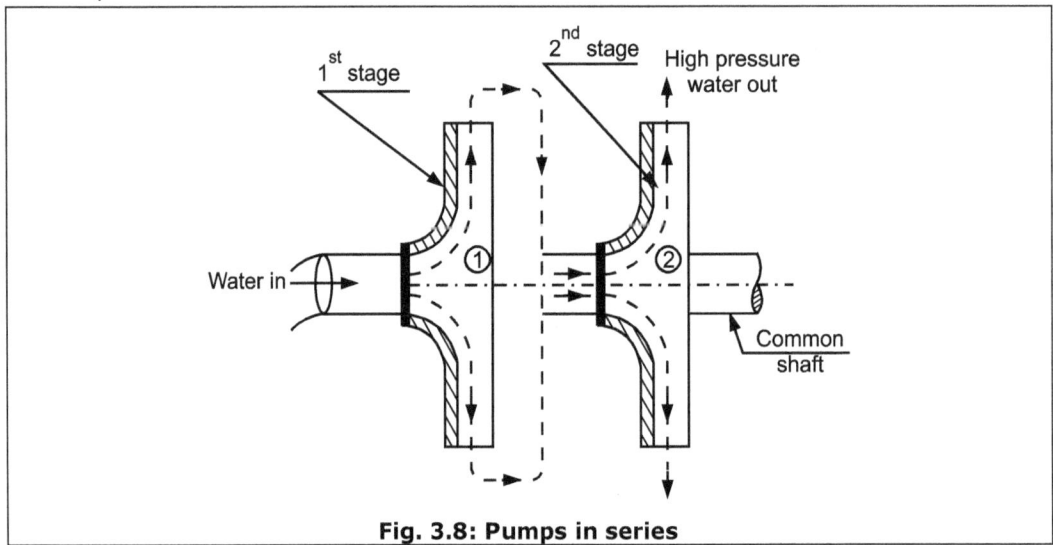

Fig. 3.8: Pumps in series

(B) Multistaging for higher discharge (pumps in parallel):

In this type of multistaging, two pumps are shown installed parallel to each other driven by separate motor.

- Q_1 is discharge of pump (1).
- Q_2 is discharge of pump (2).
- Delivery pipe is common, hence total discharge finally coming out is $Q_1 + Q_2$.
- If more pumps are installed parallel in the same manner, then total discharge will be more.
- This arrangement is done for lifting water from river and discharging it into very large size overhead tank used in water supply to town or city.

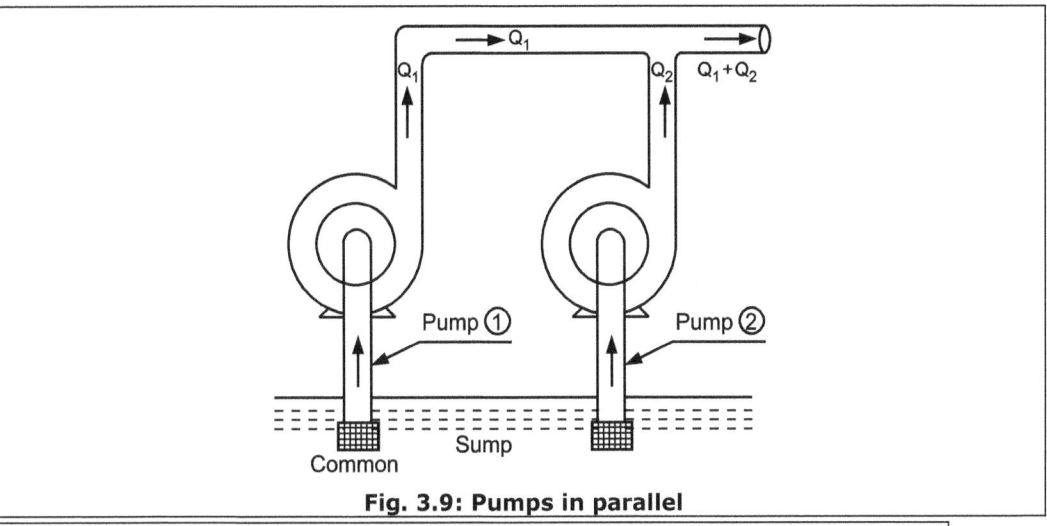

Fig. 3.9: Pumps in parallel

3.1.8 Work Done by Impeller of Centrifugal Pump on Water (Velocity Triangles of Centrifugal Pump)

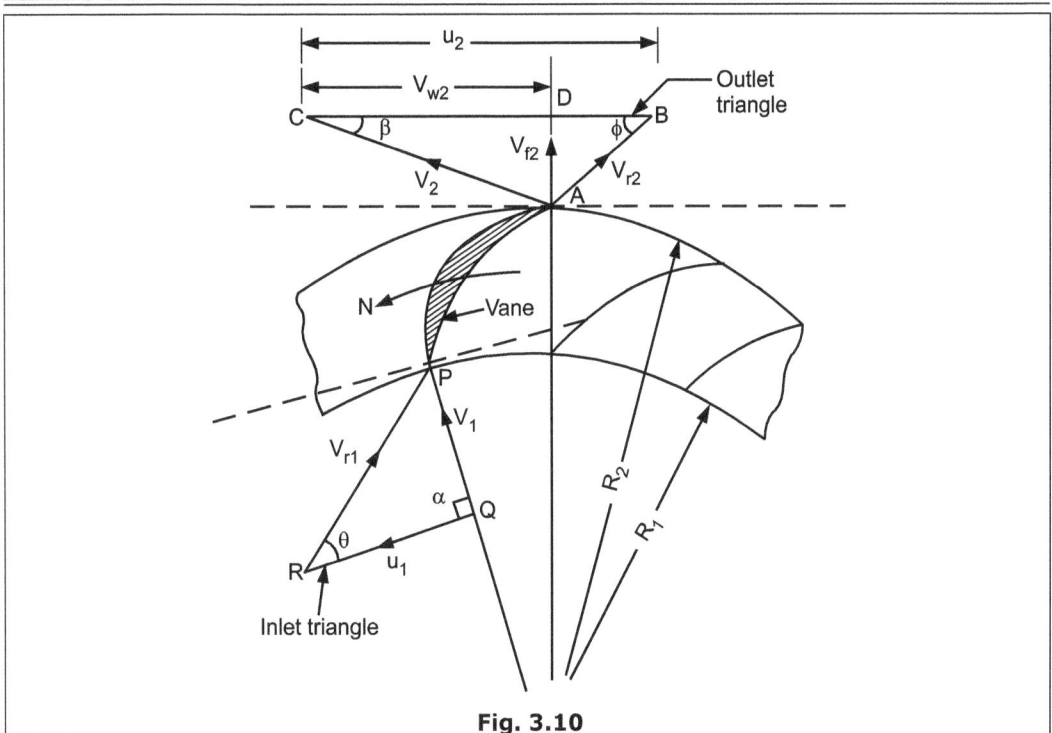

Fig. 3.10

- In centrifugal pump, impeller is rotated by electric motor/engine/turbine.
- Hence, impeller is doing work on water.
- To find out this work done, we have to draw inlet and outlet velocity triangles for centrifugal pump.

- ΔPQR – Inlet triangle.
- ΔABC – Outlet triangle.
- Water enters radially to obtain best efficiency of pump.
- Now let

  N = RPM of impeller

  D_1 = Diameter of impeller at inlet $\qquad D_2$ = Diameter of impeller at outlet

  u_1 = Tangential velocity of impeller at inlet
  $$= \frac{\pi D_1 N}{60}$$

  u_2 = Tangential velocity of impeller at outlet
  $$= \frac{\pi D_2 N}{60}$$

  V_1 = Velocity of water at inlet

  V_2 = Velocity of water leaving the impeller at outlet

  V_{w1} = Velocity of whirl at inlet $\qquad V_{w2}$ = Velocity of whirl at outlet

  $\alpha = 90°$ for centrifugal pump $\qquad \beta$ & ϕ are respective angles at outlet triangle

  θ = Angle PRQ With this data,

- Work done by impeller on water per second, per unit weight of water
$$= \frac{1}{g}(V_{w_2} u_2 - V_{w_1} u_1)$$

  but for centrifugal pump from inlet triangle, $V_{w1} = 0$

  ∴ Work done by impeller on water per second, per unit weight of water
$$= \frac{1}{g}(V_{w_2} u_2)$$

  [**Note:** This equation also gives head imparted by impeller on water.]

- If Q is discharge of pump then
  $$Q = \pi D_2 B_2 \times V_{f_2} \qquad \ldots B_2 = \text{width of impeller}$$
  $$V_{f_2} = \text{velocity of flow at outlet}$$

- Work done by water/sec. by impeller on water
$$= \frac{\rho g Q}{g} V_{w_2} u_2$$

  where, W = weight of water = $\rho g Q$.

- Power required to drive the pump,
$$S.P. = \frac{\rho Q g H_m}{1000 \times \eta}$$

3.1.9 Various Heads of Centrifugal Pump

1. **Suction Head (h_s):** Refer Fig. 3.11 of this chapter. 'h_s' is the vertical distance between centre line of pump and water surface in tank or sump. It is also known as 'suction lift'.

2. **Delivery Head (h_d):** Refer Fig. 3.11 of this chapter. 'h_d' is the vertical distance between centerline and pump of water surface in the tank to which water is delivered. It is also called 'delivery lift'.

3. **Static Head (H_s):** It is the sum of suction head (h_s) and delivery head (h_d).

   $\therefore \quad H_s = h_s + h_d$

4. **Manometric Head (H_m):** It is the head against which a centrifugal pump has to work. 'H_m' can be expressed in two ways:

   (i) $\quad H_m = \dfrac{\text{Head imparted by the impeller to water}}{} - \text{Loss of head in pump}$

   $\quad H_m = \dfrac{V_{w_2} u_2}{g} - \text{Loss of head in pump}$

   (ii) $\quad H_m = h_s + h_d + h_{fs} + h_{fd} + \dfrac{V_d^2}{2g}$

   where, $\quad h_s$ = Suction head

   h_d = Delivery head

   h_{fs} = Head loss due to friction in suction pipe (use Darcy's formula)

   h_{fd} = Head loss due to friction in delivery pipe

   $\dfrac{V_d^2}{2g}$ = Velocity head in delivery pipe

3.1.10 NPSH (Net Positive Suction Head)

- This head is concerned with suction head of pump.
- We know that, the water flow in suction pipe is due to vacuum created in pump. If vacuum pressure falls below vapour pressure then there is possibility of cavitation.

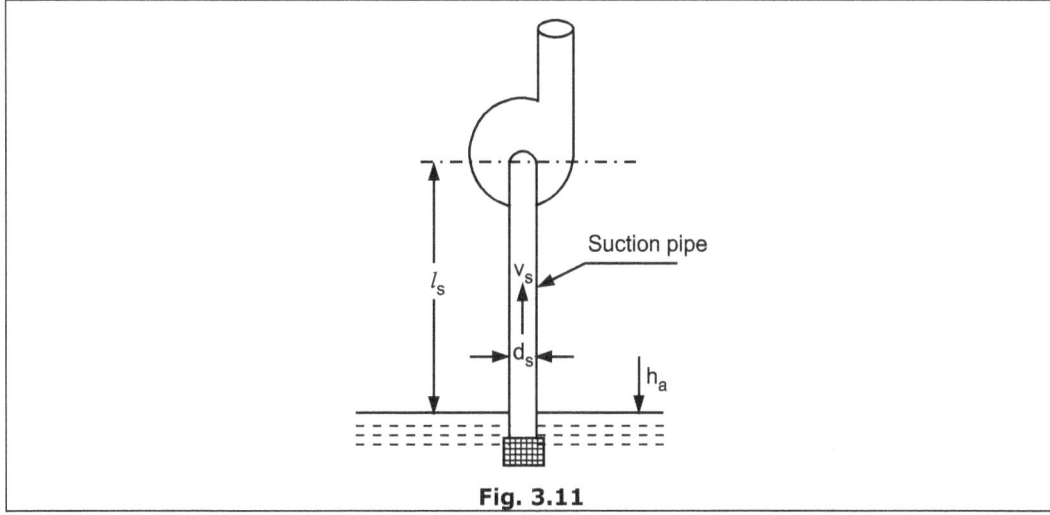

Fig. 3.11

Now, let h_s = Suction head

$\dfrac{V_s^2}{2g}$ = Velocity head in suction pipe

h_v = Vapour pressure head of liquid corresponding to the temperature of liquid.

Then,

Net Positive Suction Head = Suction Head + Velocity Head
− Vapour Pressure Head

$$\boxed{NPSH = h_s + \dfrac{V_s^2}{2g} - h_v}$$

NPSH can also be determined by applying Bernoulli's theorem at liquid level in sump and in inlet of pump. In that case,

$$\boxed{NPSH = h_a - h_v - h_s - h_{fs}}$$

where, h_a = Atmospheric pressure head at sump

h_{fs} = Head lost due to friction in suction pipe
$= \dfrac{4 f\, l_s\, V_s^2}{2g\, d_s}$

3.1.11 Efficiencies of Centrifugal Pump

Similar to reaction turbine, we can calculate following efficiencies for centrifugal pump.

(a) Manometric efficiency (η_{mano})

(b) Mechanical efficiency (η_m)

(c) Overall efficiency (η_o)

The 'power flow' in centrifugal pump can be expressed in the following flow chart.

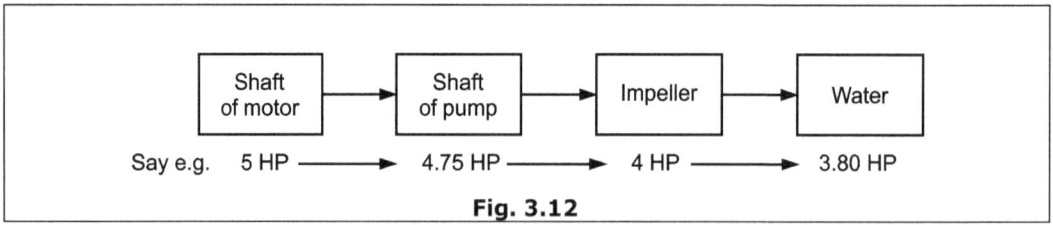

Fig. 3.12

From above flow chart of power and example given, it is clear that entire power of motor does not reach to water. There is power loss. Hence, we must calculate efficiencies at various stages.

(a) Manometric Efficiency (η_{mano}): It is the ratio of manometric head (H_m) to the head imparted by impeller to water.

$$\eta_{mano} = \frac{\text{Manometric head}}{\text{Head imparted by impeller to water}}$$

$$\eta_{mano} = \frac{H_m}{V_{w_2} u_2/g}$$

$\therefore \qquad \boxed{\eta_{mano} = \frac{g \cdot H_m}{V_{w_2} \cdot u_2}}$ ... Refer sub-article on velocity triangles.

where, $\quad H_m = h_s + h_d$
$\qquad u_2$ = Tangential velocity of impeller at outlet
$\qquad \quad = \frac{\pi D_2 N}{60}$
$\qquad V_{w2}$ = Velocity of whirl at outlet.

(b) Mechanical Efficiency (η_m): It is the ratio of power available at impeller to the power at shaft of pump.

$$\eta_m = \frac{\text{Power available at impeller}}{\text{Power at shaft (S.P.)}} \quad ...\text{SP = Shaft Power}$$

$$\eta_m = \frac{\frac{W}{g}\left(\frac{V_{w_2} u_2}{1000}\right)}{\text{S.P.}}$$

where, $\quad W$ = Weight of water
$\qquad \quad = \rho \times g \times Q$
$\qquad$ S.P. = Shaft power
$\qquad V_{w_2}, u_2$ = Same as stated earlier

(c) Overall efficiency (η_o): It is the ratio of power output of pump to power input of pump.

$\therefore \qquad \eta_o = \frac{\text{Power output}}{\text{Power input}}$

Now, $\quad$ Power output of pump $= \frac{WH_m}{1000}$ .... $W = \rho g Q$

$\qquad$ Power input = S.P.

$\therefore \qquad \eta_o = \frac{\frac{WH_m}{1000}}{SP}$

Also, $\qquad \eta_o = \eta_{mano} \times \eta_{mech}$

Priming and its method: Filling of suction pipe, entire casing and portion of delivery pipe by the liquid to be lifted from outside source is called 'priming'.

- Refer Fig. 3.11 of this chapter. Priming cup is shown on delivery pipe.
- If the liquid to be handled by pump is water then pouring of water through this cup and filling the suction pipe casing and portion of delivery pipe upto priming cup is called 'priming'.

- Remember that priming needs to be done only once. Every time before starting of pump priming is not necessary because we have fitted non-return valve called 'foot valve at the end of suction pipe'. It will not allow the flow from delivery pipe to sump when pump stops.
- If every time we need priming then the foot valve is faulty. We have to repair or change the foot valve.

3.1.12 Why Priming is Necessary in Centrifugal Pump? [S-15]

We know that head imparted by impeller on water is $\frac{1}{g}(V_{w_2} u_2)$ meters. This equation is independent of density. This clearly indicates that, if pump is handling water then this above stated head will be in terms of water (meters of water). If pump is handling oil then head will be meters of oil. Now,

(a) Let, pump be handling say water.

(b) Initially pump is empty i.e. there is only air present in casing and suction pipe. (But the strainer and foot valves are immersed in water sump).

(c) Let the pump be started. Impeller starts rotating. Since only air is present in the casing, the head imparted by impeller will be in terms of air (meters of air) i.e. 'h_{air}'.

(d) Now let us fill the suction pipe, casing and part of delivery pipe by water. Then start the pump. Now, water is present in the casing and head imparted by impeller will be meters of water i.e. 'h_{water}'.

(e) The density of air is lower than water, naturally $h_{air} < h_{water}$.

(f) So if priming is not done then 'h_{air}' will not be sufficiently strong to lift the water by opening the foot valve through suction pipe. Hence, if water is filled then the head imparted by impeller on water is sufficient to suck the water from sump. So priming is necessary.

Methods of Priming:

(a) Through priming cup.

(b) Through special type of delivery valve having priming chamber.

(c) In self-primed monoblock pumps there is special arrangement i.e. water storing chamber, near casing. When there is no water in casing, the water from this chamber automatically flows into casing and suction pipe.

(d) In concentrated acid handling chemical factories, to avoid priming, the pump itself is kept submerged in the liquid i.e. acid. In this case, the pumps are made from high non-corrosive metals and there is perfect sealing.

3.1.13 Cavitation in Centrifugal Pump

During suction of centrifugal pump, there is a possibility of falling the liquid pressure below vapour pressure. If it falls below vapour pressure then, vapour bubbles start forming in flowing liquid. These bubbles 'explod' when they come across any metal surface (inside surface of casing or surface of impeller). During this momentary explosion, very high pressures are created which result into pitting of metal surface. During this explosion, considerable noise and vibrations are created.

The falling of pressure below vapour pressure, forming of bubbles, movement of bubbles in pump and their collapse with high pressure. This entire phenomenon is called 'CAVITATION'.

3.1.14 Performance Characteristics of Centrifugal Pump [W-14]

If you visit any centrifugal pump manufacturing industry, you will find that, before despatch of pump; pump is tested on Test Bench. The pump is tested under various conditions like:
1. Performance for different suction and delivery heads (H_m).
2. Performance under various speeds of impeller (N).
3. Performance under various values of flow rate (Q).
4. Performance under change in power of pump.

The simple way to understand these tests is to plot graph of it. Hence, characteristic curves of pump are the plotted curves on graph paper from the results of number of tests on pump.

Following are the main characteristic curves for centrifugal pump:
(a) Main characteristic curves.
(b) Operating characteristic curves.

(a) Main characteristic curves:
- On X-axis, speed of pump is taken.
- On Y-axis, 3 quantities are taken: Q, H_m and Power.

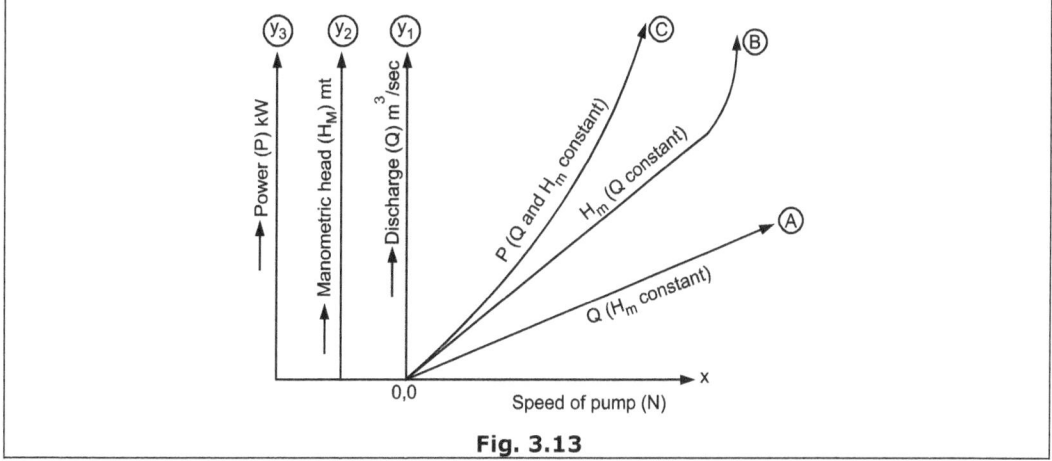

Fig. 3.13

- **Curve A:** Variation of discharge Q with respect to speed of pump when H_m and Power are constant [x axis – y_1 axis].
- **Curve B:** Variation of H_m with respect to speed of pump when Q and Power are kept constant [x axis – y_2 axis].
- **Curve C:** Variation of power P with respect to speed of pump when Q and H_m are kept constant [x axis – y_3 axis].

(b) Operating characteristic curves:

While plotting these curves, we have to keep RPM i.e. speed of impeller constant and we have to plot discharge (Q) for efficiency variation, power variation and head variation. These curves are called 'Operating characteristic curves'.

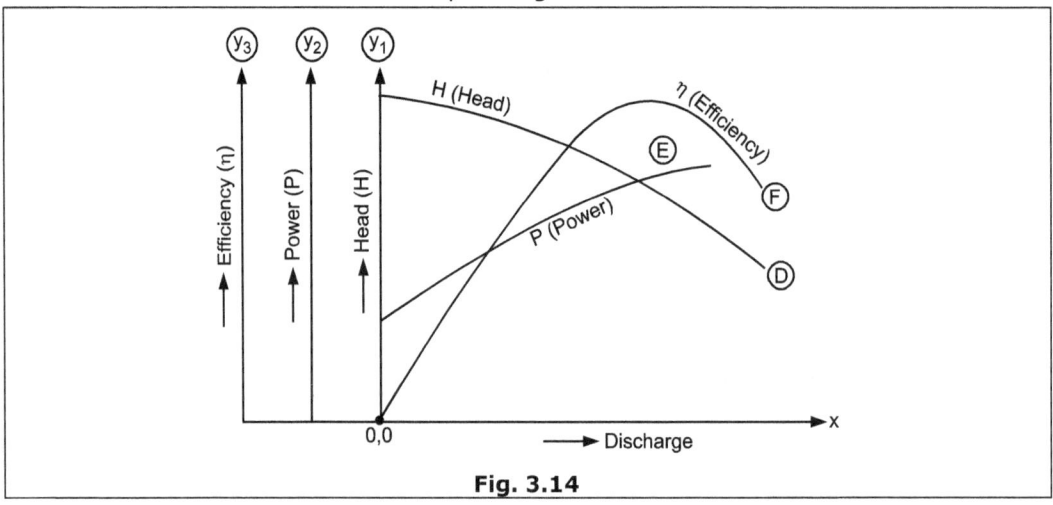

Fig. 3.14

- **Curve D:** Discharge against head (How discharge varies when head increases and decreases) [x-axis – y_1].
- **Curve E:** Discharge against power (How discharge varies when power varies) [x-axis – y_2].
- **Curve F:** Discharge against efficiency (How efficiency varies when discharge varies) [x-axis – y_3].

3.1.15 Trouble Shooting [W-14, S-15]

While operating a centrifugal pump some troubles arise. Following table gives possible troubles and their remedies (way of solving the troubles).

Trouble	Possible fault	Remedy
Pump not starting	(a) Power off. (b) Loose connection in pin of wire of motor. (c) Faults in motor.	Start DG set if available. Repair the connections. Check the motor and if required replace it.

contd. ...

Pump starts, works for some time and then stops delivering water	(a) Leakage in suction pipe. (b) High suction head. (c) Air pockets in suction pipe.	Check leakage. Make it low by installing the pump at lower level. Prime the pump.
Insufficient pressure at delivery pipe	(a) Low speed. (b) Air in pipe system. (c) Impeller damaged.	Check the speed of motor. Remove air by priming. Check and repair the impeller.
Noisy operation of pump	(a) Loose connections of casings, impellers. (b) Cavitation.	Make proper connections. Check suction pressure.
Pump does not delivering water	(a) No water in casing, suction pipe. (b) High delivery head than capacity of pump. (c) Pump may be running at lower speed. (d) Foot valve may be clogged. (e) Impeller may be running in wrong direction.	Priming may be done. Lower the delivery head. Check the motor speed and adjust it. Check foot valve remove clogging. Check and make the direction proper.
Low discharge through delivery pipe	(a) Leakage through delivery pipe. (b) High suction lift. (c) Impeller/suction pipe partly clogged.	Check the leakage and stop it. Place the pump at lower level. Check and clear the clogging.

3.2 RECIPROCATING PUMPS

- As we have already discussed in part (A) i.e. centrifugal pump that, pump converts Mechanical Energy into Hydraulic Energy, which is mainly in the form of 'Pressure Energy'.
- When high pressure is required and comparatively low quantity is required to handle then reciprocating pump is used.
- You are regularly visiting vehicle service station for washing your vehicle. There you see the water in the form of spray is coming out of nozzle which when strikes the vehicle, the mud and dirt of the vehicle immediately drops down. You can easily understood that the water coming out of that nozzle is with high force i.e. high pressure. This high force or pressure is provided by 'Reciprocating Pump'. Service station uses this pump only for vehicle washing.
- Tube well is a small well (diameter 6") drilled in the ground (bore well); for water availability. The water from this well is taken out by hand pump on bore well. This hand pump is actually a reciprocating pump.
- Reciprocating pump can create very high pressures, hence are used to achieve high pressure to inject fluids in pipes or tanks.
- A new ultra high pressure plunger pump (sort of reciprocating pump) can create pressure upto 2500 bar and is used for surface preparation before lamination and coating.
- This very high pressure pump is used for creating spray to cut the metal plates and also to cut concrete.
- Reciprocating pumps, comes into the category of piston pumps which are high pressure pumps. In hydraulic circuits high pressure is required. So piston pumps are having wide applications in hydraulic circuits.
- For handling of very thick liquids like tar, reciprocating pumps are used.

3.2.1 Construction and Working of Single Acting Reciprocating Pump

- **Principle of working of reciprocating pump:** This pump is driven by power from external source. It consists of cylinder in which piston or plunger is moved backward and forward. This movement of piston creates vacuum pressure and positive pressure alternately in the cylinder, by means of which the water is raised with pressure.

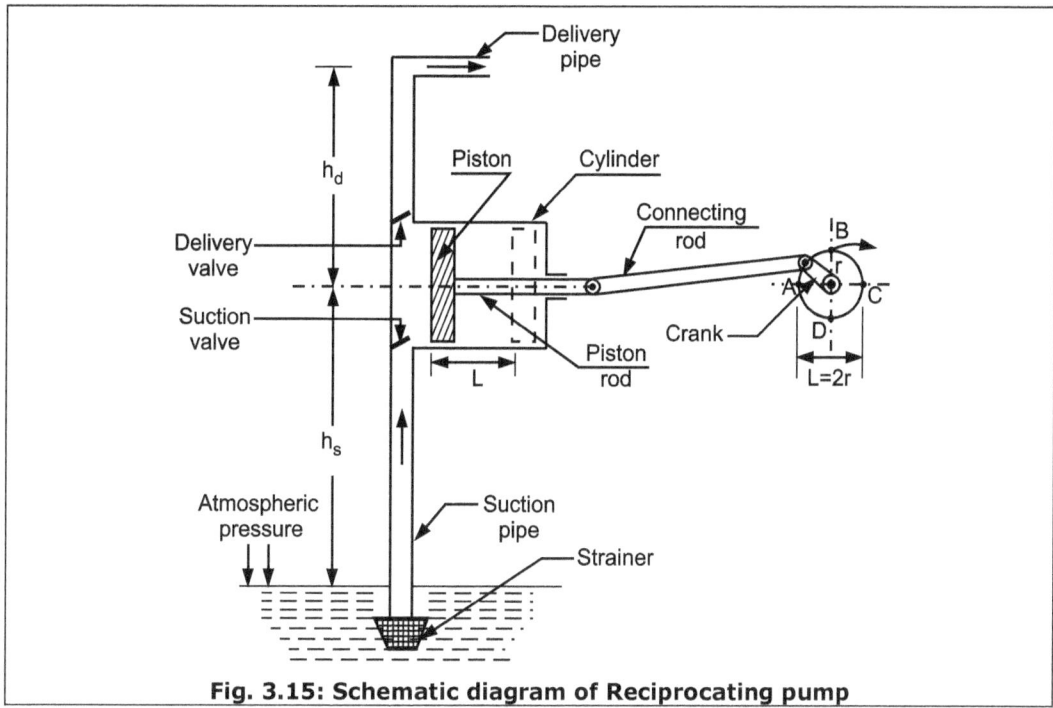

Fig. 3.15: Schematic diagram of Reciprocating pump

Construction: Fig. 3.15 shows single acting reciprocating pump. Following are the parts of the pump:

(a) A cylinder with piston and 4 bar mechanism i.e. piston rod, connecting rod, crank.
(b) Suction pipe with suction valve.
(c) Delivery pipe with delivery valve.
(d) Strainer.
(e) Prime mover (preferably motor) with belt pulley arrangement for speed reduction.

Cylinder is closed vessel in which piston reciprocates. Piston is connected to crank through connecting rod and piston rod. Electric motor (with pulley belt arrangement) is connected to crank. Suction and Delivery valves are one-way valves or non-return valves, which allow the water to flow in one direction only.

Working: When crank starts rotating, piston will reciprocate in cylinder. When crank is at 'A' piston will be on extreme left position in cylinder.

Suction stroke: As crank rotates from A to C through 180°, angle piston will move towards right. This movement of piston from left to right creates vacuum in cylinder. The pressure acting on water in sump is atmospheric, which is more than the pressure in cylinder. Hence, water rushes in suction pipe from sump. This water opens the suction valve and will fill the entire cavity of cylinder. Here completes the suction stroke.

Delivery stroke: Now crank will rotate from C-D-A (i.e. from 180° to 360°), the piston will move from right to left. During this movement, pressure on the water in cylinder will increase. This high pressure water will close suction valve and will open the delivery valve. The water forces in delivery pipe and will be raised to required height.

3.2.2 Discharge through Single Acting Reciprocating Pump

Let,
D = Diameter of piston or inside diameter of cylinder
N = RPM of crank
L = Length of stroke
= 2r
ρ = Density of liquid
h_s = Suction head (mt.)
h_d = Delivery head (mt.)

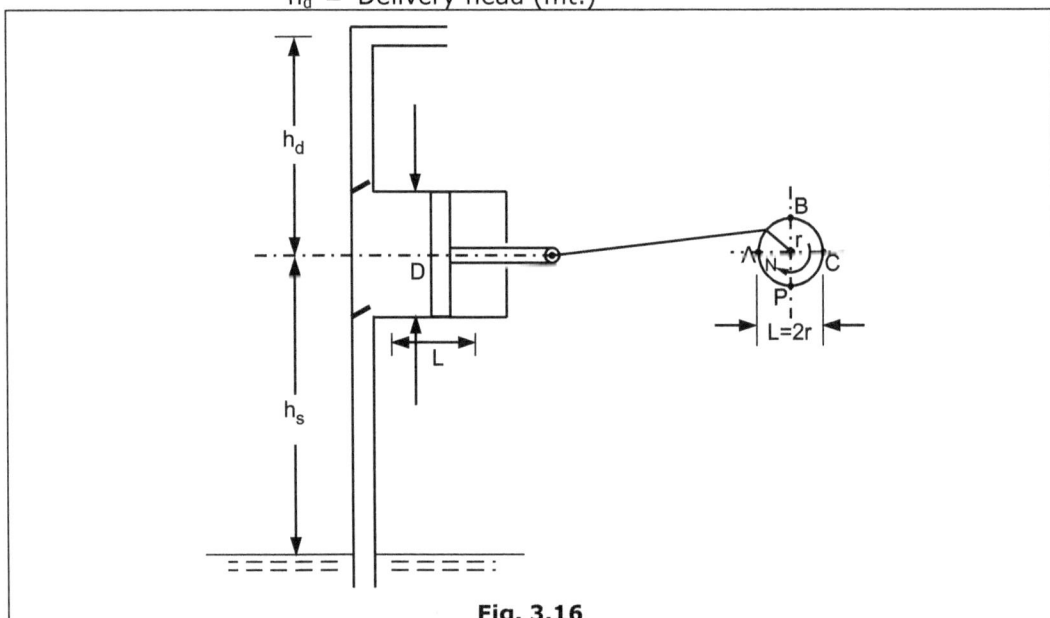

Fig. 3.16

- Then discharge of pump per second,

$$Q = \frac{A \cdot L \cdot N}{60} \qquad \ldots(A)$$

where, A = cross-section of cylinder = $\frac{\pi}{4} D^2$

- Weight of water delivered per second,

$$W = \rho \cdot g \cdot Q$$

$$\therefore \quad W = \frac{\rho g A L N}{60} \qquad \ldots(B)$$

- Work done by reciprocating pump/sec. $= \dfrac{\rho g ALN}{60}(h_s + h_d)$

- Power required to drive the pump

$$\boxed{P = \dfrac{\rho g ALN(h_s + h_d)}{60 \times 1000}} \text{ kW}$$

If liquid is water then $\rho = 1000$ kg/m^3

$\therefore \qquad P = \dfrac{\rho ALN(h_s + h_d)}{60}$ kW

3.2.3 Construction and Working of Double Acting Reciprocating Pump

- **Principle of working:** Same as that of Single Acting Reciprocating Pump.

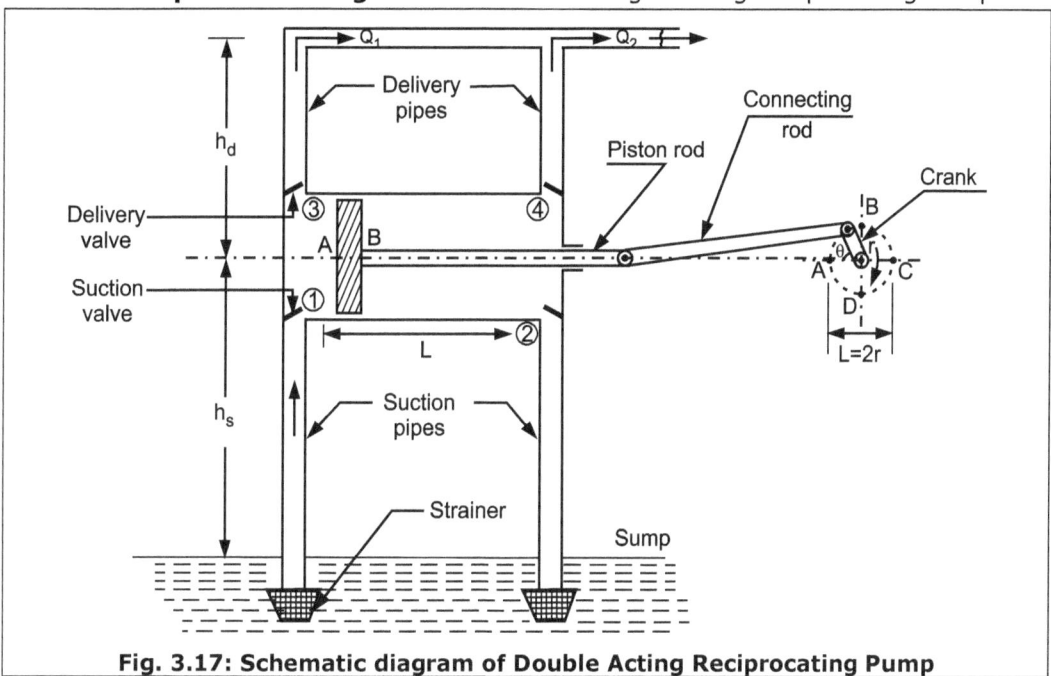

Fig. 3.17: Schematic diagram of Double Acting Reciprocating Pump

Construction: Fig. 3.17 shows Double Acting Reciprocating Pump. Following are the parts of the pump:

(a) Cylinder with piston, 4 bar mechanism i.e. piston rod, connecting rod, crank.

(b) 2 suction pipes with 2 suction valves.

(c) 2 delivery pipes with 2 delivery valves.

(d) 2 strainers.

(e) One prime mover (preferably motor) with belt pulley arrangement for speed reduction.

Cylinder is closed vessel in which piston is reciprocating. Piston is connected to crank through piston rod and connecting rod. Electric motor drives the crank. Since water will be there on both sides of piston, there are 2 suction and 2 delivery pipes with valves in each pipe. Similar to single acting pump the valves are non-return type (unidirectional). There are two strainers as shown which will arrest the foreign particles before entering into suction pipe.

Working: Crank rotates from A to C through 180° in clockwise direction. Naturally, piston will move from left to right. This movement creates vacuum on 'A' side of piston in cylinder. Due to vacuum cylinder and atmospheric pressure acting on sump, water rushes in through suction pipe by opening valve (1). The cavity on side 'A' will be filled by water.

Now crank will rotate from C-D-A (i.e. from 180° to 360°). The piston will move from right to left. During this movement, pressure on A side of piston will increase. The pressurised water will open the delivery valve (3) and goes out. But during this stroke, vacuum is created on 'B' side of piston (piston rod side) and due to pressure difference, the water rushes in by opening suction valve (2) and will occupy all space in the cylinder on 'B' side.

Now, crank will rotate from A-B-C through 180°. During this stroke, piston will move from left to right, thereby increasing the pressure of water on 'B' side. Delivery valve (4) will open and pressurised water goes out through delivery pipe.

In short, when there is suction on one side of piston there is delivery of pressurised water on other side of piston.

Thus for one complete revolution of crank there are two suction strokes and two delivery strokes.

3.2.4 Discharge through Double Acting Reciprocating Pump [W-14]

Let,
- D = Diameter of piston or inside diameter of cylinder
- N = RPM of crank
- L = Length of stroke = $2r$
- ρ = Density of liquid
- h_s = Suction head (mt.)
- h_d = Delivery head (mt.)

Then,

- Discharge through pump/sec. = $Q = 2\left[\dfrac{ALN}{60}\right]$ ...(C)

- Weight of water delivered per second = $2\left[\dfrac{\rho g ALN}{60}\right]$ ...(D)

- Work done by reciprocating pump/sec. $= 2\left[\dfrac{\rho g ALN}{60}\right](h_s + h_d)$

- Power required to drive the pump $= 2\left[\dfrac{\rho g ALN}{60 \times 1000}\right](h_s + h_d)$ kW

- If liquid is water then $\rho = 1000$ kg/m^3.

  Then power $P = 2\left[\dfrac{gALN}{60}\right](h_s + h_d)$ kW

3.2.5 Concept of Slip (Slip of Reciprocating Pump) [S-15]

Definition: Slip of pump is defined *as the difference between theoretical discharge (Q_{th}) and actual discharge (Q_{act}) of pump.*

$\qquad$ Slip of pump = (Theoretical discharge) − (Actual discharge)

$\qquad\qquad$ Slip $= Q_{th} - Q_{act}$

- Note that in almost all cases, generally theoretical discharge is more than actual discharge because of leakages in pump systems and pipings.
- **What is Theoretical Discharge:** The discharge calculated on paper by knowing dimensions of cylinder and RPM of crank is theoretical discharge.
- For single acting pump, $\quad Q_{th} = \dfrac{ALN}{60}$
- For double acting pump, $\quad Q_{th} = \dfrac{2ALN}{60}$
- Actual discharge is measured quantity of liquid coming out of delivery pipe.
- Since $Q_{th} - Q_{act} \Rightarrow +$ ve, this slip is positive slip.
- To calculate percentage slip, use the following formula:

$$\% \text{ Slip} = \dfrac{Q_{th} - Q_{act}}{Q_{th}} \times 100$$

$$= \left(\dfrac{Q_{th}}{Q_{th}} - \dfrac{Q_{act}}{Q_{th}}\right) \times 100$$

So, $\qquad$ Percentage slip $= (1 - C_d) \times 100$ ... where $\dfrac{Q_{act}}{Q_{th}} = C_d$

Negative slip:

Definition: When actual discharge is more than theoretical discharge, then that pump is said to be having negative slip.

$$-\text{ve slip} \Rightarrow Q_{th} < Q_{act}$$

- Negative slip occurs when:
1. Delivery pipe is short.
2. Sunction pipe is long.
3. When pump is running at high speeds.

3.2.6 Use of Air Vessels on Reciprocating Pump

- Air vessel is a closed chamber made up of cast iron containing air in the top portion and liquid at the bottom of chamber.
- At the base of chamber there is an opening through which liquid flows into the vessel or out of vessel. When liquid enters into the vessel, the air above liquid gets compressed.

When liquid comes out of vessel, air expands in the vessel.

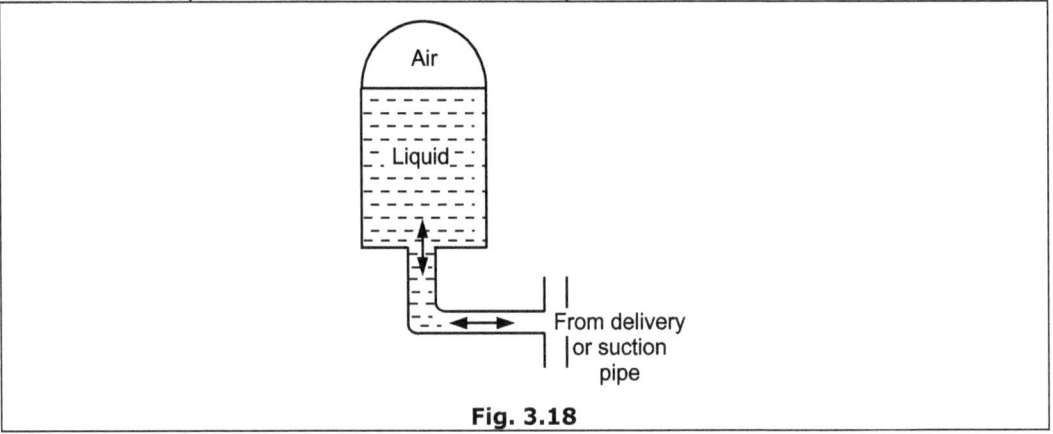

Fig. 3.18

Location of Air Vessel: Air vessel is fitted to suction pipe and to delivery pipe at a point close to cylinder of a single acting reciprocating pump.

- **Function of Air Vessel:** It acts like intermediate reservoir. It smoothens the pulsating flow of reciprocating pump.

3.2.7 Working of pump when air vessels are fitted

Fig. 3.19 shows two air vessels are fitted to suction and delivery pipe.

- **First Half of Delivery Stroke:** Piston moves from C to D and we know it moves with acceleration. It clearly means that the velocity of water in the delivery pipe is more than mean velocity and naturally more quantity of water is entering into delivery pipe as compared to mean discharge (Q_{mean}). This excess water moves into air vessel No. (2). The water compresses the air in air vessel.

- **Second Half of Delivery Stroke:** In this second half, piston moves from D to A. We know that this movement is with retardation. Velocity in delivery pipe is less than mean velocity and naturally less quantity of water enters into delivery pipe as compared to mean discharge (Q_{mean}). During this period the pressure of water on air in pressure vessel reduces which results into expansion of air in air vessel and excess quantity stored in vessel in 1st half stroke comes out of vessel and flows into delivery pipe, thus maintaining average discharge and reducing pulsation.

- Similar flow of water in and out of air vessel takes place in suction pipe.
- **Important:** It may be noted that the pressure of air in the air vessel will vary as the water flows in and out. This variation can be reduced by making the air vessel large as compared with area of delivery pipe.

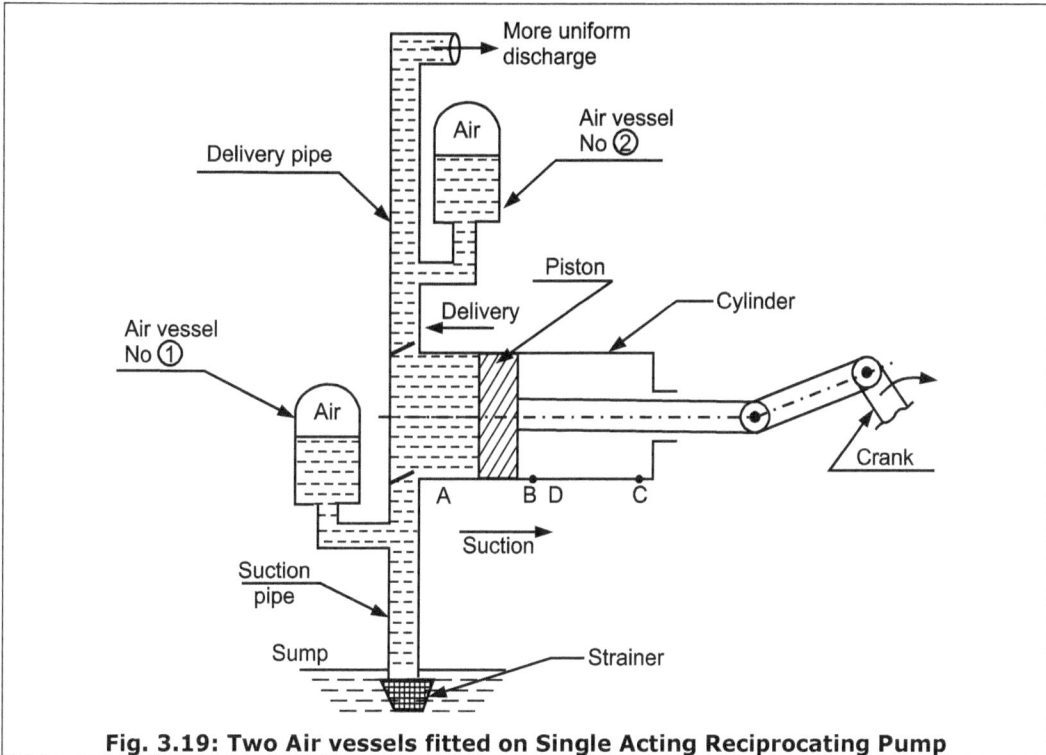

Fig. 3.19: Two Air vessels fitted on Single Acting Reciprocating Pump

- In single acting reciprocating pump the discharge is intermittent or pulsating. It is not continuous flow or smooth flow through delivery pipe.

3.2.8 Why flow through Single Acting Reciprocating Pump is Pulsating?

- The delivery of pressurized water is only in half stroke. In remaining half stroke, there is only suction of water. Hence, when crank rotates from $0°$ to $180°$ there is only suction. When crank rotates from $180°$ to $360°$ the water goes out through delivery pipe. Hence, the flow is pulsating.
- There is another reason for pulsation. During suction or delivery stroke, in the first half of the stroke piston accelerates and in second half it retards. Water is in contact with piston. Hence, naturally velocity of water does not remain uniform. Hence, flow is pulsating.
- When we use air vessel, the flow pulsation reduces and flow is almost uniform.

3.2.9 Separation in Reciprocating Pump

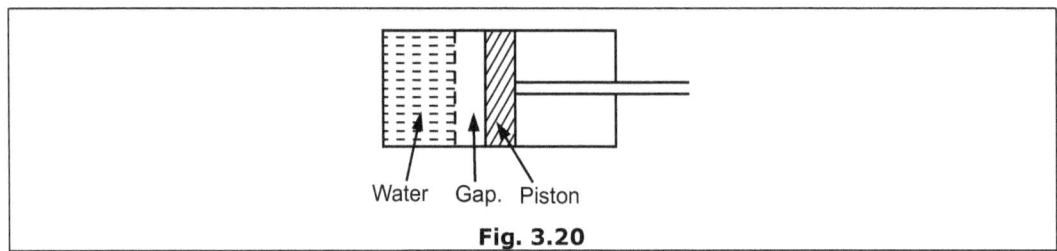

Fig. 3.20

- Separation means separating piston and water by a gap. If pump runs at high speed, there is a possibility of separation during the start of suction stroke and end of delivery stroke. Hence, there are limitations on the speed of pump. The pressure head at which separation takes place is called 'separation pressure head (h_{sep})'. For water limiting value of this head h_{sep} = 7.8 mt. below atmospheric head.

3.2.10 Cavitation in Reciprocating Pump

- As we have already seen that cavitation is vaporizing the liquid when pressure of liquid falls below vapour pressure. If the speed of pump is high then during suction stroke, there is possibility of falling the pressure of liquid below vapour pressure. If so happens then vapour bubbles are formed in liquid and carried along the flow. They explode when they touch inside surface of cylinder or piston surface. During this explosion, momentary very high pressures are created and which results in pitting of surfaces. This phenomenon is called 'cavitation'.
- To avoid cavitation, the speed of reciprocating pump is low.

Important Points

- Casing is an air-tight passage surrounding the impeller. Casings are generally made up of Graded cast iron. Casings are also known as chamber.
- **Volute Casing (Volute Chamber:** It is a spiral type casing in which the area between impeller and casing goes on increasing. The water leaving the impeller flows over the circumference of the impeller.
- **Vortex Casing (Vortex Chamber) (Whirlpool Chamber:** This is a modification of volute casing. In this casing, a circular chamber is provided in between impeller and spiral casing.
- Pump fitted with guide blades is called 'Turbine Pump'.
- NPSH can also be determined by applying Bernoulli's theorem at liquid level in sump and in inlet of pump.

- **Manometric Efficiency (η_{mano}):** It is the ratio of manometric head (h_m) to the head imparted by impeller to water.
- **Mechanical Efficiency (η_m):** It is the ratio of power available at impeller to the power at shaft of pump.
- **Overall efficiency (η_o):** It is the ratio of power output of pump to power input of pump.
- **Priming and its method:** Filling of suction pipe, entire casing and portion of delivery pipe by the liquid to be lifted from outside source is called 'priming'.
- **Reciprocating pumps,** comes into the category of piston pumps which are high pressure pumps.
- **Concept of Slip (Slip of Reciprocating Pump:** Slip of pump is defined as the difference between theoretical discharge (Q_{th}) and actual discharge (Q_{act}) of pump.
- **Negative slip:** When actual discharge is more than theoretical discharge, then that pump is said to be having negative slip.
- **Air vessel** is a closed chamber made up of cast iron containing air in the top portion and liquid at the bottom of chamber.
- **Separation** means separating piston and water by a gap. If pump runs at high speed, there is a possibility of separation during the start of suction stroke and end of delivery stroke.

Practice Questions

1. Define a centrifugal pump. Explain the working of single-stage centrifugal pump with sketches.
2. Differentiate between volute casing and vortex casing for the centrifugal pump.
3. Define the terms: suction head, delivery head, static head and manometric head.
4. What do you mean by manometric efficiency, mechanical efficiency and overall efficiency of a centrifugal pump?
5. What is the difference between single-stage and multistage pumps? Describe multistage pump with (a) impellers in parallel and (b) impellers in series.
6. What is priming? Why is it necessary?
7. What do you understand by characteristic curves of a pump?
8. Define cavitation. What are the effects of cavitation?
9. Why are centrifugal pumps used sometimes in series and sometimes in parallel?
10. Draw and discuss the operating characteristics of a centrifugal pump.
11. What is cavitation and what are its causes?
12. With a neat sketch, explain the principle and working of a centrifugal pump.
13. What is a reciprocating pump? Describe the principle and working of a reciprocating pump with a neat sketch.
14. Why is a reciprocating pump not coupled directly to the motor? Discuss the reason in detail.
15. Differentiate: between a single acting and double acting reciprocating pump.

16. Define slip-percentage slip and negative slip of a reciprocating pump.
17. What is the effect of acceleration of the piston on the velocity and acceleration of the water in suction and delivery pipes?
18. What is an air vessel? Describe the function of the air vessel for reciprocating pumps.
19. What is negative slip in a reciprocating pump? Explain with neat sketches the function of air vessels in a reciprocating pump.
20. Why is it that the speed of a reciprocating pump without air vessels is not high? Explain with sketches.

Chapter 4

SIMPLE HYDRAULIC DEVICES

Weightage of Marks = 12, Teaching Hours = 06

Learning Objectives
- Apply Pascal's law in various hydraulic devices
- Know working of other types of pumps.

Contents
Simple Hydraulic Devices
- Working Principles, Construction and Applications of Hydraulic Jack, Hydraulic ram, Hydraulic Lift, Hydraulic Press.

Other Pumping Devices
- Gear Pumps used in Hydraulic Circuits, Vane Type, Swash Plate Type Pump. Comparison of above Pumps for various characteristics and their applications.

4.1 HYDRAULIC DEVICES

- Hydraulic devices are the devices in which power is transmitted with the help of fluid which may be water or oil or gas under pressure.
- All these devices work on the principles of fluid statics and fluid kinematics.
- We will study following Hydraulic Devices:
    (a) Hydraulic Press
    (b) Hydraulic Ram
    (c) Hydraulic Lift
    (d) Hydraulic Jack

4.1.1 Hydraulic Press (Ref. Fig. 4.1)

Hydraulic press uses hydraulic energy created by pressurizing the fluid called 'hydraulic oil'.

Construction: It consists of Hydraulic System i.e. main cylinder and two lifting cylinders. The ram of press is attached to main cylinder and two lifting cylinders by means of bolting. There are two pressure pipes, one of which is going to lifting cylinders and other is going to main cylinder.

Working: Pressurized oil will enter through port (A) and its force will act on piston. Piston will move down with force. The steel sheet kept on die, will take the shape due to the meeting of die and punch.

Then pressurised oil will enter through port (B). Oil pressure will act on pistons of lifting cylinders. Due to this main piston will move up and entire assembly will move up. When die and punch separate we can take out pressed component.

Applications: Hydraulic presses are having wide applications. Some of them are as given below:

(a) Manufacturing of crank case.
(b) Bottom cup of hermetically sealed compressor.
(c) Hoods over big tractor tyres.
(d) Forging operation (press forging) is done by using these presses.
(e) For removal of axle or shaft bends.
(f) For manufacturing of car doors, front and side pannels etc.

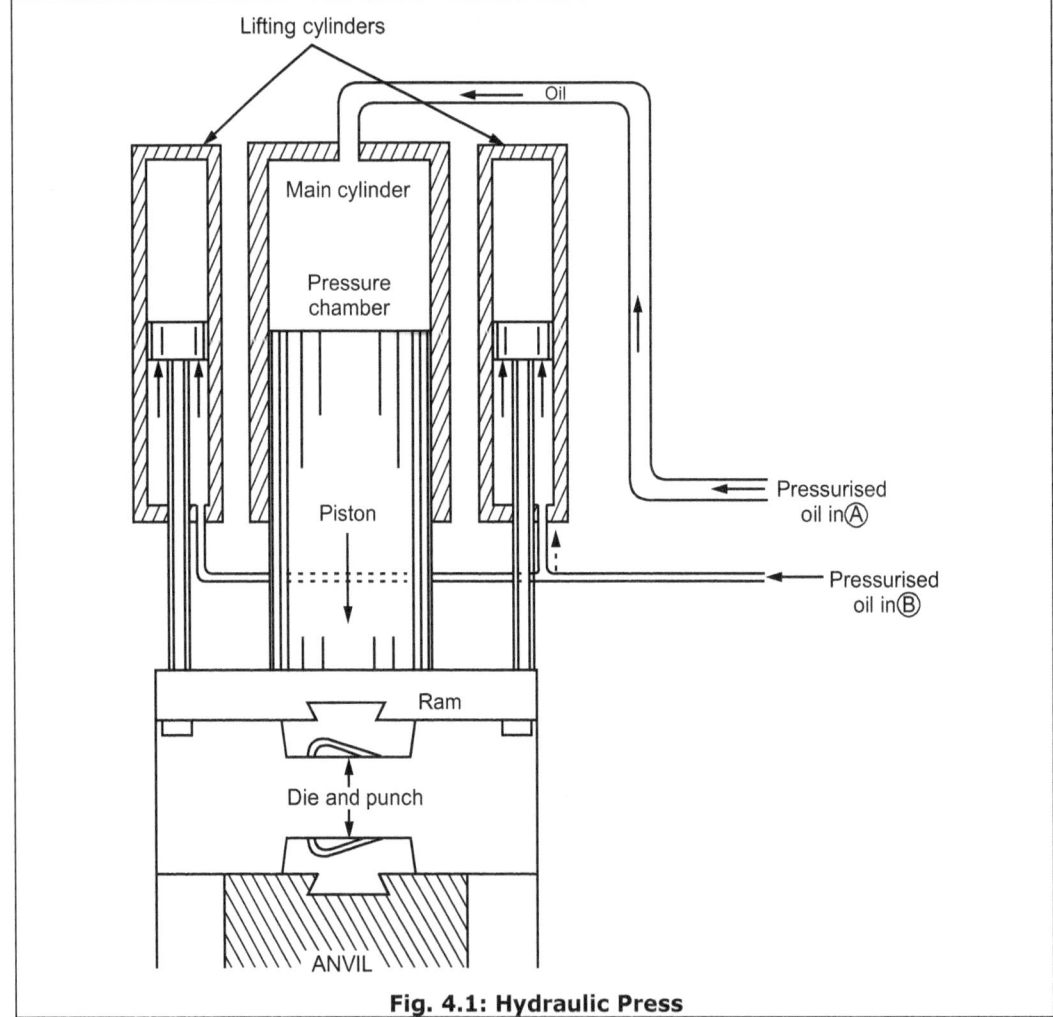

Fig. 4.1: Hydraulic Press

4.1.2 Hydraulic Ram

[W-14, S-15]

It is non-power operated pump used to lift the water. The details of the same are as given below:

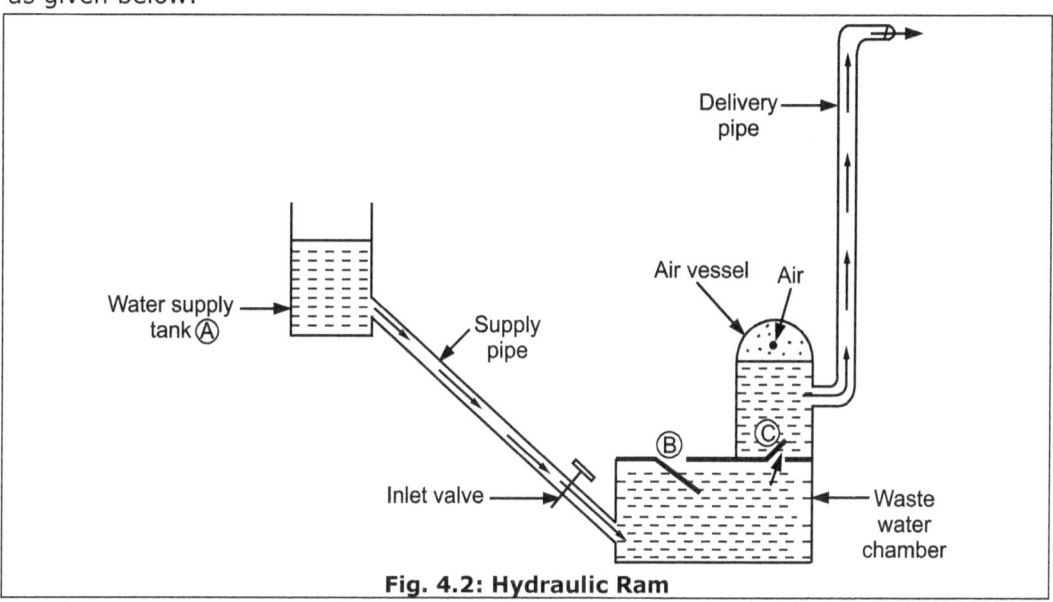

Fig. 4.2: Hydraulic Ram

Principle of working: It works on the principle of water hammer. Water hammer is actually an operational defect. If water is flowing through pipe, and if the valve at the end of the pipe is suddenly closed then the momentum of water is suddenly destroyed and a wave of high pressure is set up in the pipe. This wave propagates and creates an effect of hammer. On this principle, hydraulic ram works.

Construction: There is supply water tank (A). Waste water chamber is connected to tank (A) by water supply pipe. There are two flap valves (B) and (C) in this chamber. Air vessel is fitted on this chamber. Delivery pipe is fitted to air vessel.

Working:

1. When huge quantity of water is available at small height, a small quantity of water (from this huge quantity) can be raised to a greater height with the help of hydraulic ram.
2. Open the inlet valve on water supply line.
3. Water starts flowing from tank (A) to waste water chamber. Valve (B) is open and valve (C) is closed due to its hinged position.
4. Waste water tank will be filled and valve (B) will start closing due to force of incoming water.
5. A stage will come when valve (B) will be suddenly closed. This sudden closure will create a water hammer effect. A wave of high pressure will set inside the chamber. This pressure will force valve (C) to open.

6. Water from chamber will enter into air vessel and compress the air inside the air vessel. This compressed air will expert pressure force on water in the air vessel and small quantity of water will be raised to a greater height in delivery pipe.
7. **Applications:** When there is no electric power and non-availability of diesel engine pump set, this ram is useful.

4.1.3 Hydraulic Lift

Hydraulic lift is a device used for following purposes:
(i) Lifting Cars / Trucks at elevated height for servicing / repair works.
(ii) Carrying passengers from ground level to top floor.
(iii) Carrying storage foods viz. potato, kismis, manuka in multistoried cold storages.
(iv) Carrying engineering goods in multistoried storage buildings/material handling.
(v) Carrying workers in coal mines.

Types of Hydraulic Lifts:
1. Direct Acting Hydraulic Lift
2. Suspended Hydraulic Lift

1. Direct Acting Hydraulic Lift: This lift works on Pascal's law which states that the intensity of pressure in a static fluid is transmitted equally in all directions.

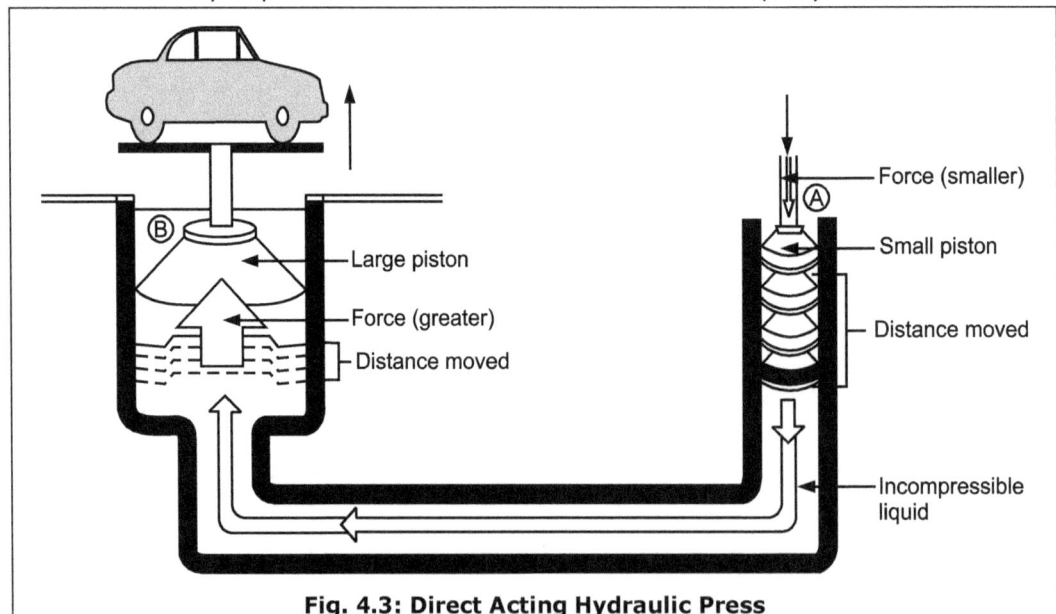

Fig. 4.3: Direct Acting Hydraulic Press

Construction: It consists of two chambers connected by means of pipe. One chamber is small and other is big one. Two chambers and pipe contain incompressible fluid. In a small chamber there is piston (A) and in big chamber there is piston (B). At the end of big piston rod, a platform is connected on which a car/vehicle can be placed.

Working: When small force is applied on piston (A) in downward direction, then a pressure will produce on the liquid in contact with plunger. The pressure is transmitted equally in all directions and acts on big piston (B). Due to this force piston (B) will move upwards.

2. **Suspended Hydraulic Lift:**

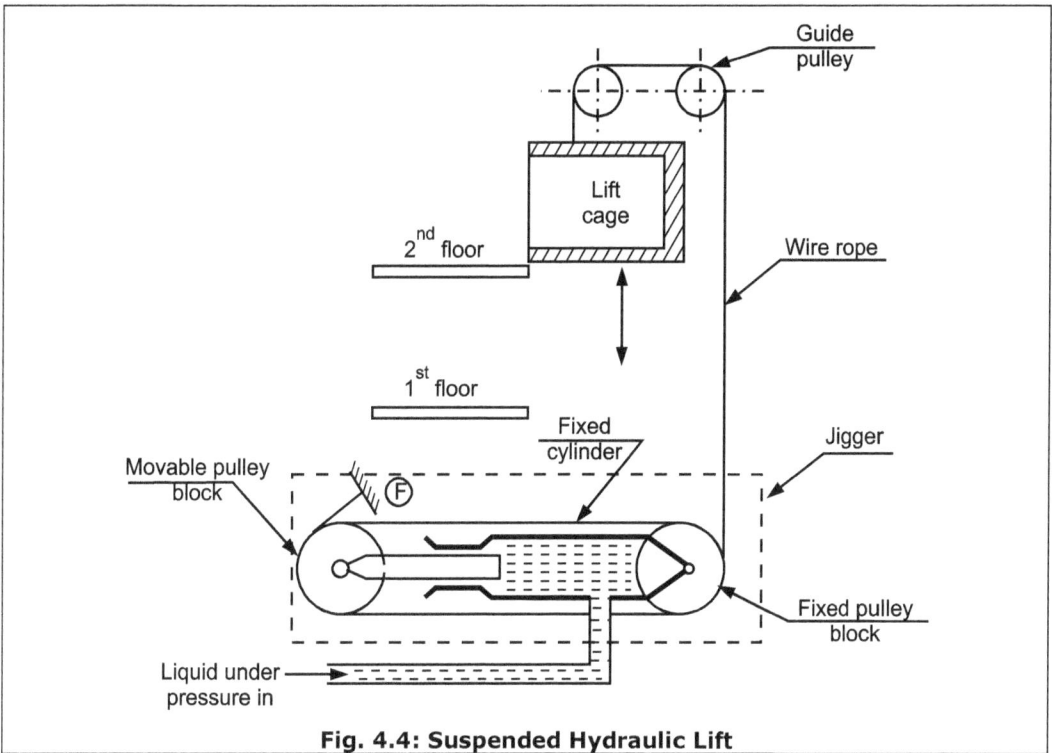

Fig. 4.4: Suspended Hydraulic Lift

Construction: It is a modified version of direct acting lift. It consists of lift cage suspended from a wire rope. Main part of lift is 'Jigger'. It consists of a fixed cylinder, sliding ram and set of two pullies. One of these pulley block is movable and other is fixed one. The end of sliding ram is connected to the movable pulley block. Wire rope, one of its end is fixed at (F) and other end is taken round all the pulleys of movable and fixed block and finally over the guide pulleys. The lift cage is suspended from the other end of rope.

Working:

- When water under pressure is admitted into fixed cylinder of jigger, the sliding ram will move towards left.
- As one end of sliding ram is connected to movable pulley block and hence the moveable pulley block moves towards right.
- Due to these two opposite direction movements, the distance between two pulley blocks of jigger will increase.
- The wire rope connected to cage is thus pulled and cage will be lifted up.
- For lowering the cage water from fixed cylinder is taken out. Now sliding ram will move towards right and movable pulley will move towards left. This decreases the distance between two pulleys and cage will be lowered.

When work after raising the load is complete, we have to take down the load. This is achieved by pressing foot lever of unloading valve (V_3). This valve will open and pressurised oil from big cylinder will be passed to oil reservoir. Due to this bypass (or unloading) of oil big piston (P_2) will come down and load will be lowered.

(d) Hydraulic Jack:

Hydraulic jack is another modification of direct acting lift. It works on the same principle of Pascal's law. But in addition it uses hand-operated reciprocating pump.

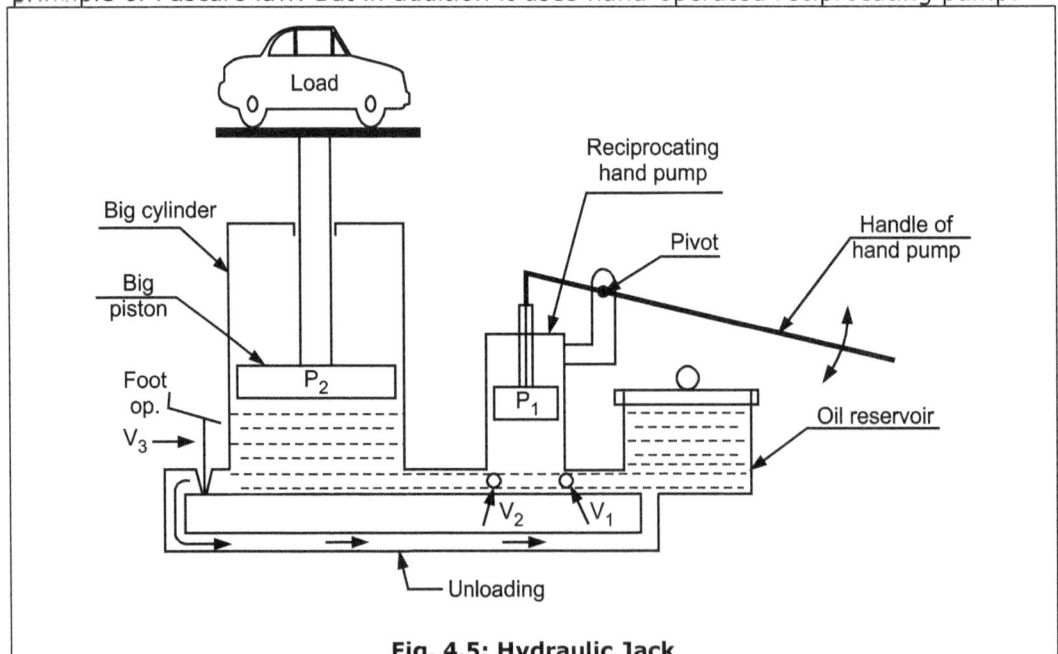

Fig. 4.5: Hydraulic Jack

Construction: It consists of pair of big cylinder – piston and hand lever operated reciprocating pump (similar to bore well hand pump fitted on bore well). There is oil reservoir fitted to hand pump. There are three valves V_1, V_2 and V_3 as shown. Valve V_3 can be open by pressing foot lever.

Working: Hand lever is moved up and down. Due to this movement, piston in hand pump will move up and down. During upward movement of piston (P_1), oil from reservoir will be sucked in via valve (V_1) due to vacuum created in cylinder. During downward stroke of piston (P_1), valve (V_1) will close and valve (V_2) will open and pressurised oil will enter into big cylinder via valve (V_2). The pressurised oil will lift the piston (P_2) upward with more force and load will be lifted up.

Applications:

This hydraulic jack is having wide applications. Some of them are:

(a) Hydraulic jack for lifting vehicles (4 wheelers) for removal of tyre.

(b) Hydraulic pallet for material handling.

(c) Stationary material lifting platform.

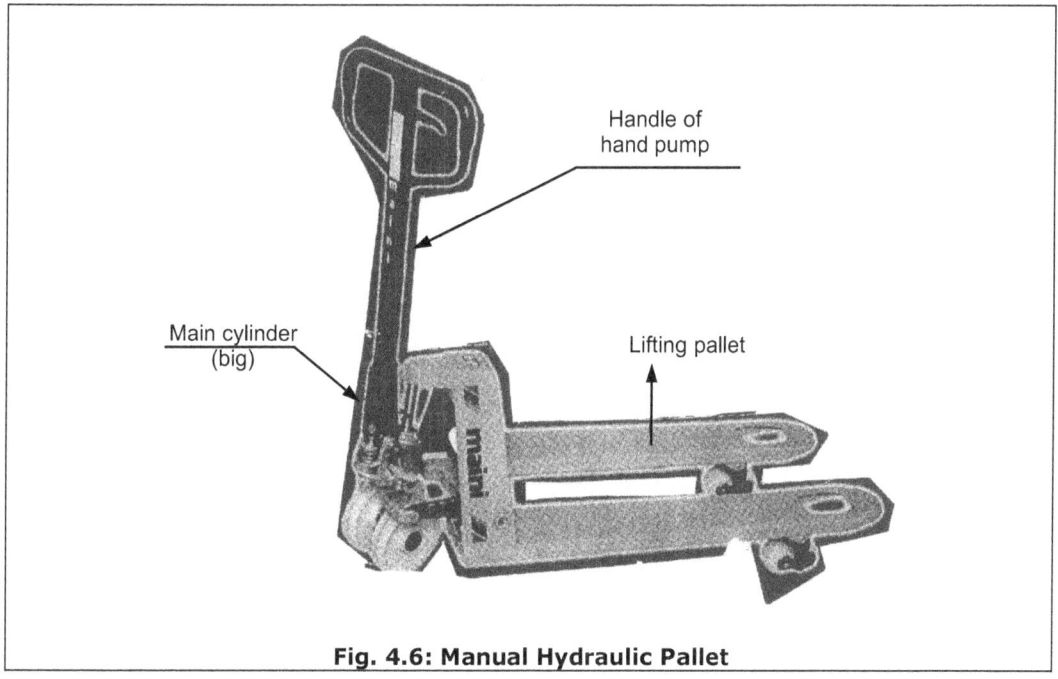

Fig. 4.6: Manual Hydraulic Pallet

4.1.4 Hydraulic Bottle Jack

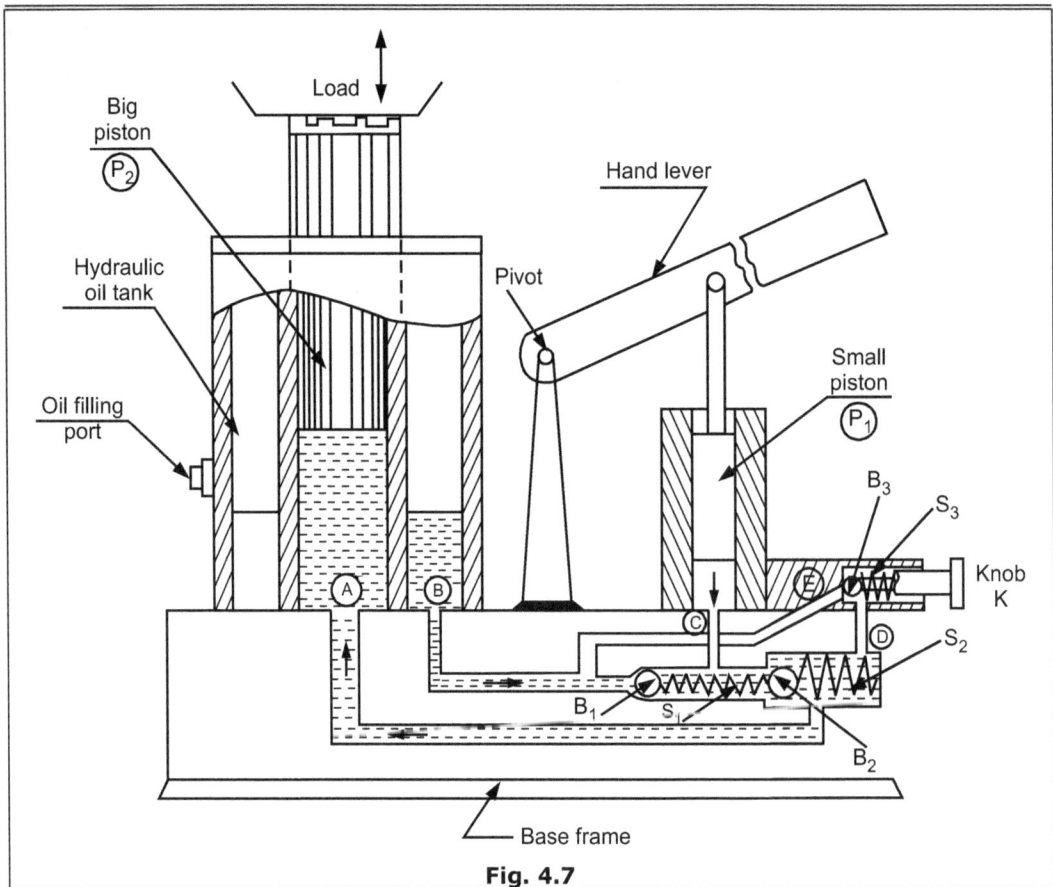

Fig. 4.7

Construction:

It consists of following components:
(a) Big piston and cylinder (P_2).
(b) Around big piston/cylinder pair there is hydraulic oil storage tank.
(c) Small piston and cylinder (P_1).
(d) A special valve with balls (B_1) and (B_2) and springs (S_1) and (S_2).
(e) Release valve having ball (B_3) and knob (K).
(f) Oil passages (A), (B), (C) and (D).
(g) Hand lever to operate small piston (P_1) with pivot fixed on Base frame.
(h) Oil used in this jack is Turbo 32 (shell) oil. Brake oil should not be used in this jack.

Working:
1. Close the knob (K) tightly. Due to this ball will close the opening.
2. When piston P_1 will move up with the help of lever; vacuum is created in small cylinder and oil from hydraulic oil tank will rush into small cylinder via oil

passage (B). This oil is under vacuum pressure, it will push the ball (B_1) towards right by compressing the spring (S_1). Due to this the oil will come into small cylinder via passage (C).

3. Immediately due to operation of hand lever, small piston will come down. Due to the movement oil in small cylinder will go down with pressure (because oil is incompressible) via oil passage (C). Due to oil pressure ball (B_2) will move towards right by compressing the spring (S_2). The pressurised oil will move in big cylinder via passage (A) and this pressurised oil will push the big piston (P_2) upwards.
4. When we reciprocate the small piston by hand lever, the cycle repeats and piston (P_2) will move up and up which will lift the load (most probably the car or small 4 wheeler/3 wheeler for removal of tyre).
5. To take the load down. Open the knob (K). Due to the knob opening, ball (B_3) will be loose. Pressurised oil in big cylinder will now return via passage (A). It will come in the cavity around spring (S_2). Then it will flow to cavity around spring (S_3) via passage (D). This oil will then flow to hydraulic oil tank around big piston via passages (E) and (B). The oil level in tank will rise and big piston will come down.
6. The typical feature of this bottle jack is that same passages are used for oil movement. The valve comprising of balls (B_1), (B_2) and springs (S_1) and (S_2) is a typical design to make the jack compact.

Applications:
- This valve is a replacement to toggle jack (mechanical – power screw jack) for lifting the 4 wheeler / 3 wheeler for tyre removal/repairs.
- 20 Ton and above bottle jacks are used for lifting the machines during maintenance work.

Specifications of Bottle Jack:

Bottle jacks are specified according to its tonnage, lowest height, extended height, stroke length, base frame dimensions and weight of jack.

Weight that jack can lift (Tonnage)	Lowest height of jack (mm)	Stroke length (mm)	Extended length (mm)	Weight of jack (kg)	Base frame dimensions (L x W) mm
2T	180	120	300	2.72	100 × 90
3T	187	125	312	4.63	115 × 90
5T	232	160	392	5.45	125 × 110
8T	230	155	385	7.27	127 × 115
20T	275	168	443	14.09	165 × 150
50T	305	170	475	40.45	230 × 190

4.2 OTHER PUMPING DEVICES

- Pump plays a specific and unique position in the system. It is a 'Heart' of Hydraulic system.
- The main function of pump is to take oil from tank and deliver it to rest of the hydraulic circuit. In doing so, it raises oil pressure to required level.
- It is important to note that – fluid or oil is incompressible (cannot be compressed opposite to air in pneumatic systems). Then how pressure of oil increases? The simple answer to this question is that, the load on fluid creates the pressure. If load is more, pressure is more. If load is less, pressure is less.

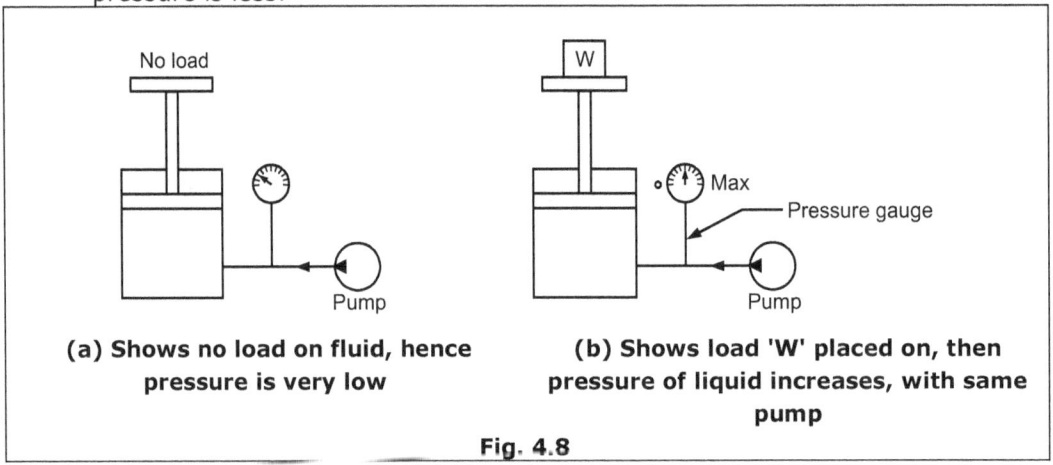

(a) Shows no load on fluid, hence pressure is very low

(b) Shows load 'W' placed on, then pressure of liquid increases, with same pump

Fig. 4.8

Symbol of Pump:

1. **Unidirectional Fixed Displacement Hydraulic Pump**

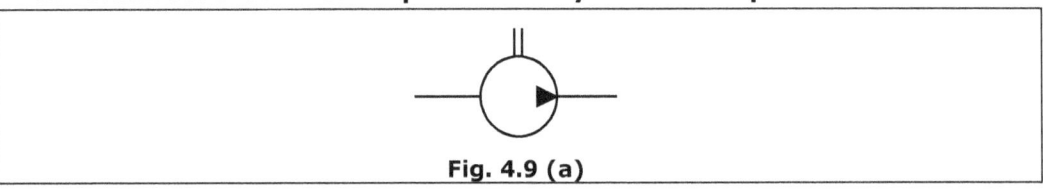

Fig. 4.9 (a)

2. **Bi-directional Fixed Displacement Hydraulic Pump**

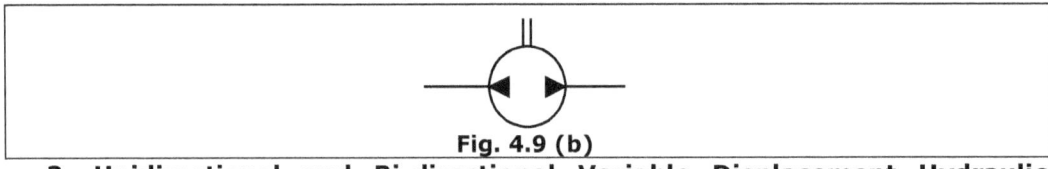

Fig. 4.9 (b)

3. **Unidirectional and Bi-directional Variable Displacement Hydraulic Pump**

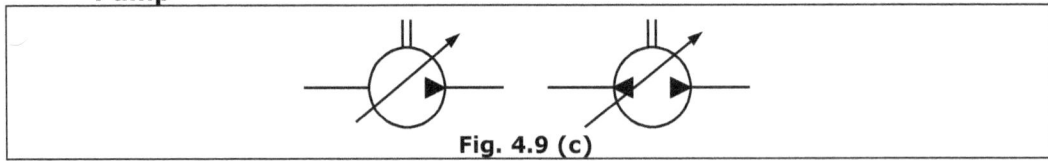

Fig. 4.9 (c)

4.2.1 Classification of Pumps

Pumps can be well classified into two major categories:

(a) Positive Displacement Pumps.

(b) Non-Positive Displacement Pumps (Rotodynamic):

- Pressure is major consideration in Hydraulic system, hence majority pumps used in hydraulic systems are 'Positive Displacement Pumps'.

- The classification of Positive Displacement Pumps is as under:

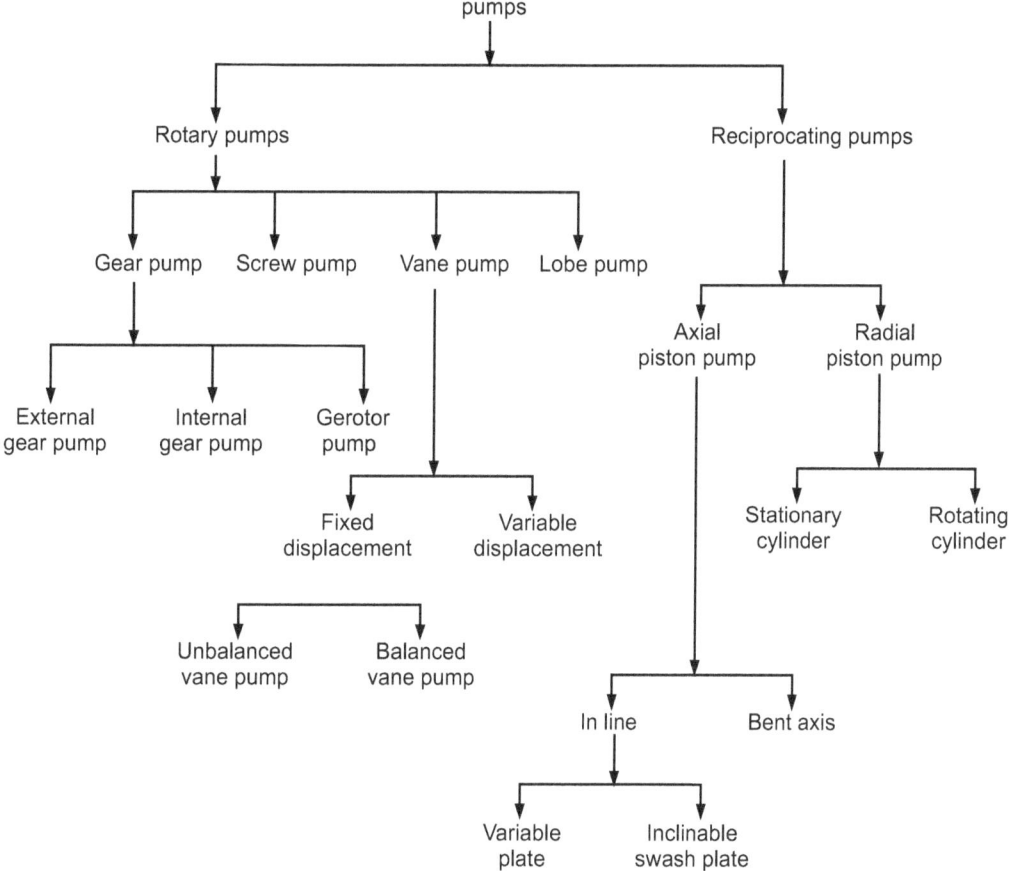

- The pressures that can be created by various positive displacement pumps and their efficiencies are given in following table.

Pump Type	Pressure (Bar)	Efficiency
External Gear Pump	300	60%
Internal Gear Pump	350	85%
Fixed Vane Pump	175	75%
Variable Vane Pump	125	85%
Screw Pump	175	75%
Axial Piston Pumps	700	85%
Bent Axis Pumps	700	90%

- Non-Positive Displacement pumps are centrifugal pump, Radial flow pump. These are used for very low pressure. In fact, these pumps are very rarely used in Hydraulic system. These pumps cannot create pressure above 40 Bar (40 kg/cm^2).
- Now we will see important pumps one by one.

4.2.2 External Gear Pump

Construction: It consists of two meshing gears, housing, two cover plates, bearings and shaft for gear mounting and a drive motor. The housing is having two ports (inlet and outlet). Gears are either spur or helical gears. If pressure angle is $14\frac{1}{2}^\circ$ then minimum number of teeth are 16.

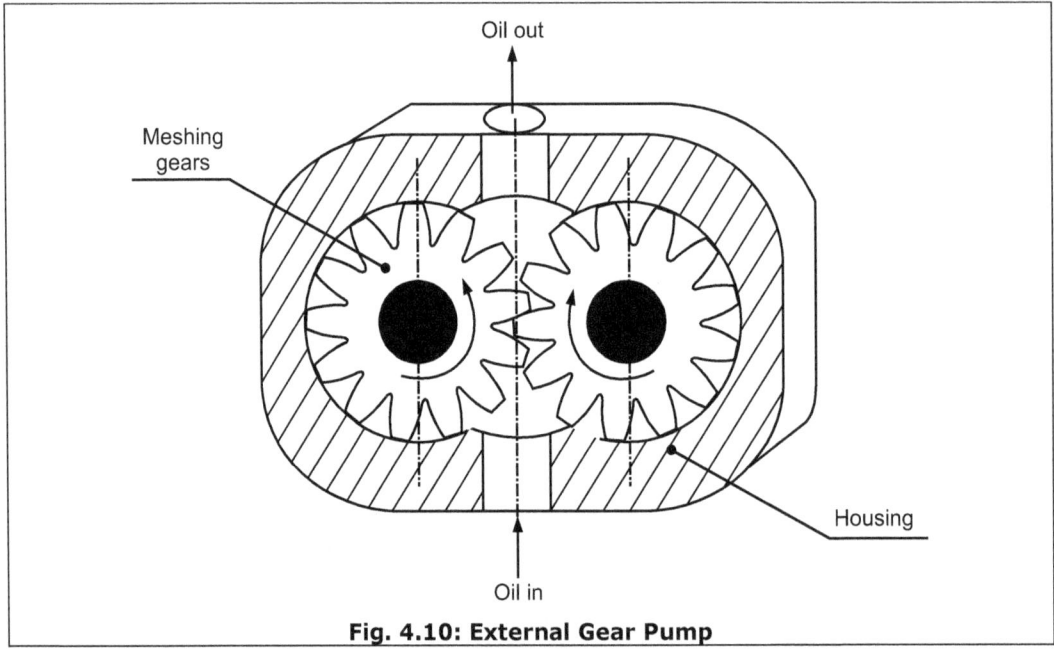

Fig. 4.10: External Gear Pump

Working: Tooth space of one gear is filled by tooth of other gear. Motor drives one gear which in turn rotates other gear. As meshed gears start rotating, one tooth space after another is evacuated resulting in vacuum. Atmospheric pressure in the tank forces the oil into the tooth space. Now tooth space is full of oil. Due to rotation of gear, oil is carried around the periphery of the gear until the teeth again mesh and the oil is forced out through delivery port location on opposite side of suction port. This pump can create pressure upto 300 bar.

4.2.3 Internal Gear Pump

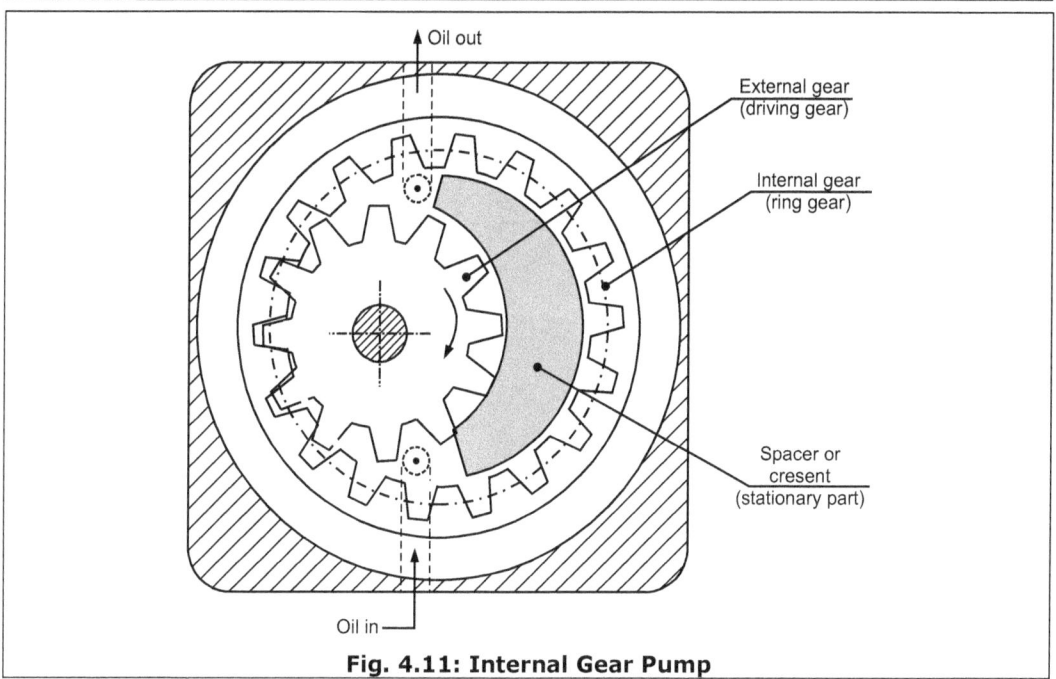

Fig. 4.11: Internal Gear Pump

The basic principle of working is same as that of external gear.

Construction: It consists of one external and one internal meshing gear pair. External gear is connected to electric motor and hence is driving gear. Internal gear or Ring gear is driven gear which rotates in same direction as that of external gear. Between two gears a spacer called 'cresent' is located which is stationary piece connected to housing. Inlet and outlet ports are located in end plates.

Working: External Gear (Driving Gear) drives the Internal Gear (Ring Gear). Portion where teeth starts meshing, a tight seal is created. Near inlet port the vacuum is created due to quick unmeshing and oil enters from oil tank through inlet port. Oil is trapped between the internal and external gear teeth on both sides of cresent (spacer) and is then carried from inlet to outlet port. Meshing of gear near outlet port reduces the volume or gap and oil gets pressurised. These pumps can create pressure upto 350 bar and one other speciality of this pump is that it makes very less noise.

4.2.4 Gerotor Pump

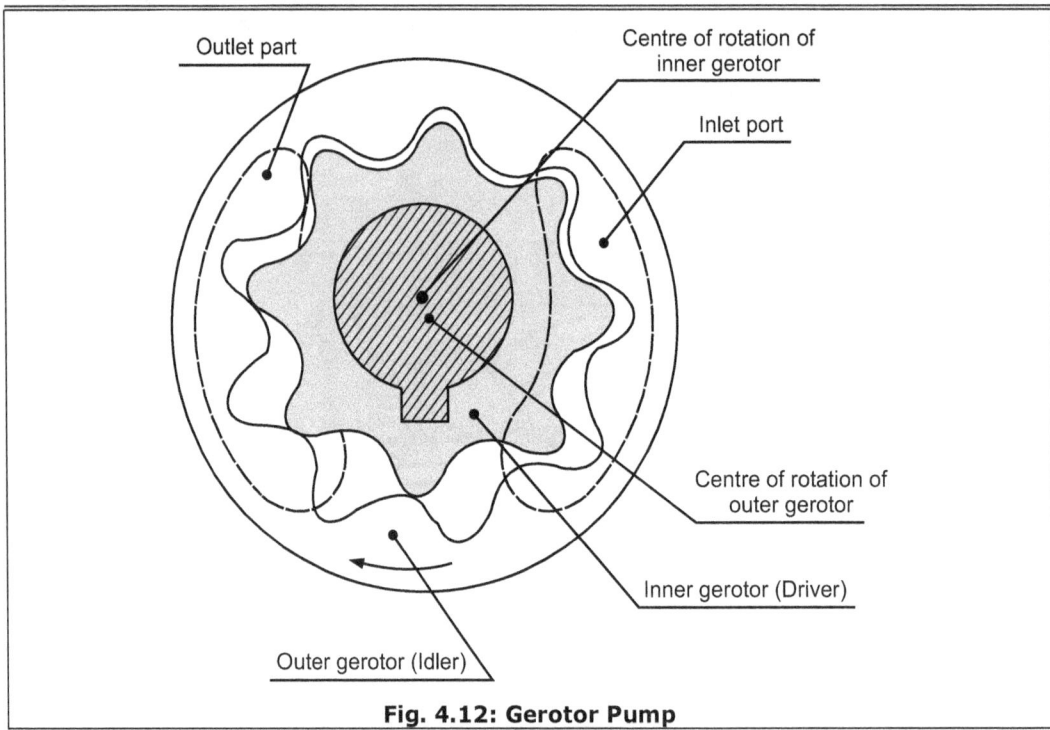

Fig. 4.12: Gerotor Pump

Construction: It is similar to internal gear pump. But in this pump cresent is absent. It is dispenced by using inner gerotor with one less tooth than outer gerotor.

Working: When inner gerotor rotates, the pockets go on increasing in size due to motion. These pockets create suction and oil comes in through inlet port. On outlet side this pocket area goes on decreasing and the trapped oil is forcefully discharges through outlet port. So continuous motion causes continuous discharge. This pump can create pressure @120 Bar.

4.2.5 Unbalanced Vane Type Pump [S-15]

- Vane pump operates on the principle of increasing and diminishing volume.

Construction: The pump shown in Fig. 4.12 is unbalanced vane pump because its rotor is eccentric to housing. (There is distance between centre of rotor and centre of housing.) Its main parts are:

(a) Driving rotor with slots for vanes: The electric motor is coupled to rotor.

(b) Sliding vanes: Its steel flat piece is shown in Fig. 4.13.

(c) Cam ring to constrain the outward movement of vanes.

(d) Housing with inlet and outlet ports.

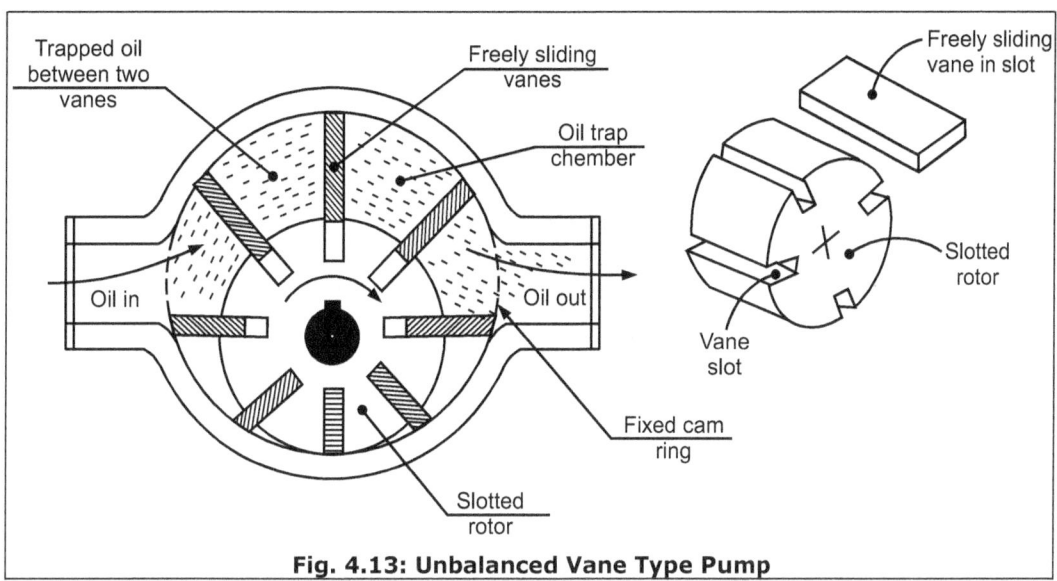

Fig. 4.13: Unbalanced Vane Type Pump

Working: The rotor is having number of vanes which are free to slide in or out in slots. When rotor starts rotating, vanes flow out in slots due to centrifugal force. Now vanes touch the cam ring. As one can see number of oil trap chambers are formed between two consecutive vanes. Since rotor is offset with cam ring the area of these oil trap chambers diminishes and increases as rotor rotates.

In the beginning due to rotation of rotor the air moves out quickly and partial vacuum is created near inlet port. Oil rushes in and is trapped in each oil chamber. As the area of chamber reduces further the trapped oil gets pressurised.

Important: The oil leakage in this pump is low as compared to gear pump.

4.2.6 Balanced Vane Pump

A little consideration will show that in unbalanced vane pump, the pump is subjected to low pressure on inlet side and high pressure on outlet side. This pressure difference results in unbalanced pressure on vanes of pump and shaft.

To avoid this problem, unbalanced vane pump is modified to create balanced forces. Such construction is called 'Balanced Vane Pump'.

Construction: Similar to unbalanced vane pump it has following parts. The only difference is that instead of circular cam ring, an elliptical cam ring is used.

  (a) Driving rotor with slots for vanes

  (b) Sliding vanes

  (c) Elliptical cam ring

  (d) Housing with crossed inlet and outlet ports (2 each)

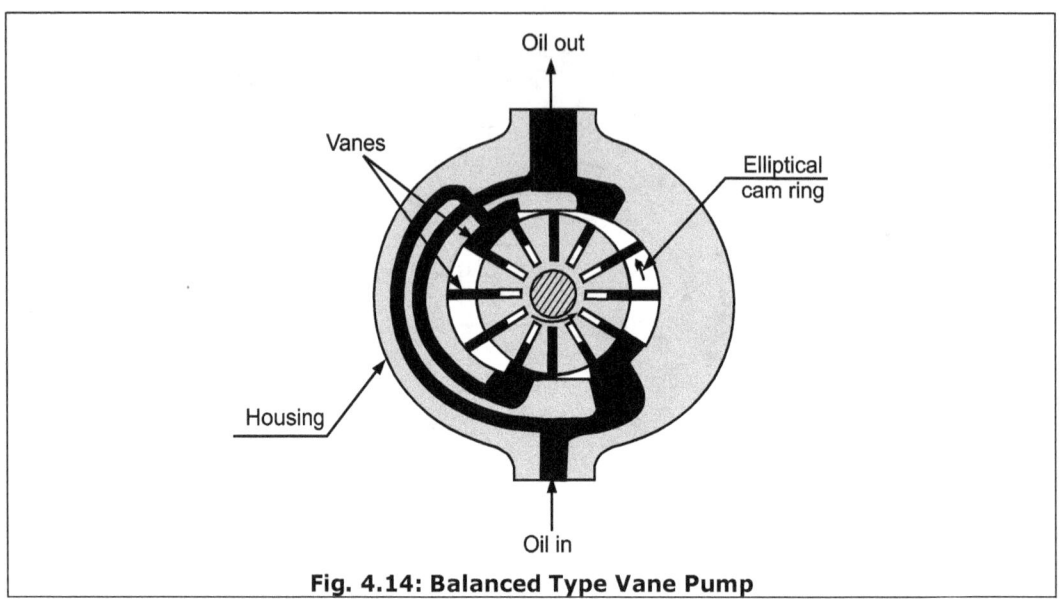

Fig. 4.14: Balanced Type Vane Pump

Working: In this type, rotor and housing are concentric (having same centre. No eccentricity). When rotor rotates, vanes move out due to centrifugal force and touch to cam ring. Oil trap chambers are formed between two consecutive vanes. In the beginning air goes out and partial vacuum is created. The oil comes in through two inlet ports. Due to diminishing and increasing trap chamber volume, oil gets pressurised and goes out through two delivery ports. Due to pressure action created by two ports, the unbalanced force on vane and shaft is nullified.

4.2.7 Variable Displacement Vane Pump

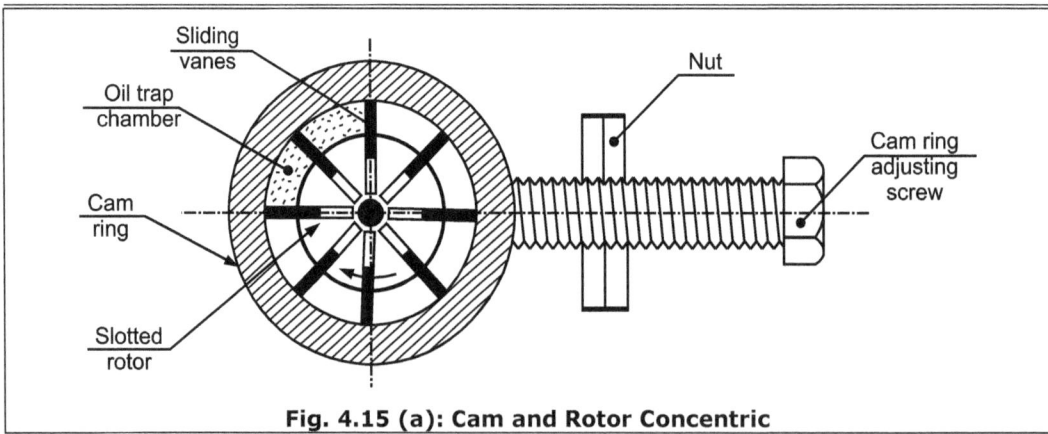

Fig. 4.15 (a): Cam and Rotor Concentric

In many hydraulic circuits, the flow rate of pump needs variable. This can be done by changing the speed (RPM) of motor which drives the pump. But variable speed electric motor is a costly affair. An alternative method is to vary the displacement of pump. This is possible very easily with vane pump as depicted in Fig. 4.15 (a).

If we change the geometric position of cam ring relative to slotted rotor, we can achieve delivery volume as per the need of circuit.

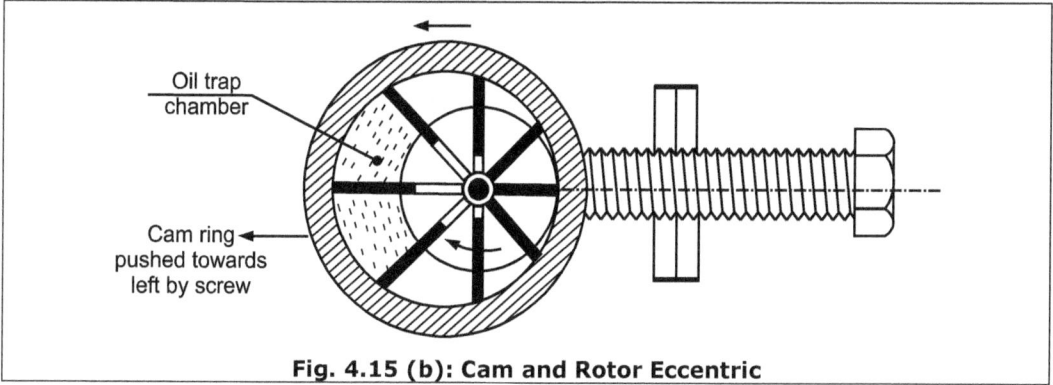

Fig. 4.15 (b): Cam and Rotor Eccentric

Construction: It is similar to unbalanced vane pump but the only difference is that we can adjust or shift the cam ring to left or right. Its main parts are:

(a) Driving motor with slots for vanes

(b) Sliding vanes

(c) Adjustable cam ring with adjusting screw

(d) Housing with inlet and outlet ports.

Working: Fig. 4.15 (a) shows cam ring and rotor are concentric. In this position, all oil trap chambers will be having same volume and oil will not be pressurised.

Fig. 4.15 (b) shows cam ring is shifted towards left by using screw and fixed nut pair. Now the pump will act exactly similar as unbalanced vane pump we have already seen. The volumes of 'trap oil chamber' will increase and diminish which will pressurise the oil.

By adjusting screw we can increase or reduce the eccentricity between cam ring and rotor. By doing so we can change or vary the flow output of pump.

4.2.8 Screw Pump

Construction: The special screws having 'right hand' and 'left hand' threads on same shank are used in this pump. Fig. 4.16 shows two such meshing screws. These are encased in closely machined housing. One screw is connected to prime move (motor). This is driving screw and since it meshes with other it is driven screw. Below the screw there is intake port; which is bottom of housing similar to crank case of engine. Timing gears on screw shaft provide the turning force between driving and driven screw.

Working: In this pump, oil entering into pump does not 'rotate' but move 'linearly' (similar to nut slides on rotating screw) as screw starts rotating, in the beginning air moves out and due to vacuum created oil draws in from suction chamber into pump housing. This oil moves on the helical grooves of screw. Due to close meshing of screw, oil moves in tight gap (very small gap) between meshing threads as well as threads and inside surface of housing. Due to special design of screw, oil gets divided into two compartments and advances towards the centre of pump and pressurised oil comes out through discharge port at centre.

- Sometimes for creating heavy pressures, 3 screws are used. This pump can create pressure upto 400 bar.
- Timing gears are generally 'Herring bone' type gears.
- The usual operating speed of this pump is about 1500 to 1700 RPM.

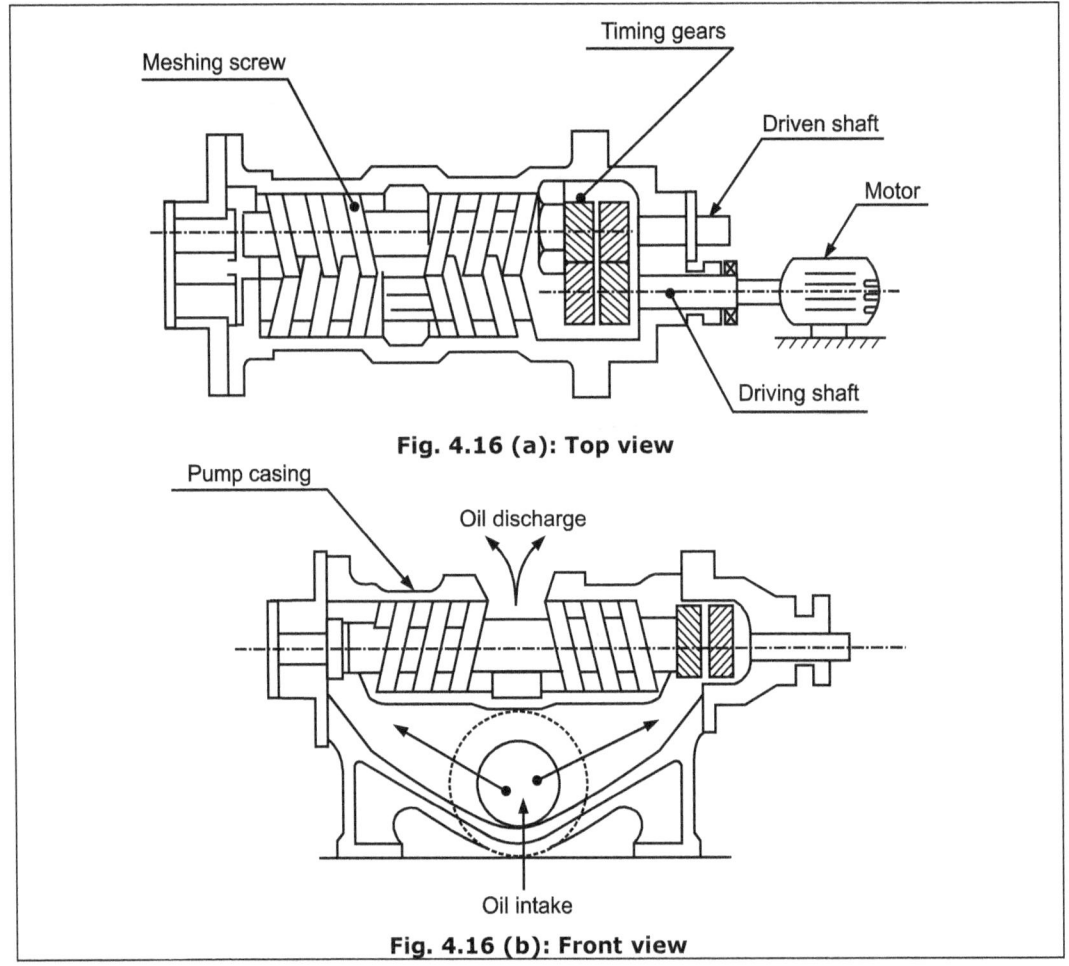

Fig. 4.16 (a): Top view

Fig. 4.16 (b): Front view

4.2.9 Lobe Pump

There are two lobes meshing with each other, driving lobe shaft is attached to motor. This pump is low pressure pump. When both lobes start rotating a vacuum created near inlet port draws the oil in. It is trapped between lobes and casing surface. Oil goes out with force due to high RPM of lobes. This pump is used when more quantity of oil is required at low pressure.

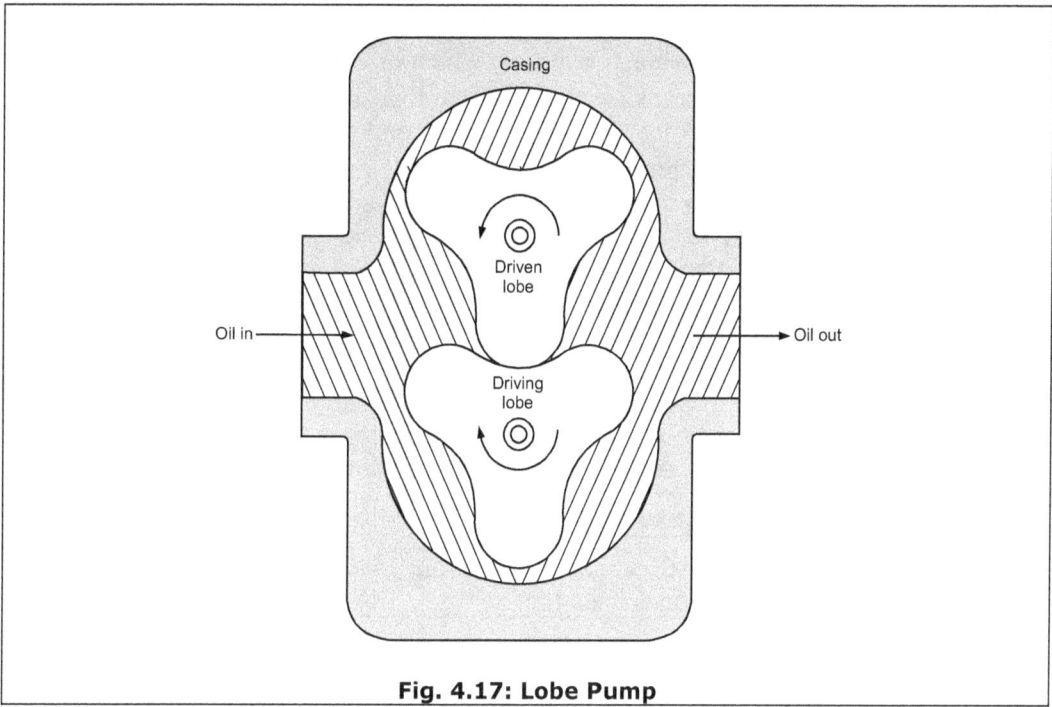

Fig. 4.17: Lobe Pump

4.2.10 Simple Piston Pump

This piston pump is exactly similar to reciprocating pump as well have studied in this same topic.

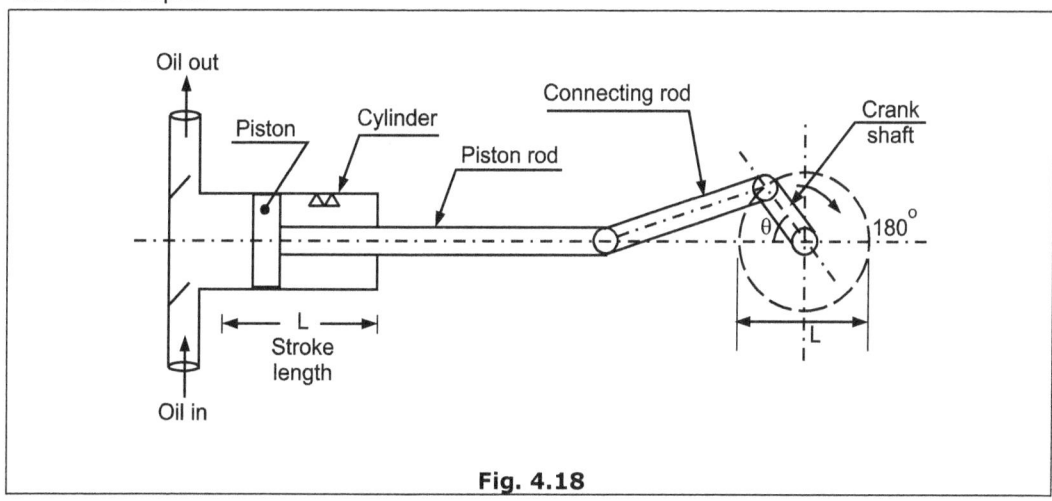

Fig. 4.18

Construction: It consists of:
- Finely finished cylinder barrel.
- Piston or plunger.
- 4 bar mechanism – piston rod, connecting rod, crank shaft.
- Prime mover (generally electric motor) which drives crank shaft.

Working: Motor drives crank shaft. Due to four bar mechanism, this rotary motion is converted into reciprocating motion of piston in cylinder.

- **When piston moves from left to right:** Vacuum is created. Suction valve opens and oil comes in the cylinder cavity.
- **When piston moves from right to left (in second half):** Suction valve closes and delivery valve opens. The pressurised oil goes out.
- As we know that, in reciprocating pump, the piston travels distance equal to 'L' in half revolution of crank ($\theta = 0$ to $\theta = 180°$). This is stroke length. This distance is fixed and hence piston pump is fixed displacement pump.
- We also know that in piston pump, piston moves in cylinder with acceleration and retardation. Hence, delivery of oil is intermittent.
- Piston pumps are adopted when pressure requirements are very high.

4.2.11 Multicylinder Piston Pumps

In this type 2, 3, 4, 6 or 8 cylinders are either inline or in 'V' shape and their piston are operated on common crank shaft.

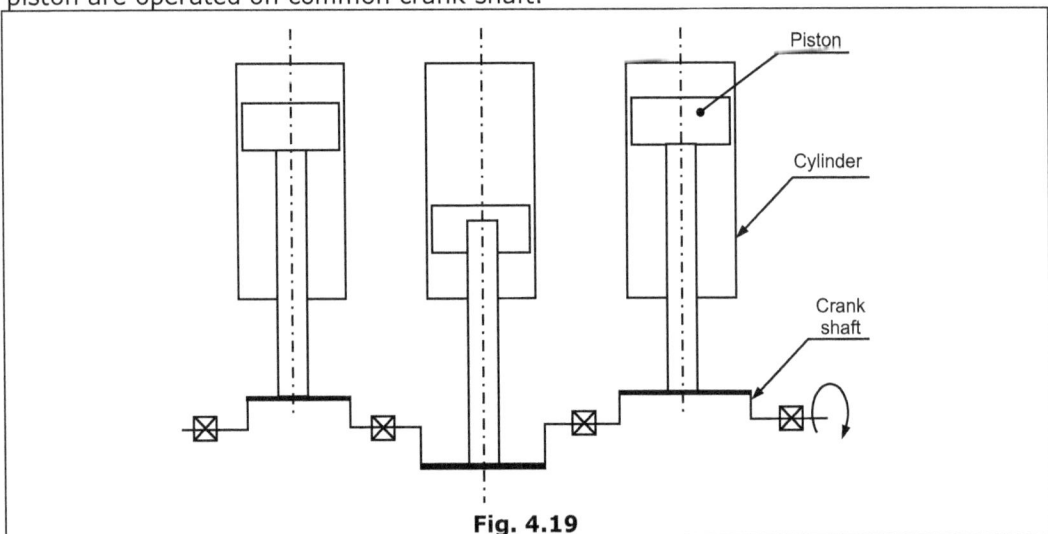

Fig. 4.19

- The arrangement is similar to Petrol or Diesel engine block.
- These pumps can create pressure upto 450 bar.
- Generally, two cylinder piston pumps are used in fork lifters, simple loaders etc.

Working: Crank is rotated by motor. According to timer adjustment, the piston reciprocates in definite order.

4.2.12 Axial Piston Pumps

In these type of pumps, pistons (or cylinder bores) are arranged axially parallel to each other around the circumferential periphery of the cylinder block.

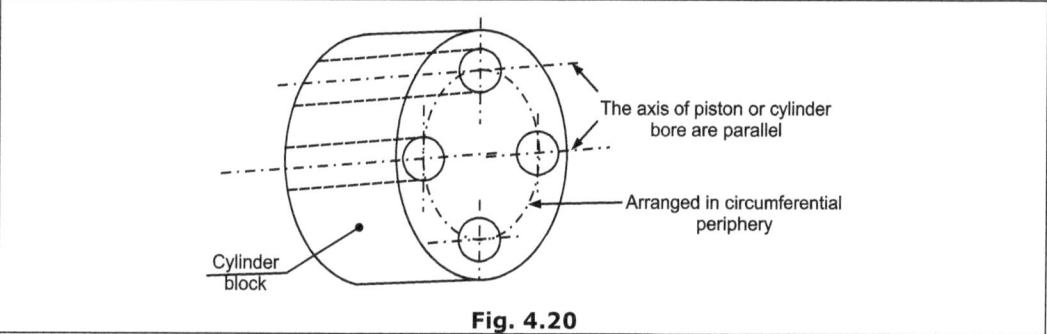

Fig. 4.20

Note: Number of cylinder bores are generally even numbers (6, 8 or 10).

Axial Piston Pumps are subdivided into:
(a) Swash Plate Axial Piston Pump
(b) Bent Axis Piston Pump

The general Axial piston pump is depicted in Fig. 4.21.

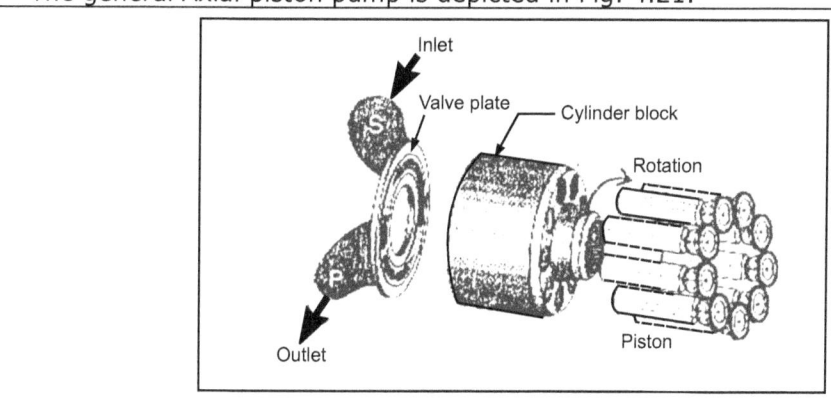

Fig. 4.21: Showing Valve Plate, Cylinder Block and Pistons

4.2.13 Swash Plate Axial Piston Pump [W-14, S-15]

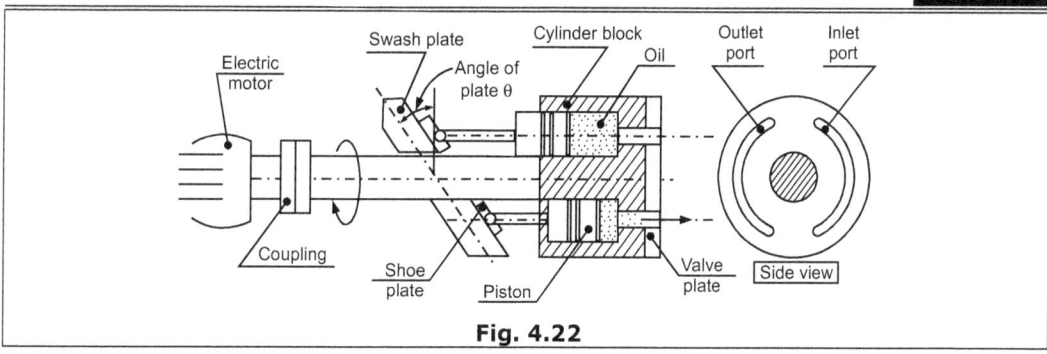

Fig. 4.22

Construction: The pump consists of following parts:

(a) Cylinder Barrel having circumferentially arranged cylinder bores (6, 8 or 10).

(b) Pistons (6, 8, or 10).

(c) Swash plate with shoe plate for piston rod connection. The angle of swash plate can be changed.

(d) Prime mover (Electric motor).

Working: Motor drives the shaft, which in turn rotates entire cylinder block.

- The pistons are connected to inclined swash plate through piston rod.
- Now one can easily understand that since swash plate is inclined and block is rotating, the pistons reciprocate inside the barrel.
- The reciprocating motion of pistons causes suction and delivery of fluid through the inlet and outlet ports which come infront of outlet of piston.
- We can change the angle of swash plate i.e. θ if

    (a) θ = 0 then no flow of oil, because pistons are at same level. When θ = 0 swash plate is vertical. No reciprocation of pistons, hence no flow.

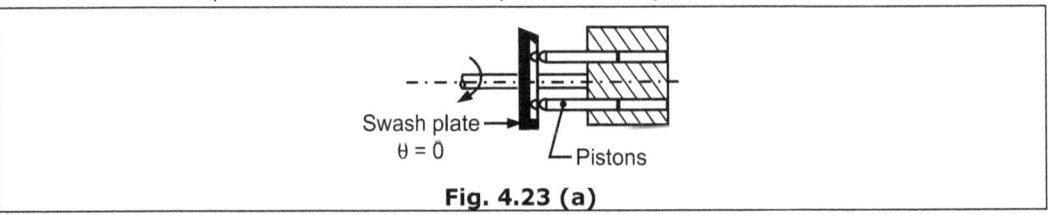

Fig. 4.23 (a)

(b) θ = max or +ve, then x will be stroke length which is maximum and there will be maximum forward flow.

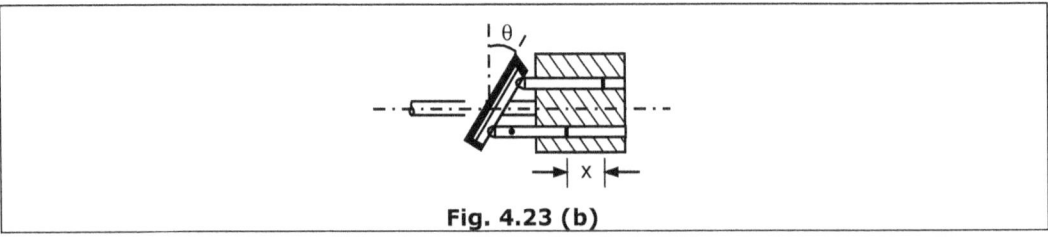

Fig. 4.23 (b)

(c) θ = −ve, then 'x' → i.e. stroke length will be maximum in reverse direction and hence there will be reverse flow.

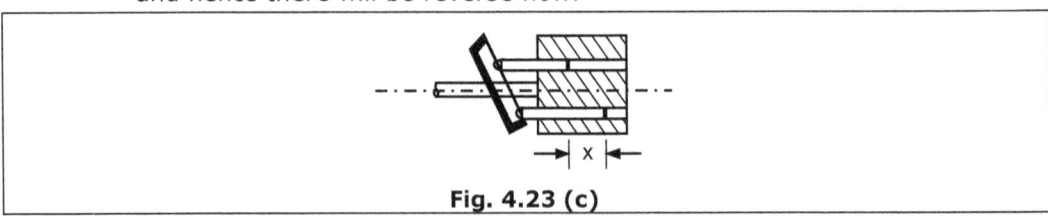

Fig. 4.23 (c)

- By changing the swash plate angle, we can vary the stroke length of piston. It may be noted that maximum swash plate angle is limited to $17\frac{1}{2}°$.

By changing the angle of swash plate the pump output flow can be changed, hence we can use this pump as variable displacement pump also.

4.2.14 Bent Axis Type Axial Piston Pump

In swash plate axial pump, the axis of cylinder block is horizontal and angle is given to swash plate. Opposite to it is Bent Axis Type Axial Piston Pump, the cylinder block is at an angle and driving flange (similar to swash plate) is horizontal.

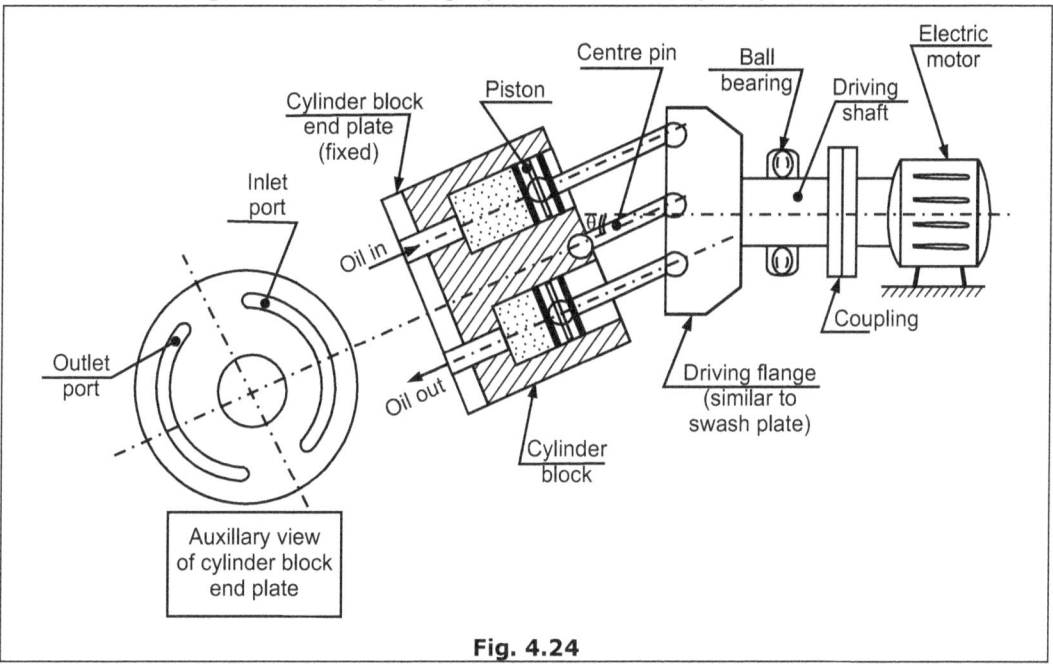

Fig. 4.24

Construction: This pump consists of following parts/components:

(a) Cylinder block having circumferentially arranged cylinder bores (6, 8 or 10).

(b) Pistons (6, 8 or 10 Nos).

(c) Driving flange (similar to swash plate of Axial piston pump).

(d) Cylinder block end plate in which inlet and outlet ports are arranged as shown in Auxillary view.

(e) Prime mover (Electric Motor).

In this pump, axis of cylinder block is arranged in such a manner that it will form an angle θ with horizontal axis of driving staff and driving flange.

Working: When driving shaft rotates, it will rotate cylinder block because it is connected to driving flange by using centre pin. When this whole assembly starts rotating, one can easily understand that pistons in the cylinder block will start reciprocating (because of inclination of cylinder axis).

The rotating cylinder block will come infront of inlet and outlet port of end plate (it is fixed) and pressurised oil will flow out through outlet port.

- The angle between drive shaft and cylinder block 'θ' can be fixed or we can change it.
- The maximum value of θ is $30°$.
- Similar to swash plate axial pump of angle $\theta = 0$ then axis of cylinder block and driving shaft coincide and there will be no flow.

4.2.15 Radial Piston Pump

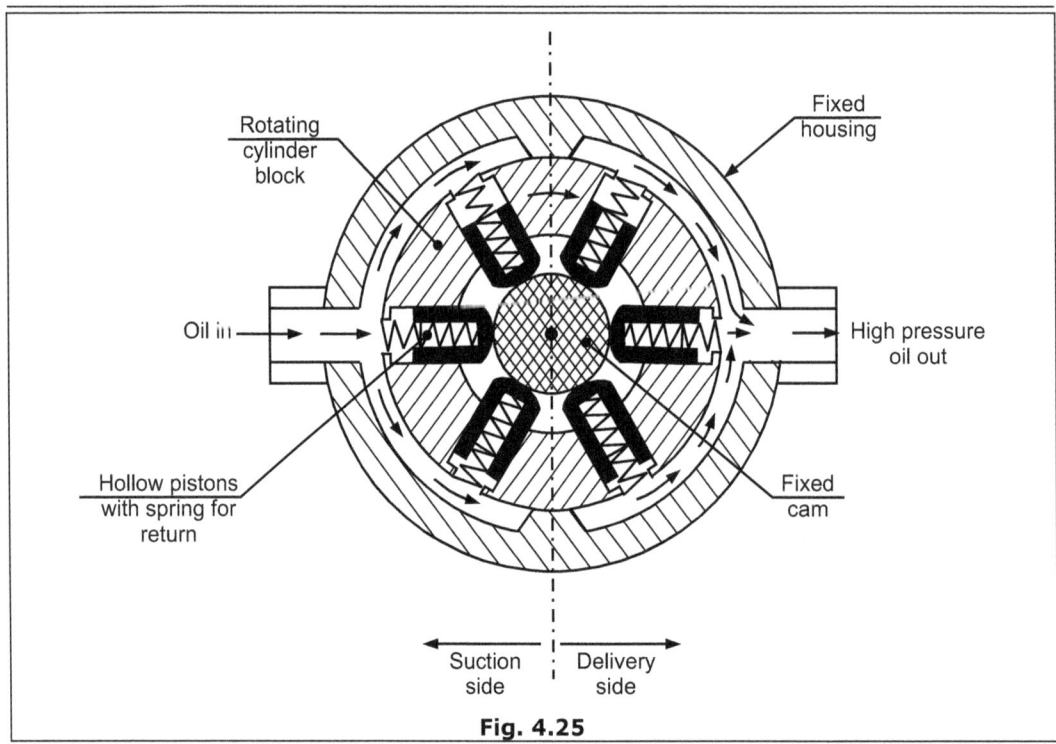

Fig. 4.25

Construction: The radial piston pump consists of following components:
(a) Rotating cylinder block having number of cylinder bores radially created.
(b) Fixed or stationary cam which is eccentric with cylinder block.
(c) Fixed or stationary housing in which suction oil and discharge oil moving paths are machined.
(d) Prime mover (Electric motor).
(e) Each cylinder barrel is having hollow piston with spring for return as shown in Fig. 4.25.

Working: When cylinder block starts rotating in clockwise direction the eccentricity between fixed cam and rotating cylinder blocks causes the piston to reciprocate. Piston on suction side (left portion in Fig. 4.25) moves towards the centre of cam and sucks the oil in the cylinder. Pistons on delivery side (right portion in Fig. 4.25) move away from the centre of cam thereby pressurizing the oil which goes out through outlet port.

- When eccentricity between cam and cylinder block is fixed then flow is fixed or the pump is fixed displacement pump or constant delivery pump.
- If we change the eccentricity by shifting the cam position then the flow of pump will change.
- We can obtain pressures upto 500 bar with this pump.

4.2.16 Characteristic Curves for few Hydraulic Pumps [S-15]

- Characteristic curve is a graphical representation of behaviour of pump under certain conditions on which pump operates.
- The graphs are obtained by testing the pumps in ideal condition as well as under actual conditions.

(a) Characteristic Curve of Vane Type Pump at Constant Speed:

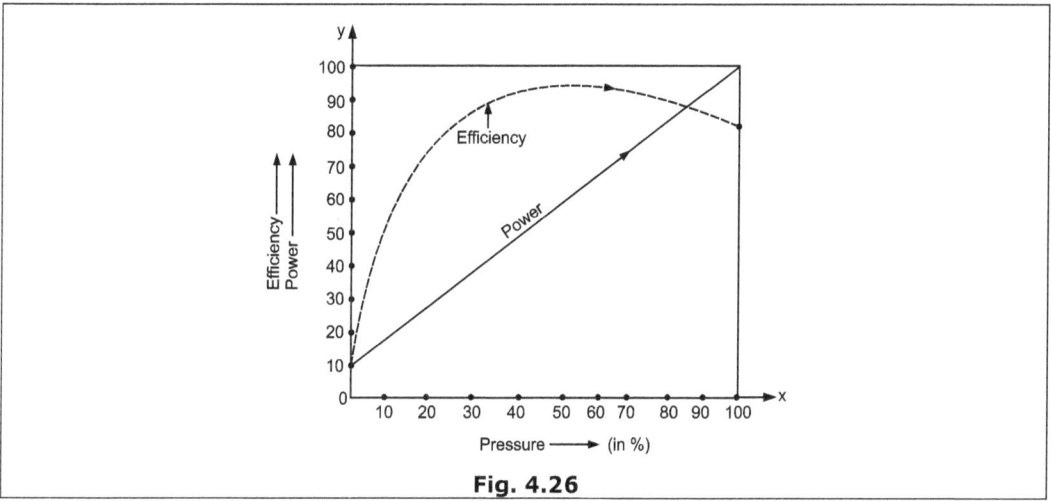

Fig. 4.26

It is clear from Fig. 4.26 that:
- Power increases at higher pressure.
- Efficiency increases at medium pressure but drops to some extent if pressure further increases.

(b) Characteristic Curve of Gear Pump at Constant Speed:

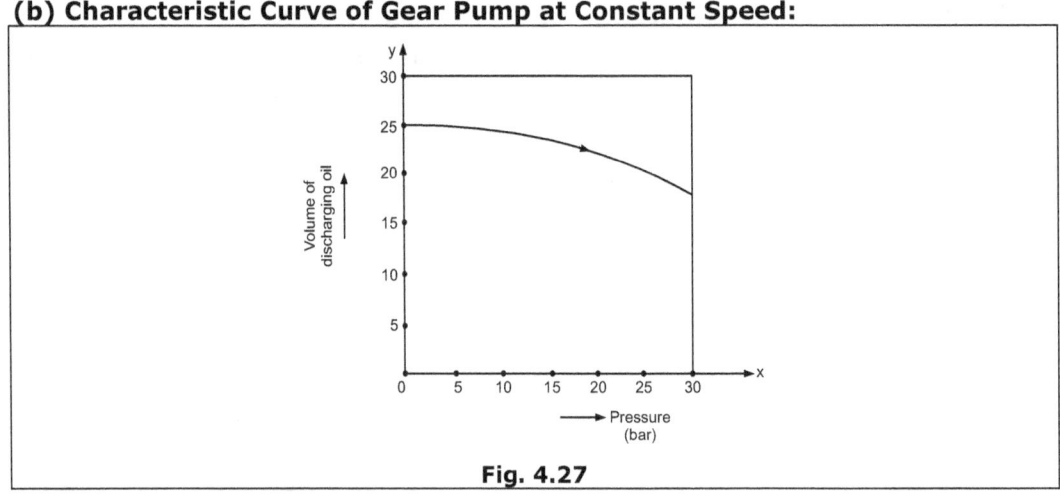

Fig. 4.27

In this curve, we have plotted pressure on x-axis and volume of discharging oil on y-axis. It is clear from the graph that when pressure is higher, the discharge volume reduces to some extent.

4.2.17 Criterias for Selection of Pump in Hydraulic Circuit (or Basis of Pump Selection)

In hydraulic circuit we use actuators to do useful mechanical work. For every different application the actuators are different and so also load on actuator is different. Hence, selection of pump (it is a heart of hydraulic system) is of high importance. Following are the criterias for selection of pump.

- **(a) Pressure:** Pump is pressurizing the hydraulic oil to the level required by actuator. When pressures upto 300 bar are required, we can select gear pumps. If pressure requirement is still low then we can choose vane pumps. But if pressure is very high (more than 500 Bar) then we have to go for piston pumps.

- **(b) Flow of pressurised oil:** It is the volumetric output of pump measured in litres per min (LPM). The flow of oil is deciding the speed of actuator. Hence, this criteria is also of importance.

- **(c) Speed of pump:** If we increase the speed of pump beyond its rated speed, we have to face the problems like cavitation or separation (as we have studied in reciprocating pump). These problems hamper the efficiency and overall working of hydraulic system. Hence, proper speed pumps need to be selected.

(d) Efficiency of pump: We should select the pump in such a manner that it should not work with low efficiency. Generally, three efficiencies are observed:

(i) Volumetric efficiency (η_v) = $\dfrac{\text{Actual discharge volume}}{\text{Theoretical discharge volume}}$

(ii) Mechanical efficiency (η_m) = $\dfrac{\text{Power output}}{\text{Power input}}$

(iii) Overall efficiency (η_o) = $\eta_v \times \eta_m$

(e) Oil compatibility: The meaning of the word compatibility is 'acceptance'. If we use diesel in Petrol engine as a fuel then the engine will not start. That means Petrol Engine is compatible only to Petrol not to Diesel. On similar lines, each pump is compatible to specific hydraulic oil. If we use different oil then the pump will not give its rated and good performance. So oil compatibility is a most important criteria.

(f) Price of pump: In modern age, many varieties of pumps are available. Circuit designer must consider its cost. If we select high cost pump then the total cost of circuit increases and in working tenure of pump, the cost of pump spares is also high. So this economical aspect must be carefully looked into.

Important Points

- **Hydraulic devices are** the devices in which power is transmitted with the help of fluid which may be water or oil or gas under pressure.
- **Hydraulic press** uses hydraulic energy created by pressurizing the fluid called 'hydraulic oil'.
- **Hydraulic Ram:** It is non-power operated pump used to lift the water.

Practice Questions

1. Draw neat sketch of hydraulic jack and label the diagram.
2. How hydraulic press works? Explain it with neat sketch.
3. Write any four applications of hydraulic press.
4. Write any four applications of hydraulic lift.
5. What is Hydraulic Ram? Explain with neat sketch.
6. On which principle centrifugal pump works?
7. Draw neat sketch of centrifugal pump and piping system to lift the water. Explain its working.

8. Why casing with Guide blades is used for centrifugal pump? Explain with neat sketch of casing.
9. Write three types of impellers used in centrifugal pump.
10. Write four types of prime movers which are used to rotate the impeller of centrifugal pump?
11. What is multi-staging of pump i.e. pumps in parallel? Explain with sketch.

Chapter 5

BASIC COMPONENTS OF HYDRAULIC AND PNEUMATIC SYSTEMS

Weightage of Marks = 18, Teaching Hours = 08

Learning Objectives

- Make them familiar with various Hydraulic and Pneumatic Symbols
- Understand Working of Actuators and Valves

Contents

Hydraulic and Pneumatic Actuators

- Hydraulic Actuators - Hydraulic Cylinders (Single, Double Acting and Telescopic) – Construction and Working, Hydraulic Motors (Gear and Piston Type) – Construction and Working.
- Pneumatic Actuators - Pneumatic Cylinders (Single and Double Acting) - Construction and Working, Air motors (Gear and Piston Type) - Construction and Working.

Valves for Hydraulic and Pneumatic Systems

- Classifications of Valves, Poppet, Ball, Needle, Throttle, Pressure Control Directional Control, Sequencing, Synchronizing, Rotary Spool, Sliding Spool, Two Position, Multi position, Non-return Valves, Proportionating Valve.
- Construction and Operation of above Valves.

5.1 HYDRAULIC AND PNEUMATIC SYMBOLS

SYMBOLS USED IN HYDRAULIC CIRCUITS

(The order in which they appear in the topic)

Oil Reservoir/Oil Tank	
Filter	

contd. ...

Component	Symbol
Heat Exchanger – Cooler	
Heat Exchanger – Heater	
Unidirectional Fixed Displacement Hydraulic Pump	
Bi-directional Fixed Displacement Hydraulic Pump	
Unidirectional Variable Displacement Hydraulic Pump	
Bi-directional Variable Displacement Hydraulic Pump	
2 × 2 Direction Control Valve (2 × 2 DC Valve)	
3 × 2 DC Valve	
4 × 2 DC Valve	
4 × 3 DC Valve (Centre Closed Position)	
4 × 3 DC Valve (Open Centre Position)	
4 × 3 DC Valve (Tandem Centre Position)	
Flow Control Valve (Non-compensated)	

contd. ...

Variable Flow Control Valve (Non-compensated)	
Pressure Compensated Flow Control Valve	
Simple Check Valve	
Pilot Operated Check Valve	
Directly Operated Pressure Relief Valve	
Pilot Operated Pressure Relief Valve	
Pressure Reducing Valve	
Unloading Valve	
Sequence Valve	
Single Acting Cylinder (SA Cylinder)	
Double Acting Cylinder (DA Cylinder)	

contd. ...

Hydraulic Ram Type SA Cylinder	
Double Acting Cylinder with Double Piston Rod	
Tandem Cylinder	
Telescopic Cylinder	
Uni-Directional Air Motor	
Bi-Directional Air Motor	
Limited Rotary Motion Motor	
Dead Weight Accumulator	
Spring Loaded Accumulator	

contd. ...

Gas Pressurized Accumulator	
Working Pipe Line	
Drain Line / Pilot Line	
Flexible Line (Hose)	
Line Junction	
Pressure Gauge	
Push Button Control	
Pedal Control	
Roller Operated Control	
Plunger Control	
Spring Control	
Hydraulic Oil Signal Control (Pilot)	
Solenoid Control	

SYMBOLS USED IN PNEUMATICS

Compressor (Irrespective of the type of compressor the symbol is same)	

contd. ...

Air receiver or Air Tank	
Water Trap – Manual Drain	
Water Trap – Automatic Drain	
Filter (F)	
Regulator (R)	
Lubricator (L)	
Combined F-R-L Unit	
2 × 2 Direction Control Valve (2 × 2 DC Valve)	
3 × 2 DC Valve	
4 × 2 DC Valve	
5 × 2 DC Valve	
5 × 2 DC Valve (Pilot operated)	
Non-Return Valve	

contd. ...

Component	Symbol
Fixed Type Flow Control Valve	
Variable Flow Control Valve	
Variable Flow Control Valve with Built-in-Check Valve	
Pilot Operated Check Valve	
Shuttle Valve (Double Check Valve)	
Pressure Relief Valve	
Pressure Regulator (Non-Relieving)	
Pressure Regulator (Relieving)	
Single Acting Cylinder	
Diaphragm Cylinder	
Rolling Diaphragm Cylinder	
Double Acting Cylinder	

contd. ...

Turn Cylinder	
Tandem Cylinder	
Bi-Directional Air Motor	
Uni-Directional Air Motor	
Oscillating Air Motor	
Shut-Off Valve	
Muffler (Silencer)	
Working Pipe Line	
Drain Line	
Flexible Line (Hose)	
Line Junction	
Pressure Gauge	
Push Button Control (used with DC Valves)	

contd. ...

Pedal Control	
Roller Operated Control	
Plunger Control	
Spring Control	
Air Signal Control	
Solenoid Control	

5.2 AIR MOTORS

These are rotary actuators and are used to generate 'ROTARY MOTION' by using force of compressed air. We can achieve the speed of 10,000 rpm with the help of Air Motors.

Air motors are classified according to its construction and mechanism. These types are:
   (a) Vane motors
   (b) Gerotor motor
   (c) Turbine motors
   (d) Piston type motors

5.2.1 Vane Motor

The construction of vane motor is similar to vane compressor.

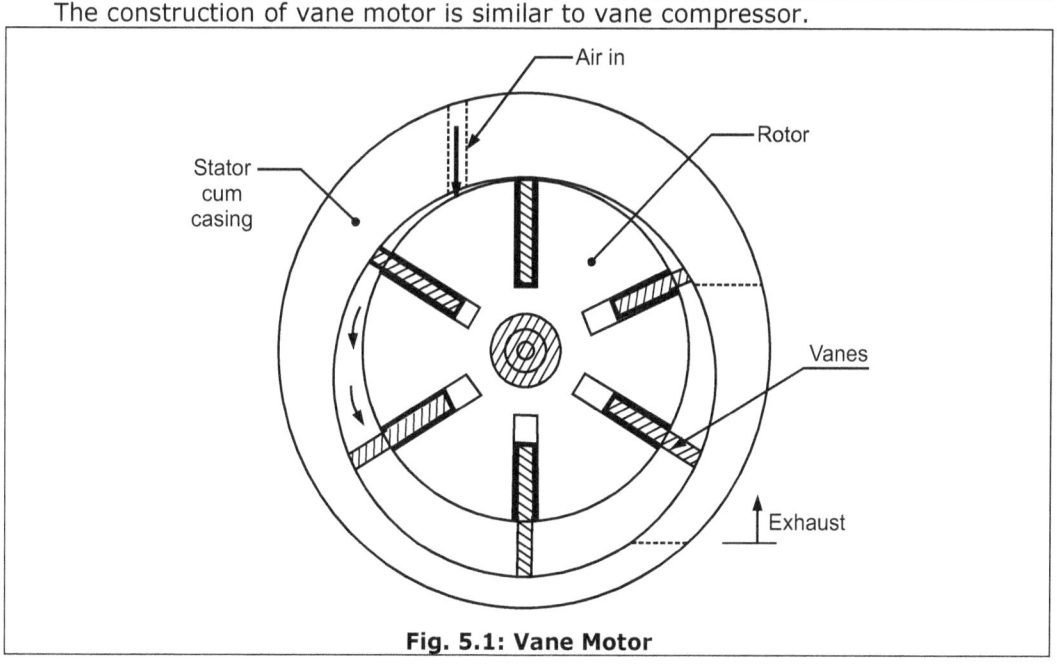

Fig. 5.1: Vane Motor

Construction: It consists of simple Vane Rotor which is having slots in which vanes (flat piece of steel) slide freely. The rotor is eccentrically located inside the stator housing.

Working: When pressurised air comes in through inlet port, the pressure of air distributes equally in all directions. Since vane is sliding freely in slots of rotator, the vane comes into way of pressurised air and air pushes the vanes so that rotor starts rotating with speed. The used low pressure air is exhausted through exhaust port. This is unidirectional motor. Since vanes are freely sliding in slots, there is possibility of leakage of air. With the help of these motors, we can achieve the speeds upto 25000 r.p.m.

5.2.2 Gerotor Motor

In this type, two specially shaped gerotor blades meshing to each other are used. When pressurised air comes in, the force of air rotates one blade. Since it is meshing with other, the other blade also rotates.

These air motors are mostly used for low r.p.m. such as 200-300 r.p.m. Hence they are not suitable for high torque applications.

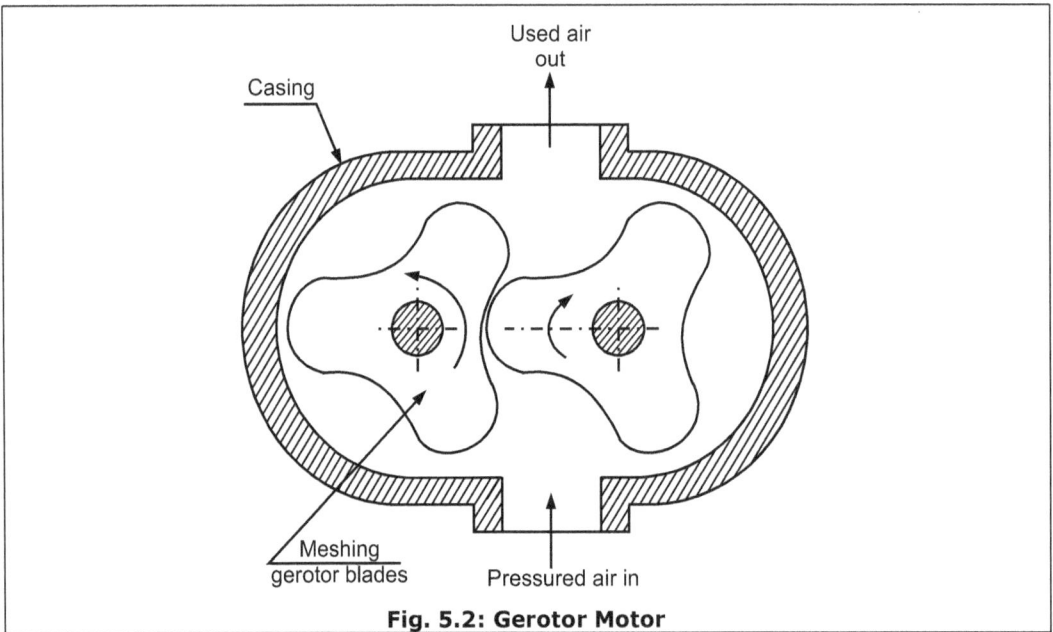

Fig. 5.2: Gerotor Motor

5.2.3 Turbine Motors

In this type of Air motor, light weight impeller having curved vanes is used. This pressurised air is passed through nozzle. The impact of jet will rotate the impeller. These motors are high speed low torque motors; and being simple in construction are used in many applications.

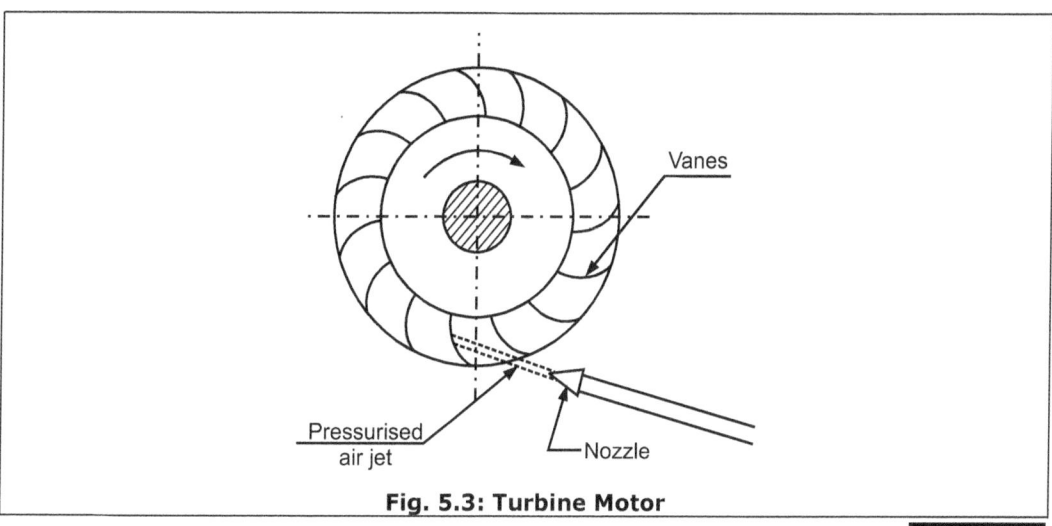

Fig. 5.3: Turbine Motor

5.2.4 Piston Motors [W-14, S-15]

There are two types of Piston motors:

(i) Axial Piston Motors

(ii) Radial Piston Motors

Piston type motors may have 4, 5 or 6 cylinders. The power developed by these motors is dependent on the inlet air pressure, number of pistons, the cross-sectional area of piston, the stroke of piston and linear speed of piston.

Axial piston motors are generally manufactured upto 3.5 HP power, while radial piston motors are upto 25 HP.

Radial piston motors can achieve speed upto 3000 rpm.

Working: The piston reciprocates in sequence and they actuate wobble plate. This in turn imparts a rotary motion to output shaft through gear train.

5.2.5 Applications of Air Motors

(i) In all pneumatic power tools like screw drivers, angle grinders, straight grinders.

(ii) To rotate conveyor belts in food industry.

(iii) Power device in printing press machine.

(iv) Agitators and mixers.

(v) Vibrators.

5.2.6 Comparison between Air Motor and Electric Motor

Air Motor	Electric Motor
(a) Air motor rotates with the help of compressed air.	(a) Electric motor rotates with electric current which in turn creates electromagnetic effect.
(b) This is shock proof motor.	(b) Some shock is possible during starting.
(c) This motor is explosion proof.	(c) Motor can be exploded or burn due to short circuit.
(d) If continuously run then temperature of motor does not increase.	(d) If continuously run then temperature of electric motor increases.
(e) Speed of air motor can be varied without using complicated mechanisms.	(e) Speed variation requires complicated circuits which increases cost of motor.
(f) The power to weight ratio of this motor is high.	(f) The power to weight ratio is low.
(g) Motors are simple in design and hence not costly.	(g) Motors are complex in design and construction and hence fetches more cost.
(h) Since the weight of motor is low, this motor can accelerate and retard quickly.	(h) Electric motor takes more time to accelerate or retard.
(i) Air motors are less efficient.	(i) Efficiency of electric motor is high.
(j) Makes more noise while working.	(j) Makes low noise.
(k) High power air motors are not available.	(k) High power electric motors (500 HP/800 HP) are available.

5.2.7 Symbol of Air Motor

	This is the symbol similar to Hydraulic pump/motor. The symbol shown in 'Air motor – Bi – Directional' (can rotate in clockwise or anticlockwise direction). Carefully see the position of triangle. The triangle is hollow.
	This is the symbol of uni-directional air motor (It can rotate in clockwise or anticlockwise direction only.)
Fig. 5.4	This is the symbol of half rotation or oscillating motor.

5.3 HYDRAULIC MOTORS (ROTARY ACTUATORS)

- Hydraulic motors provide rotational motion.
- Hydraulic motor converts Hydraulic energy (processed by pressurised oil) into Rotary Mechanical energy used in many industrial applications.
- There is not much difference in Hydraulic motor and Hydraulic pump.
    - In hydraulic pump the rotation of the fluid is done by rotary element connected to electric motor.
    - In hydraulic motor the rotating element (vanes, gear, pistons) are pushed by the pressurised oil, which results into continuous rotary motion of shaft.
- Hydraulic motors are classified on the basis of construction:
  (a) Gear motor (similar to gear pump)
  (b) Vane motor (similar to vane pump)
  (c) Swash plate piston motor (similar to swash plate pump)
  (d) Bent axis piston motor (similar to bend axis piston pump)
  (e) Radial piston motor (similar to radial piston pump)

5.3.1 Gear Motor [W-14]

Construction: Similar to gear pump, the motor is having two meshing gears, housing and two cover plates. The gears are mounted on two shafts and rotary motion is obtained from one shaft.

Working: Pressurised oil enters from bottom port and entire chamber is pressurised. The force of oil exerts pressure on teeth of two gears which causes imbalance of forces on the two gears which in turn results in rotation of gears. The low pressure oil (used oil) goes out of upper port.

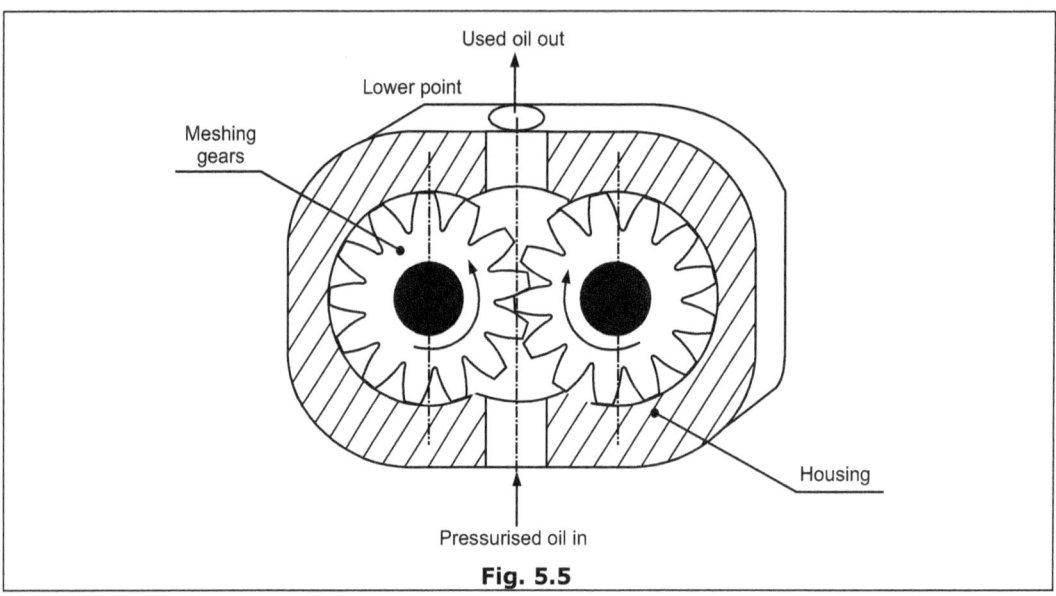

Fig. 5.5

5.3.2 Unbalanced Vane Type Motor

Construction: The construction is similar to unbalanced vane type pump. The rotor is eccentric to housing. Its main parts are:

(a) Slotted motor installed on shaft
(b) Housing
(c) Fixed cam ring to constrain outward movement of vanes
(d) Sliding vanes

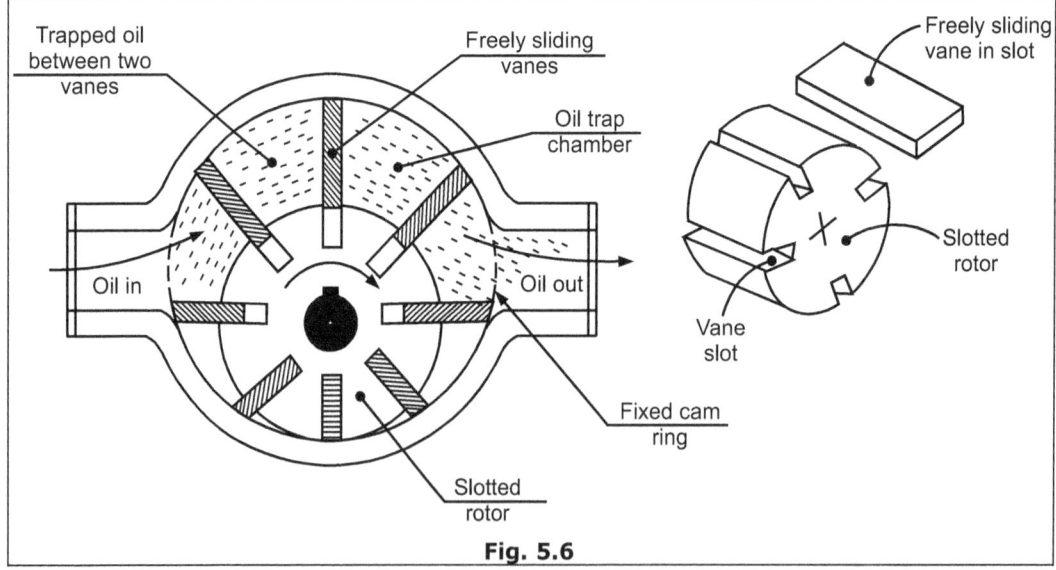

Fig. 5.6

Working: Pressurised hydraulic oil enters from left port and causes the force on vanes which imbalances the rotor which then results in rotation. Due to rotation the vanes flow and through slots because of centrifugal force. In vane motor the imbalance is caused by difference in area exposed to hydraulic energy, which is due to eccentricity between rotor and housing. Imbalance results in torque on shaft.

5.3.3 Axial Piston Motors

Similar to Axial Piston pumps there are two types:

(a) Swash Plate Axial Piston Motor

(b) Bent Axis Piston Motor

The general Axial Piston Motor is shown below. Similar to Axial Piston Pump, the axis of all pistons are parallel to each other and are arranged on circumferencial periphery of the cylinder blocks.

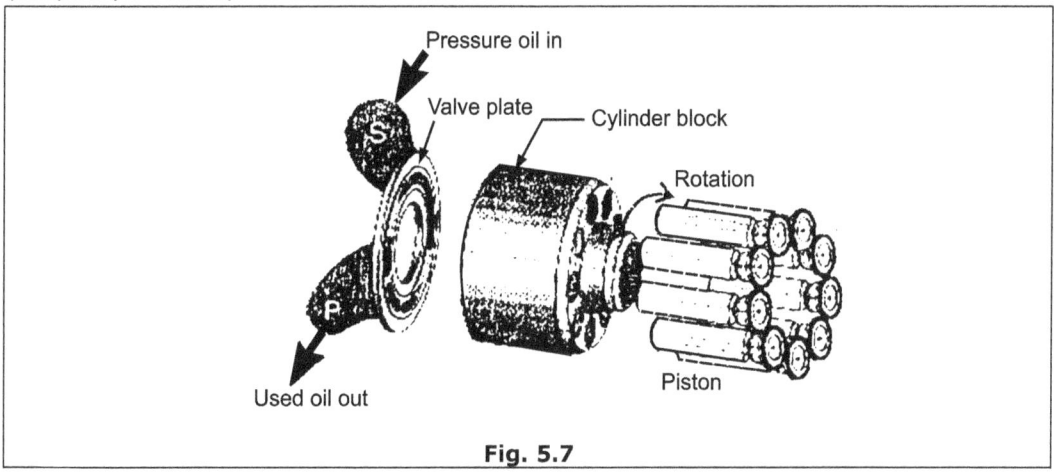

Fig. 5.7

5.3.4 Swash Plate Axial Piston Motor

Construction: The motor consists of following components:

(a) Cylindrical barrel having circumferentially arranged pistons.

(b) Pistons (minimum 3 Nos.)

(c) Swash plate with shoe plate for piston rod connection.

Working: The swash plate is making an angle θ with main Shaft Axis as shown. When pressurised oil comes in, it acts on piston in front of inlet port pushing the piston out of piston bores. This movement causes the piston shoe to slide across the swash plate surface. As the piston shoe slides on swash plate, it is able to develop the torque at the shaft attached to the barrel. The torque is proportional to ∠θ and pressure of hydraulic oil.

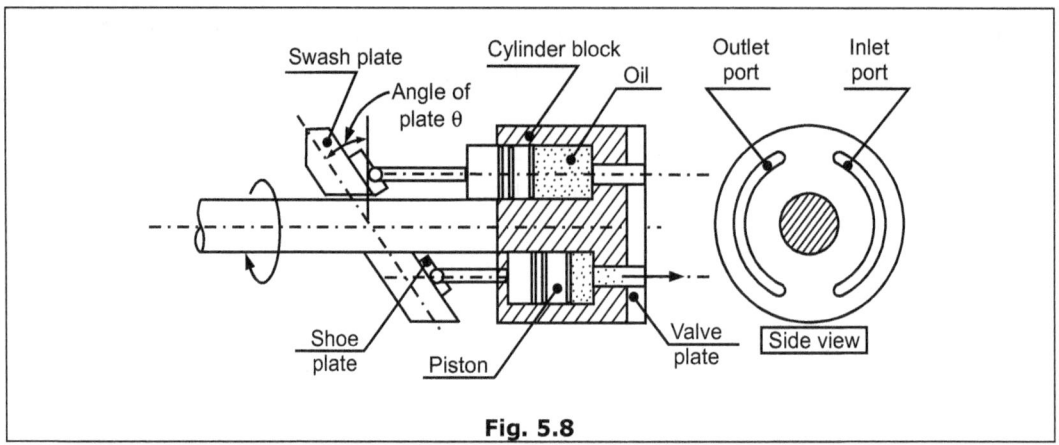

Fig. 5.8

Note: For uniform motion, number of pistons must be above 7 Nos.

5.3.5 Bent Axis type Axial Piston Motor

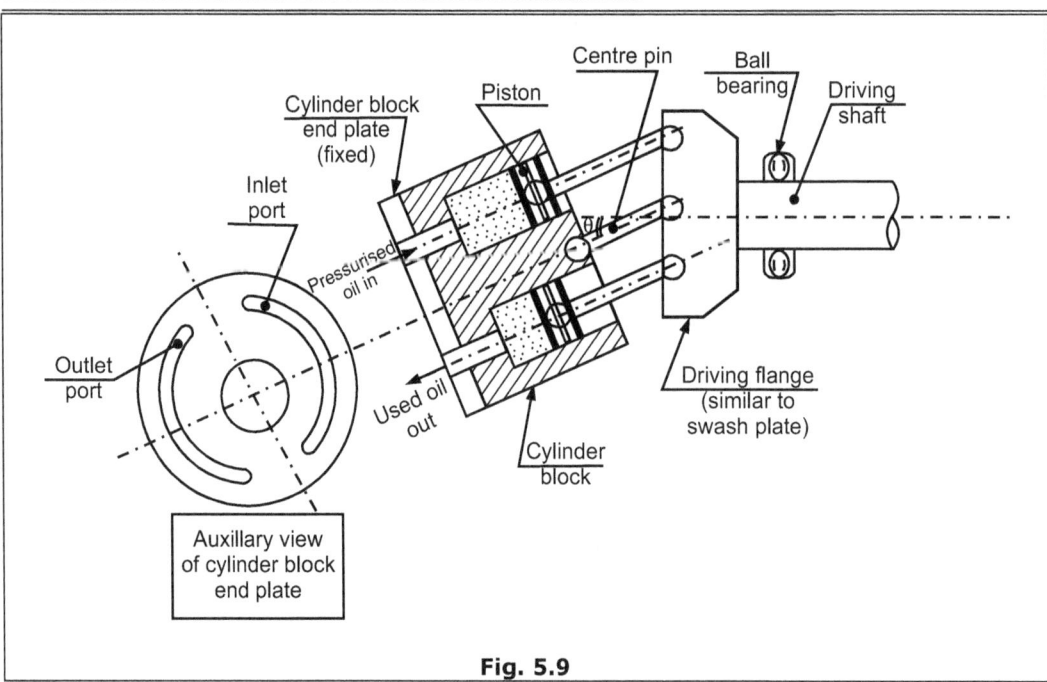

Fig. 5.9

Construction: Similar to Bent Axis Pump, this motor consists of following components.

(a) Cylinder block having circumferentially arranged cylinder bores.

(b) Pistons

(c) Driving flange similar to swash plate

(d) Cylinder block end plate (fixed)

Working: When pressurised oil comes through inlet port it acts on pistons in front of it. The oil pushes the pistons out of piston bores. This movement causes the piston rod to slide on driving flange. As this piston rod slides, it is able to develop torque at the shaft attached to driving flange. The torque is proportional to $\angle \theta$ and pressure of Hydraulic oil. If number of pistons are more the shaft will get more uniform motion.

5.3.6 Radial Piston Motor

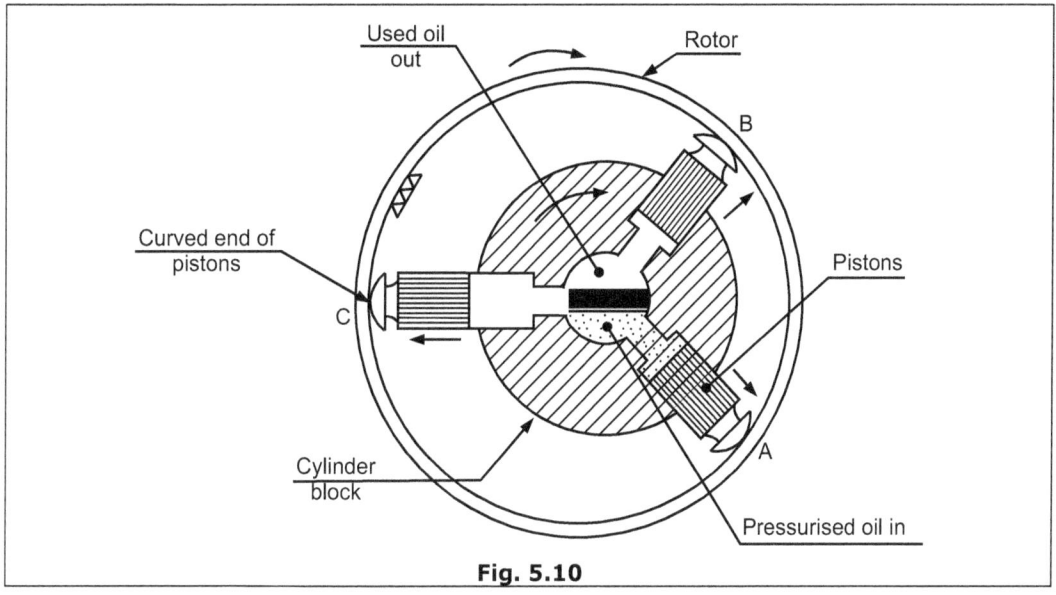

Fig. 5.10

Construction: Three pistons are fitted in cylinder block. The curve ends of pistons can rest on smooth (3 triangle finish) surface of rotor. Cylinder block and Rotor are rotating members of motor.

Working: 'If fluid is introduced in the cylinder under pressure, the piston will pushed outward'. This principle is used in this motor.

Suppose the fluid under pressure is admitted to cylinder No. (A). The piston will move outward in its cylinder. We know that fluid i.e. Hydraulic oil is incompressible; and two bodies (oil and piston) cannot occupy the same space in cylinder. Naturally curved end of piston will slide inside the rotor with force and rotor will turn in clockwise direction. Then cylinder B will occupy the position of A since cylinder block also starts rotating. And same cycle will start which results in rotational motion of rotor.

This is low speed high torque motor.

5.3.7 Limited Rotary Actuators

Hydraulic motors are 'Full' rotary actuators. The shaft of Hydraulic motor turns completely through 360°. But for some hydraulic circuits we need limited rotary motion (say 180°, 270° etc. but less than 360°). In such cases, we have to use Limited Rotary Actuators, which are described below.

5.3.8 Dual Piston Type Limited Rotary Actuator OR Limited Rotary Actuator using Rack and Pinion and SA Cylinder Pair

This actuator uses SA cylinders (2 Nos), Rack and Pinion mechanism and DC valve.

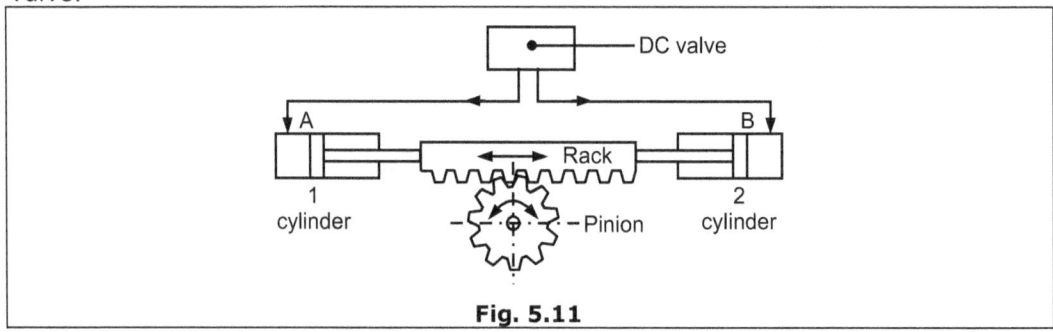

Fig. 5.11

Working: When pressurised oil is supplied through port A of cylinder 1, then its piston will move from left to right. During this movement, since rack is attached to the piston rod, it will move towards right. The pinion is meshed with rack and hence pinion will rotate to limited angle in clockwise direction.

When pressurised oil will be supplied through port B of cylinder 2 then piston will move from right to left and so the rack. The pinion will rotate in anticlockwise direction through limited rotation.

5.3.9 Single Vane Type Limited Rotary Actuator

This Limited Rotary Actuator consists of a stationary body, having rotor shaft at centre. This shaft hold one vane. There are two inlet ports.

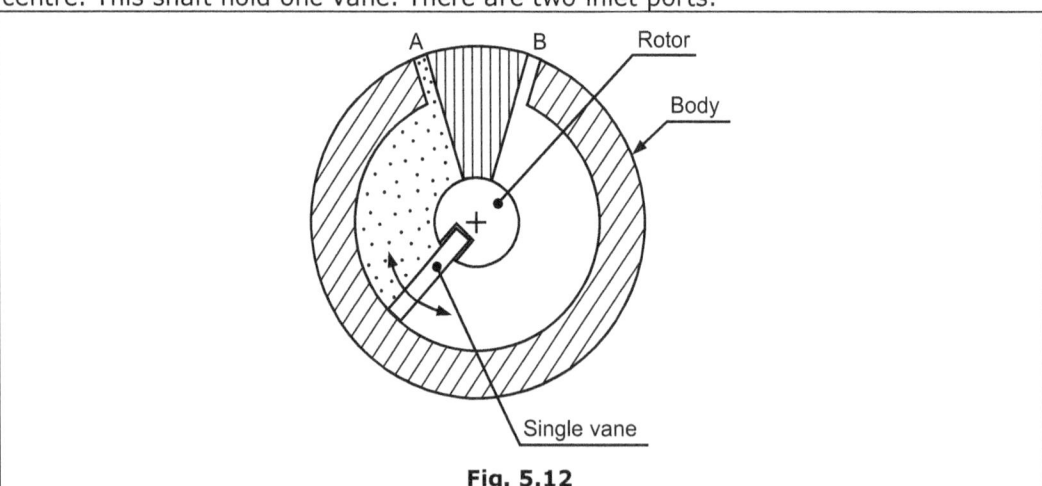

Fig. 5.12

Working: When oil comes in through port A, the force of oil pushes the vane in anticlockwise direction to obtain limited rotary motion. When oil enters through port B, we can obtain limited rotary motion of shaft in clockwise direction.

5.3.10 Criterias for Selection of Motors in Hydraulic Circuit (or Basis of Hydraulic Motor Selection)

(a) Amount of torque needed decides the type of motor. The starting torque is higher than running torque.

(b) Speed is another important criteria for selection. When we require low speed high torque motor, we have to use Radial Piston Motor. For high speed requirement use Vane Motors.

(c) System pressure is another important criteria. We have to select suitable pressure to create required torque.

(d) Application of motor is also an important criteria.

(e) Power generated by a motor is another criteria. For moderate power ranges, Axial piston motors are preferred. Vane motors or gear motors are low power motors.

(f) Cost of motor should be moderate.

5.3.11 Symbol of Hydraulic Motor

Symbol of Hydraulic motor (irrespective of type of motor) is nearly similar to symbol of hydraulic pump. The only difference is that the triangles shown are in opposite direction.

(a) Symbol of Uni-directional Hydraulic Motor:

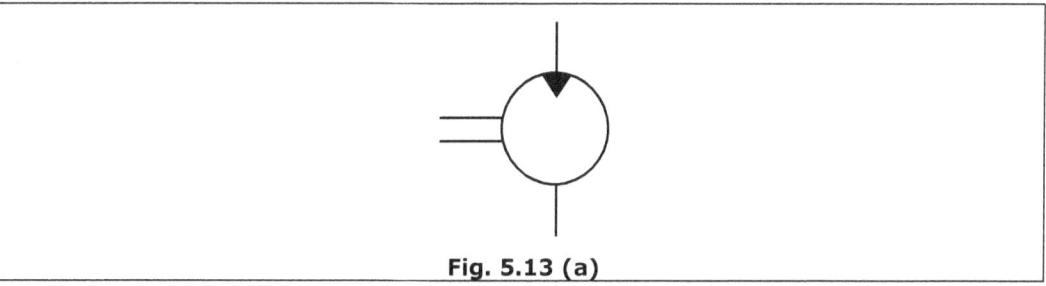

Fig. 5.13 (a)

(b) Symbol of Bi-directional Hydraulic Motor:

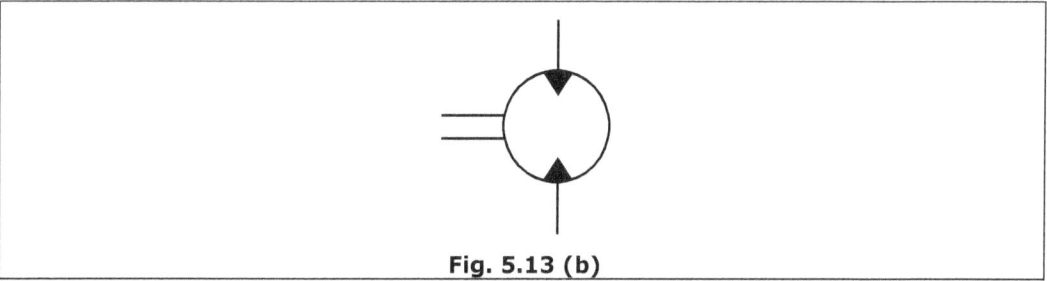

Fig. 5.13 (b)

(c) Symbol of Limited Rotation Hydraulic Motor:

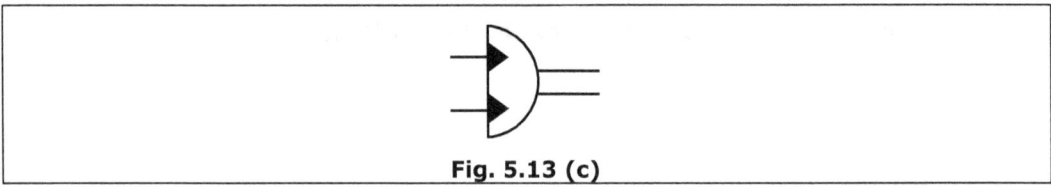

Fig. 5.13 (c)

5.4 FLUID CONTROLLING ELEMENTS SUCH AS DIRECTION CONTROL VALVES (DC VALVES), PRESSURE REGULATING VALVES, FLOW CONTROL VALVES [S-15]

- Pump pressurizes the hydraulic oil. This oil flows to hydraulic actuator. Actuator works and produces useful mechanical work. This is the general outline of hydraulic system.

- But, one must remember that when pressurised hydraulic oil with full of hydraulic energy travels towards actuator, it must be controlled to suit the requirements of Actuator (also known as consumer). So let us see 'what' to and 'how' to control this 'energetic' hydraulic oil.

(a) Direction control: The linear actuator creates to and fro i.e. Reciprocating motion. This is depicted in Fig. 5.14 (a).

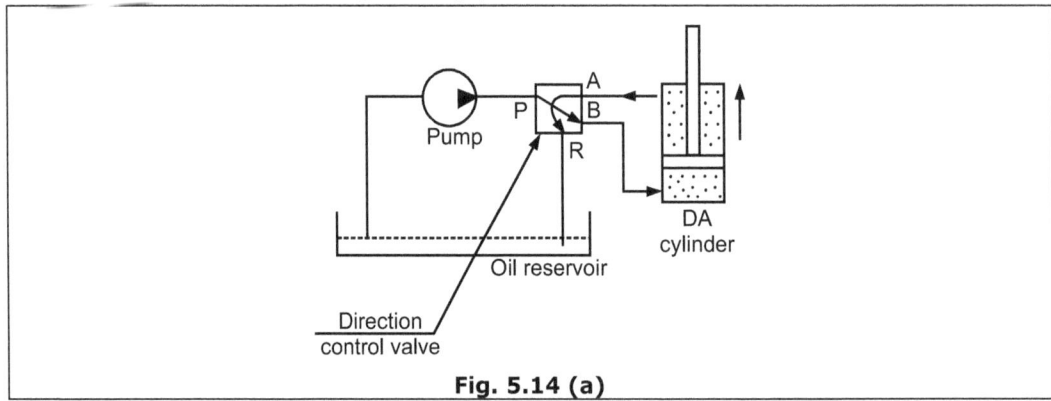

Fig. 5.14 (a)

Hydraulic oil from pump will flow from Port 'P' to Port 'B'. Piston of DA cylinder will move upwards. During this stroke oil on the other side of piston (Piston rod side) will return through port 'A' via port 'R' to Oil Reservoir.

In the next stroke port 'P' will be connected to port 'A' and oil will move the piston downwards. During this stroke oil present on the side of piston will return to oil reservoir through port 'B' via port 'R'.

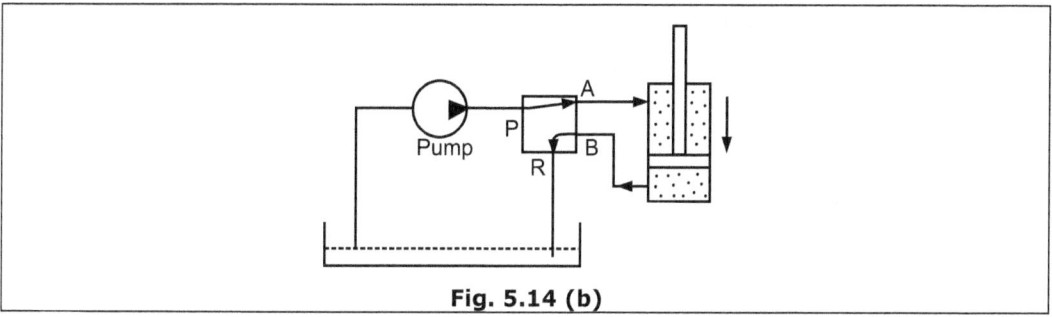

Fig. 5.14 (b)

From above it is clear that oil must be 'Directed' first through port B and then through port 'A'. At the same time port R must be connected to remaining port. All this is done by 'Direction Control Valve' or simply called as 'DC Valve'.

(b) Flow Control: Fig. 5.15 shows double acting cylinder. When oil will enter through port A, piston will move from left to right with certain linear speed-say 6 mt/min. Suppose, we have to increase this speed from 6 m/min. to 7 m/min. How we can achieve this? The answer to this question is by admitting more quantity of fluid through port A, so that piston will move faster. To admit additional hydraulic oil we have to use valve V_1 which is known as 'Flow Control Valve'. This valve will control flow (lit./sec.) or quantity of oil.

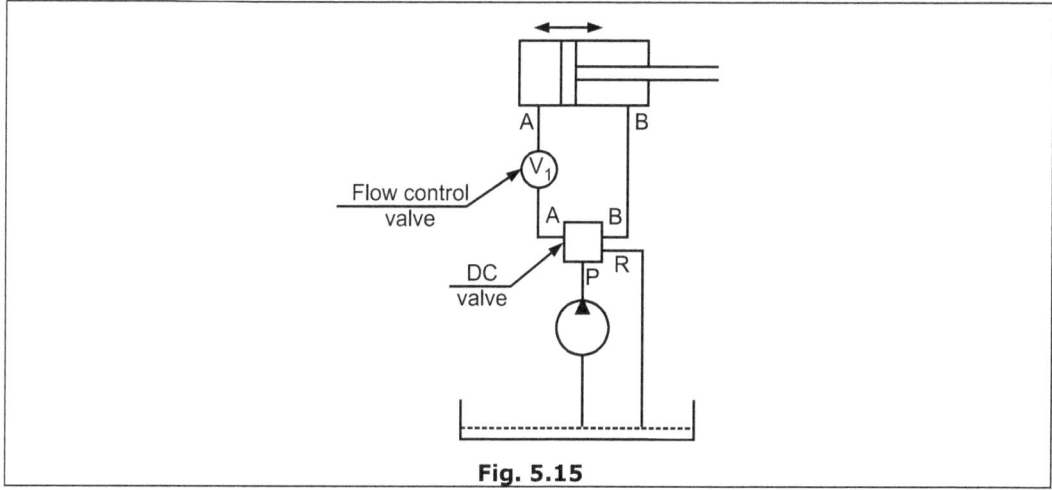

Fig. 5.15

(c) Pressure control: The pump creates higher pressure. Suppose a piston pump in a hydraulic circuit creates 30 bar pressure. The actuator in the circuit can operate at 20 bar pressure. Then we must reduce the oil pressure from 30 bar to 20 bar for that particular actuator. The second actuator in the same circuit operates on 10 bar pressure. Then we have to reduce the pressure of oil from 30 bar to 10 bar for that 2nd Actuator. This clearly means we have to control the pressure of oil after pump to a suitable level for actuator. This is done by **Pressure Regulating Valve.** Some pressure control valves are safety valves which do not allow the system pressure to increase beyond specific set level. These valves are called as Pressure Relief Valves.

Now we will see following valves in detail:
(i) Direction control valves
(ii) Flow control valves
(iii) Check valves
(iv) Pressure control valves
(v) Unloading valve
(vi) Sequencing valve

5.4.1 Direction Control Valves

- The name of this valve itself clarifies its function.
- This valve is like a 'Traffic Police'. It directs the flow of pressurised as well as used oil to actuator and oil reservoir respectively.

Classification of Direction Control Valves (DC Valves)

(A) Classification based on Construction:
(i) Seat or Poppet type
(ii) Spool type:
- Sliding spool
- Rotary spool

(i) Seat or Poppet Type DC Valve: In this valve, a poppet or ball or similar item like plate or cone is made to seat over a specially constructed finely machined and polished seat.

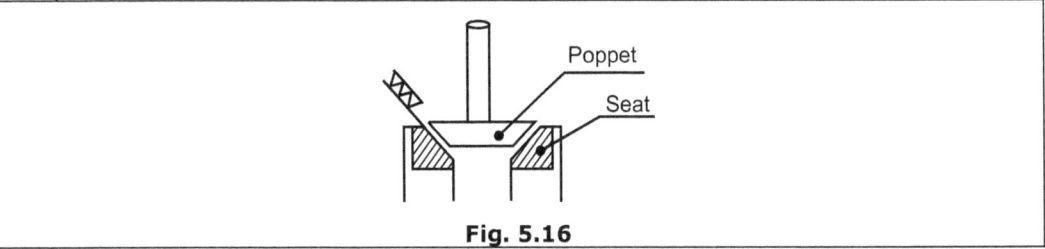

Fig. 5.16

Advantages:
(a) Suited for very high pressure applications.
(b) Very minor leakage.

Disadvantages:
(a) Not suitable for large valve sizes.
(b) Due to complicated construction, valves are costly.

(ii) Sliding Spool Type DC Valve: In this valve there is small piston inside a valve casing which slides inside the casing thereby opening or closing the ports (drilled holes) in valve body.

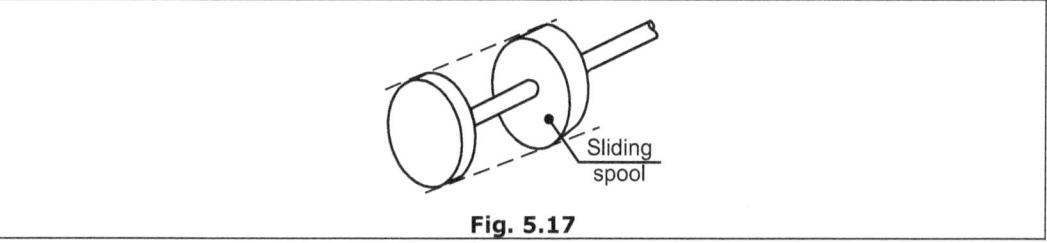

Fig. 5.17

Advantages:

(a) Simple in construction.

(b) Cost is low.

(c) These valves are permanently balanced.

Disadvantages:

(a) Leakage inside the valve is possible.

- Sliding spool type DC valve is most widely used valve.

(iii) Rotary Spool Type DC Valves: Rotary spool valves consist of a rotating spool which aligns with ports in the stationary valve casing, so that fluid is directed to required port. A/B/P/R are the ports in casing. Port 'P' is a pressure port through which pressurised oil is coming in the valve. 'R' port is the port through which used oil is returning to oil tank. In Fig. 5.18 it is clear that:

Port P is connected to Port B (P → B) and

Port A is connected to Port R (A → R).

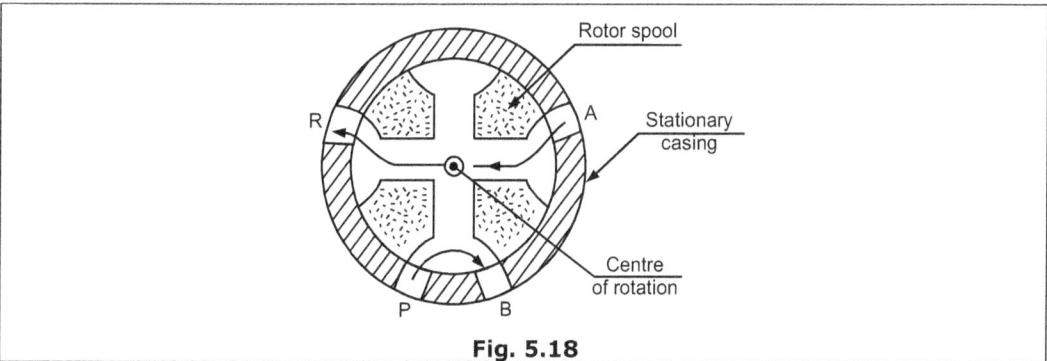

Fig. 5.18

Advantages:

(a) Are compact and simple in design.

(b) Are having low operating forces.

Disadvantages:

(a) Due to rotary motion of spool, leakage inside this valve is possible.

(b) These valves are not suitable for high pressures because sometime pressure of oil rotates the valve in unwanted directions.

- Rotary spool valves are generally manually operated.

TYPES OF DC VALVES BASED ON NUMBER OF PORTS (Generally Spool Type)

1. 2 × 2 DC valve
2. 3 × 2 DC valve
3. 4 × 2 DC valve
4. 4 × 3 DC valve

Now we will see the valves one by one in detail alongwith symbols.

5.4.2 2 × 2 DC valve (Read as Two by Two DC Valve)

Fig. 5.19 shows 2 × 2 spool type DC valve, push button operated.

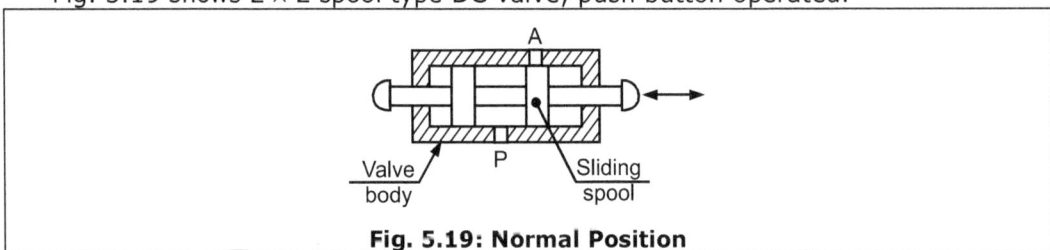

Fig. 5.19: Normal Position

Construction: It consists of sliding spool in a finely finished bore. The actuation is by push button.

Operation: Through port P, pressurised oil is coming in. This oil will go out (directed) through port 'A'. Fig. 5.19 shows port 'P' is not connected to port 'A'. Hence no flow from P to A.

Now left push button is pressed. The spool will shift towards right and port 'P' will be connected to port 'A' and oil will start flowing from port P to A. (Ref. Fig. 5.20).

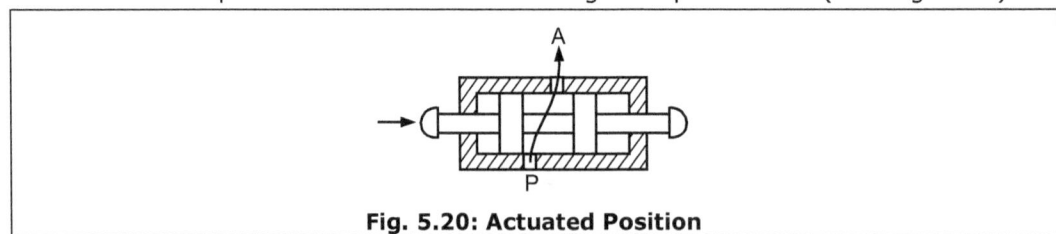

Fig. 5.20: Actuated Position

Important: This valve is normally closed.

- 2 × 2 DC valve can be best compared with our domestic **water tap**. The water tap in bathroom is always closed. This is its normal position i.e. it is normally closed. When we open it, water starts flowing.

- **Symbol of 2 × 2 DC valve:** The symbol concept is explained below.
- The valve position is shown by squares. (Remember while drawing these squares, it should be exact square you should not draw it as rectangle).
- The direction of flow of oil is shown by arrows in these squares.

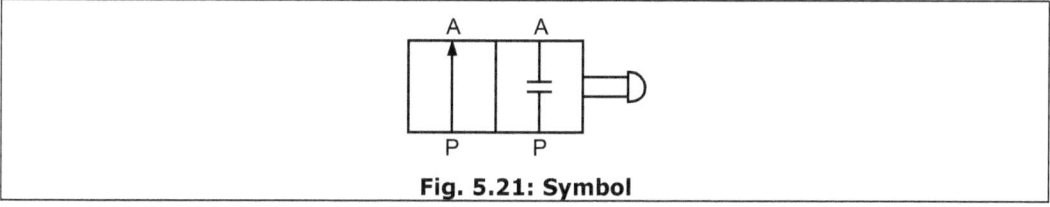

Fig. 5.21: Symbol

- Actuation arrangement i.e. push button in above case must be shown outside.
- **Remember:** At a time think of only one square i.e. one position.

5.4.3 3 × 2 DC Valve (Read as three by two DC Valve)

Similar to 2 × 2 DC valve, in this valve also, a spool reciprocates in a finely finished bore. The spring is attached to front spool. Fig. 5.22 shown is actuated position. Push button pressed in the port P is connected to port A and no flow through port R. When spool is pressed in, spring is compressed.

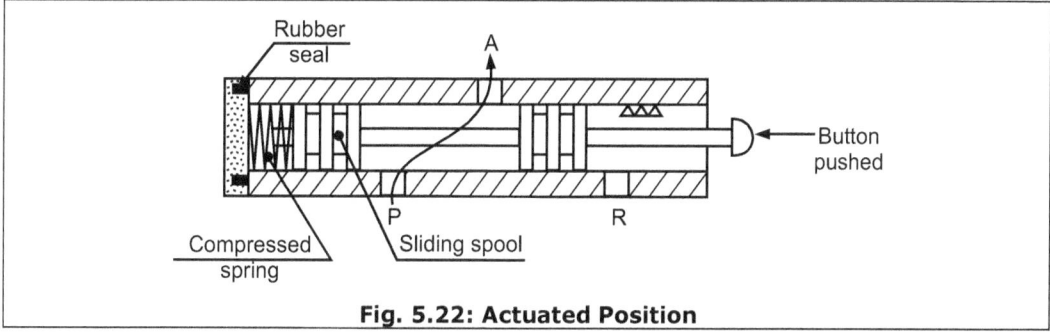

Fig. 5.22: Actuated Position

- **Now push button is released:** When push button is released, spring will expand and spool will move towards right. Now port A will be connected to port R and port P will be disconnected, so that flow of used oil will start from port A to R and then to oil reservoir. (Refer Fig. 5.23)

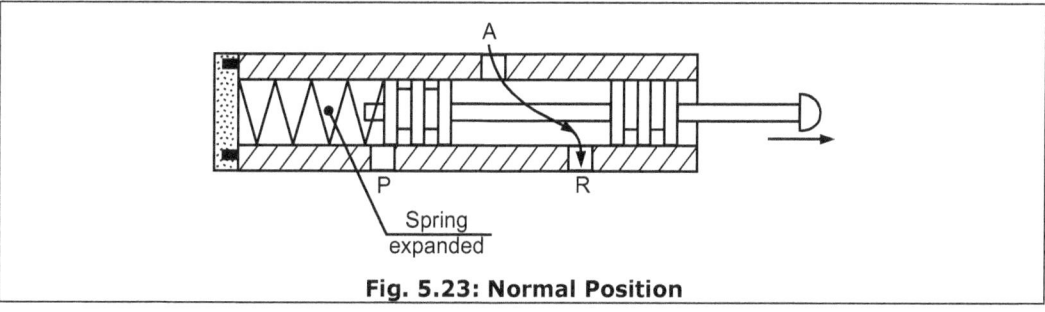

Fig. 5.23: Normal Position

Symbol of 3 × 2 DC valve: 3 × 2 means 3 ports and 2 positions. Two positions means 2 squares. Look at square (1) It shows actuated position. Port P connected to A and port R is disconnected. Similar square (2) shows normal position i.e. Port A → R, port P is disconnected.

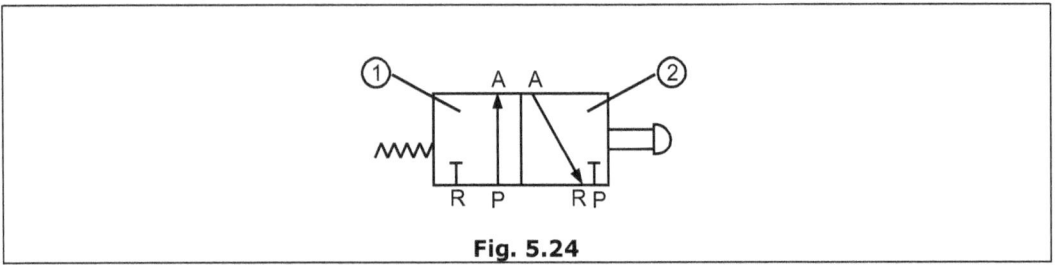

Fig. 5.24

5.4.4 4 × 2 DC Valve (Read as four by two DC Valve can also be read as '4 way 2 position' DC Valve) [S-15]

4 × 2 DC valve is shown in Fig. 5.25. It is in normal position. There are 4 ports, A and B are consumer ports (ports going to actuator). P is pressure port through which pressurized oil goes in. Port 'R' is used oil returns to oil reservoir. The valve is push button operated (manually). Valve regains its normal position by spring expansion. From figure it is clear that spring is fully expanded to its free length. Port P is connected to port A and port B is connected to port R. Now push button is pressed as shown in Fig. 5.26. This is actuated position. Now sliding spool will move towards left thereby compressing the spring. Now as we can see port P is connected to port B and port A is connected to return oil port R.

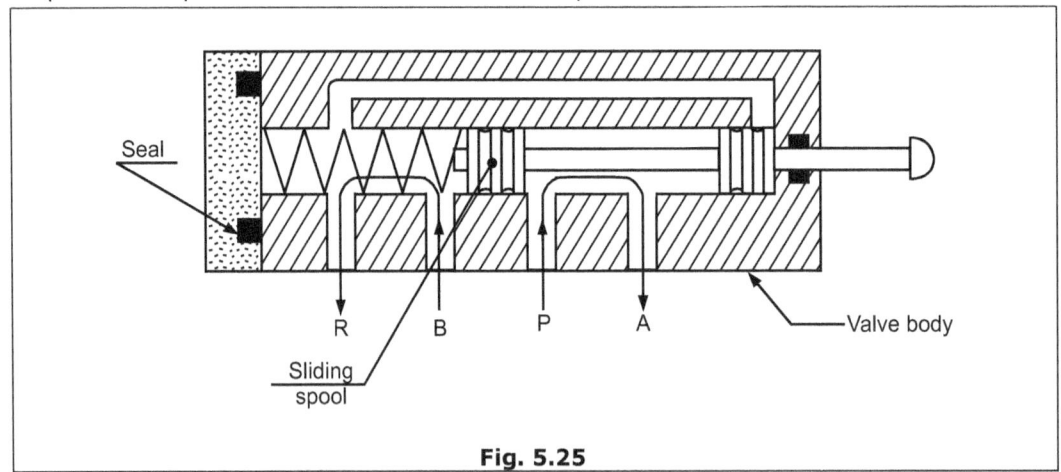

Fig. 5.25

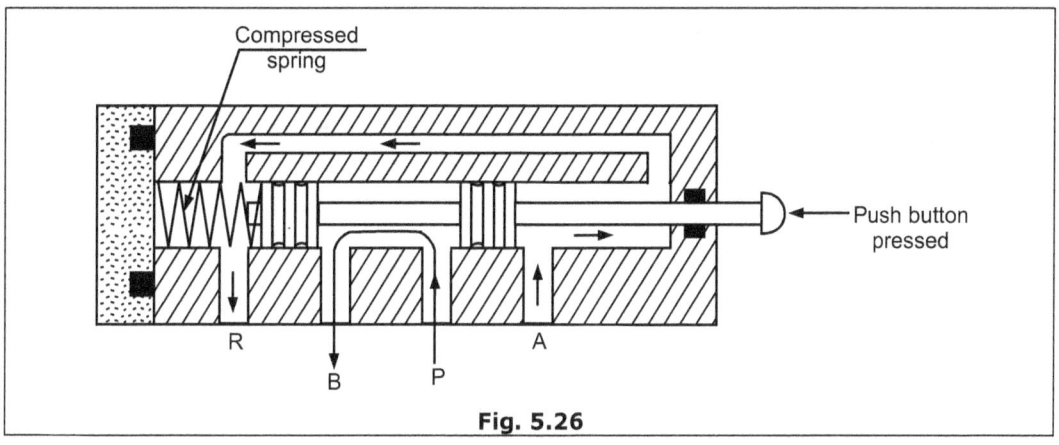

Fig. 5.26

Symbol: 4 × 2 means **4 ports** and **2 positions**.

Two positions means two squares. Look at square (1) which shows normal position P → A / B → R.

At square (2) we can see actuated position P → B / A → R.

Push button and spring are shown outside.

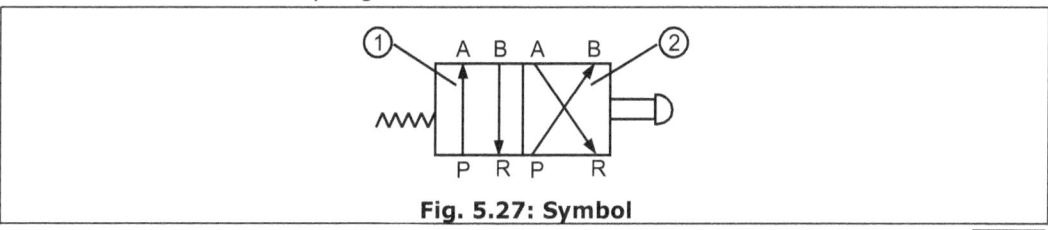

Fig. 5.27: Symbol

5.4.5 4 × 3 DC Valve   [W-14]

We have seen 4 × 2 valve. This is slight modified version of 4 × 2 DC valve. Similar to 4 × 2 valve there are 4 ports (A/B/P/R). But one position is added i.e. centre position. Figs. 5.28 and 5.29 are showing similar positions as we have seen in 4 × 2 DC valve.

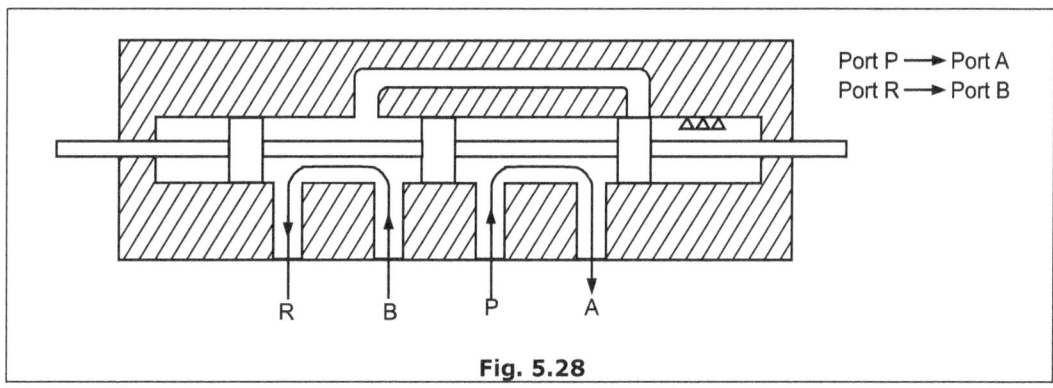

Fig. 5.28

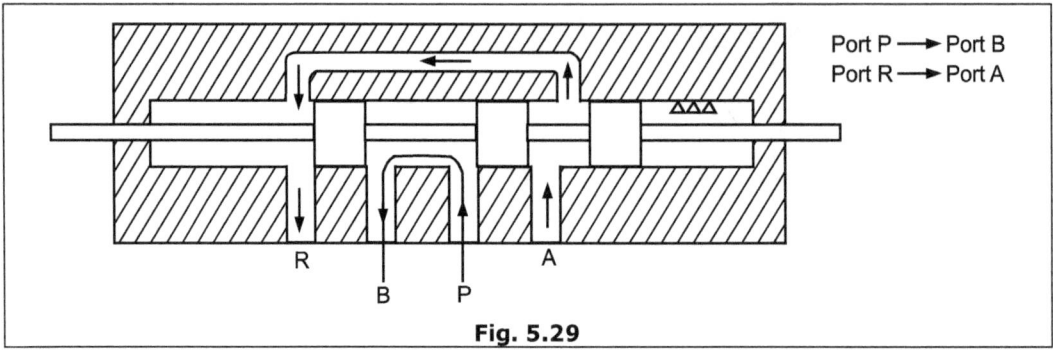

Port P ⟶ Port B
Port R ⟶ Port A

Fig. 5.29

As we can see that, the spool of this valve is having 3 positions. The spool is so selected because we have to obtain 3rd position also called as 'Closed Centre Position'. This position is shown in Fig. 5.30. We have shifted the spool in such a manner that all ports are closed to each other. No flow from port P to A or B and no flow from port A and B to R.

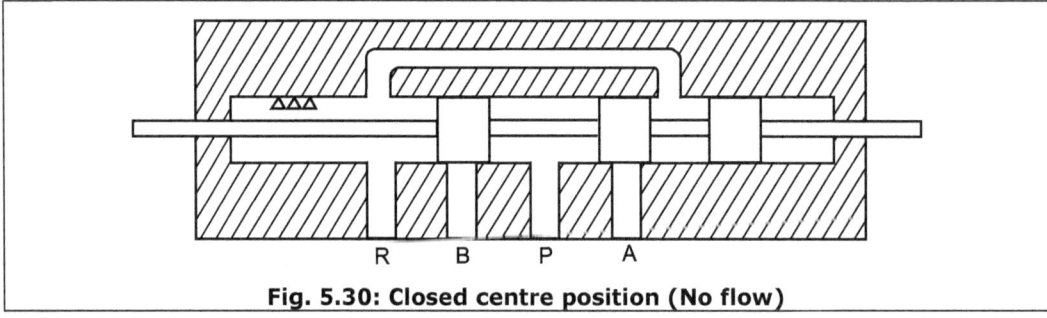

Fig. 5.30: Closed centre position (No flow)

When DC valve attains this position, pressurised oil returns to reservoir via pressure relief valve.

Applications of this valve:

Centre closed position DC valve is suitable for:

(a) Immediate closing of movements of actuator.

(b) 'Inching' operation in raising or lowering the heavy loads e.g. Dumper trolly lifting/lowering.

Symbol of 4 × 3 DC valve (Centre Closed Position)

4 × 3 means 4 ports and 3 positions. Three positions mean 3 squares.

Square (1):   Port P → Port A
              Port R → Port B

Square (2):   Port P → Port B
              Port R → Port A

Square (3):   Shows all ports closed to each other.

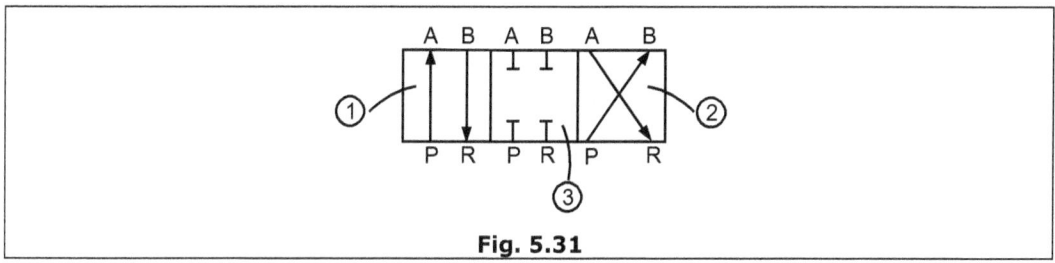

Fig. 5.31

Other versions of 4 × 3 DC valve: We can have different combinations of centre port (square (3)) for various applications.

(I) This version is 'open centre position' of 4 × 3 DC valve. In this arrangement, sliding spool is so designed that when it attains centre position 'all ports are open to each other'.

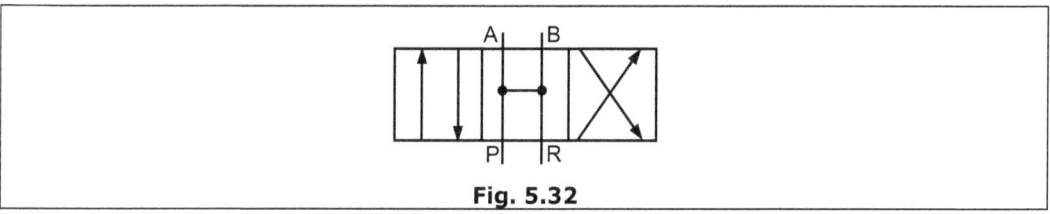

Fig. 5.32

(II) This version is 'Tandem Centre Position' of 4 × 3 DC valve. In this arrangement, as we can see, pressure port is connected to Return port and consumer ports A and B are blocked.

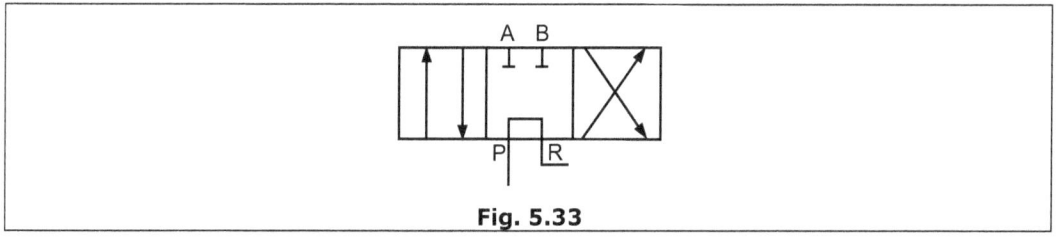

Fig. 5.33

5.4.6 Flow Control Valves

- Flow control valves (as we have seen) are used to regulate the flow of hydraulic oil in hydraulic circuit for controlling the 'SPEED' of actuators.
- For Linear Actuators, speed is measured in m/sec.
- For Rotary Actuators, speed is measured in RPM.
- **Importance of flow control:** Control of pressurised oil flow is extremely important because the rate of movement of machine element depends on rate of flow of pressurised hydraulic fluid.
- Flow control is achieved by 'throttling' or 'diverting'.
- **Throttling:** Throttling is passing the pressurised oil through small restriction like 'orifice' (Hole). Fig. 5.34 (a) shows that oil flow is restricted through orifice.

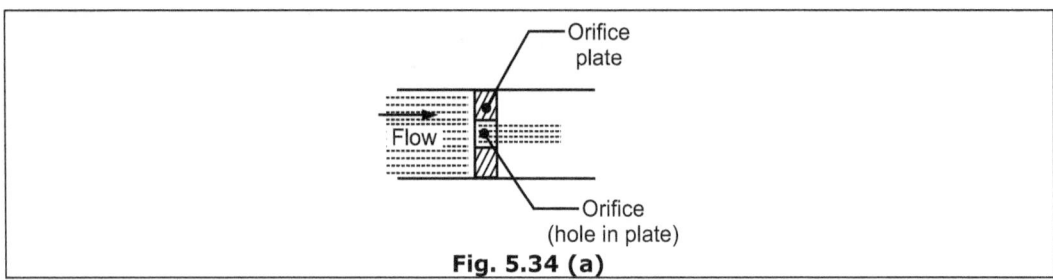

Fig. 5.34 (a)

- In venturimeter the throat of venturi does the work of throttling.

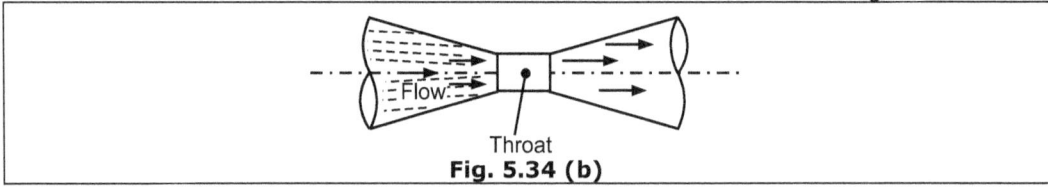

Fig. 5.34 (b)

During throttling the oil looses its part pressure. But the speed of fluid increases.

- Other throttling arrangements are:

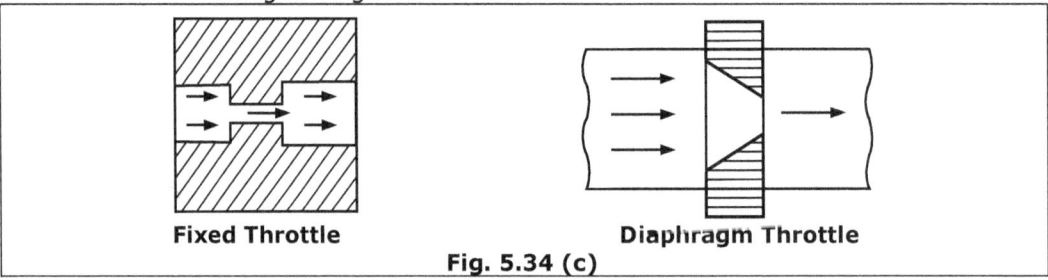

Fig. 5.34 (c)

- **Diversion:** Diverting is by-passing the part of flow so that the actuator receives only the portion to perform its task. 'Bleed-off-Circuit' is the best example of diversion of flow. Fig. 5.35 shows how flow is diverted. Suppose from DC valve quantity of oil going out is say 5 lit/min. Flow of 1 lit/min. is diverted. Hence actuator will receive 4 lit./min.

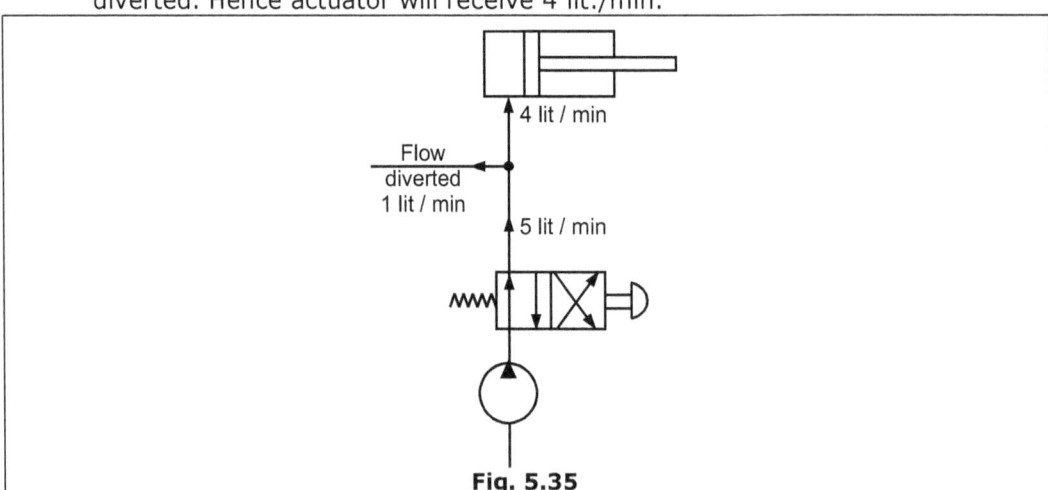

Fig. 5.35

Types of Flow Control Valves: Following are the types of flow control valves:

(a) Needle valve (Basic two-way flow control valve).

(b) Pressure compensated flow control valve.

(c) Non-compensated flow control valves.

(d) Check valves.

Now we will see one by one.

5.4.7 Needle Valve

It has a pointed stem or needle that can be adjusted upward or downward by rotating the handwheel. Since stem is threaded we can accurately control the needle which in turn controls the outflow.

This is most commonly used flow control valves in many hydraulic systems.

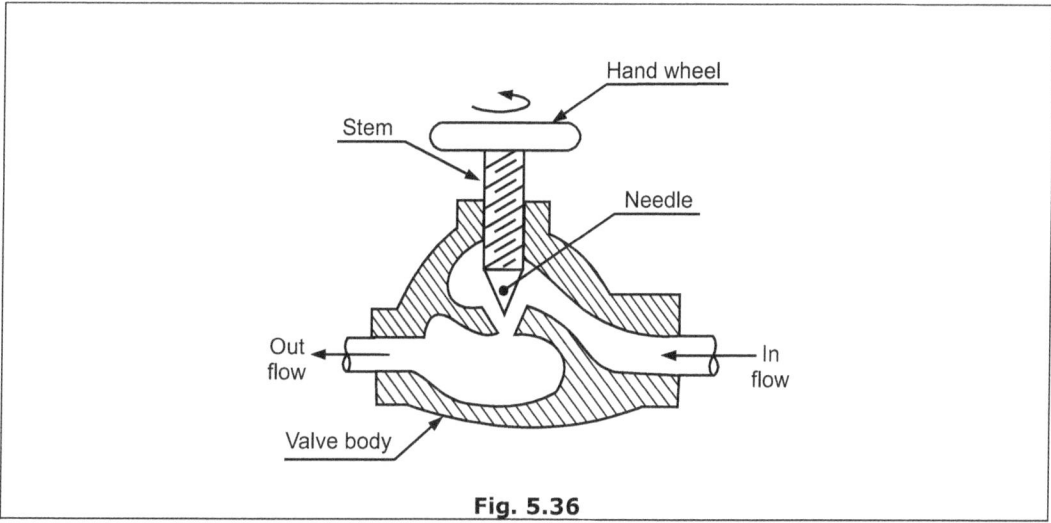

Fig. 5.36

- This valve is also used as 'stop valve' to stop or 'shutt-off' the flow.

5.4.8 Pressure Compensated Flow Control Valve

In any hydraulic circuit there are slight variations in pressure of oil. When pressure changes, the rate of flow changes. But many circuit requires constant flow regardless of input or output pressure variations in circuit. Then we must use pressure compensated flow control valve. Such valve is depicted in Fig. 5.37.

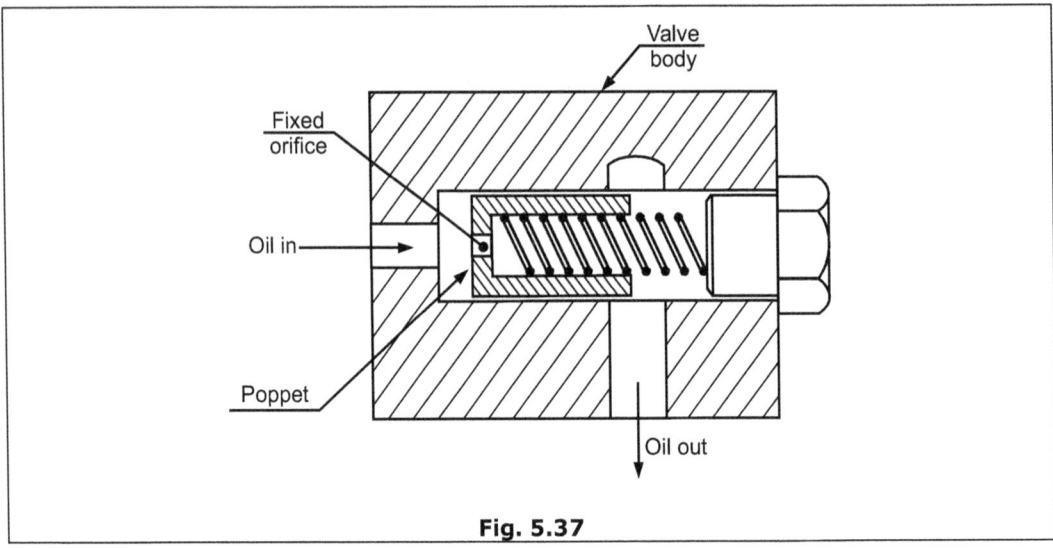

Fig. 5.37

Construction: It consists of hollow cylinder shaped poppet at the bottom of which there is fixed orifice (hole). There is spring inside the poppet as shown.

Working: Pressurized oil entering through inlet port will apply full force on the bottom of poppet and will try to compress the spring, by shifting the poppet to right. The poppet will move to right and will close the outlet port. Then movement of poppet towards right will stop.

Now flow of oil through orifice will start. Oil will occupy the bore of poppet cylinder. This flow of oil will equalize the pressure on both ends of poppet. The poppet will then balance.

During the process of poppet balancing, spring will expand and poppet will move towards left thereby uncovering the outlet port.

A balance will automatically be established between quantity of oil through orifice and quantity of oil going out through outlet port.

Even if the pressure of incoming oil changes, the rebalancing will be established automatically and constant flow of oil will come out.

Applications:

These valves are used in Material handling systems e.g. lowering the speed of pallets where there are pressure variations.

5.4.9 Non-compensated Flow Control Valve

Non-compensated flow control valves that control the flow by throttling or restricting. Needle valve we have seen is non-compensated valve.

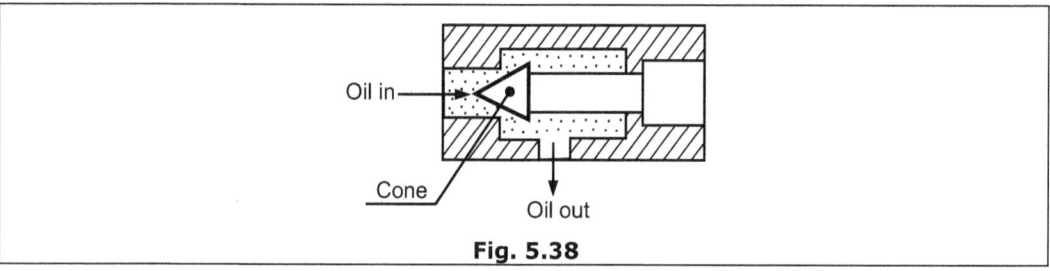

Fig. 5.38

Non-compensated: It gives oil flow; which will vary if pressure increases or decreases.

Non-compensated Flow Control Valve: A simple variable non-compensated flow control valve is shown above. The restriction is constant or variable. The flow is restricted by cone. For adjustment i.e. forward or backward movement of cone we can use screw. When pressure of incoming oil changes the flow of outgoing oil will change. No compensation for pressure changes.

Applications: These valves are used where accuracy in actuator movement when speed of actuator is not important.

Symbol: Following are the symbols of flow control valves.

(a)    Flow control valve (Non-compensated)

(b)    Variable flow control valve (Non-compensated)

(c) 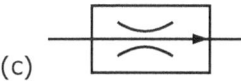   Pressure compensated flow control valve with fixed orifice

5.4.10 Check Valves (Also Known As Non-Return Valves) [S-15]

- **Function of check valve:** The main function of check valve is to allow the flow of fluid in one direction only. Flow of fluid in reverse direction is completely blocked or restricted. Due to this function only they are also termed as 'Non- return valves'.
- In topic 3 of this book you have studied 'foot valve' of centrifugal pump. This foot valve is non-return valve or you may call it as a check valve.

We will study two types of check valves:

5.4.11 Simple Check Valve

This valve consists of valve body in which valve element like cone (we can use ball or special poppet) is incorporated with specifically designed spring as shown.

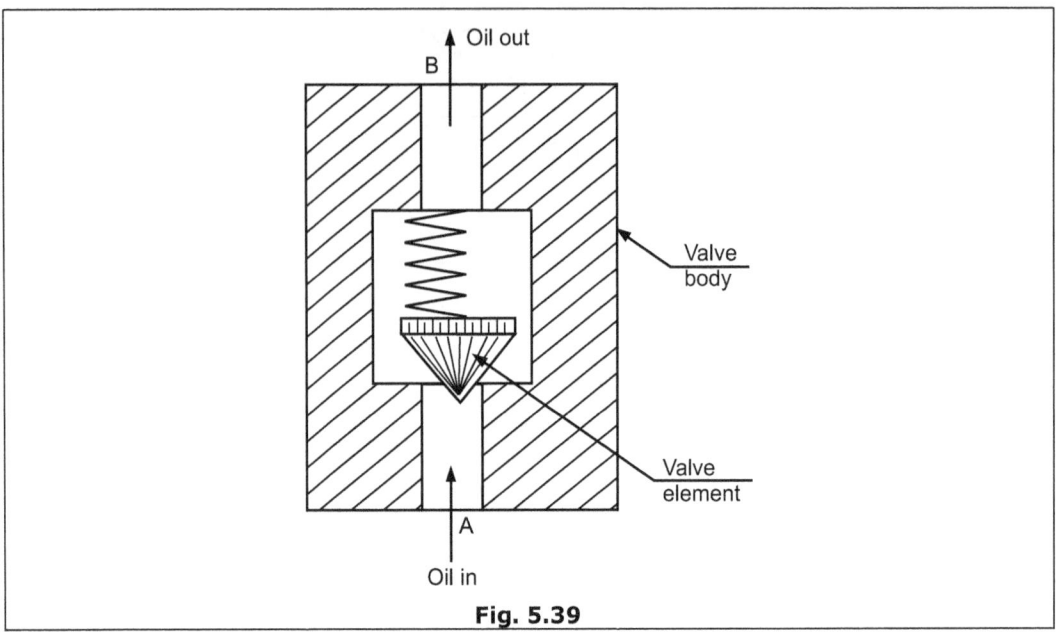

Fig. 5.39

Working: When pressurised oil comes in through port A, it will lift up the cone by overcoming spring force and flow will start from port A to port B. When flow from A stops, spring will expand and cone will block the flow.

It is easily understood that no flow is possible from port B to port A; flow in only one direction is possible.

Symbol of simple check valve: The symbol is designed based on construction itself.

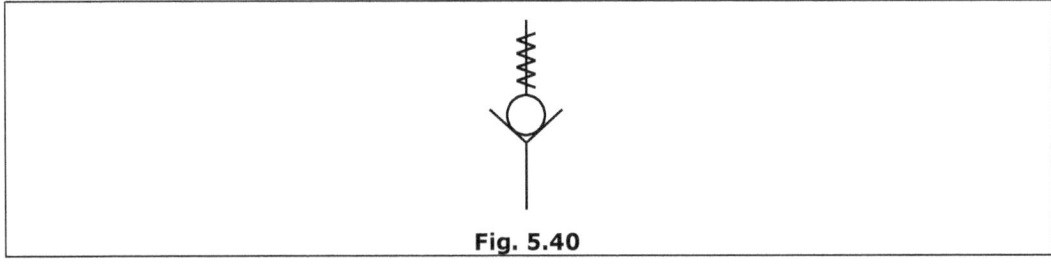

Fig. 5.40

5.4.12 Pilot Operated Check Valve

- Directly operated check valve cannot be kept open because it is safety valve. It will open when dangerous situation arises.
- If we want continuous oil flow from port (A) to (B) for some specific period then we have to modify the directly operated check valve. (Refer Fig. 5.41 and 5.42).

- Fig. 5.41 shows the pilot operated check valve. A pilot piston is introduced below moving poppet (we can see that upper part of valve is similar to directly operated check valve). This pilot piston can move up by introducing pilot signal (it is nothing but pressurised oil) from port C.

Working: As we can see in normal position shown there is no flow from (A) to (B) because the movable valve poppet has blocked the flow.

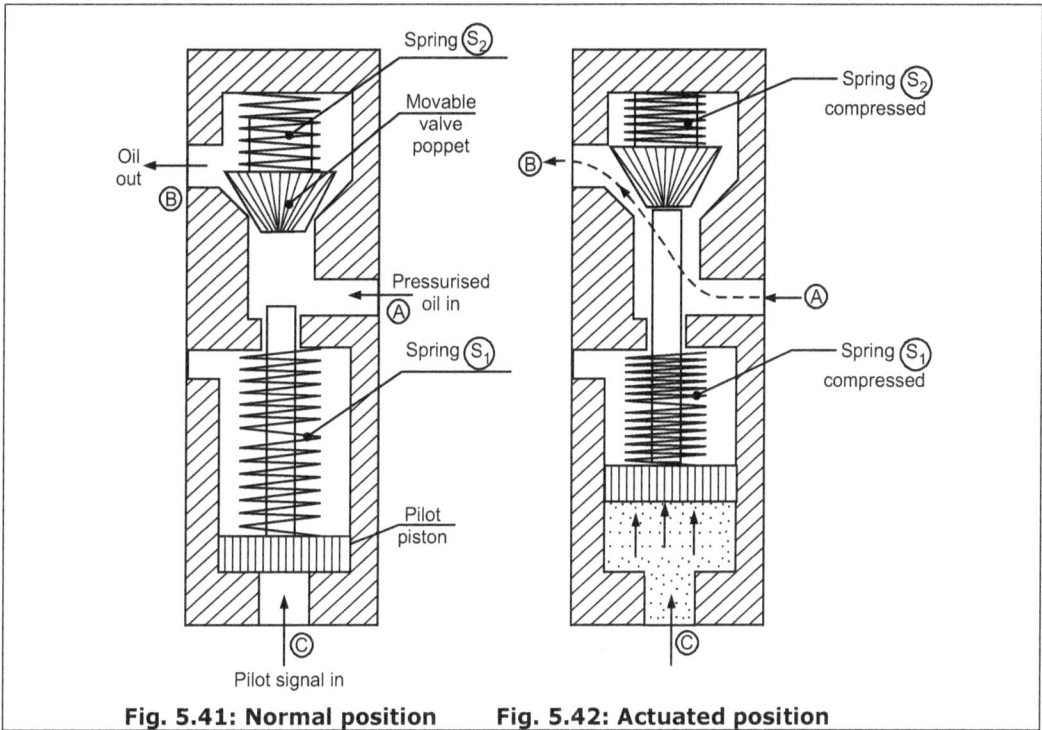

Fig. 5.41: Normal position   **Fig. 5.42: Actuated position**

Now pilot signal is given through port (C). This oil will push up the pilot piston upwards, thereby compressing spring (S_1). The piston road of pilot piston will push the movable poppet in upward direction thereby compressing the spring (S_2). Now the flow from (A) to (B) will start.

As and when we cut-off the pilot signal the flow from (A) and (B) will continue. When pilot signal will be cut-off, springs S_1 and S_2 will expand and moving poppet will again block the flow from (A) to (B).

- **Symbol of Pilot Operated Check Valve**

While drawing this symbol in hydraulic line show correctly the pilot line.

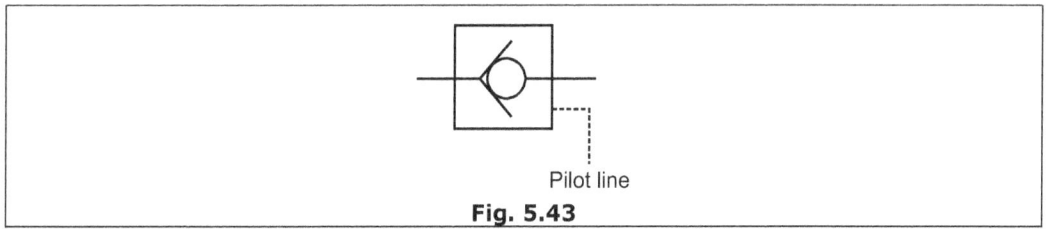

Fig. 5.43

5.4.13 Pressure Control Valve

- Pressure control valves maintain the desired pressure level in the various parts of hydraulic circuit.
- Functions of pressure control valves:
    (i) Limiting the maximum or set pressure limit and thus protecting the system.
    (ii) Regulating or Reducing the pressure in certain portions of circuit.
    (iii) Unloading the system pressure.
    (iv) Any other pressure related function to perform.

We will study the following pressure control valves:
(a) Pressure Relief Valve (Directly Operated)
(b) Pressure Relief Valve (Pilot Operated).
(c) Pressure Reducing Valve.

(a) Pressure Relief Valve (Directly Operated)

Pressure Relief Valves are found in almost every hydraulic circuit. It is normally closed valve and it is connected between the pressure line (after pump) and the oil reservoir.

Main function of pressure relief valve: Its main function is to limit the pressure in the system and thus to protect the individual component and hydraulic oil carrying lines from overload and danger of bursting. It is safety valve. It takes care of safety of hydraulic system.

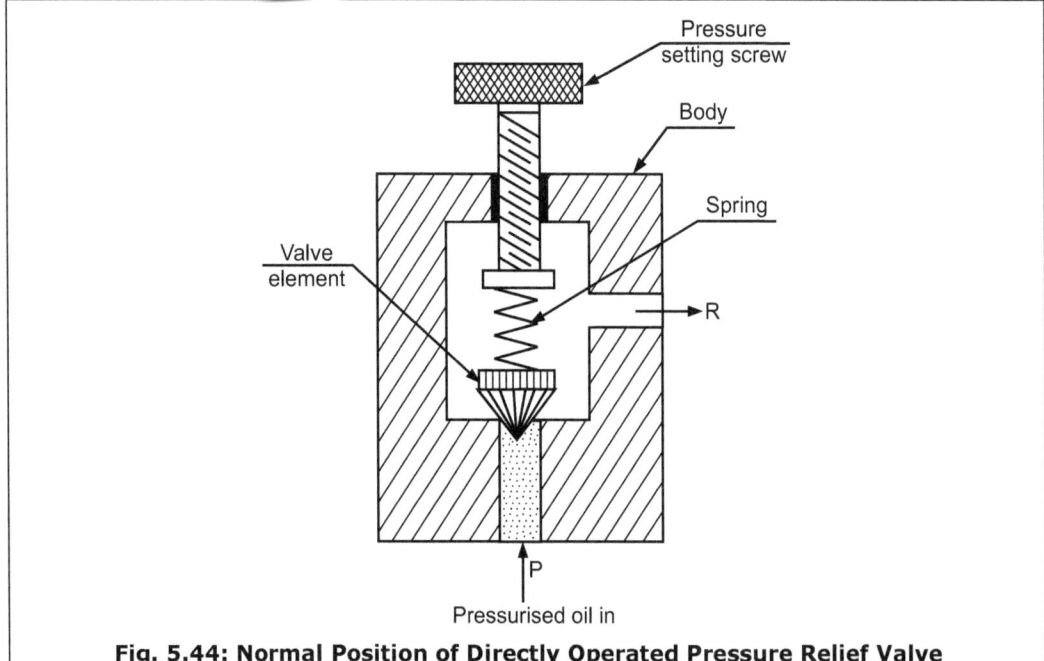

Fig. 5.44: Normal Position of Directly Operated Pressure Relief Valve

Construction: It consists of a valve body in which valve element (cone or ball) is fitted with spring. The compression of spring can be adjusted by pressure setting screw. There are two ports. P is pressure port connected to pump, R is oil return port connected to reservoir.

Working: The valve element is seated in valve body, by the compressive force of spring. When inlet pressure of oil is insufficient to overcome spring force, valve will remain close. (No flow from port (P) to (R)). Hence normally this valve is closed. When pressure of input oil through port (P) increase due to some unpredicted blockages, then this increased pressure of oil will overcome the spring force and will lift the valve element in upward direction by compressing the spring. Due to lifting of valve element, port P will be uncovered and flow from port (P) to port (R) will start. Since port (R) is connected to oil reservoir, the oil will be discharged into it. This flow will continue unless and until system pressure falls below the set value. Then again spring force will be dominating and valve will close.

The pressure level in system is thus controlled by spring force.

Symbol of Directly operated pressure relief valve:

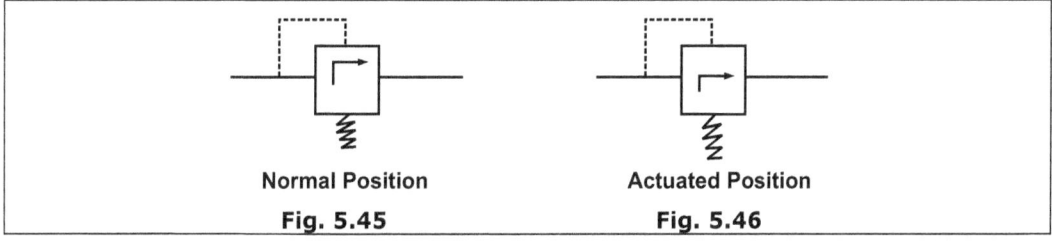

Normal Position　　　　　Actuated Position
Fig. 5.45　　　　　　　　Fig. 5.46

5.4.14 Pressure Relief Valve (Pilot Operated)

What is the need of Pilot operated Pressure Relief Valve?

When we are using high pressure oil and large flow, then we have to use heavy spring in directly operated pressure relief valve. Due to the use of heavy spring, the size of valve increases considerably. To keep the size of valve limited and to use normal size spring, the directly operated valve is modified to pilot operated valve.

Principle of Pilot Operated Pressure Relief Valve

Pilot operated valve works on the principle of flow through orifice. It is well known fact that when the pressurised fluid flows through orifice its pressure drops. So pressure difference is setup across an orifice. This principle is used in this valve.

Construction: The upper part of valve is pilot stage and lower part is main stage. The main spool is bigger in size with bigger spring to allow more flow whereas pilot spool (cone) is smaller in size with light spring. There is orifice in main spool. (Refer Fig. 5.47).

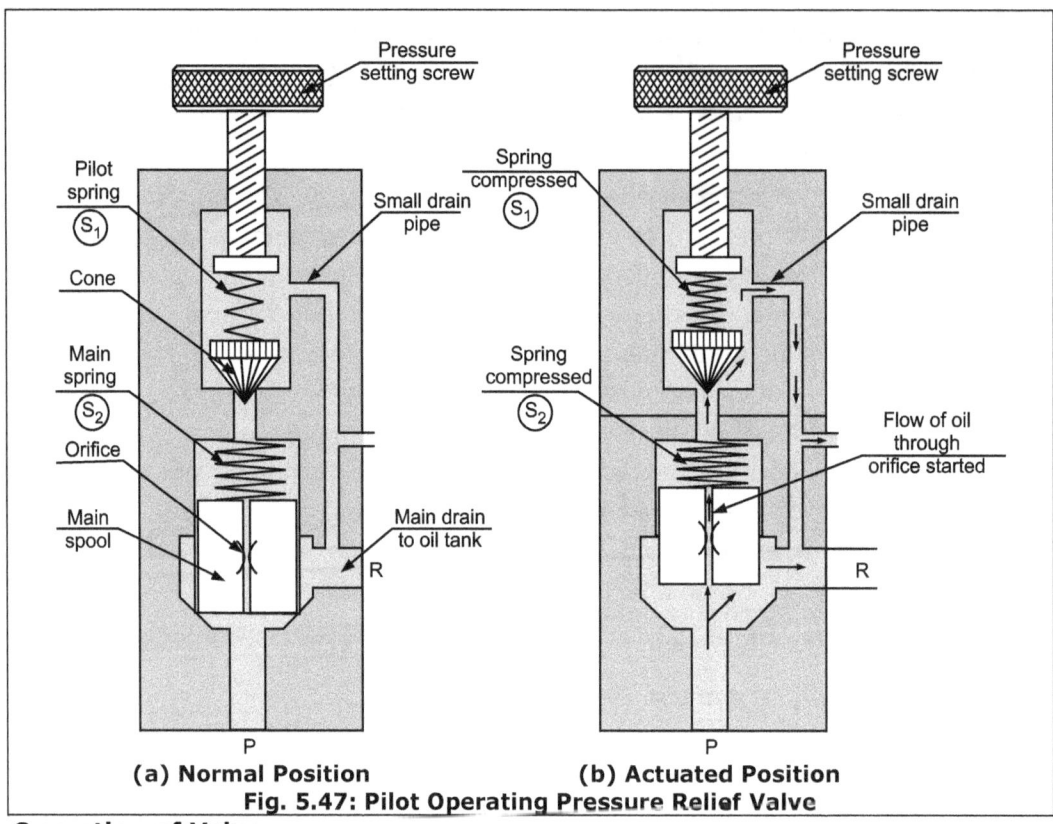

Fig. 5.47: Pilot Operating Pressure Relief Valve

Operation of Valve:

- **Normal position:** In normal position i.e. when system pressure is in constant state, the pressure on bottom of main spool and on the bottom of cone is same. There is no flow of oil across the orifice. Hence, there is no flow from port P → R. Everything is safe.
- **Actuated position:** Now suppose due to some problem of blockage, pressure of oil started increasing, oil flow will start from port P through orifice towards cone. Then due to light weight of cone and light spring attached to it, cone lifts up and small drain flow starts as shown in Fig. 5.47 (b). Naturally, flow through orifice is starting. This flow through orifice creates pressure difference across main spool and automatically main spool lifts up, by compressing the spring (S_2). Due to lifting of main spool, main flow from port P to port R starts. Oil returns to oil reservoir.

Symbol of Pilot Operated Pressure Relief Valve

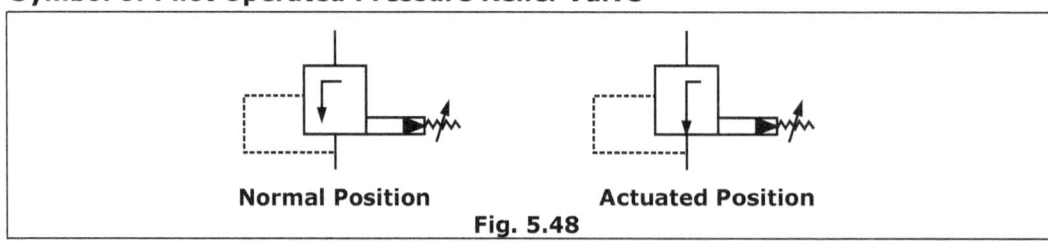

Fig. 5.48

5.4.15 Pressure Reducing Valve

The main function of pressure reducing valve is to reduce the pressure in particular branch of the circuit to different level as demanded by consumer in that branch.

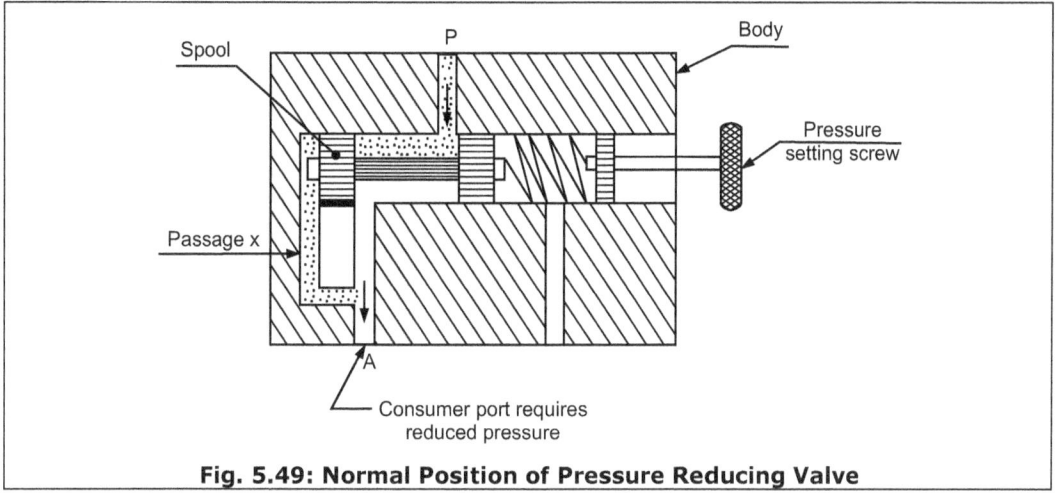

Fig. 5.49: Normal Position of Pressure Reducing Valve

Construction: It consists of spool and spring enhoused in the bore of valve body. Spring compression can be adjusted by pressure setting screw. Port P is pressure port connected to pump. Port A is consumer port requiring reduced pressure.

Working: As shown in normal position, port P is supplying oil to consumer port A. If the main supply pressure is below the set pressure, there will be continuous flow from P → A. Hence normally this valve is open.

When outlet pressure rises to valve setting, then oil will flow through 'passage x' and will act on spool and spool will shift to right thereby partly closing the port A. Now only enough flow will pass through port 'A' so that consumer connected to A will receive reduced pressure.

Use of Pressure Reducing Valve in Circuit and Symbol

The circuit shown in Fig. 5.50 shows that reduced pressure P_2 is available to second branch of circuit. ($P_2 < P$).

Unloading Valve

Function of unloading valve: The power of oil in terms of pressure of flow can be given by following expression:

$$\boxed{\text{Power} = \text{Pressure} \times \text{Flow rate}}$$

If we allow excess flow of oil through pressure relief valve (in case of blockages) then it is wastage of 'Energy'. This can result into rise in temperature of fluid, because wastage energy, generally converts into heat.

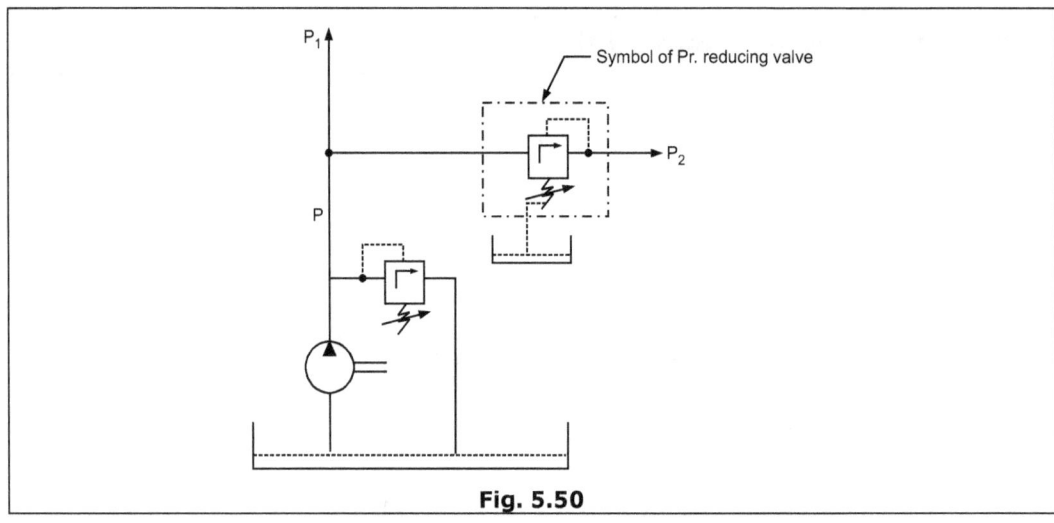

Fig. 5.50

To overcome this difficulty, additional valve called 'unloading valve' is used before pressure relief valve. This unloading valve is opened or closed by external electrical circuit. By using this valve we can unload the pressurised oil from pump at much lower pressure and there is very low wastage of energy. Naturally, there is no much heating of oil.

Unloading valve is on-off type and operated by external electrical energy source. The hydraulic circuit using unloading valve is as under.

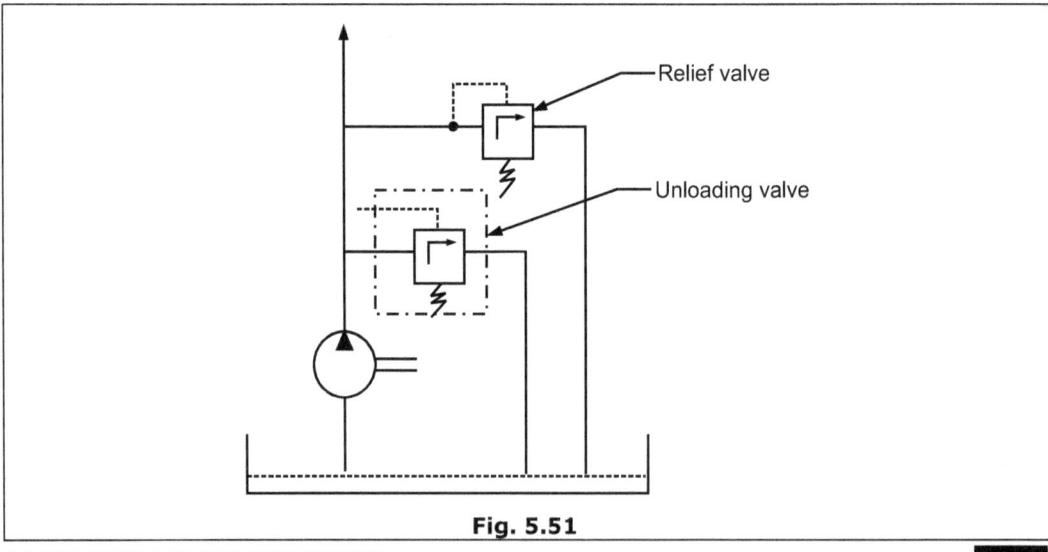

Fig. 5.51

5.4.16 Sequence Valve [W-14]

The main function of sequence valve is to operate 2-3 operations in sequential order i.e. one after the another. Suppose we have to carry out drilling a hole in a block. Then first operation must be clamping and second operation is drilling. Third operation is de-clamping. These three operations must be done in a specific sequence. This task is carried out by sequence valve in the circuit. (Refer sequencing operation in Topic 7).

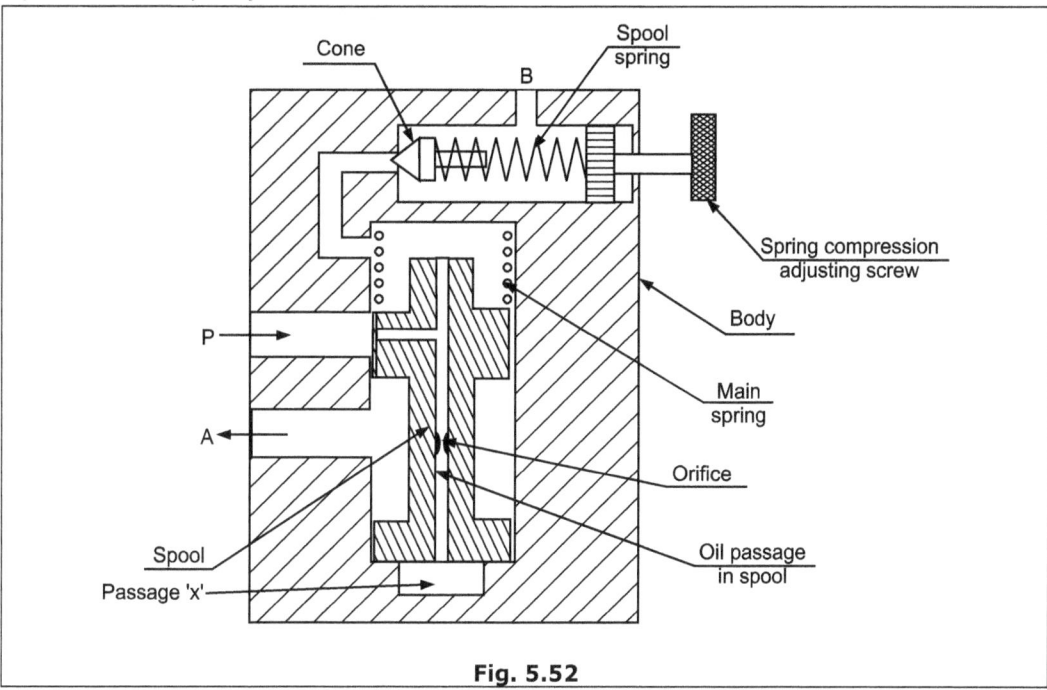

Fig. 5.52

Construction: The construction is similar to 'Pilot Operated Pressure Relief Valve'. It has a special spool having specifically drilled oil passages.

Operation: Oil under pressure goes inside through port P. It will pass through oil passage to space 'x'. When pressure is sufficiently build-up, oil flow will start from 'x' because cone will move towards right. Due to orifice, pressure difference will set up across the spool and spool will lift up by compressing main spring. And flow will start from port P to port A.

Symbol of Sequence Valve:

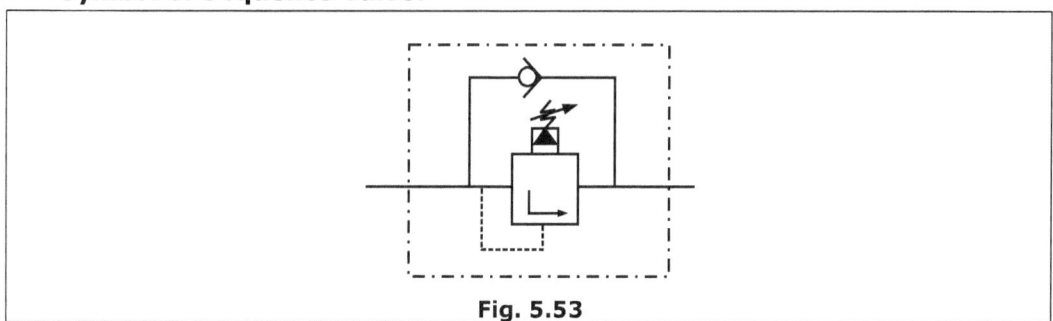

Fig. 5.53

5.5 FLOW CONTROL VALVES / DIRECTION CONTROL VALVES / PRESSURE CONTROL VALVES AND OTHER VALVES IN PNEUMATIC CIRCUITS

Pneumatic energy i.e. compressed air from air receiver and FRL unit goes to pneumatic equipment or simply called as 'consumer'. Consumer (also known as an Actuator) uses compressed air and gives us an 'useful work'.

But when air travels from FRL unit to equipment, it needs to be controlled to suit the requirement of consumer. This control of air is a function of various pneumatic valves.

Now let us make this concept more clear by studying following examples.

Example 1: Fig. 5.54 shows double acting cylinder. (It is actuator). When compressed air enters through port (inlet) A piston will move from left to right. When compressed air will enter through port B, piston will move from right to left. So at first air will enter through port A and then through port B, then we can achieve reciprocating movement of piston. So to 'direct' the air first through port A and then to port B, we have to use **Direction Control Valves** or simply called as 'DC valves'.

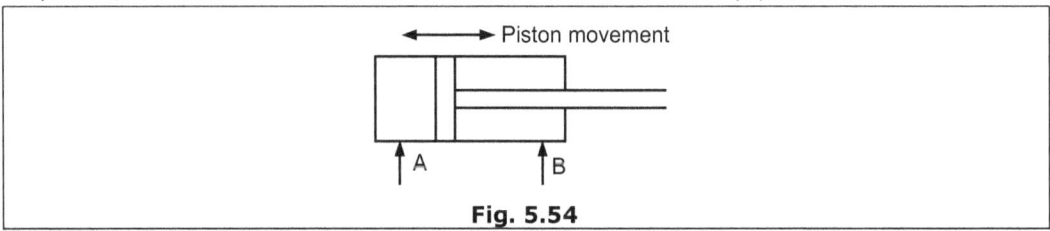

Fig. 5.54

Example 2: Fig. 5.55 shows double acting cylinder. When air enters through port 'A' as stated above piston will move from left to right. The linear speed of piston moving from left to right is say 3 m/sec. Suppose we have to increase this speed from 3 m/sec to 5 m/sec. then we have to admit more quantity of air through port 'A' so that piston will move faster from left to right, and we can achieve more linear speed of piston (5 m/sec). So here we have to use additional valves which will control the **quantity of air** entering into cylinder. This valve is known as **Flow Control Valve**.

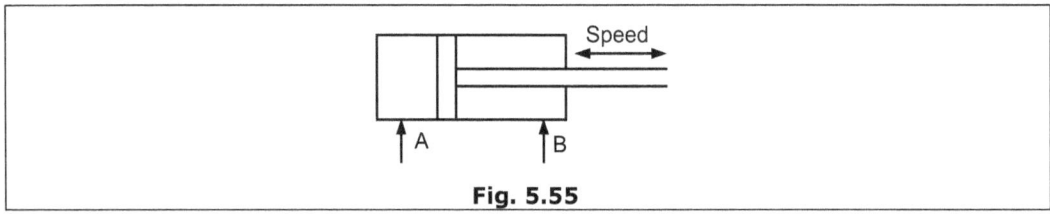

Fig. 5.55

Example 3: Consider two actuators (air cylinder or air motor) No. (1) and (2) shown below. The air pressure developed by air compressor is say 8 bar. Actuator

(1) operates on 4 bar pressure and Actuator (2) operates on say 5 bar pressure. So for Actuator (1) we have to reduce the pressure of air from 8 bar to 4 bar and for Actuator (2) we have to reduce the pressure of air from 8 bar to 5 bar. So we have to control pressure of air. We must introduce another additional valve to make changes in pressure. This valve is known as **pressure control valve**.

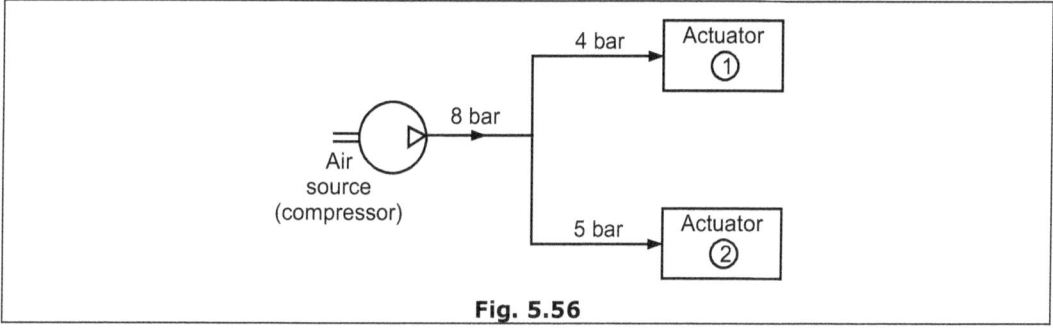

Fig. 5.56

Classification Pattern of Valves

- Now we will see the classification pattern of valves.
- As stated above valves in pneumatic circuit are divided into three main categories. Each valve will be either spool type or seat type.
  (a) Direction Control Valves (Spool/Seat).
  (b) Flow Control Valves (Spool/Seat).
  (c) Pressure Control Valves (Spool/Seat).
- Note that spool or seat type is concerned with the construction of valve. Irrespective of its construction, each valve will perform the function for which it is made.

Spool type valve: Spool is an element similar to piston and piston rod; which slides in a closely finished bore of cylinder. The wear of these elements is uniform and are most widely used.

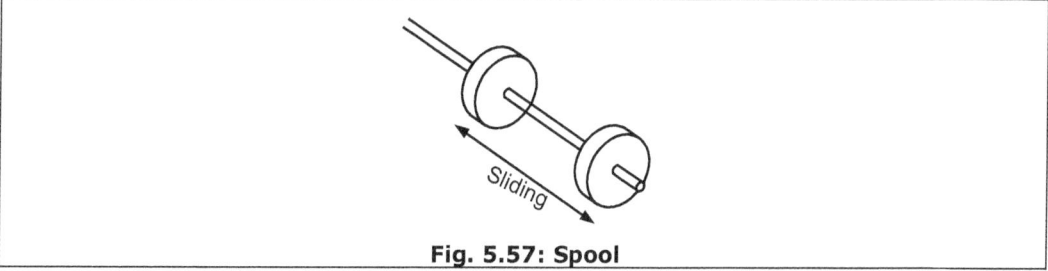

Fig. 5.57: Spool

Seat type valve: You must have seen the valves of IC engines. It is exactly a similar valve. The valve element (either poppet/cone or ball), sits on specially machined and finished seat. The wear of these valves is not uniform, hence used on very selective basis.

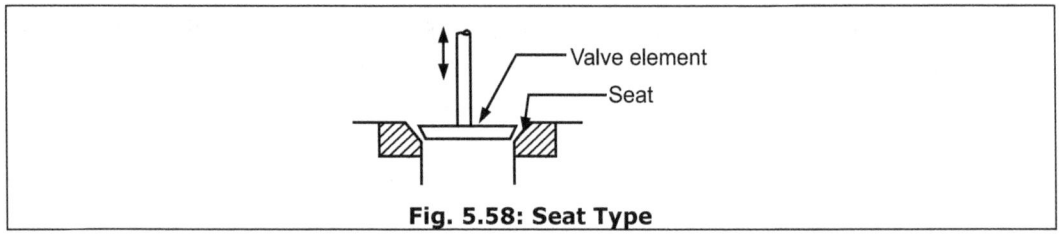

Fig. 5.58: Seat Type

Classification of Direction Control Valves (DC Valves)
(Either spool type or seat type)
1. 2 × 2 DC valve (spool type)
2. 3 × 2 DC valve (seat type and spool type)
3. 4 × 2 DC valve (seat type)
4. 5 × 2 DC valve (spool type)
5. 5 × 2 pilot operated DC valve (Impulse valve).

Classification of flow control valves:
1. Fixed type flow control valve.
2. Variable flow control valve with built-in check valve
3. Check valve (Directly operated)
4. Check valve (Pilot operated)
5. Double check valve (shuttle valve)

Classification of pressure control valves:
1. Relief valve
2. Pressure regulator (Pressure reducing valve)
3. Non-relieving pressure regulators
4. Relieving pressure regulators.

5.5.1 Direction Control Valves (DC Valves)

1. 2 × 2 (Read as 'two-by-two') DC valve (spool type)

Fig. 5.59 shows '2 × 2 spool type push button operated DC valve'.

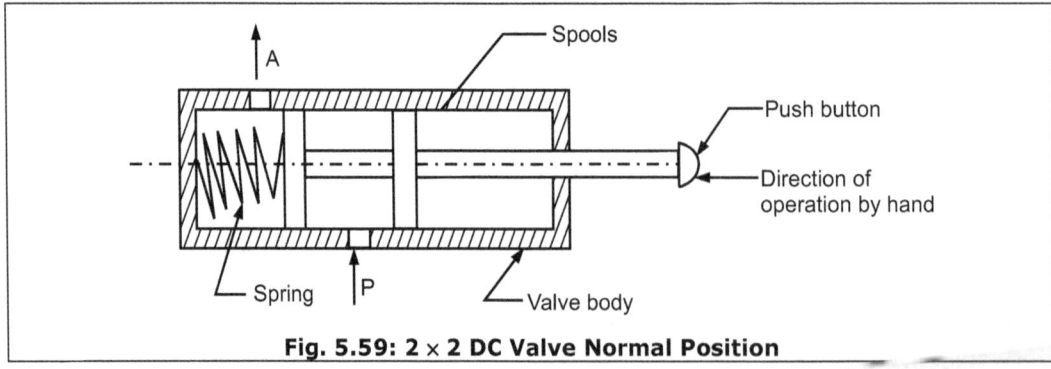

Fig. 5.59: 2 × 2 DC Valve Normal Position

Construction: It consists of a spool sliding in a finitely finished bore. The actuation of spool is by push button. Spring is attached to front spool.

Operation: Through port P, pressurised air has already entered into inside bore of valve.

- When push button is pressed, spool will move forward (right to left). Spring will compress. And air will move out through port A, because port P is connected to port A.

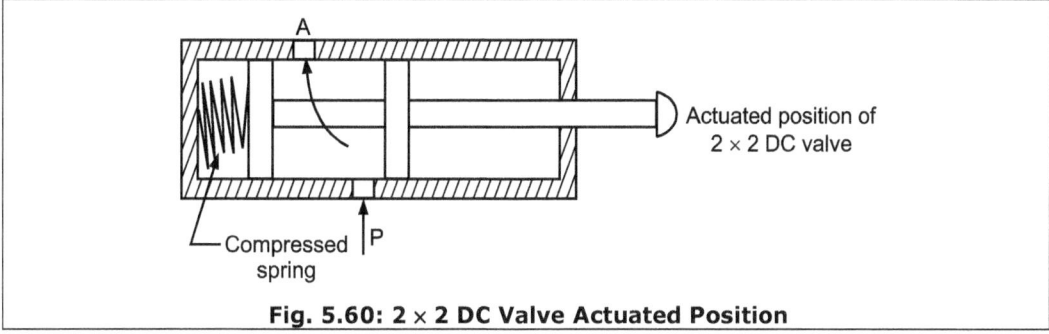

Fig. 5.60: 2 × 2 DC Valve Actuated Position

- When push button is released, spring will expand and the spool will regain its original position. Port P will be disconnected from A.
- Normal position of this valve is closed.
- 2 × 2 DC valve can be compared with ON-OFF water tap is house. The water tap on basin is always closed. When we open it the water starts flowing (Port P of water connects to Port A). Fig. 5.61 clarifies this concept. Remember that tap is normally closed; and it is 2 × 2 DC valve.

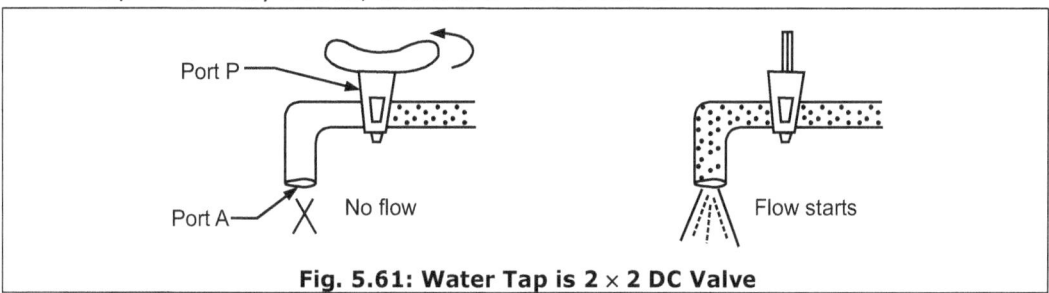

Fig. 5.61: Water Tap is 2 × 2 DC Valve

- **Symbol of 2 × 2 DC valve:** The symbol generation concept can be explained as under.
- The valve position is shown by squares.

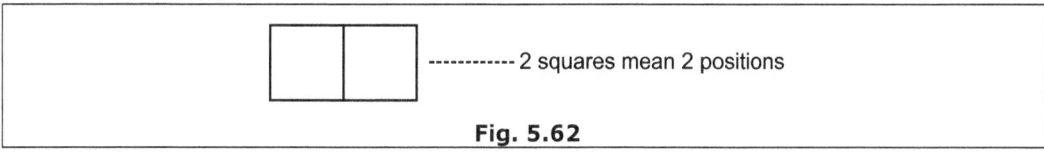

Fig. 5.62

In above valve, there are two positions:

One: Air pressure port P is connected to consumer port A (On)

Two: Air pressure port P is disconnected from consumer port A (Off).

Hence to show 2 × 2 valve, we have to draw 2 squares (Remember: the square should be exact square having all equal sides. Student may draw squares having 10 mm (1 cm) side for suitability in drawing. Preferably use engineering plastic 'templet' to draw squares).

- The direction of flow of air is shown by 'Arrows' in the squares. In square no (1), port A is connected to port P. In square (2), port A is disconnected from port P.

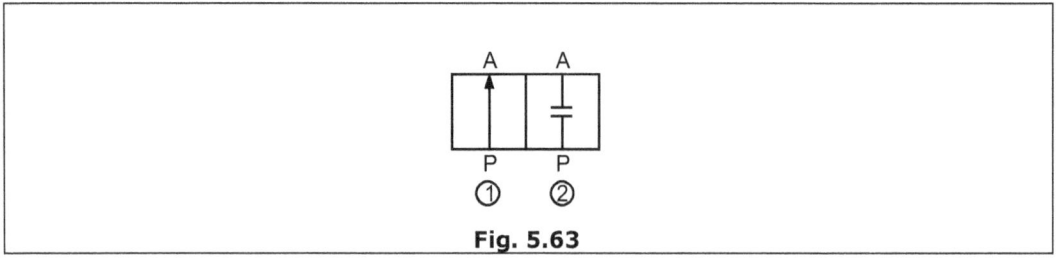

Fig. 5.63

- **Remember:** At a time think of only one square and position of arrow in it.
- So now we will have to construct complete symbol of 2 × 2 DC valve. As we know from the construction, the valve is normally closed. It is operated by push button and it regains its original position by spring force. Hence we have to attach push button and spring to the two squares, so that we will get complete symbol.

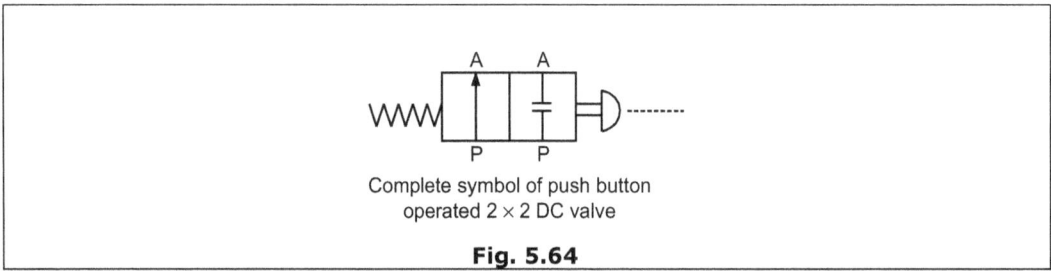

Complete symbol of push button
operated 2 × 2 DC valve

Fig. 5.64

5.5.2 3 × 2 (Read as 'Three-by-Two') D.C. Valve (Spool type)

Similar to 2 × 2 DC valve, in this valve also, spool reciprocates in infinely finished bore of valve body (machining quality is shown by two triangles). The spring is attached to front spool. In Fig. 5.65, port A is connected to port R. Remember that port R is exhaust port. After doing work, the air is returning from port A to port R and going into atmosphere, that means air is exhausting.

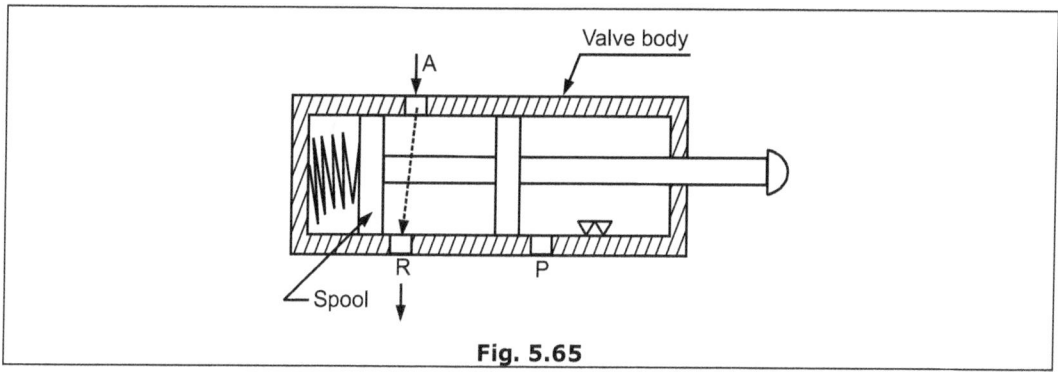

Fig. 5.65

Now push button is operated:

When push button is pressed, spool will move from right to left, thereby compressing the spring. With this movement of spool, port A will be connected to pressure port P. Compressed air will start flowing from port P to port A.

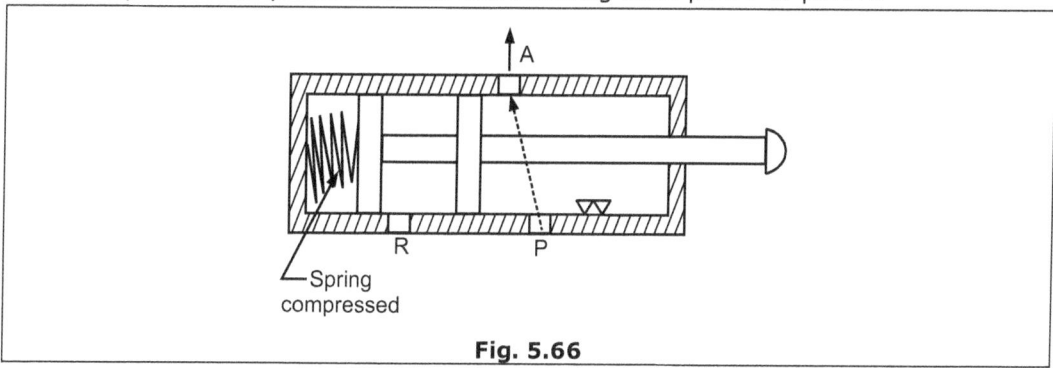

Fig. 5.66

Exhaust port R is disconnected from port A.

Now it can be easily understood that, when push button is released, spring will expand and spool will regain its original position.

Symbol of 3 × 2 DC valve:

Three-by-Two means there will be 2 positions and 3 ports, 2 positions means 2 squares. 3 ports are shown in a specific manner.

Square (1) shows 1st position i.e. port A is connected to port R (exhaust port) and port P is disconnected. Square (2) shows 2nd position i.e. operated position. Push button is operated. Port P is connected to port A and port R is disconnected. In this manner, symbols are formed.

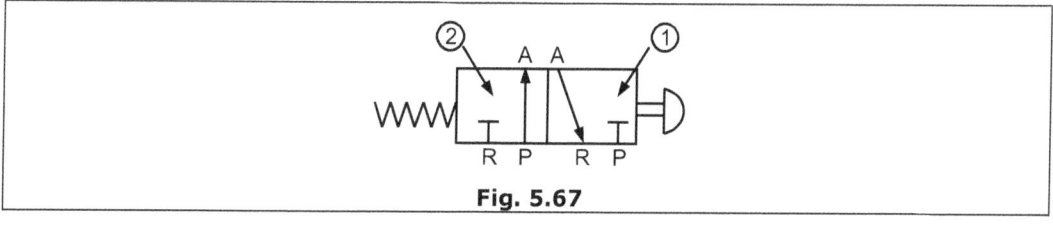

Fig. 5.67

Let us see the application of 3 × 2 DC valve

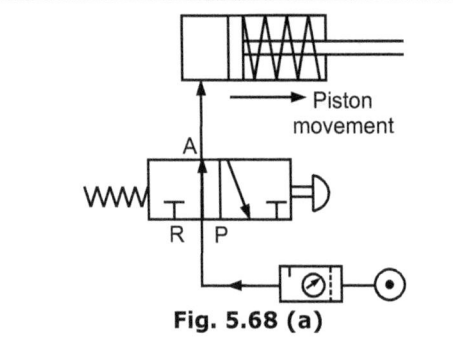 **Fig. 5.68 (a)**	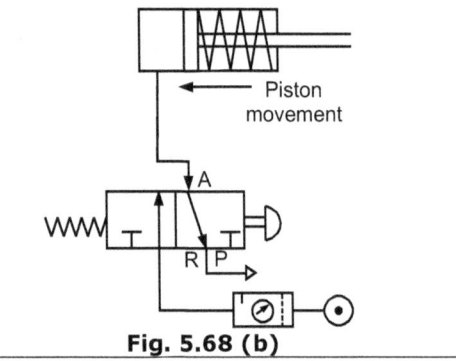 **Fig. 5.68 (b)**
3 × 2 DC valve is used here to operate single acting pneumatic cylinder (SA Cyl.) Port P is connected to port A. Compressed air will push the piston from left to right thereby compressing the spring (power stroke).	Now power stroke is complete. Push button of DC valve is released. Spring of cylinder will expand. Piston will move from right to left, thereby pushing out the air out of cylinder through port A. This port is now connected to port R i.e. Exhaust port. Air will return to atmosphere.

5.5.3 3 × 2 Seat Type DC Valve

3 × 2 DC valve can also be seat type as shown in Fig. 5.69. There are two valve seats shown, on which cones of valve element rest. There is no spring. The valve element can move up-down. At present position shown port A is connected to exhaust port R. Pressure port P is disconnected. Now air starts entering from port P. Due to pressure force the valve element will lift up. Due to this movement, port P will be connected to port A and port R will be blocked by upper cone of valve element.

The symbol of seat type valve is same as that of spool type valve.

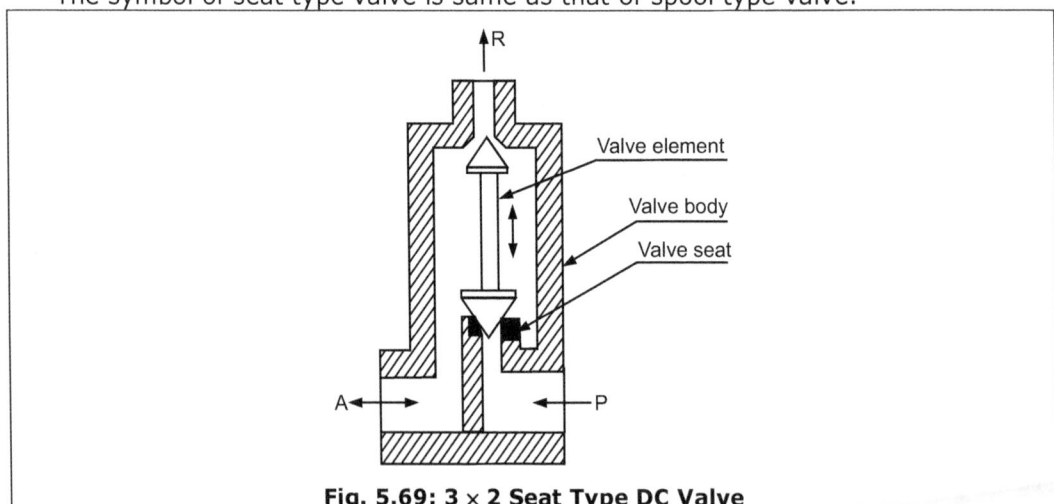

Fig. 5.69: 3 × 2 Seat Type DC Valve

5.5.4 4 × 2 DC Valve (Seat and Poppet Type)

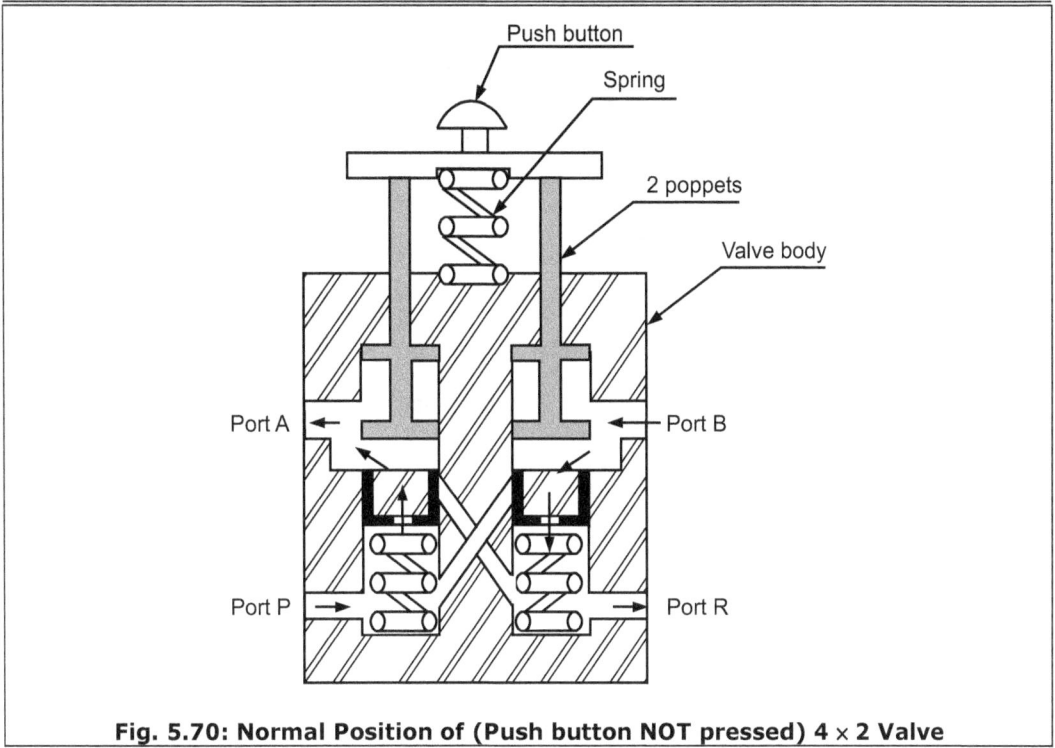

Fig. 5.70: Normal Position of (Push button NOT pressed) 4 × 2 Valve

Fig. 5.70 shows normal position of 4 × 2 DC valve. There are two poppets. A and B are consumer ports. (Ports attached to actuator to obtain useful work).

Port P is pressurised compressed air inlet port.

Port R is exhaust port.

The present position shows that:

- Port P is connected to port A.
- Port B is connected to port R.

Now push button is pressed downwards.

It shows actuated position of valve. See Fig. 5.71.

As push button is pressed downwards, all springs will be compressed. And spool will be in such a position that:

- Port A will be connected to port R.
- Port P will be connected to port B.

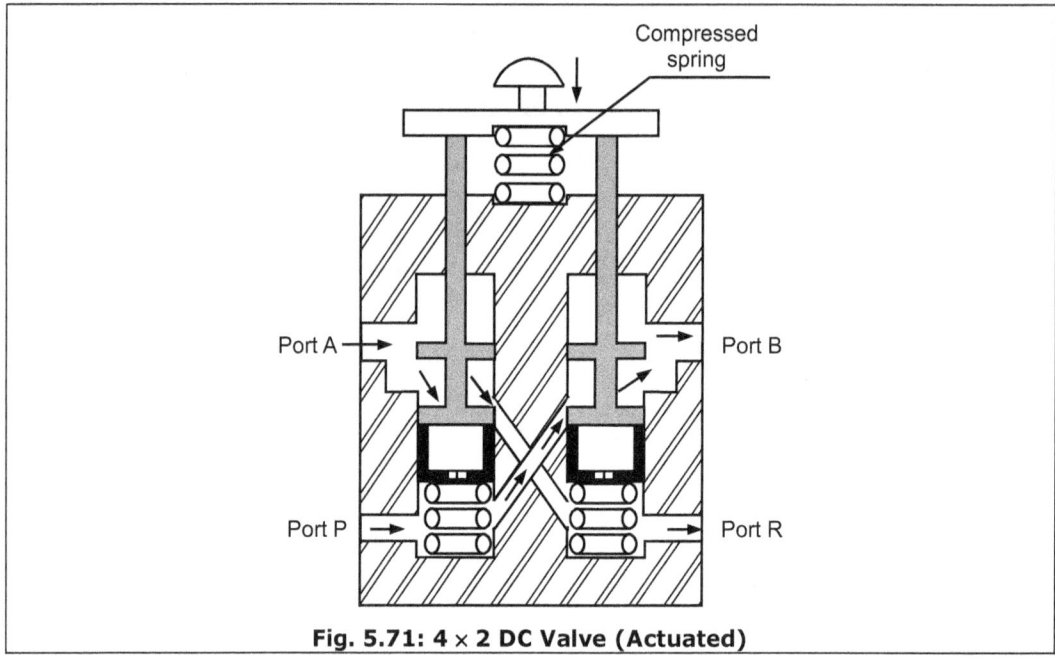

Fig. 5.71: 4 × 2 DC Valve (Actuated)

- When button will be released, spring below button will expand and spool will regain its original position i.e. normal position.

Symbol of 4 × 2 DC valve: Four-by-Two means there will be 2 positions and 4 ports. 2 positions mean 2 squares. 4 ports are shown in specific manner as shown in Fig. 5.72.

Square (1) shows – Normal position of valve i.e.

    Port P connected to Port A

    Port B connected to Port R

Square (2) shows – Actuated position of valve i.e.

    Port A connected to Port R

    Port P connected to Port B

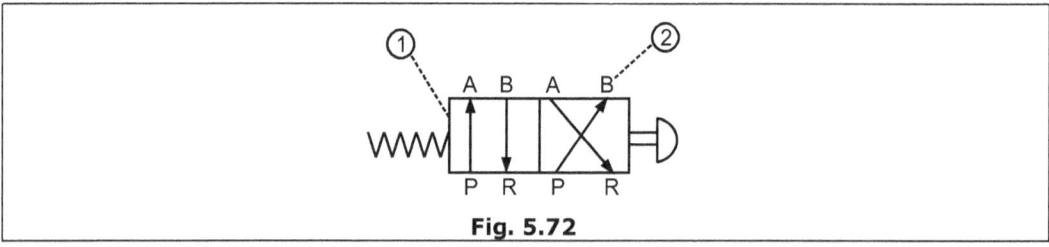

Fig. 5.72

Application of 4 × 2 DC valve: This valve can be used to operate Reciprocating actuator called 'Double Acting Cylinder' (DA cylinder). 4 × 2 DC valve is most widely used valve in pneumatic applications/circuits.

Observe the following figures.

Forward stroke of DA cylinder (Normal position)	Retract stroke of DA cylinder (Actuated position)
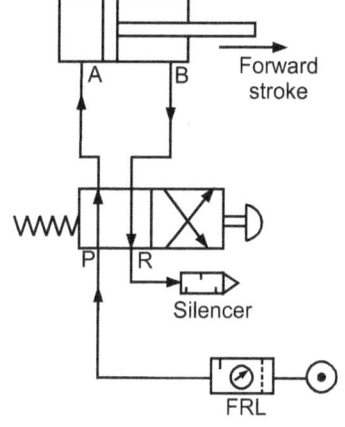 Fig. 5.73 (a)	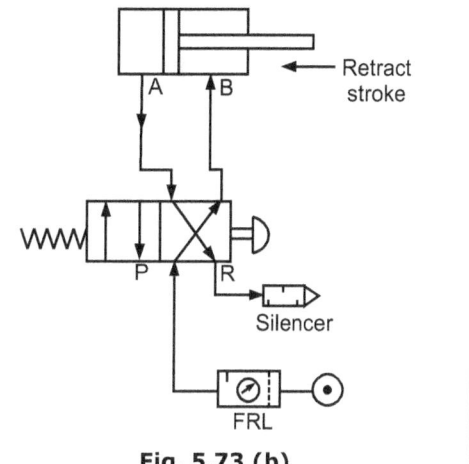 Fig. 5.73 (b)
Working: In normal position Pressure port P is connected to port A. Compressed air is entering into DA cylinder through port A. Due to pressure force, piston of DA cylinder will move from **left to right**. During this movement air on other side of piston will come out through port B and will be exhausted via DC valve into atmosphere through silencer.	**Working: In actuated position (press button of DC valve is pushed)** Pressure port P is connected to port B. Compressed air is entering into DA cylinder through port B. Due to pressure force, piston of DA cylinder will move from **right to left**. During this movement air on other side of piston will come out through port A and will be exhausted via DC valve into atmosphere through silencer.

Important

What is the meaning of 'Piston of DA cylinder is forwarding'?

Ans. When compressed air is admitted in the bore of DA cylinder from piston side then, movement of piston (left to right as shown in Fig. 5.74) is called forward stroke, it is said that piston is forwarding. Two cases are shown in two figures. In Fig. 5.74 (b), piston is moving from right to left. Even then it is forwarding, because air is admitted from piston side.

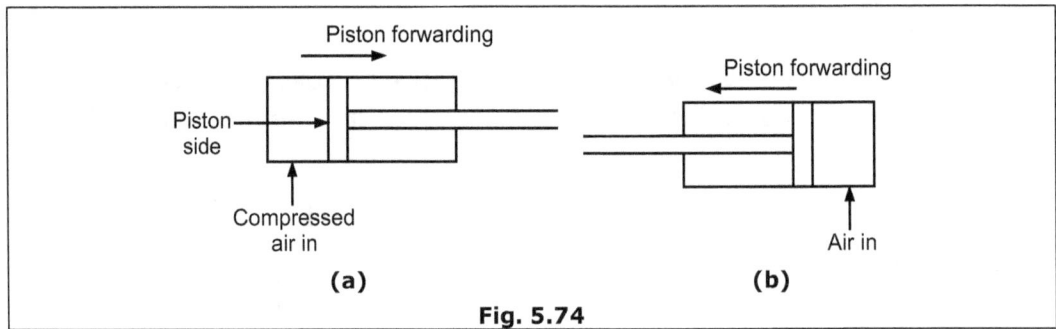

Fig. 5.74

What is the meaning of 'Piston of DA cylinder is retracting?

Ans. When compressed air is admitted in the bore of DA cylinder from piston-rod side, then movement of piston from left to right (or right to left) is called Retract movement and piston is said to be 'Retracting'.

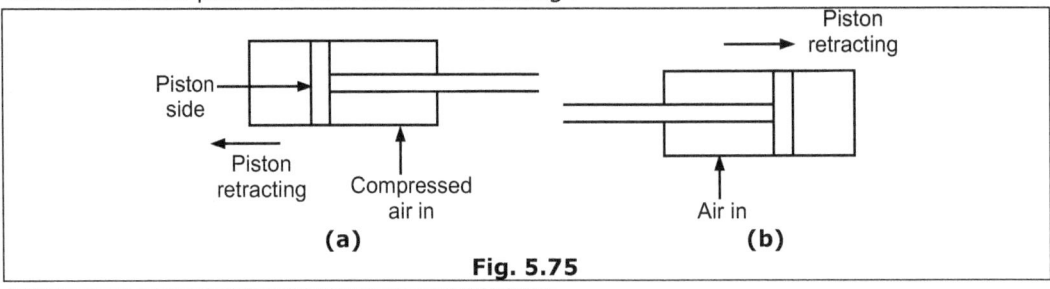

Fig. 5.75

5.5.5 5 × 2 DC Valve (Spool Type)

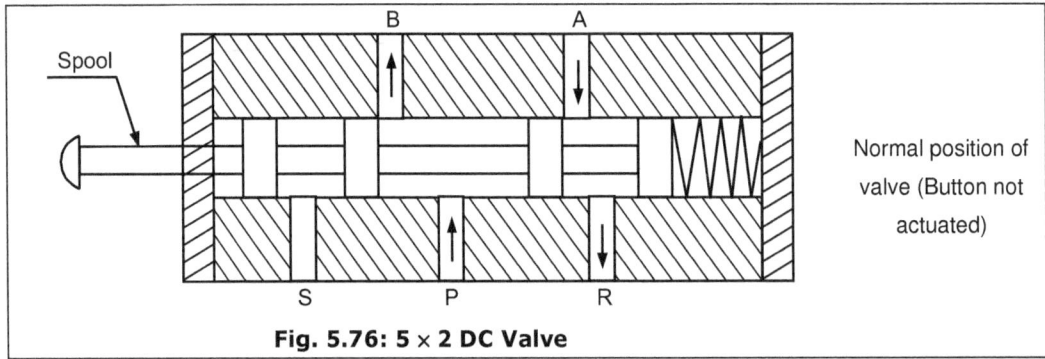

Fig. 5.76: 5 × 2 DC Valve

Spool type 5 × 2 DC valve (push button operated) is shown in Fig. 5.76. There is single spool. A and B are consumer ports (ports attached to actuator to obtain useful work). P is pressure port, R is normal exhaust port and S is EASY EXHAUST port.

The normal position shown in Fig. 5.76 shows that:
- Port P is connected to port B.
- Port A is connected to port R (Air is exhausting)
- Port S is closed or disconnected.

Now if push button is operated, spring will compress due to movement of spool from left to right and then

- Port P will get connected to port A.
- Port B will get connected to port S.
- Port R will close or will be disconnected.

Symbol of 5 × 2 DC valve: Five-by-Two means there will be 2 positions and 5 ports (A, B, P, R, S), 2 positions mean 2 squares. 5 ports are shown in specific manner.

Square (1) shows – Normal position.

Square (2) shows – Actuated position (push button is operated).

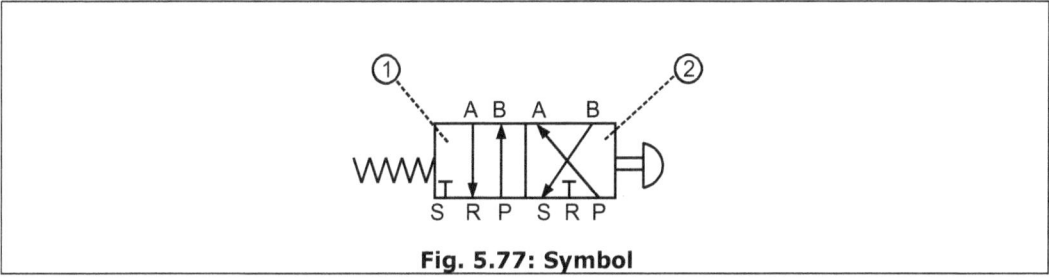

Fig. 5.77: Symbol

Note: At a time only one position (connections shown in one square) is in operation. So while studying the circuit, respective one square is considered.

5.5.6 5 × 2 Pilot Operated DC Valve (Impulse Valve)

- Pilot operated means instead of push button, the spool movement is done by compressed air. This compressed air entering into valve to operate spool of valve is called 'air signal'.
- For entry of air signal there are separate ports.

Fig. 5.78 will clarify the concept.

This valve is similar to push button operated 5 × 2 DC valve, except push button and spring. Instead of push button and spring there are x and y and air signal ports. When pressurised air enters from port x, spool will move from left to right, and when air enters through port y, spool will move from right and left. By controlling the pressurised air through port x or y, we can control movement of spool and can obtain connections of ports i.e. B to P/A to R or A to P/B to S etc. The operation of spool is by impulse (force) of air and hence it is called impulse valve.

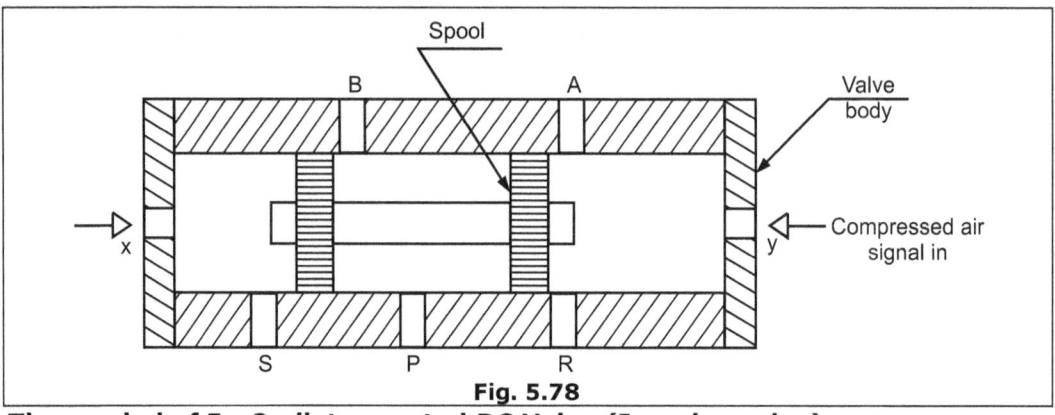

Fig. 5.78

The symbol of 5 × 2 pilot operated DC Valve (Impulse valve)

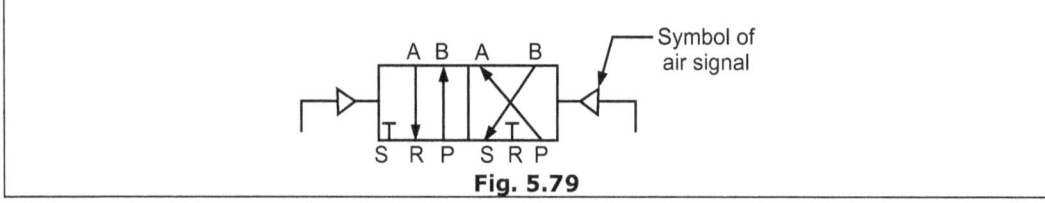

Fig. 5.79

5.5.7 Flow Control Valves

Fixed Type Flow Control Valve

As we have seen that by controlling the flow of air admitting in actuator we can control the speed of actuator (linear speed in case of linear actuator or rotary speed in case of air motors).

Fixed type flow control valve is shown as below (Refer Fig. 5.80)

In this valve a special restricted passage is created. This passage is called throttle or flow restrictor passage (It is similar to throat of venturimeter). Suppose if 3 lit./min. compressed air comes into the valve, due to restricted passage entire 3 litres will not go out. Quantity less than 3 lit./min. will go out and hence flow will be controlled.

This type of flow control valve is very rarely used; or used on very selective basis because, we cannot vary the outgoing flow (outflow is fixed).

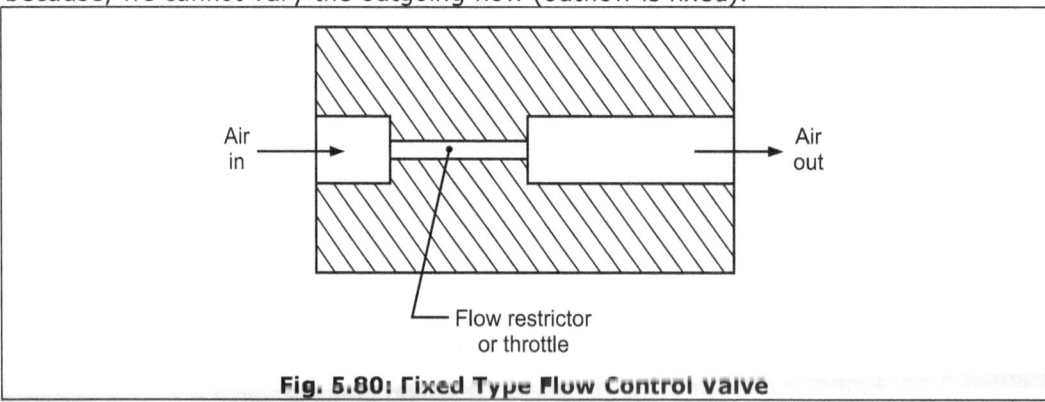

Fig. 5.80: Fixed Type Flow Control Valve

The symbol of fixed type flow control valve is as shown in Fig. 5.81.

Fig. 5.81

5.5.8 Variable Flow Control Valve with Built-in Check Valve

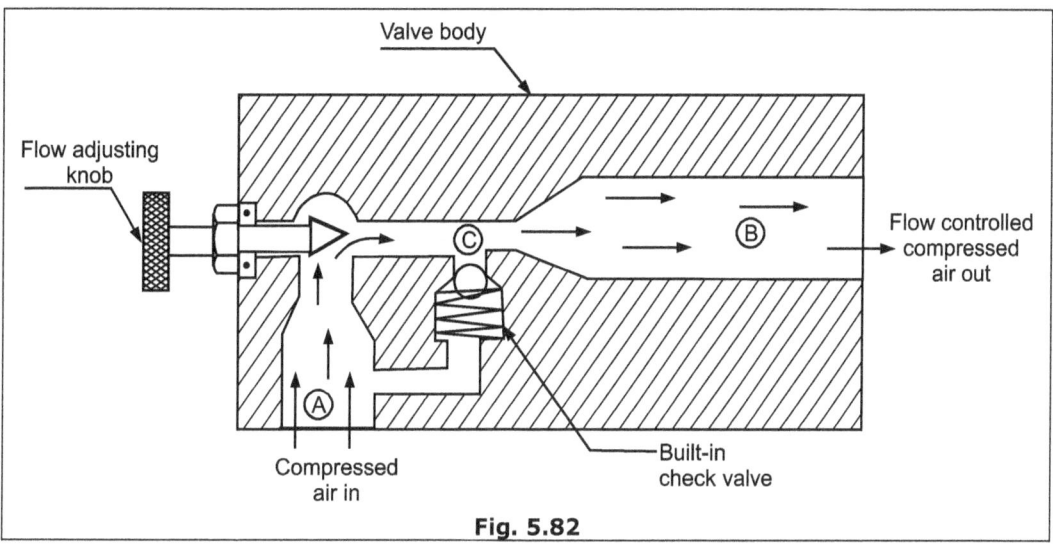

Fig. 5.82

The internal construction of valve is shown in Fig. 5.82. A built-in check valve (also called non-return valve or unidirectional valve) is incorporated in this valve.

Working: It is clear from the figure that, air comes in through port (A) and goes out through port (B). The flow can be reduced or increased by rotating 'Flow Adjusting Knob', in clockwise or anticlockwise direction.

- **Function of Built-in check valve:**

Air going out from port (B) which is connected to consumer. If due to some chocking/jamming, the consumer has stopped working; then air will not flow further and back pressure starts building. Now air starts accumulating and flow will try to reverse i.e. from port (B) to (A). But there is continuous supply of air from (A) to (B). That means, air flowing in reverse direction i.e. from (B) to (A) needs to be vented out. Look at port (C). Reverse air will act on ball and will push down the ball by compressing the spring. Due to this, the reverse flow air will flow from (C) to (A) and back pressure will be subsided.

- **Why check valve is called unidirectional valve?**

When air flows from (A) to (B), some air will try to flow towards port (C). But this air will push the ball in upward direction, thereby locking the port (C). In addition to this the spring force will also keep the port (C) locked. Hence there cannot be flow from (A) to (C). The flow is possible only from (C) to (A). Hence this valve is actually a safety valve because it vents out back pressure (If this back pressure increases beyond certain limits there is a possibility of damaging the consumer/pipelines/valves). i.e. flow from (C) to (A). And because flow cannot be possible from (A) to (C), it is called unidirectional valve.

Symbol of variable flow control valve with built-in check valve

The symbol is slightly modified by addition of an arrow to the symbol of fixed type flow control valve. Arrow represents its variable flow. The symbol of built-in check valve is similar to its construction.

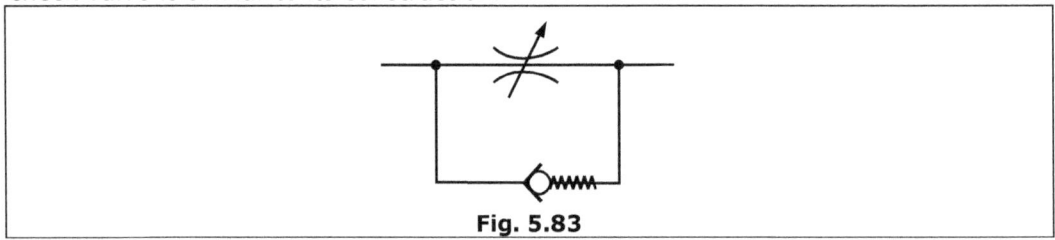

Fig. 5.83

Now let us study, the application of 'Variable flow control valve with built-in check valve'.

Let us use this valve for controlling the forwarding speed of piston of Single Acting Cylinder (SA Cylinder).

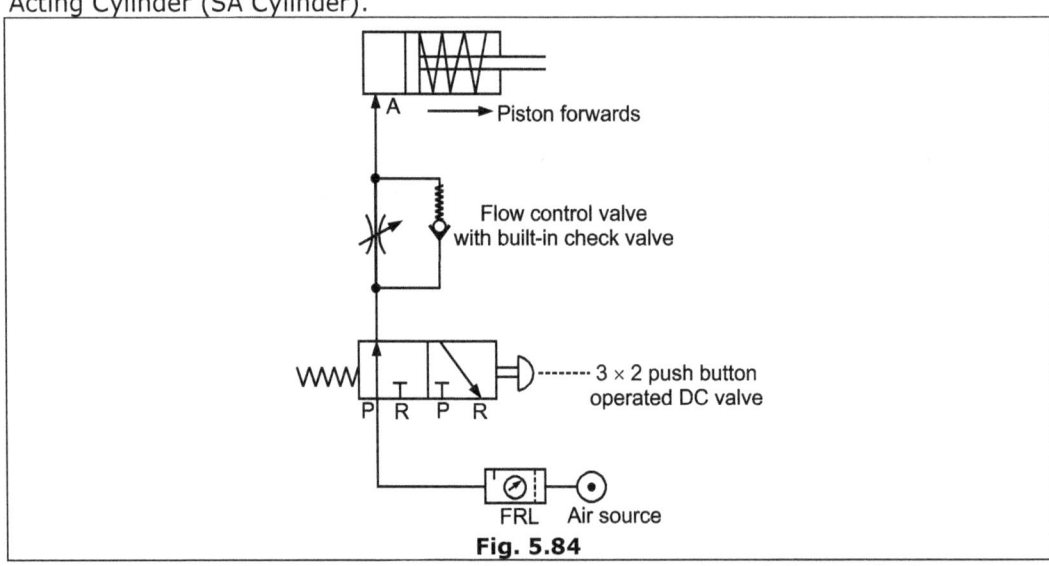

Fig. 5.84

SA cylinder is shown in Fig. 5.84. The piston moves from left to right because air is being admitted through port A. (This is forward stroke). The linear speed of piston can be controlled by flow control valve. When push button of DC valve is operated, port A will be connected to port R. Port P will be disconnected and piston will move from right to left due to expansion of spring. If suppose spring does not expand due to failure of spring, then air will be accumulated in cylinder and piston will remain on right side. Here, the check valve will operate automatically and excess air in cylinder will be by-passed through check valve to avoid damage of SA cylinder.

5.5.9 Directly Operated Check Valve

As we have seen that, check valve is a 'safety valve' because it allows the flow in one direction. This valve can be best compared with safety valve of domestic pressure cooker.

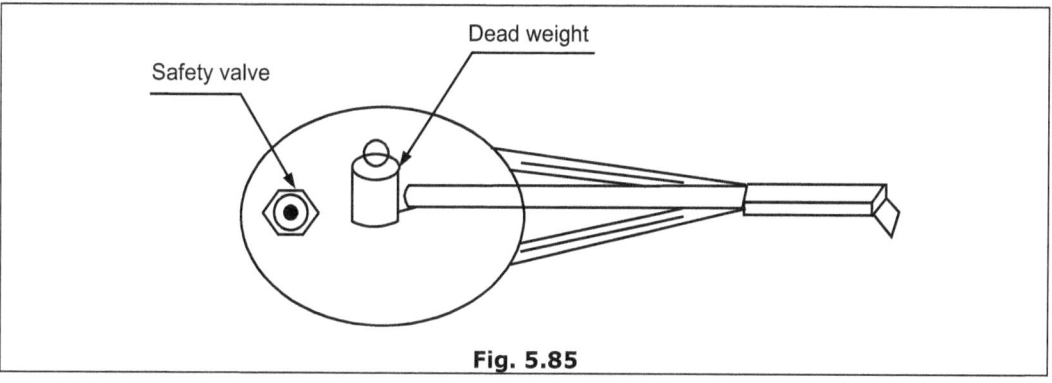

Fig. 5.85

We know that, steam formed inside the cooker pot, comes out from the opening below dead weight. If this opening is chocked, then steam starts accumulating in pot. After sometime steam superheats. Temperature increases tremendously. Then the special material below safety valve gets melted and hole is created at the centre of safety valve. Through this hole steam vents out. This safety valve is also called as fusible plug. Because it fuses (melts) at particular temperature.

Except melting, the work of check valve is to protect the pneumatic systems and circuits by blowing or by passing the extra air.

Fig. 5.86 shows construction of Directly Operated (Poppet type) check valve:

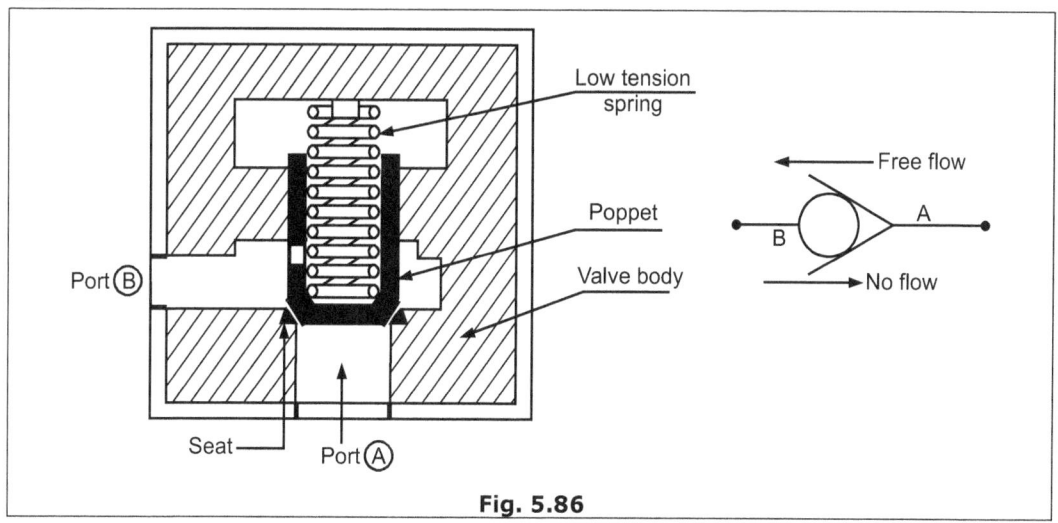

Fig. 5.86

In this valve there are 2 ports i.e. port (A) and port (B). A moving poppet is installed above port (A) with low tension spring. Poppet is rested on seat.

Working: When air pressure at port (A) starts increasing beyond rated limit then the force of air will move the poppet upward, thereby compressing the spring. When poppet moves up, air starts flowing from port (A) and port (B). Flow from port (B) to (A) is not at all possible. When air pressure at port (A) normalizes, the spring will expand and poppet will regain its original position.

5.5.10 Pilot Operated (Poppet type) Check Valve

- Pilot operated means, as we have seen, the air pressure (called air signal) is utilized in this valve for special operation.
- Directly operated check valve, cannot be continuously kept open i.e. it acts as a safety valve. But if we want continues supply of air from port (A) to (B) for some particular period of time, then we have to modify this directly operated check valve in following manner.

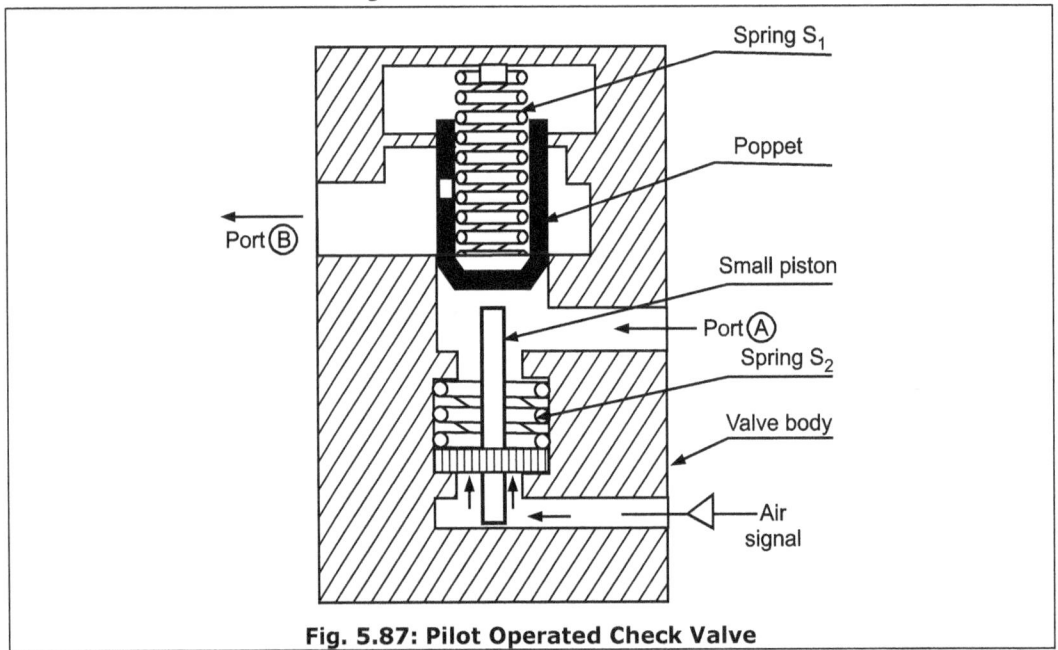

Fig. 5.87: Pilot Operated Check Valve

In the modified version of directly operated check valve, a small piston is introduced below moving poppet. (As we can see that, upper part of the valve shown in Fig. 5.87 is same as that of directly operated check valve.) This piston can move up by pressurised air signal.

Working: When air signal is operated, pressurised air will be admitted and small piston will move upward by compressing spring S_2. Piston rod of piston will in turn push the poppet upward by compressing spring S_1. And air flow from (A) to (B) will start. Unless and until we supply air signal to small piston, there will be air flow from (A) to (B). When air signal is cut off, springs S_1 and S_2 will expand and poppet and small piston will regain its original position.

It may be noted that, there cannot be air flow from (B) to (A).

Symbol of pilot operated check valve

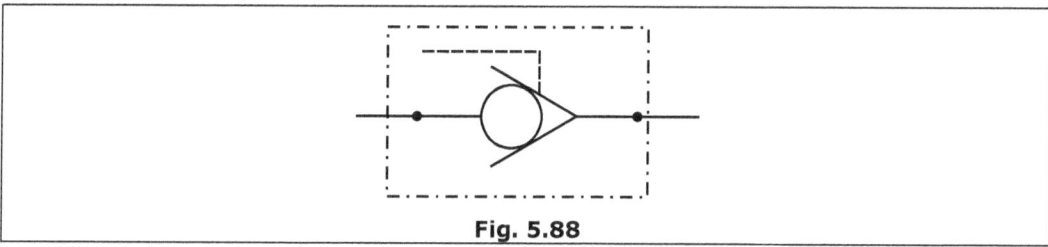

Fig. 5.88

Important:

While drawing this symbol in pneumatic circuit we must draw the outside rectangle drawn with the help of centre line (— • — • —).

5.5.11 Double Check Valve (Shuttle Valve) (Or Gate)

This valve is popularly known as Shuttle valve. (Name shuttle is used because, the valve element used in this valve is a ball and it moves in a valve in the same manner as that of Badminton shuttle). This valve is also known as **OR GATE**, because, it allows the air to flow from two alternative sources. Following figure shows construction of Double check valve (shuttle valve) (OR GATE):

Construction: In the valve body there are 3 ports. A is consumer port i.e. connected to actuator. x and y are air supply ports. The valve element is free to move in the valve.

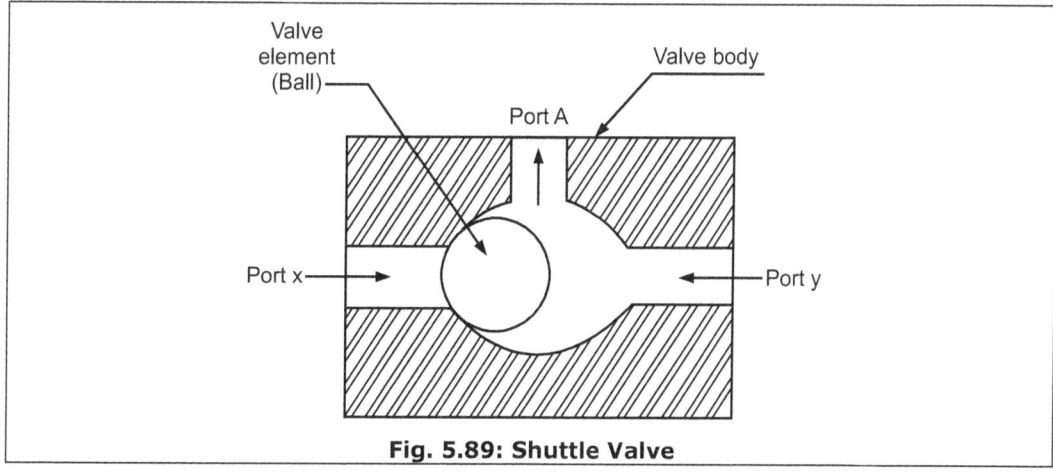

Fig. 5.89: Shuttle Valve

Working: When air is supplied through port y, the ball will move towards left and will block port x. When air will be supplied through port x, the ball will move towards right and will block the port y; and air will flow from port x to port A. Thus, port A will receive air either from port x OR from port y. Hence it is called OR Gate.

Symbol of Double Check Valve (Shuttle Valve)

The symbol is designed on the basis of the construction of valve itself.

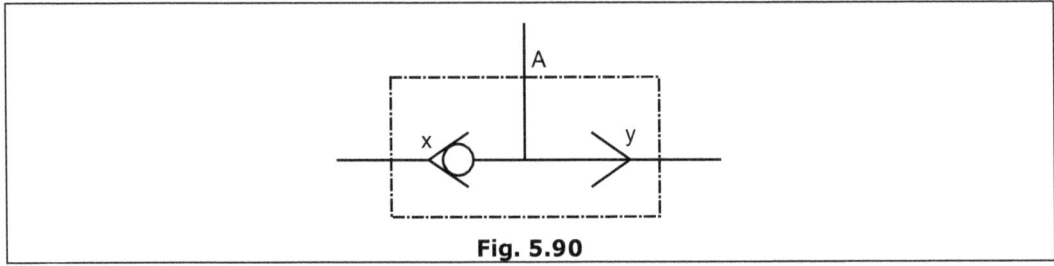

Fig. 5.90

Application of Double Check Valve

The double check valve is used to actuate Single Acting Cylinder.

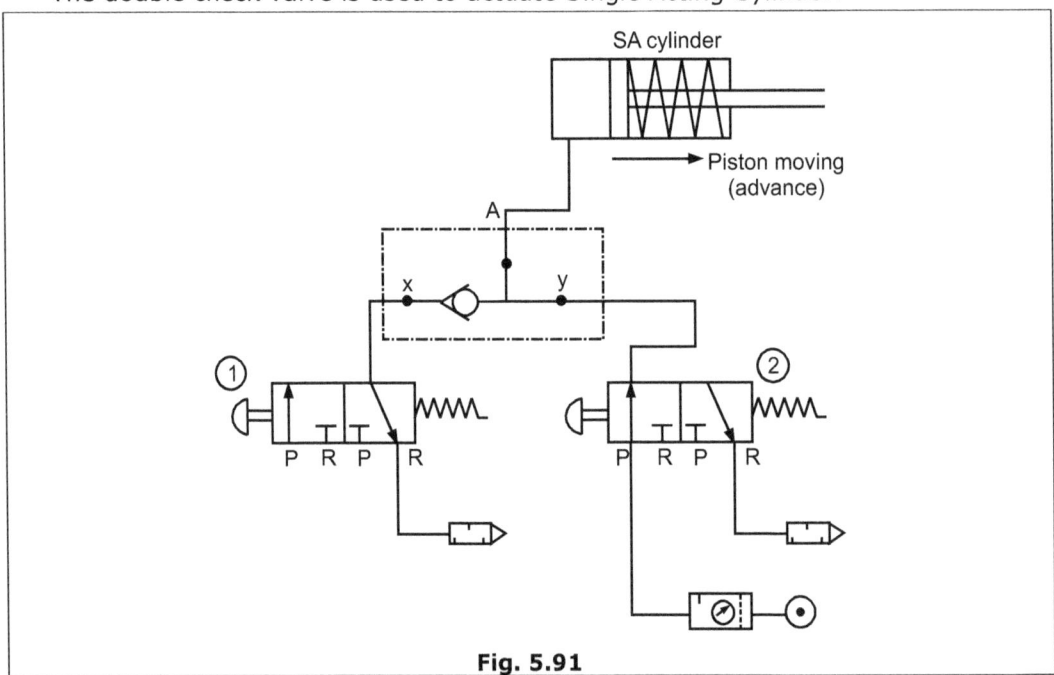

Fig. 5.91

The typical circuit shows SA cylinder, the movement of which is possible through 2 sources. The circuit uses two DC valves. At present, valve (2) is in operation. The air is supplied to SA cylinder through port y and naturally port x is blocked. When piston moves from left to right (Advance of piston), it will return to its original position due to expansion of spring. And then valve (1) is operated; so that air will be supplied through port x.

5.5.12 Pressure Control Valves

Refer Fig. 5.92.

- Here, the air travels from air receiver to consumer or load. The distance of pipe is long. Generally the air compressor is fitted outside the factory shed to avoid its Noise. During the flow of air from receiver to load, there are considerable leakages which reduces the pressure.

- It is called a 'pressure drop'. Hence, therefore, air pressure in the receiver is kept at higher level than the required by consumer or load.

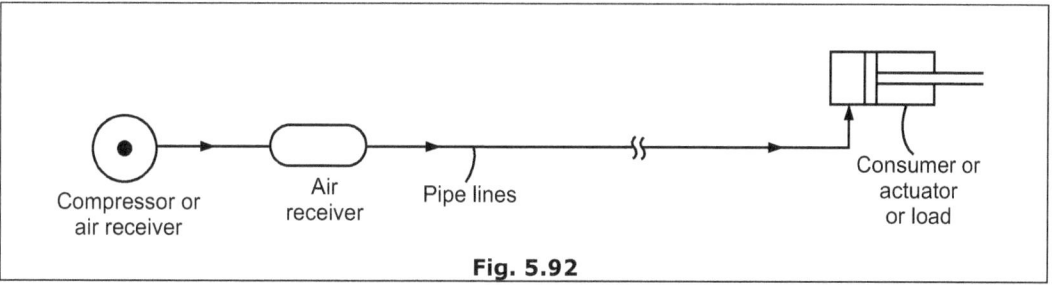

Fig. 5.92

- Suppose the pressure of air in receiver is say 8 Bar and consumer or load requires say 5 Bar then we have to reduce the pressure near that load. Here we need pressure control valve.

- Sometimes due to blockage of load, the air starts accumulating in system, which may lead to damage of system. Here to protect the system we need pressure relief valve. This valve relieves the accumulated dangerous air to atmosphere.

Important: Pressure control valve is actually a pressure reducing valve.

Now, we will see various valves which take part in pressure control.

5.5.13 Pressure Relief Valve

This valve is infact not a pressure control valve, but it is actually a safety valve. It operates when main pressure control system fails. It is a sort of stand-by arrangement.

Construction: There is threaded joint between cap and body. By rotating the cap we can adjust the tension of spring. There are two (or one) exhaust ports and one inlet port.

Working: The valve element is held closed by spring tension, according to required relief pressure. So normally there is no flow from inlet port to exhaust port.

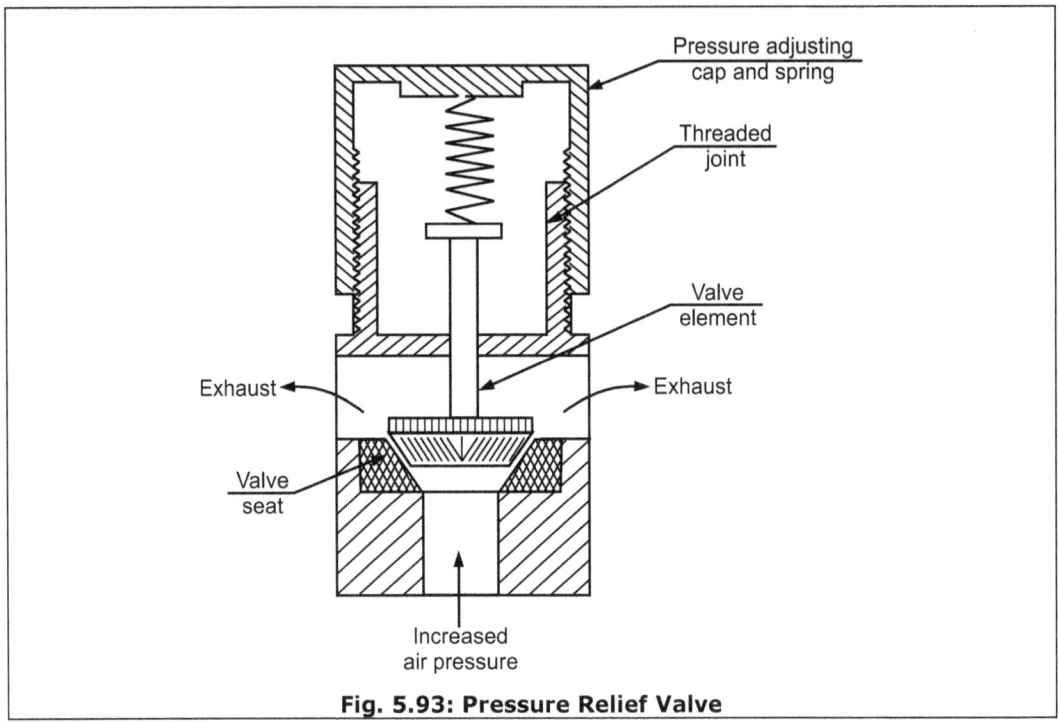

Fig. 5.93: Pressure Relief Valve

Important: Note that pressure relief valve is normally closed. When due to failure of main pressure control system, the air pressure starts increasing. When force due to air pressure exceeds the spring tension, the valve element lifts up and air starts flowing from inlet to exhaust. Once the inlet pressure falls below the safe pressure, the force of air reduces and spring expands the valve element will regain its original position so that the flow stops.

Location of valve: It is generally fitted near outlet of air receiver.

Symbol of Pressure Relief Valve

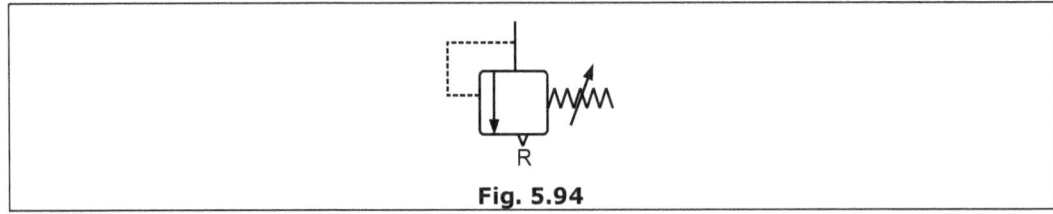

Fig. 5.94

The symbol shows exhaust port R as per construction. The arrow on spring shows that, the spring tension can be adjusted.

Pressure Regulator

Please refer Pressure Regulator in FRL unit.

5.5.14 Non-Relieving Pressure Regulator

We are aware of the fact that, pressure regulator or pressure control valve is fitted near consumer or load (SA Cyl./DA Cyl./Air Motor/Any other specially designed). We also know that, air pressure supplied to pressure regulator is of higher valve. Pressure regulator reduces this air pressure as required by consumer. To reduce the air pressure, some part of air must be vent out (exhausted to atmosphere). The venting of air is either through pressure regulator itself or through consumer.

If the regulator is designed in such a manner, that air vents through consumer only (not through regulator), then that regulator **is called Non-Relieving Pressure Regulator**.

Fig. 5.95 shows non-relieving pressure regulator.

Construction: The diaphragm is fixed in the body. Outlet pressure is preset by pressure setting spring and adjusting screw. Valve element is attached to diaphragm.

Working:

- **If outlet pressure is too low** then spring will force down the flexible diaphragm and valve element will move downward because spring force is dominating. And air starts flowing from inlet to outlet to increase the outlet pressure to required valve.

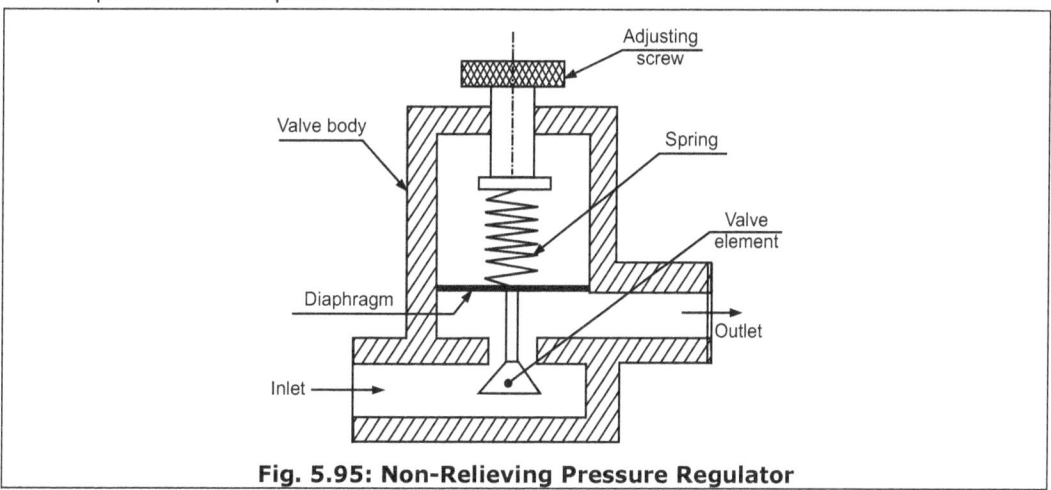

Fig. 5.95: Non-Relieving Pressure Regulator

- **If outlet pressure is too high** then this pressure forces the diaphragm in upward direction thereby reducing the air flow from inlet to outlet. Due to this reduction in flow, air vents through consumer or load.

- **If outlet pressure is regular** then the valve will balance the forces on diaphragm, and there will be continuous flow from inlet to outlet.

5.5.15 Relieving Pressure Regulator

Refer to the description given in non-relieving pressure regulator:

If the regulator is designed in such a way that, the air vents through Regulator only (Not through consumer) then that regulator is called **Relieving Pressure Regulator.**

It is similar to non-relieving pressure regulator.

Note that outlet pressure is sensed by diaphragm. The tension of diaphragm is adjusted by pressure adjusting spring.

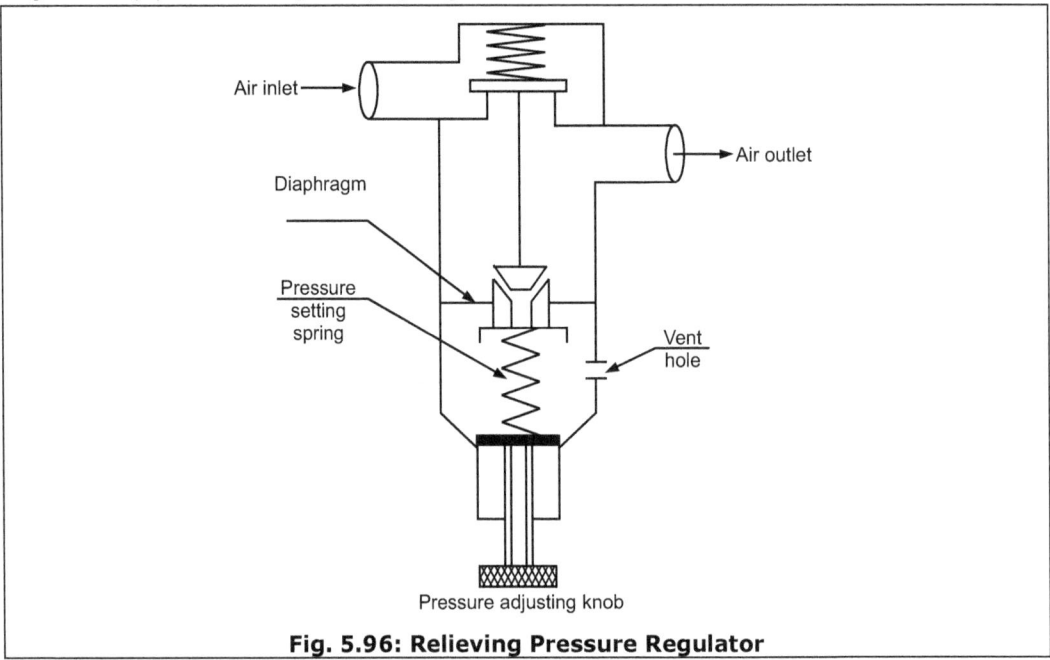

Fig. 5.96: Relieving Pressure Regulator

Working: If outlet pressure is too high, the diaphragm moves down closing the flow from the inlet to outlet.

When outlet pressure is too low, then the inlet poppet valve is pushed open admitting more air to raise the pressure.

If outlet pressure is regular then valve will balance admitting and venting small amount of air to keep load pressure at set valve.

Important: Note that vent hole is shown on valve body i.e. air is venting out through valve only and not through consumer, in Relieving Pressure Regulator.

Important Points

- **Air Motors:** These are rotary actuators and are used to generate 'ROTARY MOTION' by using force of compressed air. We can achieve the speed of 10,000 rpm with the help of Air Motors.
- **Hydraulic motor** converts Hydraulic energy (processed by pressurised oil) into Rotary Mechanical energy used in many industrial applications.
- **Symbol of Hydraulic motor** (irrespective of type of motor) is nearly similar to symbol of hydraulic pump. The only difference is that the triangles shown are in opposite direction.
- **Direction control valves:** The name of this valve itself clarifies its function. This valve is like a 'Traffic Police'. It directs the flow of pressurised as well as used oil to actuator and oil reservoir respectively.
- **Flow control valves:** Flow control valves (as we have seen) are used to regulate the flow of hydraulic oil in hydraulic circuit for controlling the 'SPEED' of actuators.
- **Diversion:** Diverting is by-passing the part of flow so that the actuator receives only the portion to perform its task.
- **Function of check valve:** The main function of check valve is to allow the flow of fluid in one direction only. Flow of fluid in reverse direction is completely blocked or restricted. Due to this function only they are also termed as 'Non- return valves'.
- **Simple check value:** This valve consists of valve body in which valve element like cone (we can use ball or special poppet) is incorporated with specifically designed spring.
- **Sequence valve:** The main function of sequence valve is to operate 2-3 operations in sequential order i.e. one after the another.
- **Pilot Operated (Poppet type) Check Valve:** Pilot operated means, the air pressure (called air signal) is utilized in this valve for special operation.
- **Double Check Valve (Shuttle Valve) (Or Gate):** This valve is popularly known as Shuttle valve. (Name shuttle is used because, the valve element used in this valve is a ball and it moves in a valve in the same manner as that of Badmington shuttle). This valve is also known as **OR GATE**, because, it allows the air to flow from two alternative sources.
- **Pressure Relief Valve:** This valve is infact not a pressure control valve, but it is actually a safety valve. It operates when main pressure control system fails. It is a sort of stand-by arrangement.
- If the regulator is designed in such a manner, that air vents through consumer only (not through regulator), then that regulator is called **Non-Relieving Pressure Regulator**.
- If the regulator is designed in such a way that, the air vents through regulator only (not through consumer) then that regulator is called **Relieving Pressure Regulator.**

Practice Questions

1. Draw symbol of:
   (a) Unidirectional variable displacement hydraulic motor.
   (b) Pressure compensated flow control valve
   (c) FRL unit
   (d) Non-return valve
2. What is Turbine Motor used in pneumatic circuits? Explain with neat sketch.
3. Differentiate between Air motor and Electric motor.
4. What is limited rotary actuator? Explain with neat sketch.
5. Differentiate between seat type and spool type DC valve.
6. What is the function of DC valve? Explain.
7. What is the function of flow control valve?
8. Draw neat sketch of needle valve and explain its working.
9. Draw labelled diagram of simple check valve?
10. Draw symbol of pilot separated check vale.
11. Write functions of pressure control valve.
12. What is the need of pilot operated pressure relief valve?
13. Draw symbol of sequence valve.
14. Draw constructional details of 3 × 2 spool type DC valve used in pneumatic circuit and explain its working.
15. Draw neat sketch of variable flow control valve with built-in check valve.
16. What is shuttle valve? What is its other name? Explain.
17. How pressure is regulated in pneumatic circuits?

■■■

Chapter 6

ACCESSORIES OF HYDRAULIC AND PNEUMATIC SYSTEMS

Weightage of Marks = 12, Teaching Hours = 06

Learning Objectives

- Understand Function of Filters, Hoses and Gaskets.
- Know use of Gaskets and Filters for Specific Applications.

Contents

- Filters
  - Hydraulic Filters and Strainers – Full Flow and Proportional Types, Function and Working, Difference Between Filters and Strainers.
  - Pneumatic Filters – Screen type and Mechanical type, Function and Working, FRL Unit.
- Hoses and Connectors for Hydraulic and Pneumatic Systems - Types, Construction and Applications.
- Seals and Gaskets for Hydraulic and Pneumatic Systems - Types, Function, Construction, Commonly used Seals and Gasket Materials.

6.1 OIL FILTERS

- An absolutely clean fluid is essential for reliable operation of hydraulic system.
- Now sophisticated machines like CNC/VMC machines use high pressure oil which demands very very clean oil.
- To clean the oil is a main function of oil filters. Filters are cleaning stations used to arrest the unwanted materials/particles.
- **The hydraulic oil is having following general contaminants:**
  (a) Particles (micron size – metallic/fibrous/dirt)
  (b) Water
  (c) Chemical reaction products such as sludge
  (d) Rubber chips or particles of seals/hoses carried by flowing oil.
  (e) Other fluids.

6.1.1 Effect of Contaminants [S-15]

Hydraulic systems are adversely affected by contamination. If we does not use filters, then all these contaminants will flow everywhere with oil, and will block or jam the moving parts. This jamming may result in damaging the entire system. Even dirt particles of 20 µ (1 µ = 1 micron = one millionth of meter) size can arrest or stop the entire hydraulic system.

- Filters can be classified as:

    (a) Full flow filters

    (b) Proportional flow filters

6.1.2 Full Flow Filters [S-15]

As shown in Fig. 6.1 oil comes in through port (A), passes through filter element and goes out through port (B). In this filter, all flow passes through filter, hence is called full flow filter.

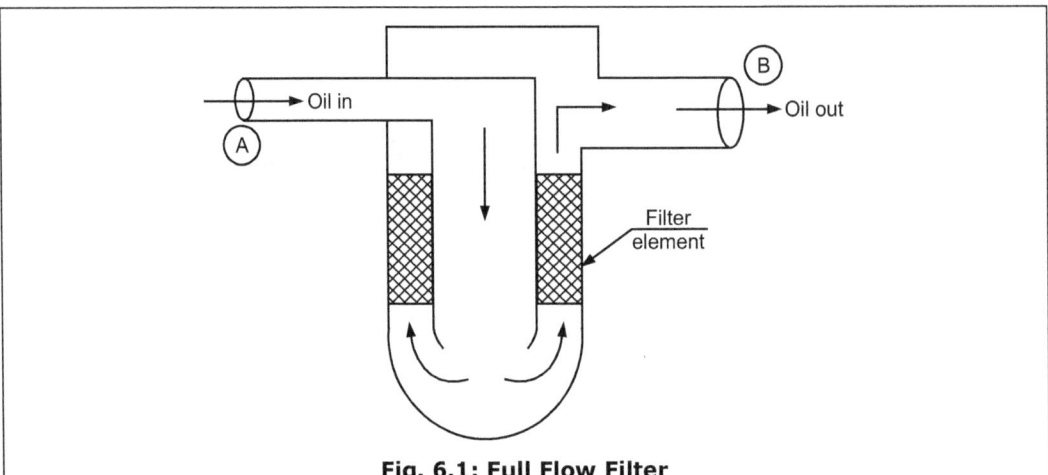

Fig. 6.1: Full Flow Filter

This is very efficient filter but the only drawback of this filter is there is a large pressure drop. When filter element of the filter is packed with arrested particle then the pressure drop still increases.

6.1.3 Proportional Flow Filters [W-14, S-15]

In this type main oil flow passes through venturi, which creates localized low pressure area inside the filter element. We can see that on outside of filter element there is high pressure oil.

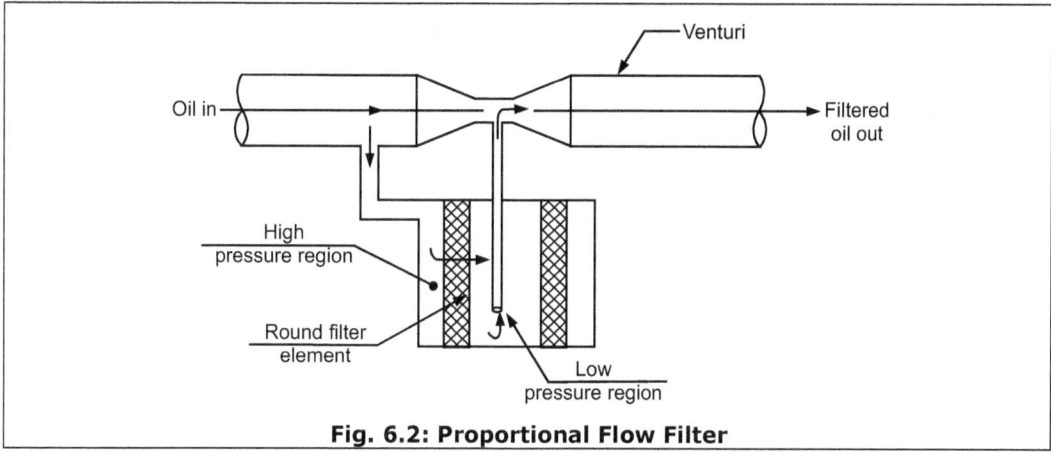

Fig. 6.2: Proportional Flow Filter

Due to pressure difference created across filter element 'proportionate' quantity of oil passes through filter element. In this filter the pressure drop across the filter is very low. Hence is having wide applications.

- **Filtration materials:** Filter material is wire mesh/screen or paper, cotton, cellulose. Following is the list of filtration materials or filter media used in hydraulic oil filters.

    (a) Felt

    (b) Paper

    (c) Fabric

    (d) Wire mesh

    (e) Wire cloth

    (f) Glass fibre

    (g) Paper disc

    (h) Phenolic resin

    (i) Sintered woven wire

    (j) Sintered PTFE

    (k) Membrane filter

    (*l*) Magnetic filter cloth

- **Symbol of filter:** The symbol of filter is as shown below:

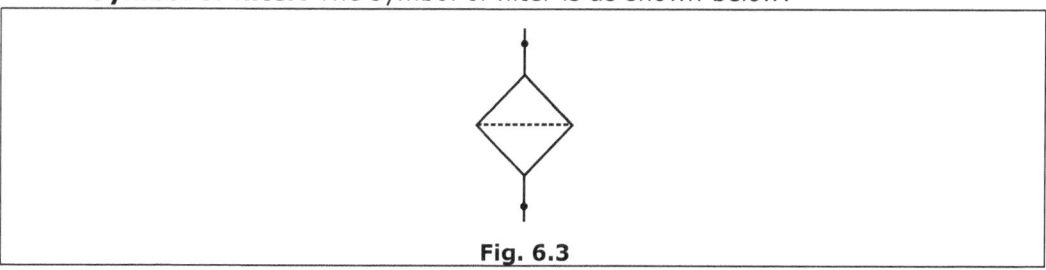

Fig. 6.3

- **Location of filter:** Filter can be located at 3 suitable locations in Hydraulic circuit.

    (a) Return line filter

    (b) Suction line filter

    (c) Pressure line filter

6.1.4 Return Line Filter

This is common location of filter. As you can see that oil is supplying to motor through port (A), motor is rotating. The oil is returning through port (B) via DC valve through filter F_1. The oil is collected in oil tank.

The major disadvantage of this location is that, contaminants are removed only after leaving the system.

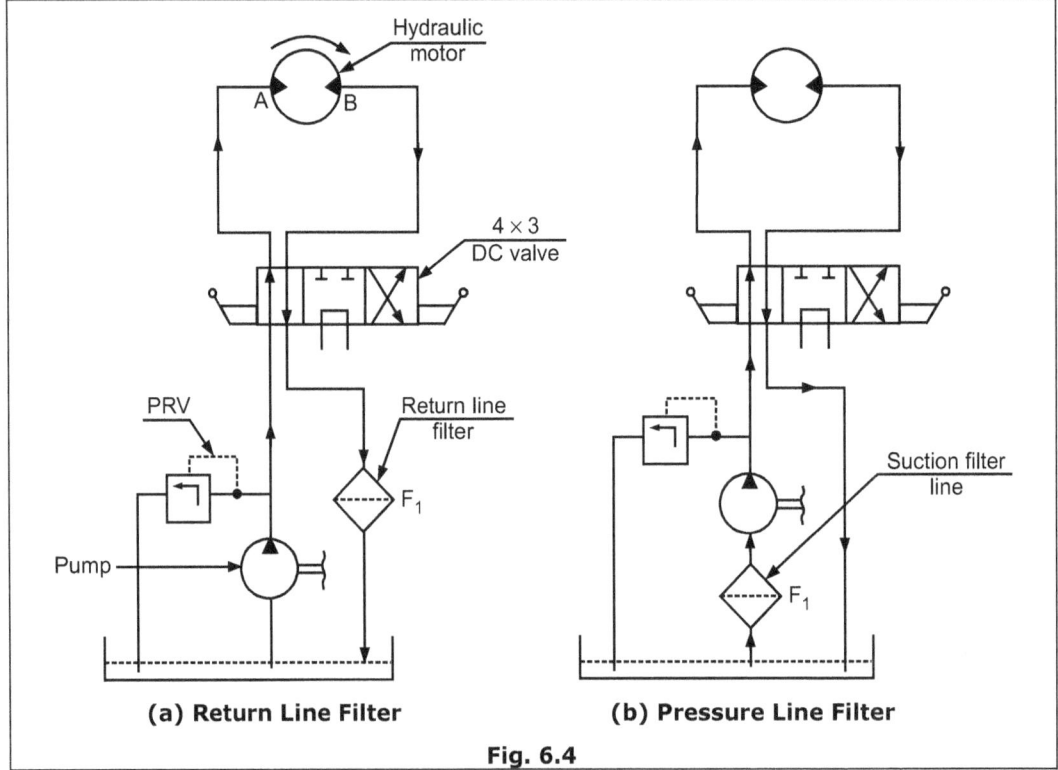

(a) Return Line Filter   (b) Pressure Line Filter

Fig. 6.4

6.1.5 Suction Line Filter

Now, in this location we have fixed the filter on suction line of pump. Hence oil will be filtered before entering into pump. This prevents random entry of large and other contaminants.

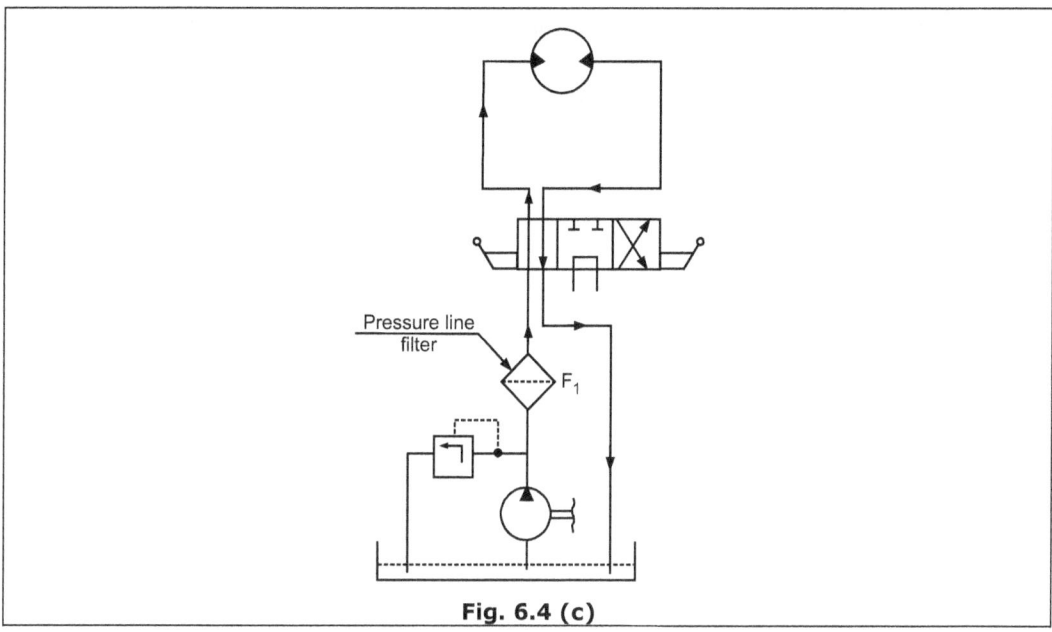

Fig. 6.4 (c)

6.1.6 Pressure Line Filter

In this arrangement, the filter is located after pump or on delivery side of pump. Full pressure is created by pump and this oil is entering into filter. This arrangement prevents entry of contaminants generated in the pump into components like valves, actuators etc. Since filter is subjected to high pressure oil, its construction must be robust.

Oil needs filtration, on the same line air in pneumatic circuits requires conditioning. FRL unit used in pneumatic circuit plays major role in conditioning of air.

6.1.7 FRL Unit [W-14, S-15]

    F – Filter

    R – Regulator

    L – Lubricator

These three units are called service unit or FRL unit. These three units are in bunch and are installed on pneumatic pipe lines. Compressed air passes through these three units one-by-one.

- First air enters into 'F' i.e. Filter. In this unit air gets filtered. The micron and submicron (very very small like dust particles) particles are arrested in filter and air gets cleaned.

- Filtered compressed air then enters into 'Regulator'. This unit regulates the pressure of air required by pneumatic mechanism or circuit. Suppose the pressure of compressed air is say 8 bar. The circuit demands 3 bar pressure. Then regulator is used to reduce the pressure from 8 bar to 3 bar. Regulator is a pressure reducing valve.
- The regulated pressure air then enters into 'Lubricator'. In lubricator a thin film of oil or very fine oil droplets are mixed with air. The oil particles are then carried with air to pneumatic circuits and lubricates the components of circuits (Actuators, valves etc.) for smooth running and to increase the life of components.

Symbols of Filter / Regulator / Lubricator and their Composite Symbol

(a) Symbol of Filter:

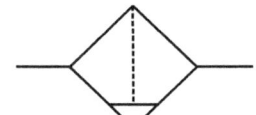

(b) Symbol of Regulator:

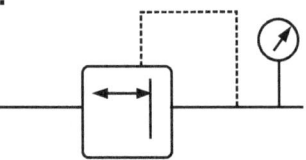

(c) Symbol of Lubricator:

(d) Combination of FRL:

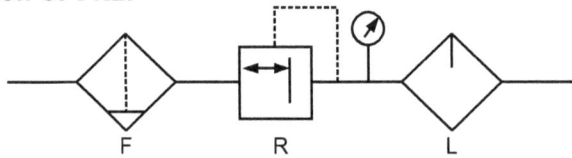

(e) Composite symbol used in Pneumatic Circuit

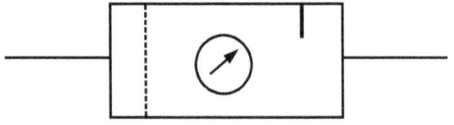

From above symbols you can easily make out that one line or figure from each unit is taken to form composite symbol. Dotted line on left is taken from symbol of filter. Pressure gauge symbol at centre is taken from regulator and small vertical line on right is taken from symbol of lubricator. Three boxes are combined in Rectangle.

Now let us see the construction and working of filter/regulator/lubricator.

6.1.8 Air Filter

The construction of simple air filter is depicted in following schematic diagram.

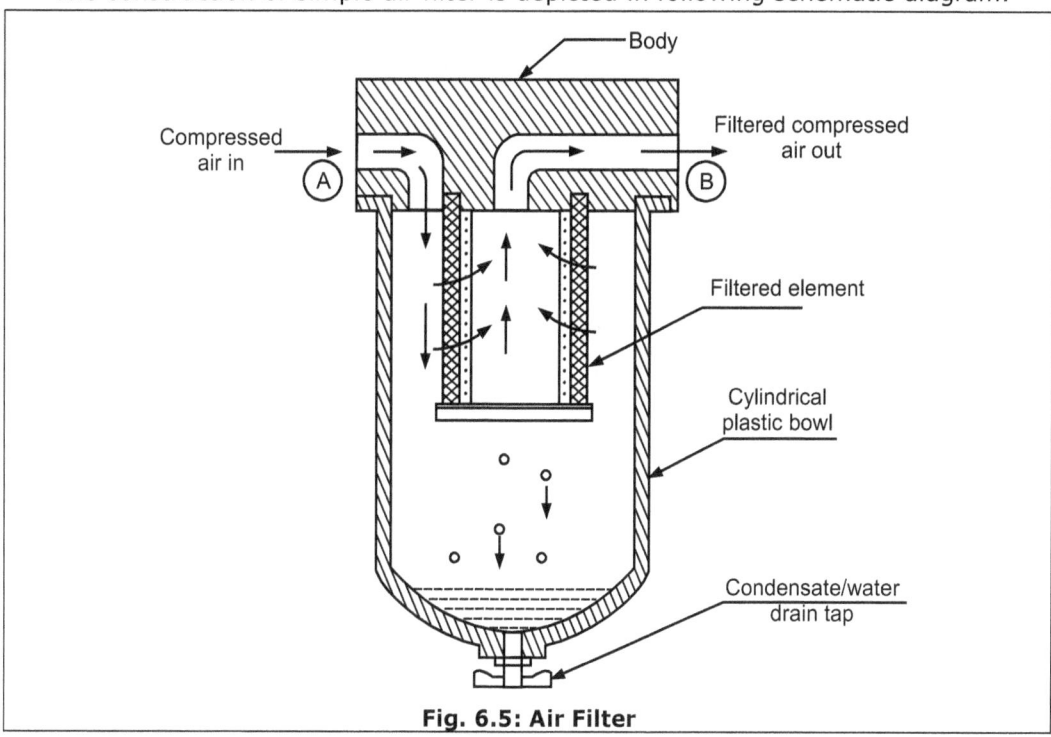

Fig. 6.5: Air Filter

Construction: Air filter consists of plastic bowl, attached to body of filter. The filter element called 'cartridge' is also attached to body at the centre. Both cartridge and bowl can be removed as and when required and can be reattached. There is water tap to remove collected condensate (water) at the bottom of bowl. The air inlet and outlet are created in body of filter.

Working: The compressed air which is unfiltered enters through port (A) and comes into bowl. It has no alternative than to enter into filtering element. The special zig-zag passages created in filtering element, arrest, the micron and sub-micron particles and clean air go out through port (B).

Filter element: It is sintered (powder metallurgy process) cylinder and uses metal-wool as a filtering material.

The filter also acts as water trap. When air enters into filter bowl through port (A), it suddenly changes its direction. During this movement the moisture particles present in air drop down due to inertia (moisture particles are heavy and they cannot change the direction with air). The moisture is collected at bottom of bowl.

6.1.9 Pressure Regulator

The construction of simple regulator is depicted in following diagram.

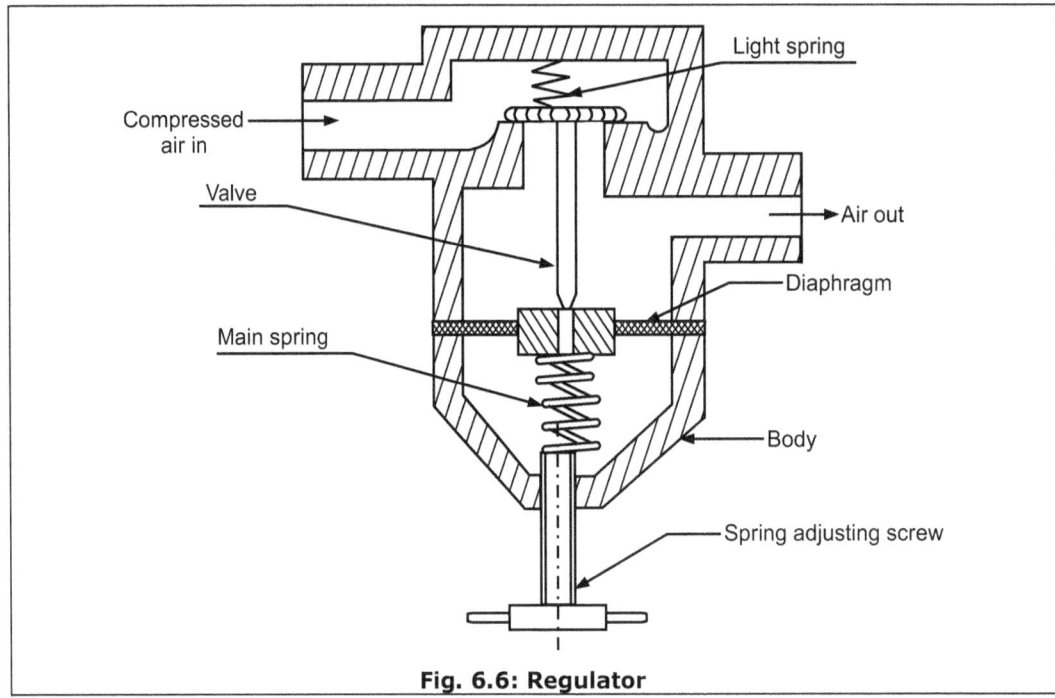

Fig. 6.6: Regulator

Construction: The metallic body of a regulator has 'inlet' and 'outlet' port. There are two springs one is light spring and other is main spring. The main spring can be compressed by spring adjusting screw. The diaphragm is attached to main spring.

Working: The compressed air coming in the regulator is having high pressure. We have to reduce it as per the requirement of circuit. When main spring is compressed by moving spring adjusting screw upward, the diaphragm will move upward. This upward movement of diaphragm will lift the valve element upward, creating an opening to allow the air flow from inlet to outlet.

The opening of the value and thereby the pressure of air flowing through it, will be directly proportional to compression of main spring. When the spring compression is less then amount of opening will be small pressure reduction will be more. Hence Regulator is actually a pressure reducing valve.

6.1.10 Lubricator [S-15]

The construction and working principle of lubricator is depicted in following diagram.

First we will see the working principle of lubricator:

As we know, the lubricator is a device which mixes mist or fine spray of lubricating oil into compressed air. This air with oil particles, enters into pneumatic equipments and oil particles lubricate the sliding/rotating parts/pairs of equipment. This arrangement enhances the life of equipment. Hence lubricator is 'must'.

How to obtain fine spray or automised spray of lubricant oil?

This spray is obtained by 'Venturi Effect'. The details of this effect is given below.

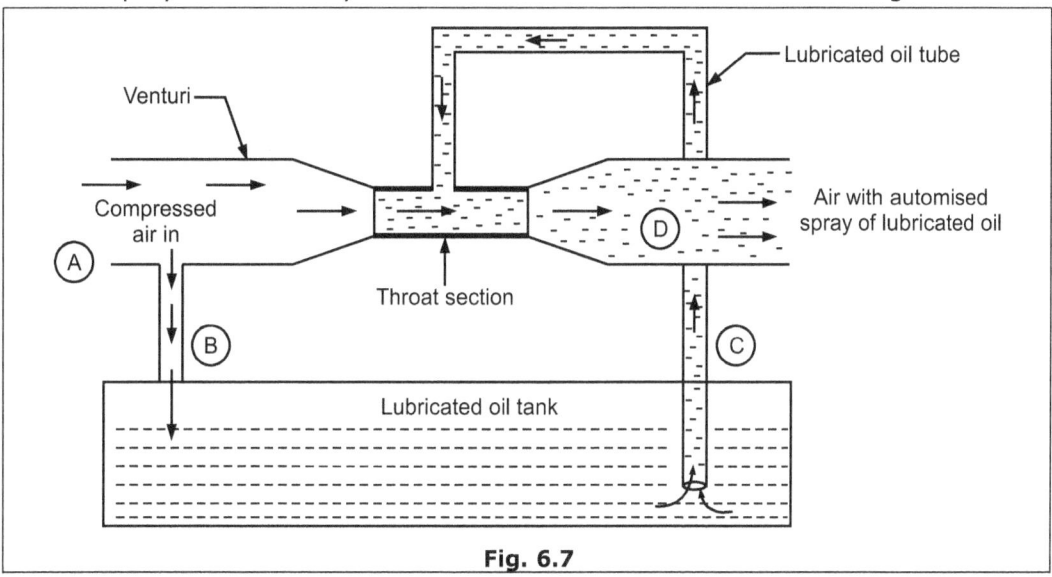

Fig. 6.7

The arrangement shows only principle of working of lubricator (The actual lubricator is having different shape). When compressed air enters through port (A), part of it goes through tube (B) and exerts pressure on surface of oil. When compressed air passes through throat section, the air pressure drops and lubricant oil from pipe (C) rushes to throat section in the form of spray. Air goes further, crosses throat section and enters into venturi portion (D). The pressure again builts up due to diverging portion and air + oil droplets go out.

Actual Construction of Lubricator

Fig. 6.8 shows actual construction of lubricator based on above discussed principle of venturi effect.

Construction: It is having transparent plastic bowl, through which we can see the level of lubricating oil. Venturi is located in the body of lubricator. There are two ports in body, one for dry 'Air in' and other for lubricated 'Air out'. Oil pickup tube is immersed in lubricant oil.

Working: Dry air comes in with pressure. The vacuum is created at the throat section. The lubricating oil rushes to throat section through oil pickup tube and fine droplets of lubricant oil mixed with dry air. Air plus oil goes out to circuit.

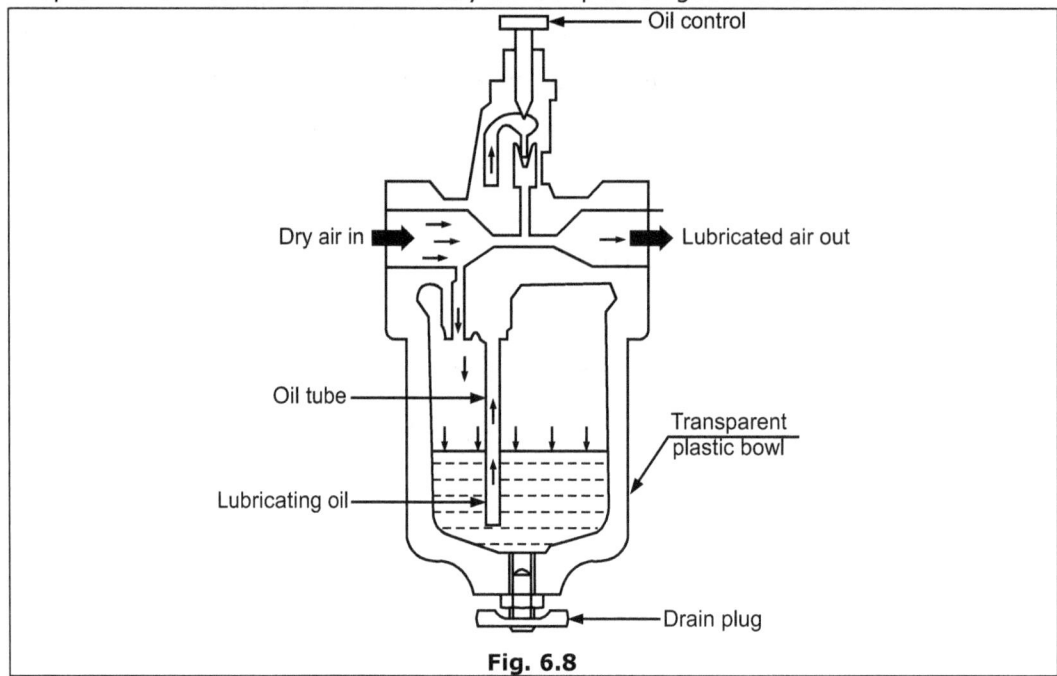

Fig. 6.8

Actual FRL unit: FRL unit is like 3 'closed friends'. They stand 'Hand in Hand' in every pneumatic circuits. Following is the view of FRL units; actually used in circuit.

6.2 HOSES AND CONNECTORS

6.2.1 Pipes/Tubes

Basically, there are three types of pipes / tubes used in Hydraulic Systems.
(i) Rigid pipes
(ii) Semi-rigid pipes
(iii) Flexible pipes

- Whether to select Rigid/Semi-Rigid/Flexible pipes depends on:
    (a) Pressure oil it will carry
    (b) Mechanical strength of pipe
    (c) Type of fluid it will carry
    (d) The location of system
    - Rigid pipe : Steel Seamless (Jointless) Pipes
    - Semi-Rigid : Tubes (Copper/Aluminium/Steel)
    - Flexible : Nylon/Plastic/PVC

Materials for Pipes:

(i) Steel: This material is most widely used pipe material in Hydraulic circuit. These are seamless pipes/tubes.

Tubes/Pipes are of Annealed Quantity (Annealing is a heat treatment in which components are heated and cooled slowly). Mild steels or Soft Ductile Carbon Steel (Ductility: Ability of material to drawn into wires).

Stainless steel is also used for pipe/tube material but is very costly. But are exclusively used in Aircraft/Marine fluid lines where pipes are exposed to varied atmosphere.

(ii) Copper: As we know copper is highly resistant to corrosion, so it can be also easily drawn into pipes/tubes. Copper tends to harden in high temperature. Hence used in medium pressures and low bore sizes. Some oils react with copper which limits the use of copper tubes. In old days, hydraulic break systems of automobiles, copper tubes were used.

(iii) Aluminium: It is also highly resistant to corrosion and similar to copper, can be easily drawn into tubes. The additional 'profitable' property of aluminum is its light weight. Hence obviously these pipes are used in Hydraulic Systems used in AirCraft. But similar to copper these pipes are costlier.

(iv) Zinc Coated Galvanised Pipes: These pipes are similar to Household plumbing GI pipes. These are preferred for low pressure oil conducting.

Size of Pipe: The pipes are specified in terms of its internal diameter (ID). Now, we will look into actual specification. The Outside Diameter (OD) of pipe is fixed. The ID varies with its type. There are three types:

(a) Standard (Schedule 40)

(b) Extra Strong (Schedule 80)

(c) Double Extra Strong (Schedule 160)

Let us take example of size $1\frac{1}{2}''$ pipe:

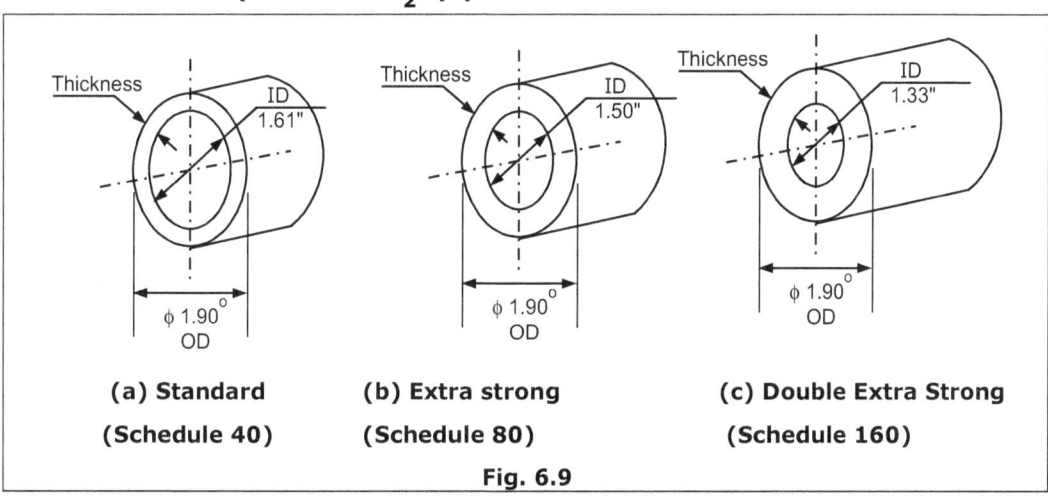

(a) Standard (Schedule 40)   (b) Extra strong (Schedule 80)   (c) Double Extra Strong (Schedule 160)

Fig. 6.9

We can easily understand that:

- Pipe having size $1\frac{1}{2}"$ will be having OD = 1.9" and the ID goes on decreasing as we go for stronger pipe. Thickness increases means ID reduces. Following are the sizes of different pipes.

(All dimensions are in inch)

Size of pipe	OD	ID Std.	ID Extra strong	ID Double Extra
$\frac{1}{2}"$	0.84	0.62	0.45	0.46
$\frac{3}{4}"$	1.05	0.82	0.74	0.61
1"	1.31	1.05	0.95	0.81
$1\frac{1}{2}"$	1.90	1.61	1.50	1.33

6.2.2 Hoses [W-14, S-15]

In many hydraulic systems, the drive units are assemblies needed to move alongwith pipelines. In such cases, flexible pipes called 'Hoses' are used.

General Construction of Hydraulic Hose

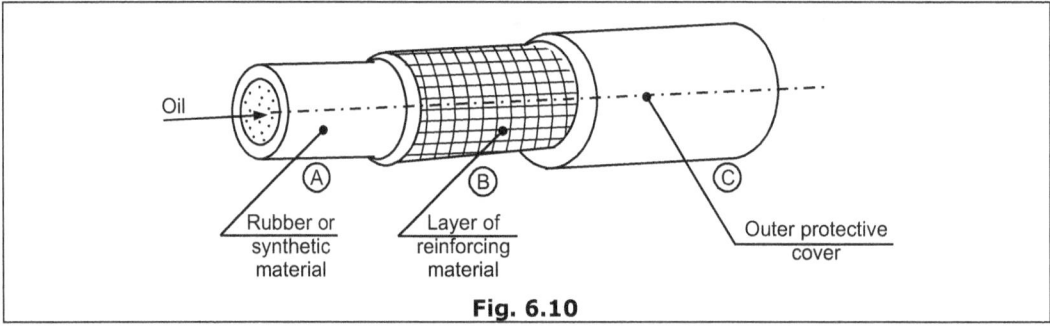

Fig. 6.10

Hydraulic hose is a compound flexible pipe having 3 layers:

Layer A: This is inner tube through which fluid/oil flows. Hence this layer comes in direct contact with pressurised hydraulic fluid. This layer is called 'Hose Material' layer. Following are the various materials used for this layer:

(a) Plastic

(b) Nylon

(c) Braided Nylon

(d) PVC

(e) Teflon

(f) Synthetic Elastomers

(g) Compounded Rubber/Natural Rubber

Layer B: This layer is called 'Hose Reinforcement'. This is middle layer and it increases strength of inner layer. This layer provides structural strength to entire hose to withstand against hydraulic pressures of oil which is very high in Hydraulic System. This layer (Polylayer) is made up of following materials:

(a) Cotton

(b) Nylon

(c) Steel wires

(d) Synthetic Yarn

(e) Rayon

Layer C: This layer is outer layer and is called protective cover. The middle layer i.e. Reinforcement layer is protected from corrosion, abrasion and other damages which can occur during accidents. Following materials are used for this layer:

(a) Neoprene

(b) Synthetic GRS rubber

(c) Cotton / Synthetic yarn.

- **Protective covers:** Many times Nylon sleeves, or plastic coil sleeves, steel coil etc. are also used over the hose. (Similar to protective plastic cover over domestic gas rubber pipe).
- **Colour of Hose:** The outer layer colour of hose is either Black or Red. Generally Black colour is preferred.

Advantages of Rubber Hose:

Generally rubber hoses are preferred all over the world. Rubber hose means layer (A) i.e. inner layer is of Rubber. Following are the advantages of Rubber Hose:

(i) Rubber hoses can be well equipped with quick connect – disconnect end fittings.

(ii) Can be manufactured in long lengths.

(iii) Capable of withstanding to very high pressures.

(iv) They can absorb very heavy shocks than rigid tubes.

Disadvantages:

(i) Very poor in abrasion resistance.

(ii) Poor in resisting whether condition.

(iii) Initial cost is very high.

(iv) They can damage due to incompatible oil.

6.2.3 End Fittings or Coupling End of Hoses (Connectors)

The end fitting or coupling end is that part attached to hose and other end is connected to the component of Hydraulic Circuit. Following are some end fittings:

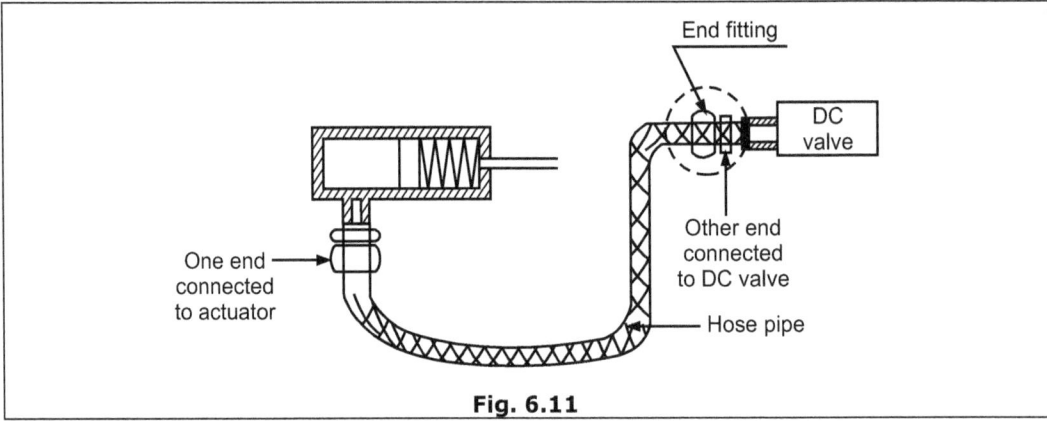

Fig. 6.11

The types of end couplings are:

(a) Male fixed coupling

(b) Compression fittings

(c) Quick coupling

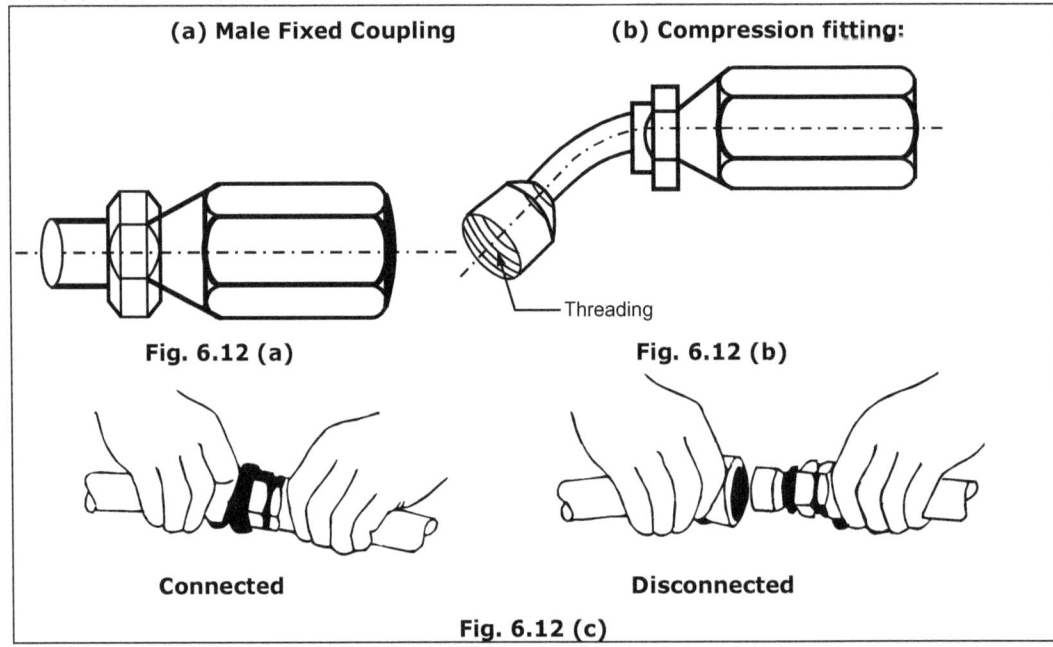

These end fittings are of steel and are crimped on rubber hose pipe by using crimping machine. (Crimping: Fixed with heavy pressure).

Pipe Fittings in Pneumatic System can be classified in four types:

(a) Bell mouth tube fitting (also called Flared Fitting)

(b) Compression type fitting (also called Ferrul Fitting)

(c) Screwed connections

(d) Quick connectors.

6.2.4 Bell Mouth Tube Fitting (also called Flared Fitting)

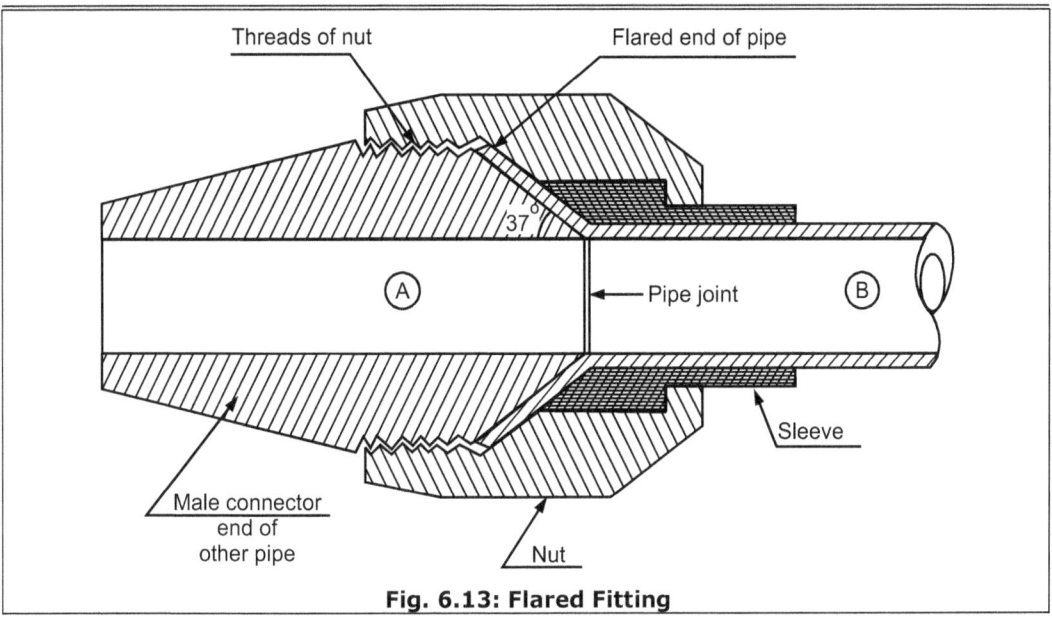

Fig. 6.13: Flared Fitting

In above figure, pipe (A) is joined to pipe (B) by using flared fitting. The end of pipe (B) is flared (made in conical shape) by using flaring tool. Flaring angle is 37° or 45°.

To pipe (A), Male Connector end is fitted. And then nut is tightened on it by using packing sleeve.

By loosening nut, we can disconnect the pipes.

6.2.5 Compression Type Fitting (Ferrule Fitting)

To avoid flaring (expanding pipe into conical shape), flareless joints like ferrule fittings are used in pneumatics. In this joint, nut and ferrule (Ferrule is a flexible member like rubber madeup of Nylon or Brass) are placed on tube and other tube which is to be joined is inserted, along with socket. Nut is tightened in socket threading. The joint is complete. The Ferrule element will occupy entire space and will make perfect seal as well as perfect joint.

By loosening the nut we can disconnect the joint.

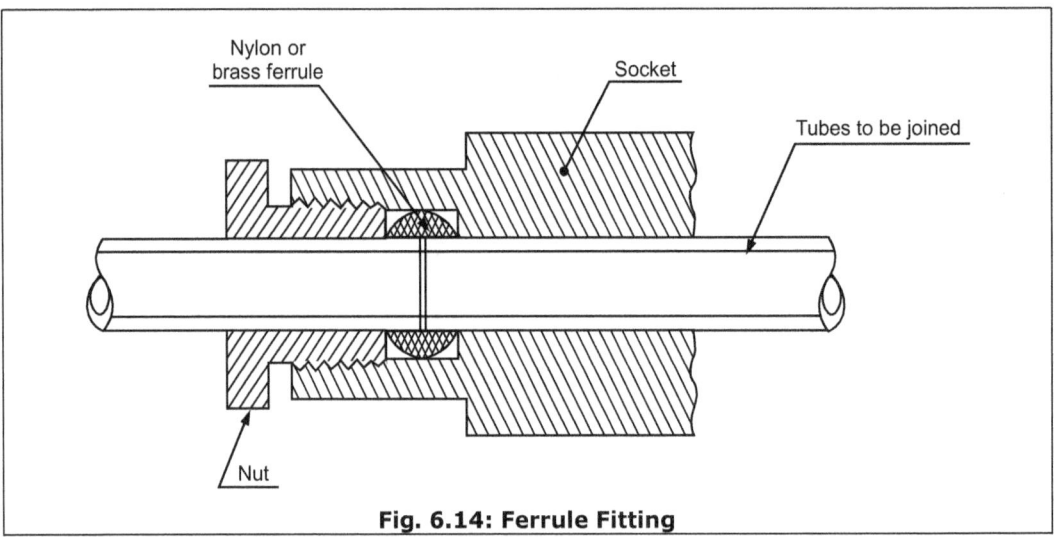

Fig. 6.14: Ferrule Fitting

Wall thickness is a limiting factor in this joint. The joint creates compressive force on pipe near ferrule which must be comfortably taken by pipe wall. If wall is too thin then there is possibility of tearing of the pipe at joint.

6.2.6 Hoses Used in Pneumatic Systems

We have seen that for higher pressures we have to use stronger non-flexible pipes like GI pipes or thick PVC pipes. But if our requirement is flexible pipe at high air pressures then 'Pneumatic Hoses' is best choice.

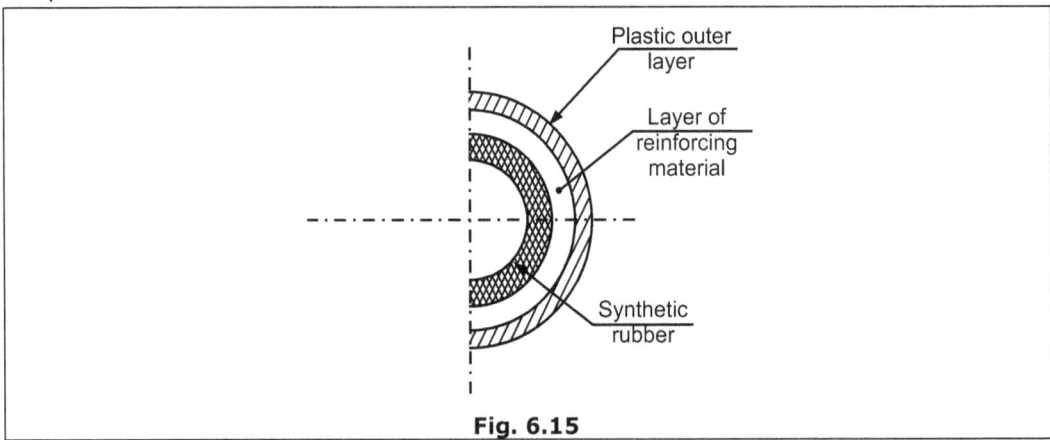

Fig. 6.15

Fig. 6.15 shows cross-section of 'Pneumatic Hose' pipe. It is specially manufactured 3 layer pipe, generally black in colour. The outer layer is of plastic. Middle layer is a layer of Reinforcing material (wire or cloth braid) and inner layer is synthetic material layer. Inner layer is actually a tube or pipe through which air passes.

Two ends of hose are special. The end metal (generally high grade steel) connectors are crimped on the basic hose. By loosening the sleeve we can easily connect or disconnect the hose from circuit. Actual hose looks like as under:

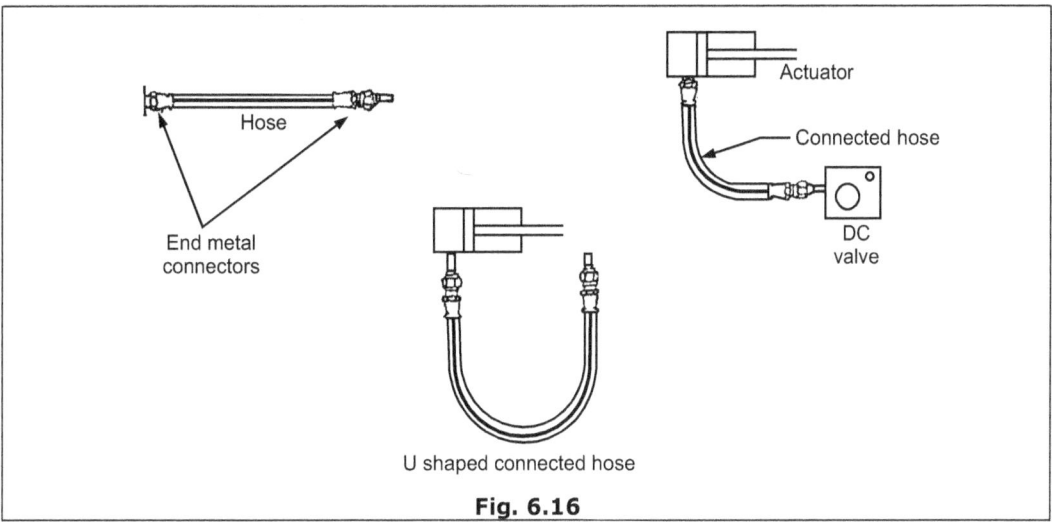

Fig. 6.16

6.2.7 Screwed Connections

Similar to water pipeline plumbing by using GI pipe or 'C' class PVC pipes, the pneumatic pipelines can be fitted. We can comfortably use GI pipes/'C' class PVC pipes. Almost all factories using pneumatic power are using GI pipes. The screwed connections can be easily disconnected. We can use 'Tee', 'Unions', 'Reducers', 'Elbow', 'Nipples' as fitting joints to take the pipe wherever we need. British Std. Pipe Threads (BSP) are most favourable screw threads used in Pneumatic Piping.

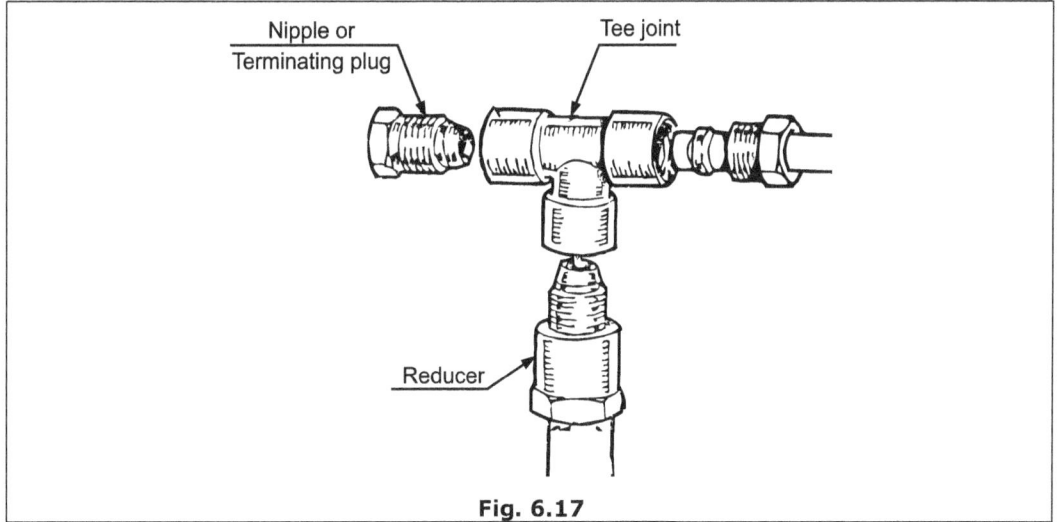

Fig. 6.17

Quick Connectors:

This type of fitting is used for plastic tubing and flexible hoses. These connectors are used where there is frequent connection and disconnection is required. It required perfect sealing arrangement to avoid leakage. Refer quick connectors given earlier in this topic.

6.3 SEALS [W-14, S-15]

Oil under pressure is moving in every hydraulic circuit. Since oil is a liquid, it has the tendency to 'leak' through every gap/slot it finds; during movement. This leakage of oil results in (Bad effects of leakage).

- Loss of efficiency of Hydraulic Circuit.
- During leakage, oil is coming out without doing any work, hence there is loss of power.
- Sometimes there is temperature rise due to leakage.
- Hydraulic oil is costly and hence when it is leaked there is loss of money (monitory loss).
- If leaked oil is dropped on 'hot' surfaces there is possibility of fire. Hence there are fire hazards due to leakage.
- When leaked oil falls on ground, it becomes slippery and there is possibility of accident.

Important: Hydraulic circuit designer has to take lot of precautions at design stage itself to select proper sealing arargement, for minimum leakage.

Seals: The seal is an agent or element which prevents leakage of oil from hydraulic elements and protects the system from dust and dirt.

Functions of Seals:
(a) To stop leakage of oil.
(b) To maintain the pressure.
(c) To keep out contamination in the system.
(d) To enhance the working life of the system.
(e) To enhance the functional reliability of components over a longer period.

6.3.1 Classification of Hydraulic Seals

These seals are classified on various basis. Let us see these basis.

(A) Classification based on Applications:
  (a) **Static seals:** Static seals are those seals which are used to 'seal' two mating parts which are not moving or which are not having any relative motion between them. These seals are stationary. These are generally installed once and forgotten ! Example is sealing end covers of DA cylinder.
  (b) **Dynamic seals:** Dynamic seals are those seals which are used to 'seal' two mating parts which are having relative motion between them. This means, seals are moving every now and then with component. For example, seals used between piston and cylinder. The motion encountered by dynamic seals may be either reciprocating or rotary or combination of both.

(B) Classification based on Degree of Sealing (Extent of Sealing):
   (a) Positive seals: Positive seals are those seals which do not allow any leakage (Internal/External).
   (b) Non-Positive seals: Non-positive seals are those seals which permit a small amount of internal leakage.

(C) Classification based on shape of seal:
   (a) 'O' Ring Seal: These are most common and simple seals with circular cross-section like 'O'. Hence called O-ring. The O-ring is used as static as well as dynamic seal.

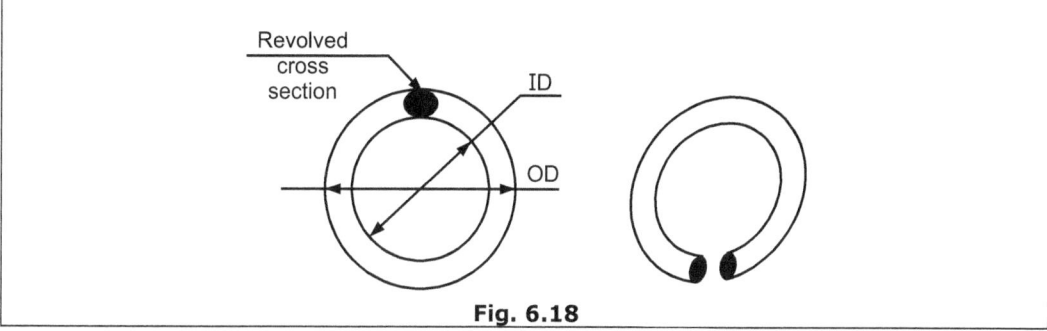
Fig. 6.18

The material used for O-ring is synthetic rubber and are specified by its ID/OD. The round cross-section of O-ring changes to oval shape under low pressure, hence O-rings are non-positive seals. O-rings are fitted with back up-ring.

Fig. 6.19 depicts sealing of cylinder and piston by using 'O'-ring with backup ring.

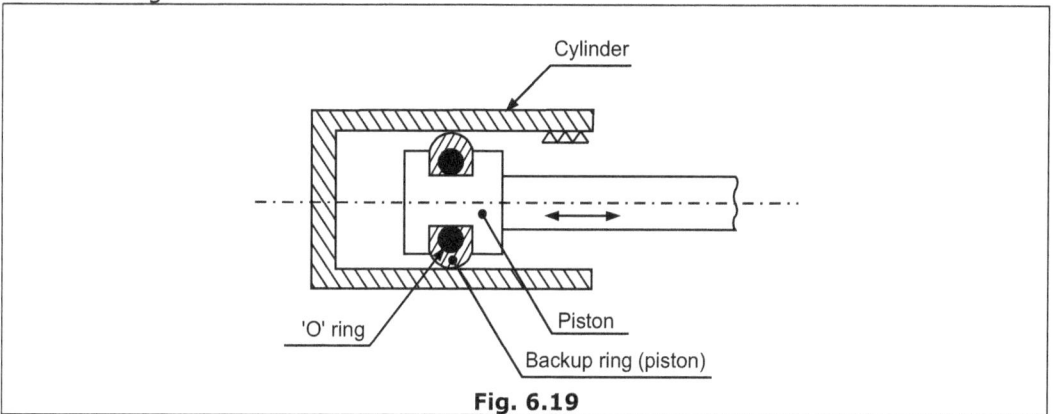
Fig. 6.19

   (b) 'V'-Ring Seal: 'V' ring seal is also called 'V' packing. It is commonly used in hydraulic systems. These seals are available in pieces to facilitate assembly and specific size. It has cross-section resembling to letter 'V'. There are male and female adapter at the extreme ends as shown. In between V-seal rings can be assembled.

   These are made up of fluorocarbon reinforced with cotton, asbestos or are made up of Neoprene reinforced with asbestos.

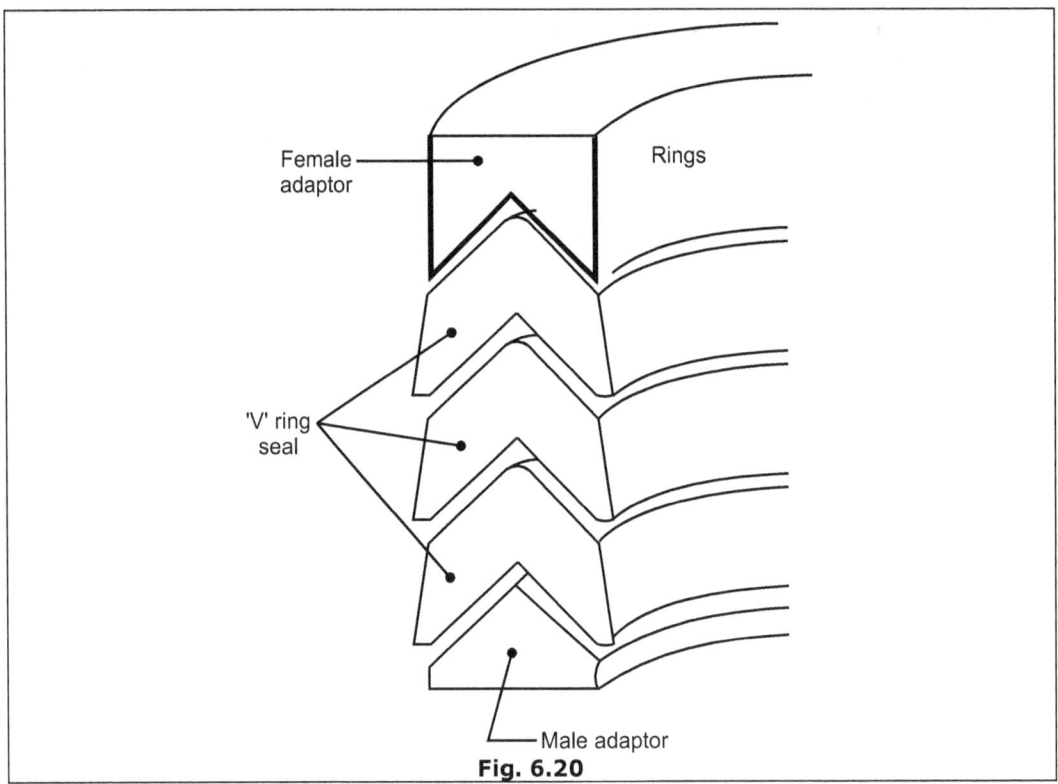

Fig. 6.20

(c) U-Packing Seal: U-packing seal is most versatile in various applications and used as ID rod seal or OD piston seal. U-packings are available in rectangular
cross-section shape to suit piston seals.
- U-packing with long lips: Suitable for eccentric operations.
- U-packing with short lips: Suitable for pressure system.

U-packings are usually made-up of leather or fabric reinforced rubber. These seals are balanced seals and no staking like V-ring seals is required.

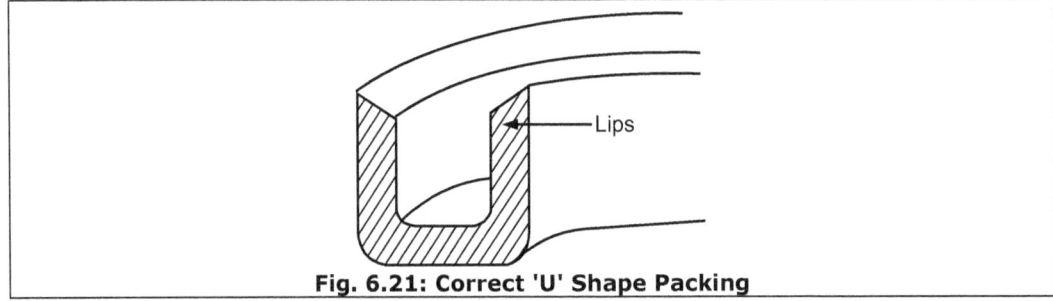

Fig. 6.21: Correct 'U' Shape Packing

(d) T-Ring Seals: These are very modern seals. These seals can be installed as 'O'-ring. But these seals are equally effective as static as well as dynamic seals.

T-Ring seals can be used on rod as well as piston.

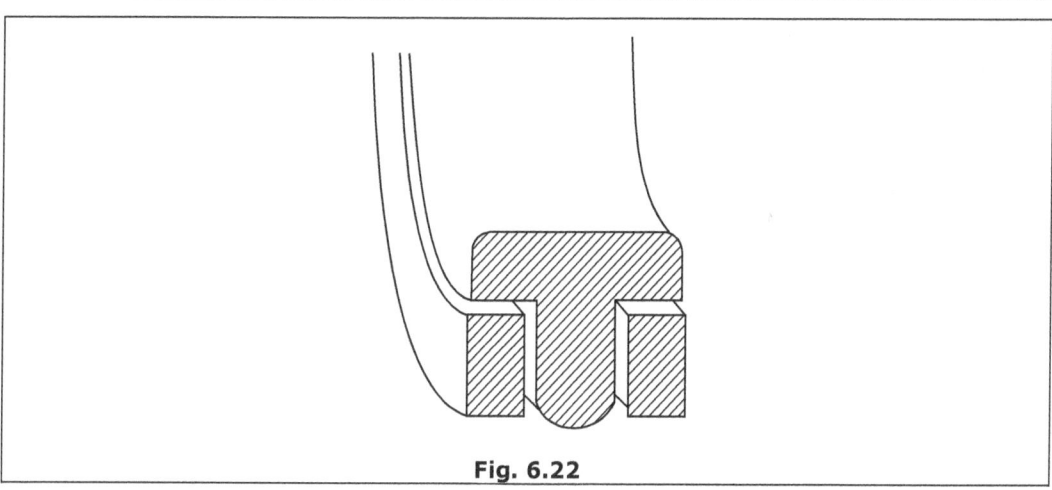

Fig. 6.22

(e) **Cup Seals:** These seals are most commonly used with piston as shown in Fig. 6.23. These are available in variety of geometric shapes to suit the applications. These seals can take higher pressures upto 700 bar. The material used for these seals is polyurethane or leather. For low pressure application, Neoprene is used.

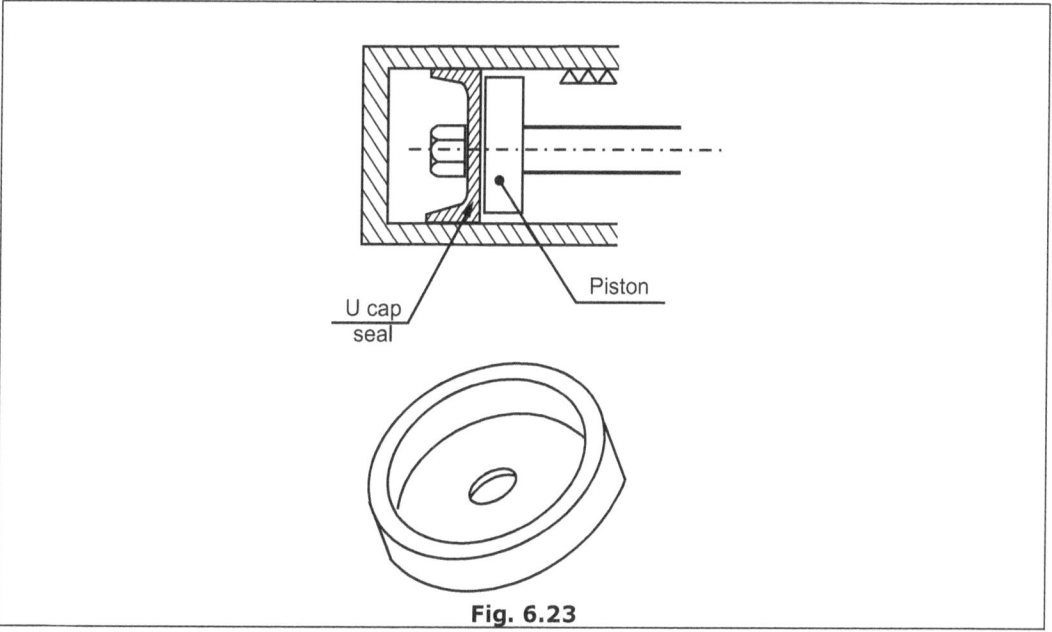

Fig. 6.23

6.3.2 Selection Criteria for Seals

Before selecting proper seal, the design engineer has to check following points for specific applications. The selection criteria for seals is as under:
 (a) Type of fluid/oil used in system. Whether it is compatible with oil used.
 (b) Maximum temperature of system in working condition.
 (c) Functional reliability expected.

(d) Expected life of seal.
(e) Cost of seal.
(f) Working pressure of system.
(g) Environmental conditions.

6.3.3 Various Reasons for Seal Failure

Many a times seal fails and heavy internal or external leakage starts. Following are the general causes of seal failure.

(a) Incompatibility of seal material with oil. If we change the type of oil then there is possibility of chemical reactions between new oil and old seal.
(b) Low speed of actuators is responsible for seal failure.
(c) If seals are not correctly installed, there is possibility of failure of seal.
(d) Unbalanced shaft, bend shaft, improper bearings, can cause vibrations on shaft and seal can fail.
(e) High temperature of oil (medium) can burn the seals.
(f) Old seals get hardened and fail.
(g) If seal is excessively squeezed then it can fail.

Important Points

- To clean the oil is a main function of oil filters. **Filters** are cleaning stations used to arrest the unwanted materials/particles.
- **Air filter** consists of plastic bowl, attached to body of filter. The filter element called 'cartridge' is also attached to body at the centre. Both cartridge and bowl can be removed as and when required and can be reattached.
- **Hoses:** In many hydraulic systems, the drive units are assemblies needed to move alongwith pipelines. In such cases, flexible pipes called 'Hoses' are used.
- **Seals:** The seal is an agent or element which prevents leakage of oil from hydraulic elements and protects the system from dust and dirt.

Practice Questions

1. What is the function of filters in hydraulic circuits?
2. What is the effect of contamination in hydraulic oil?
3. Write three locations of filters in hydraulic circuit.
4. Draw circuit diagram showing pressure line filter.
5. What is FRL unit? Explain. Draw separate symbol of each.
6. How air is filtered in pneumatic circuit?
7. Draw neat sketch of hose pipe and explain 3 layers of its construction.
8. What are the effects of oil leakages in hydraulic circuit?
9. Write any four functions of seals.
10. What is dynamic seal? Write short note on it.
11. Write types of seals.
12. Write various reasons for seal failure.

Chapter 7

HYDRO-PNEUMATIC SYSTEMS AND CIRCUITS

Weightage of Marks = 20, Teaching Hours = 10

Learning Objectives
- Compare Hydraulic and Pneumatic Circuits
- Understand various Hydraulic and Pneumatic Circuits

Contents

Hydraulic Circuits
- Hydraulic Symbols
- Meter in, Meter out, Bleed off, Sequencing.
- Introduction to Electro-Hydraulics – Concept, Principles and Applications
- Applications of Hydraulic Circuits – Hydraulic Power Steering, Hydraulic Brakes, Milling Machine, Hydraulic Press.

Simple Pneumatic Circuits
- Pneumatic Symbols
- Speed Control Circuit (Meter in, Meter out), Sequencing.
- Applications of Pneumatic Circuits – Air Brake, Low Cost Automation in Industries, Pneumatic Power Tools (Drill, Hammer and Grinder).
- Comparison of Hydraulic and Pneumatic Circuits.

7.1 COMPARISON OF HYDRAULIC AND PNEUMATIC CIRCUIT

Before going for comparison we will learn about general layout of Hydraulic System, its components and general layout of pneumatic system and its components.

7.1.1 General Layout of Hydraulic System

General layout or standard layout of any Hydraulic System is having following components/parts/equipments:
(a) Oil Storage Tank or Oil Reservoir.
(b) Oil conditioning elements such as filters, heat exchangers, heater and strainer.

(c) Pump to pressurize oil.
(d) Fluid controlling elements such as Direction Control Valves, Flow Control Valves, Pressure Relief Valves, Check Valves etc.
(e) Actuators – Reciprocating (Linear Actuators), Rotary (Hydraulic Motors).
(f) Fluid or Oil conducting elements such as pipelines, connectors, hoses etc.
(g) Medium i.e. Hydraulic oil.

7.1.2 Flow Chart of Hydraulic System

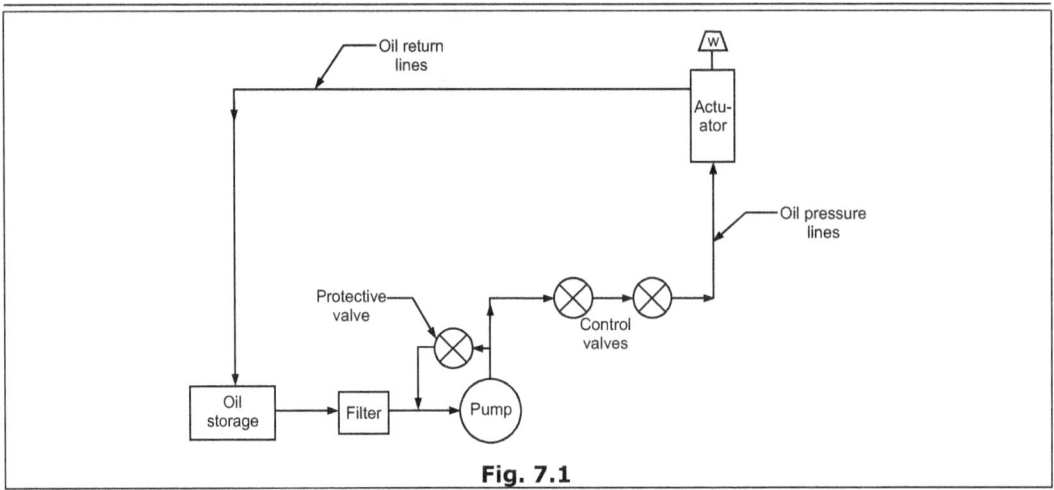

Fig. 7.1

7.1.3 Functions of each Element in Hydraulic System

(a) **Oil Tank or Reservoir:** This is an oil storage tank in which hydraulic oil is stored. The oil passes through various pipelines and after doing useful work in actuator, the oil returns back to oil tank. In the regions of low temperature, oil heaters are attached to Air tank.

(b) **Filter:** This element filters the oil before going to next element i.e. pump.

(c) **Pump:** Hydraulic pump is a heart of any hydraulic system. Its main function is to create the flow of oil under pressure through entire hydraulic system and hence to assist transfer of power and motion (i.e. useful work).

(d) **Direction Control Valves/Flow Control Valves/Pressure Relief Valves (Fluid controlling elements):** These valves are fitted in hydraulic system at a particular location. These valves control the flow of oil in the system. They also direct the flow of oil in the system as they also control the speed of actuator.

(e) **Actuators (Fluid Power Utilization Elements):** These elements are known as actuators (either rotary or linear). The pressurized oil acts on Actuator element. The oil gives or transfers its power to Actuator to create useful work or Mechanical Advantage.

(f) Pipelines (Fluid Conducting Elements): It is the functional connection for oil flow in the Hydraulic System. The efficiency of oil flow is greatly influenced by the physical characteristics of piping system.

There are two pipes:

(a) Pipes which carry pressurized oil (are called as pressure pipelines).

(b) Pipes which carry low pressure oil or used oil (are called as return pipelines).

Hoses, pipes, pipe fittings are the parts of fluid power pipeline.

7.1.4 Actual Hydraulic System Structure

To know more about Hydraulic System, we will see it with a closer view.

We have already seen the functions of each element in Hydraulic system. You can easily make out the elements. Oil reservoir is oil storage tank. Pump sucks the oil from tank and pressurizes it. The oil is directed to port (A) or (B) of Actuator by Direction control valve. When oil enters through port (A), piston will move from left to right. The oil from other side of piston will return through port (B) via Direction control valve to oil tank.

When pressurized oil enters through port (B); piston will move from right and left and oil from other side of piston will return through port (A).

Flow control valve will control the flow (lit./sec.) of oil to control or monitor the speed of piston (m/sec.). Pressure relief valve acts as a safety valve. This valve will not allow the system pressure to increase beyond set value. Filter will arrest foreign particles from oil and will keep the oil clean.

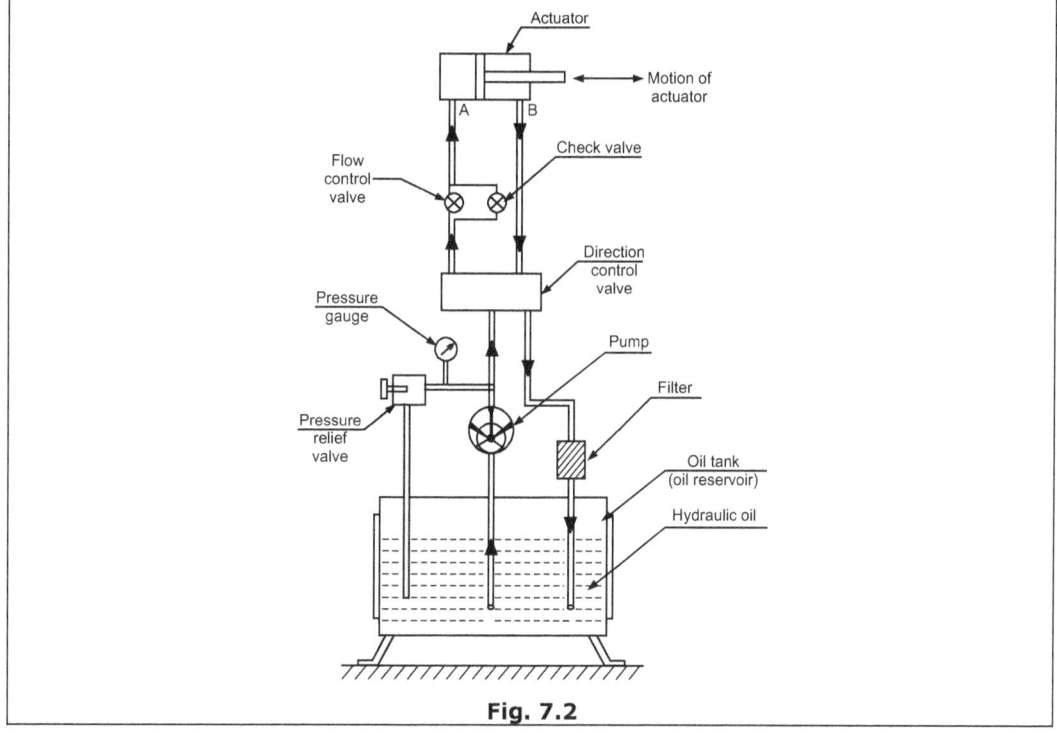

Fig. 7.2

7.1.5 Actual Hydraulic System Structure with the help of Symbols

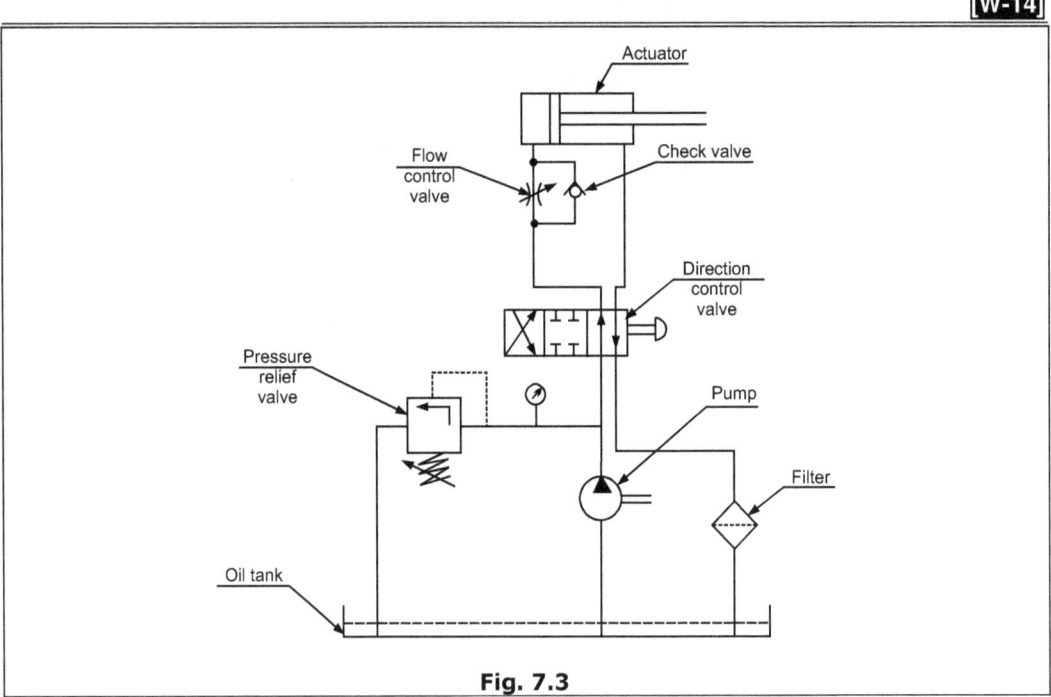

Fig. 7.3

Fig. 7.3 shows symbolic representation of actual Hydraulic System. Go through the symbols depicted in Fig. 7.3.

7.1.6 General Layout of Pneumatic System

General layout or standard layout of any pneumatic system is having following components/parts/equipments.

(a) Air compressor.

(b) Compressed Air Storage Tank or Air Receiver.

(c) Moisture separators.

(d) Air Filter – Air Pressure Regulator – Air Lubricator Unit (FRL) unit.

(e) Direction Control Valves/Flow Control Valves/Other values.

(f) Air Actuators: Reciprocating (Linear Actuators) and/or Rotary actuators (Air motors).

(g) Air conducting elements: Pipes, Valves, Joints, Bends etc.

7.1.7 Flow Chart of Pneumatic System

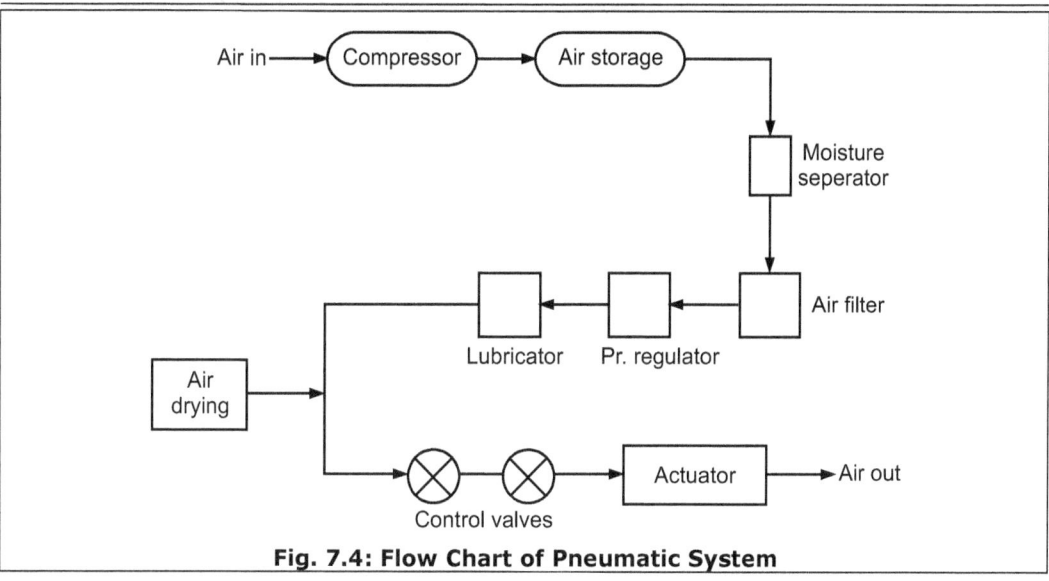

Fig. 7.4: Flow Chart of Pneumatic System

7.1.8 Functions of each Element in Pneumatic System

(a) Compressor: This unit compresses the air which is at atmospheric pressure. Due to compression the pressure of air increases. This unit runs either on Electric motor or on Diesel/Petrol Engine or Gas/Steam turbine.

Important:

- The compressors used in Engineering units/Foundry are either Reciprocating or screw compressor and run on electric motors.
- The compressors used for 'bore well' machine are generally screw compressors and run on Diesel engine or directly on truck or tractor engine on which they are mounted.
- The compressors in Sugar factory run on steam turbine.

(b) Air Tank/Air Reservoir: This is a MS cylinder (popularly known as pressure vessel) similar to Domestic Gas cylinder. This tank stores compressed air which is an output of air compressors.

(c) Moisture separator: Air contains particles of water called 'moisture'. These very fine particles of water must be removed from air otherwise, if they flow along with air, then they can rust the metal parts in the system. 'Water Trap' is a moisture separator. Other chemical or mechanical separators are also used. In these separators, part moisture is separated.

(d) Air Filter – Air Pressure Regulator – Air lubricator (F.R.L): This is a combined unit available readymade in Market. The air first gets filtered. Then its pressure is regulated and then some fine particles of lubricating oil are mixed with air in lubricator. The particles help in proper lubrication of sliding parts/rotary parts of actuator and valves.

(e) Direction control valves/Flow control valves/Other valves (Control of Air): These valves direct the flow of air, control the flow of air to control speed of actuators etc.

(f) Air Actuators: These items are the Heart of Pneumatic system. Actuators are taking part in obtaining mechanical advantage or you may say, useful work from compressed air. These are either Linear Actuators or Rotary Actuators.

(g) Air conducting elements: The compressed air flows through pipes (GI pipes/ Hoses etc.). There are on-off valves, pressure gauges attached to the pipe. All these elements come under this head.

7.1.9 Actual Pneumatic System Structure [S-15]

To know more about pneumatic system structure, we will see it with little closer view:

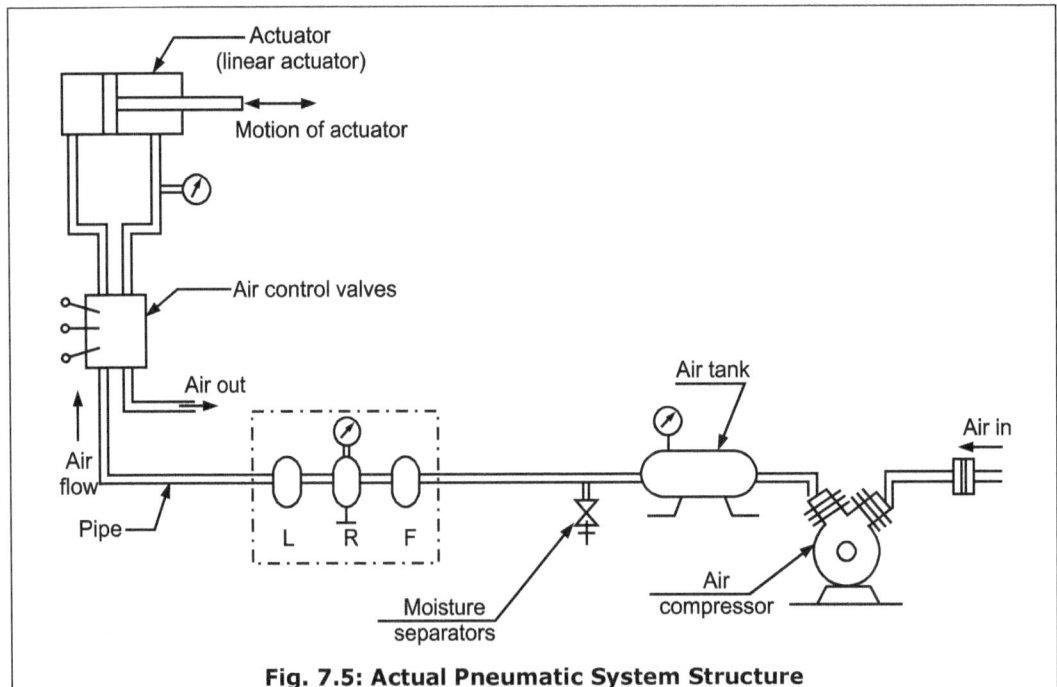

Fig. 7.5: Actual Pneumatic System Structure

7.1.10 Actual Pneumatic System Structure with the help of Symbols [S-15]

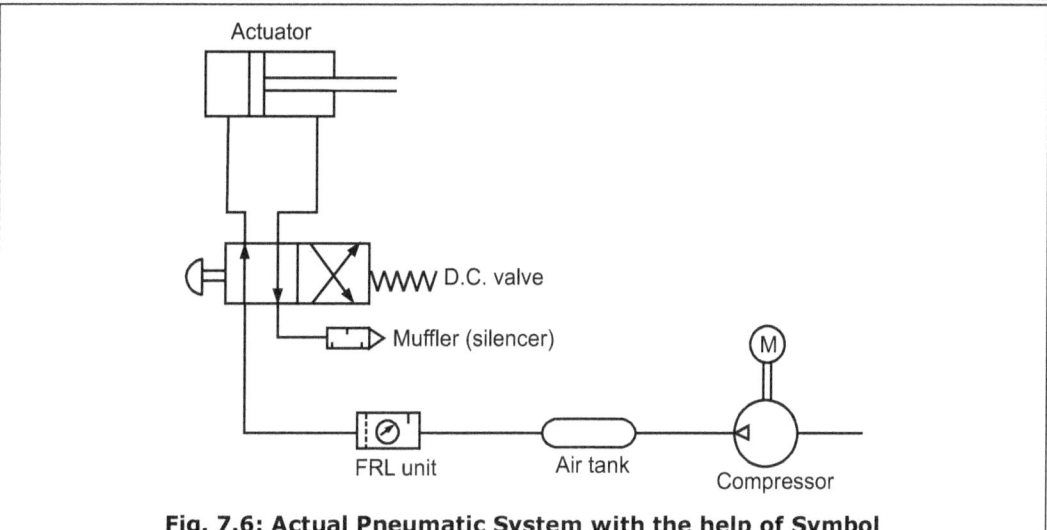

Fig. 7.6: Actual Pneumatic System with the help of Symbol

7.1.11 Comparison of Hydraulic and Pneumatic Circuits (Systems) [S-15]

Hydraulic Circuits	Pneumatic Circuits
1. Used for circuits upto 700 bar pressure.	1. Operative below 10 bar pressure.
2. Uses hydraulic oil as a medium.	2. Uses air as a medium.
3. Pump is used to pressurise the oil.	3. Compressor is used to pressurise the air.
4. Since hydraulic oil is reused in the circuit, hydraulic oil tank is a must and there are return lines (pipes).	4. Air is taken from atmosphere and is vented to atmosphere after use. Hence no return lines. Air reservoir is used to store pressurised air.
5. The rigidity of system using hydraulic circuit is good.	5. The rigidity of system using pneumatic circuit is poor.
6. Moderate operating cost.	6. Operating cost is low.
7. Maintenance is critical.	7. Maintenance is simple.
8. Very suitable for accurate speed/feed movement of cutting tool mechanism.	8. No accuracy in movement.

contd. ...

9. The system using hydraulic circuit is not clean due to oil leakages.	9. Pneumatic circuits are very clean.
10. Weight to pressure ratio is small.	10. Weight to pressure ratio is high.
11. Problem of cavitation is serious in hydraulic circuits.	11. No problem of cavitation.
12. Hydraulic circuits are used in tackling heavy loads, hence used in earthmoving equipments, CNC-VMC machines.	12. Pneumatic circuits are used when loads are much lighter. Hence used in transferring the light weight components, vacuum handling in printing press, food industry.

7.2 HYDRAULIC CIRCUITS [S-15]

Introduction:
- We have already seen the basic facts relating to Hydraulic Circuit Elements, their construction and working.
- Now let us see how Hydraulic System is constructed by using all these elements to obtain useful mechanical work.
- Hydraulic circuit is symbolic representation of system which operates on push button/pilot signal/electromechanical circuits and thereby achieving flow of pressurized oil to operate the motion of actuator.
- Hydraulic circuit is a combination of various Hydraulic elements arranged in a systematic manner to perform specific task.
- **Elements of Hydraulic Circuit:**
    (a) Oil Tank or Oil Reservoir
    (b) Oil filter
    (c) Oil pressurizing pump
    (d) Direction control valve/Flow control valves and other valves
    (e) Actuators (DA Cylinder/SA Cylinder/Motor)
    (f) Pipelines
- **We will see following Hydraulic Circuit:**
    1. Speed Control of DA Cylinder by using
        (a) Meter-in-Circuit
        (b) Meter-out-Circuit
        (c) Bleed-off-Circuit
    2. Sequencing Circuit
    3. Hydraulic Power Steering Circuit
    4. Earthmovers Hydraulic Circuit.

7.2.1 Circuit No. 1 (a) Speed Control of DA Cylinder-Meter-in-Circuit

[W-14, S-15]

- Double Acting Cylinder (DA cylinder) is cylinder-piston pair. Piston reciprocates in cylinder. It is having linear motion (meter per second). In many applications, we have to control this speed. Meter-in-Circuit is one of the speed control circuits of DA cylinder.

- **Meter-in-Circuit:** We must know that to control the speed, we have to control the flow of pressurized oil (lit/sec.) entering into DA cylinder.

  In meter-in-circuit, the flow control valve is placed in primary line (also called pressure line), directly before the load. The arrangement is depicted in circuit diagrams shown in Fig. 7.7 (a) and (b).

In Fig. 7.7 (a) position shown, the variable flow control valve with built-in check valve is placed in primary line or pressure line. (Primary line or pressure line is a pipeline which carries pressurized fluid). Pump controls many devices and its output is higher than needed by any individual actuator. So flow restrictor or flow control valve is placed to set the flow of each actuator. Hence this circuit is known as 'Meter-in-Circuit'.

Important: It should be noted that, the speed control of piston (shown in the circuit) is achieved only in Piston Advance Movement. We cannot control the speed of piston in return stroke. In return stroke, the returning oil comes out through port (A) and goes to oil tank via check valve and DC valve. Carefully look at the arrows shown in Fig. 7.7 (b).

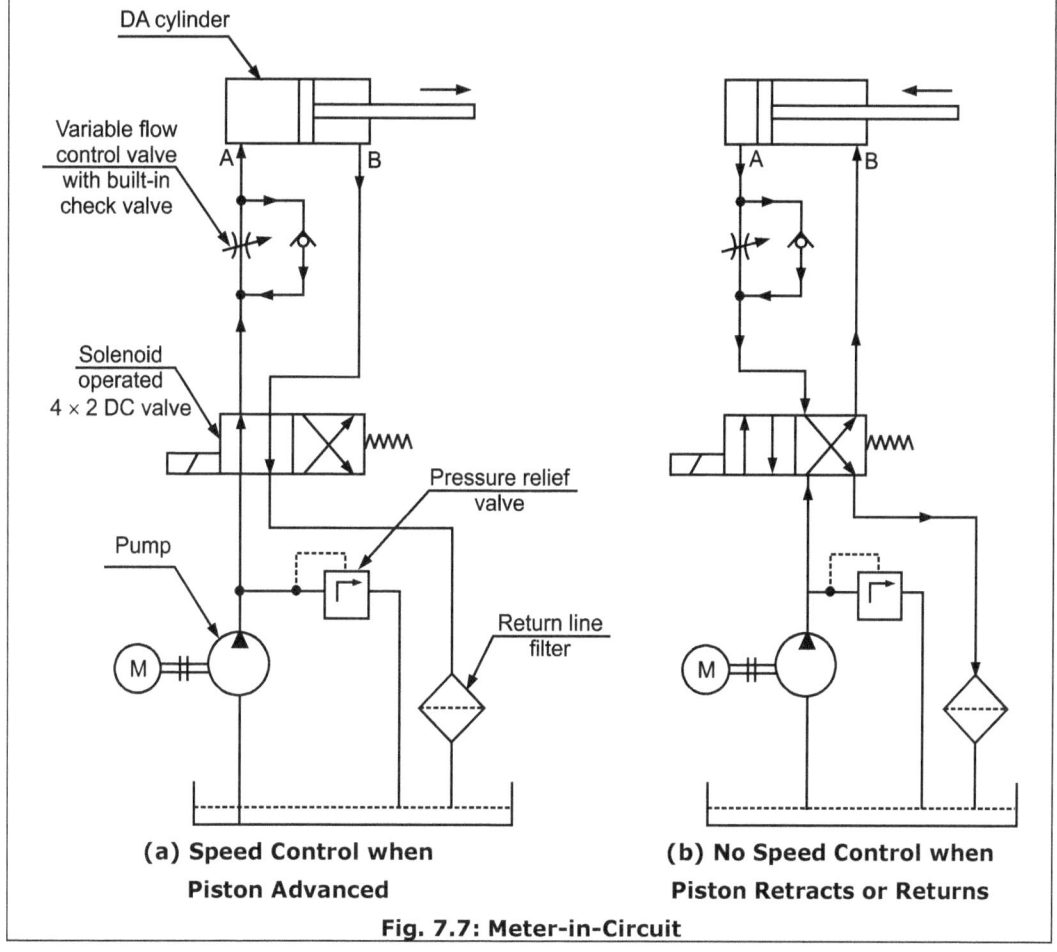

(a) Speed Control when Piston Advanced

(b) No Speed Control when Piston Retracts or Returns

Fig. 7.7: Meter-in-Circuit

Applications of Meter-in-Circuits:

(a) This circuit is used where finer speed control is required.

(b) When load is needed to move then this circuit is used.

(c) This circuit is suitable for resisting load actuated by the cylinder.

Advantages of Meter-in-Circuit:

(a) Gives best results when used in higher pressure systems.

(b) Relatively small friction to face by piston which increases life of piston.

(c) Suitable for very low piston rod speeds.

Disadvantages of Meter-in-Circuit:

(a) Not suitable for low pressure systems.

(b) We are placing flow control valve in pressure line. In this valve, throttling of fluid takes place which heats the oil and hot oil is admitted into the cylinder.

(c) There is pressure on one side of piston every time, hence load actuated by piston rod is not held firmly in position.

7.2.2 Circuit No. 1 (b) Speed Control of DA Cylinder-Meter-Out-Circuit

- This is another method of controlling the linear speed of piston of DA cylinder.
- **Meter-out-Circuit:** This is similar circuit as that of meter-in-circuit. The only difference is that we are placing flow control valve in Return lines instead of primary or pressure lines. In short we are placing flow control valve in the way where oil is going 'OUT'. Hence this circuit is called 'Meter-out-Circuit'. The arrangement is depicted in Figs. 7.8 (a) and (b).

In Fig. 7.8 (a) positions shown, the variable flow control valve with built-in Check valve is placed in Return line (the pipes through which the pressure oil returns to oil tank are called return lines or secondary lines).

- In this circuit, speed control of piston is achieved by controlling the flow control valve in such a manner that, flow coming out (and going to oil tank) is controlled by flow control valve. The oil coming out from cylinder has used its energy and is low pressure oil. Hence this circuit is called 'Meter-out-Circuit'.
- **Important:** It should be noted that, the speed control of piston is achieved only in Piston Advance movement. In return stroke shown in Fig. 7.8 (b), the flow of pump to the piston end of cylinder is through flow control valve. And oil coming out through port A directly returns to oil reservoir via DC valve. Hence in return stroke there is no speed control of piston.

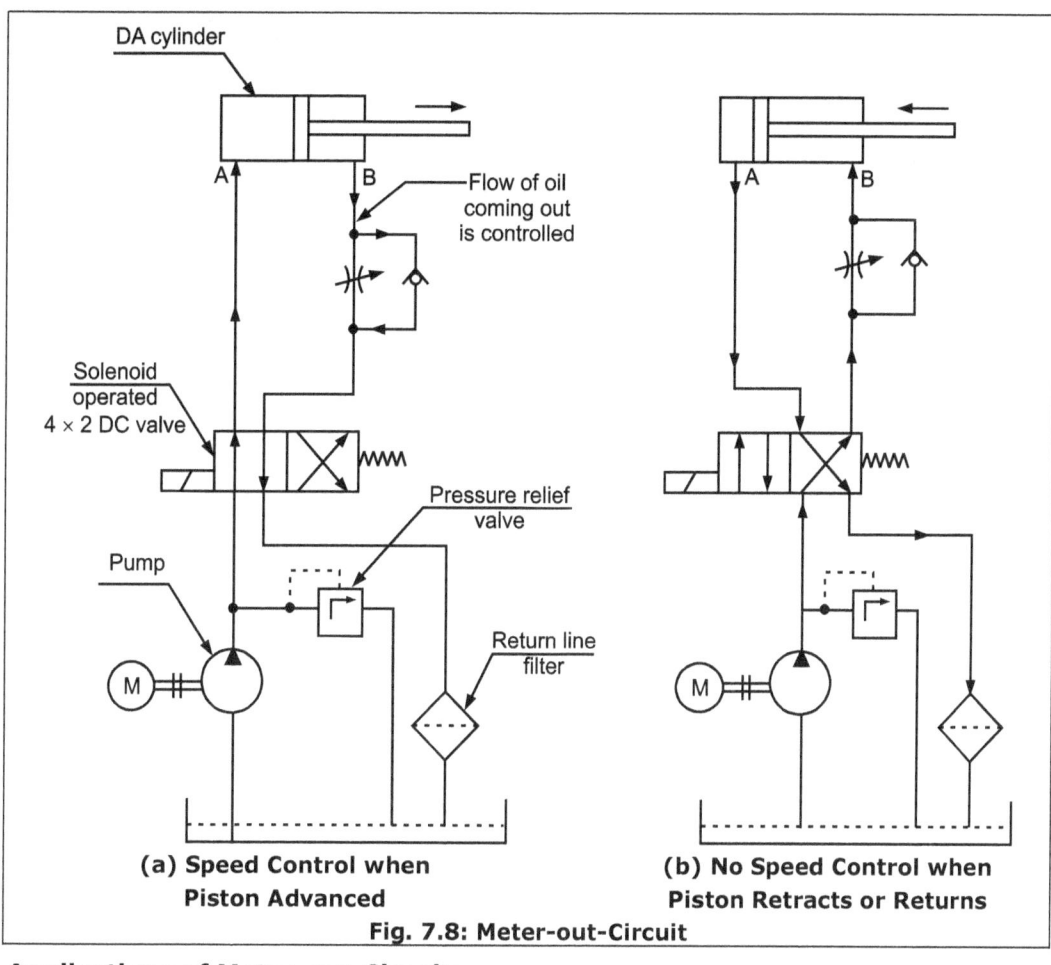

Fig. 7.8: Meter-out-Circuit

Applications of Meter-out-Circuit:

(a) This circuit is used where very stable movements of actuators are needed.

(b) Used in speed control of Hydrometer.

(c) This circuit is best suited for Drilling/boring or reaming operation. On these machines if clamping of job is loose, the tool drags the workpiece.

Advantages of Meter-out-Circuit:

(a) The actuator movement is more stable.

(b) Heat generated due to throttling at flow control valve is given to oil tank.

(c) Provides positive speed control of cylinder.

Disadvantages of Meter-out-Circuit:

(a) Since on both sides of piston there is pressure, there is possibility of higher friction.

(b) Pump works against the maximum pressure.

7.2.3 Circuit No. 1 (c) Speed Control of DA Cylinder-Bleed off Circuit

[W-14]

- This is still another method of controlling the linear speed of piston of DA cylinder.
- This is slightly different circuit than 'Meter-in' and 'Meter-out' circuit.
- In this circuit, neither the 'inflow' to the actuator nor the 'outflow' from the actuator is controlled. Instead of this, the pressurized fluid coming out of pump is diverted and by-passed to the oil reservoir. In this circuit, the flow of control valve is placed in this by-pass line.

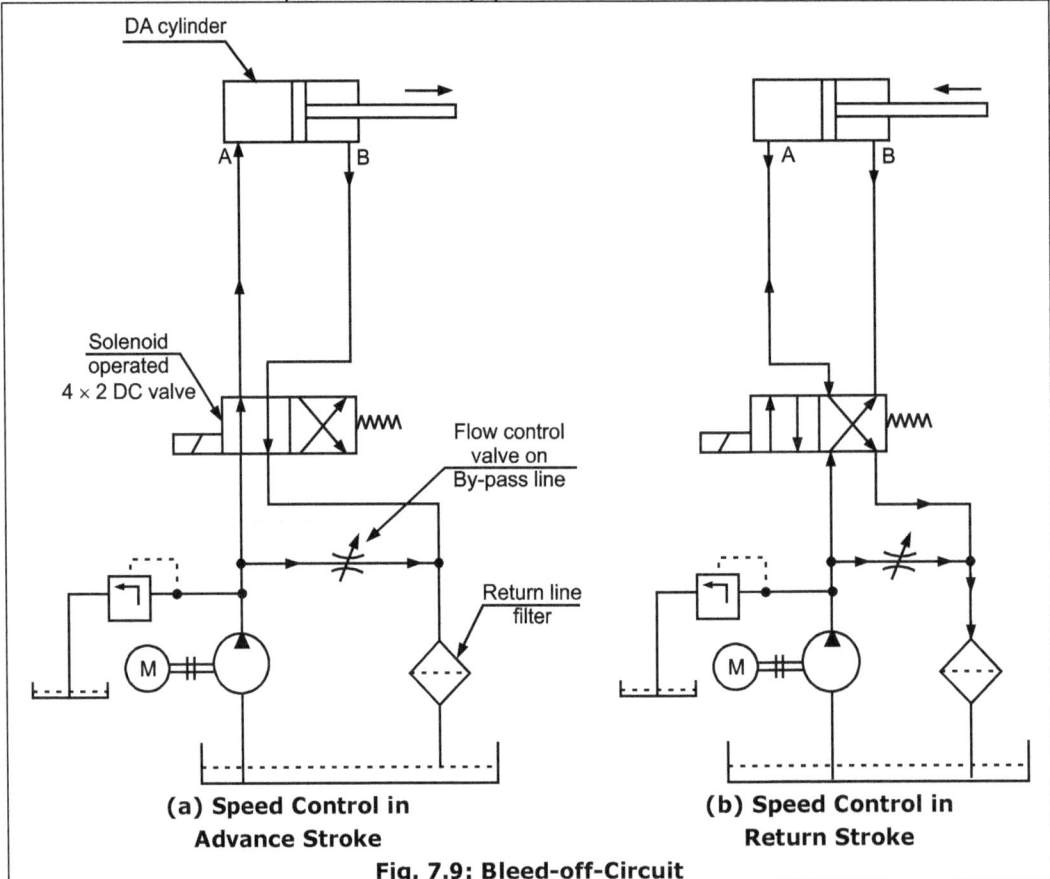

(a) Speed Control in Advance Stroke
(b) Speed Control in Return Stroke
Fig. 7.9: Bleed-off-Circuit

- Due to by-pass arrangement,

  The speed of piston ⇒ Difference between pump delivery flow and flow being by-passed to tank through flow control valve

- The oil is being by-passed immediately after pump. Another English word for by-pass flow is 'Bleed-off'. Hence this circuit is known as Bleed-off circuit. It is also called as By-Pass Control Circuit. (Refer Fig. 7.9)
- **Important:** In this circuit, we can control the speed of position in Advance Stroke as well as Return Stroke.

Applications of Bleed-off Circuit:

(a) This circuit is suitable when pressure is constant.

(b) This circuit is used where precise speed control is not required.

(c) This circuit is used for control of broach in Broaching machine. It is also used in hydraulic shaping machine.

Advantages of Bleed-off Circuit:

(a) In this circuit there is no excess flow going through pressure relief valve and the system is efficient.

(b) Heat generated due to throttling is fed to the tank.

Disadvantages of Bleed-off Circuit:

(a) The circuit does not allow positive speed control.

(b) Speed adjustment is upto average value.

(c) Does not suitable for accumulator circuit.

(d) If flow rate of pump fluctuates, the speed of actuator fluctuates.

7.2.4 Circuit No. 2 Sequencing Circuit

- Sequencing circuit is extensively used in Industrial Hydraulic Systems used especially in Mass Production.

- Sequence valve is 'close relative' of pressure relief valve; but sequence valve is used in hydraulic systems to cause various operations in sequential order i.e. one after another.

- Let us take an example of drilling a hole in a workpiece.

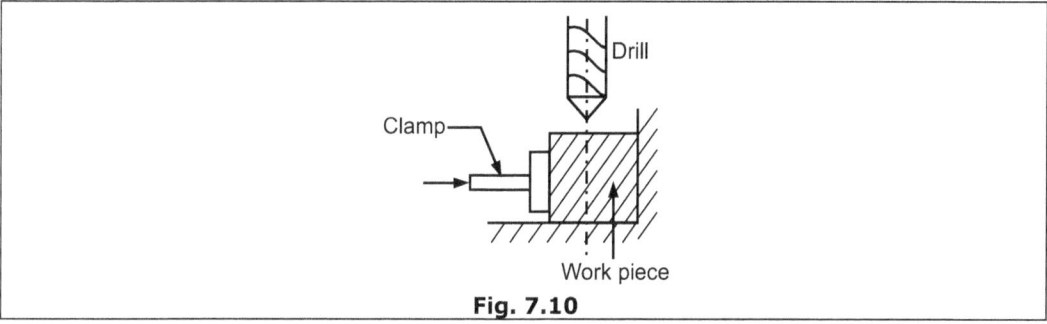

Fig. 7.10

- Before drilling we have to clamp the workpiece firmly and then we have to carry out drilling.

   (a) Step 1: Clamping of workpiece

   (b) Step 2: Drilling

   (c) Step 3: Removing drill from drilled hole and declamping.

- When an Industrial unit goes for mass production (say 20,000 jobs/month) then it has to mechanize the above three steps. For mechanization, hydraulic system is the best solution.
- There are two types of sequencing circuits:

    (a) Pressure dependant sequencing: In this circuit, second action starts when first action is complete. e.g. The above example, drilling starts only when clamping is complete.

    (b) Travel dependant sequencing: In this circuit, second action starts when first action is partly complete. This means the action overlaps but in sequential order.

- **Sequencing can be obtained by using:**

    (a) Sequencing valve

    (b) Rollar actuated DC valve with cam

    (c) Time delay valve

- Sequencing can be used for obtaining actions like bar feeding, ejecting, lifting, pushing clamping, in predetermined order.

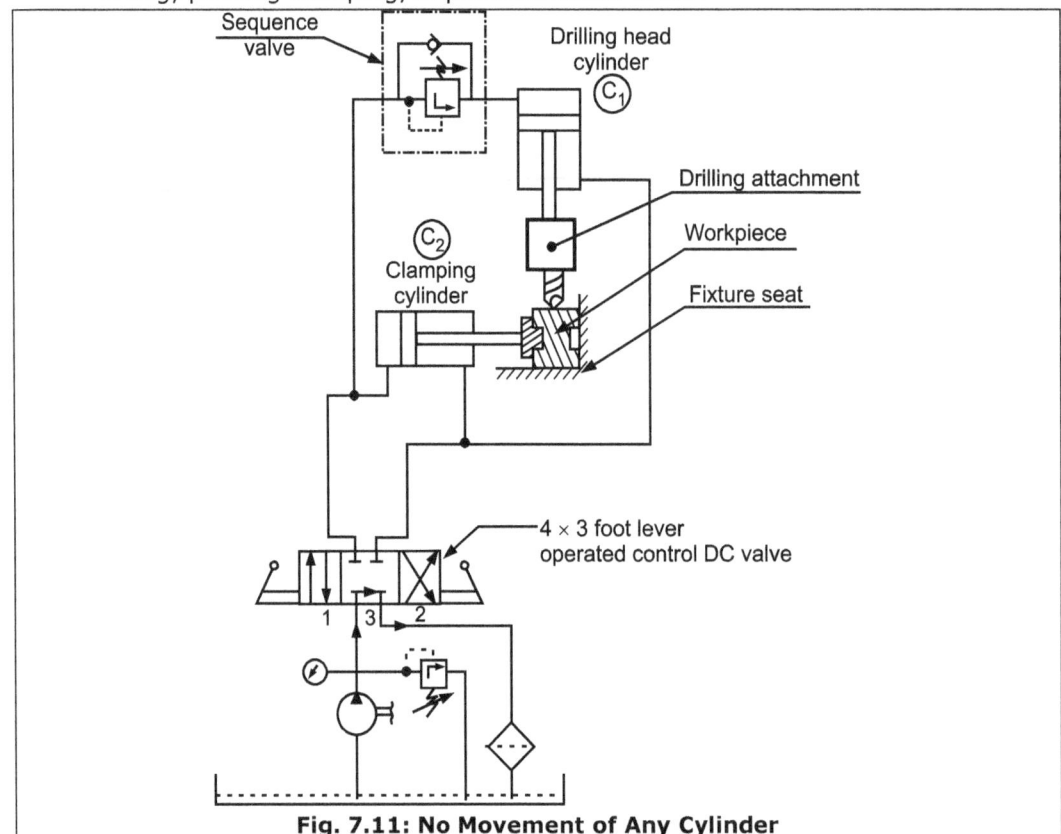

Fig. 7.11: No Movement of Any Cylinder

(a) Pressure Dependent Sequencing Circuit:

The circuit is used for drilling a hole in workpiece. The sequence of operation is:

(a) Clamping of workpiece

(b) Drilling

(c) Declamping and drill taken out from hole.

- The DC valve takes centre position (No. 3). No oil is supplied to either of cylinders C_1 or C_2. Now undrilled workpiece is kept on fixture seat. The oil from pump is going to oil tank via DC valve and return line filter. So no movement of cylinder C_1 or C_2.

Now, worker will operate foot lever of DC valve and valve takes position 1. (Refer Fig. 7.12)

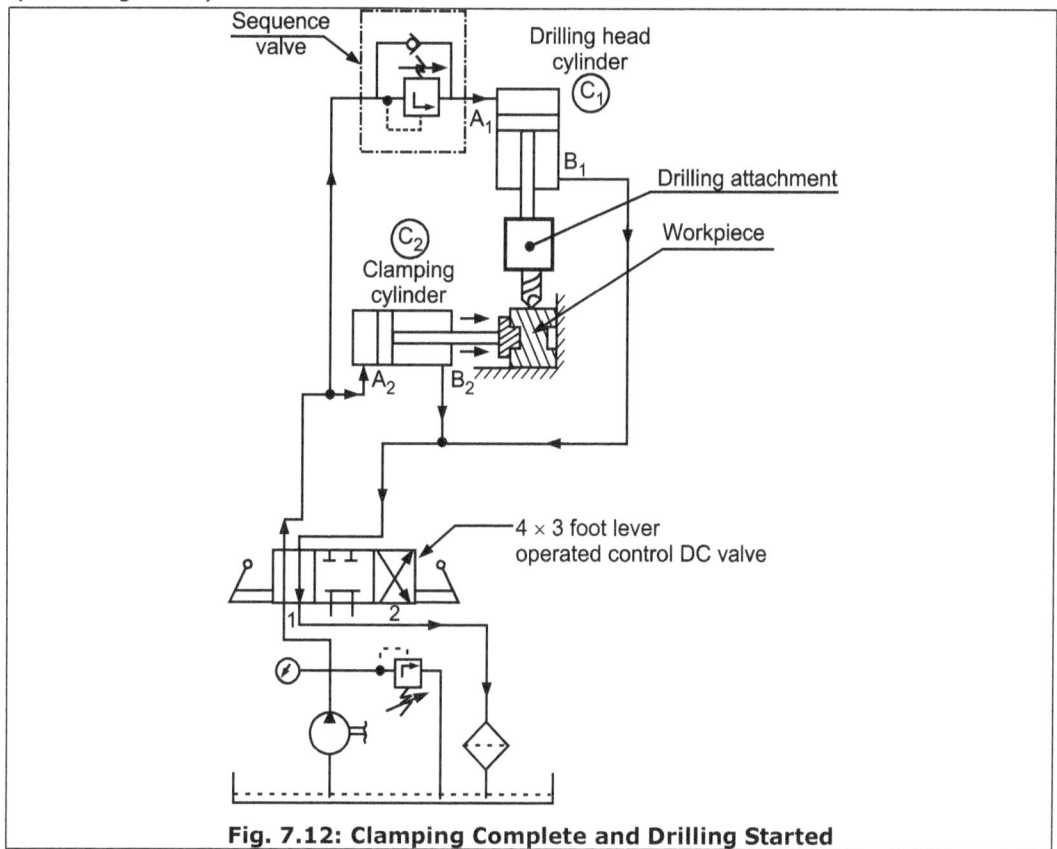

Fig. 7.12: Clamping Complete and Drilling Started

- Now, oil will start supplying directly to C_2 and through sequence valve to C_1.
- When oil enters through port A_2 of cylinder C_2, piston will advance and immediately clamps the workpiece.

- At the same time oil flows towards port A_1 of cylinder C_1; but through sequence valve. Some higher pressure is set at pressure relief valve of sequence valve. When the pressure of flowing liquid reaches this set value the sequence valve opens and oil enters through port A_1 into cylinder C_1. Due to this piston advances and comes down, so that drilling starts.
- When operator again operates foot lever of DC valve, it takes position 2 and both pistons retract and workpiece declamps and drill comes out of drilled hole.

7.2.5 Travel Dependant Sequencing Circuit using Cam

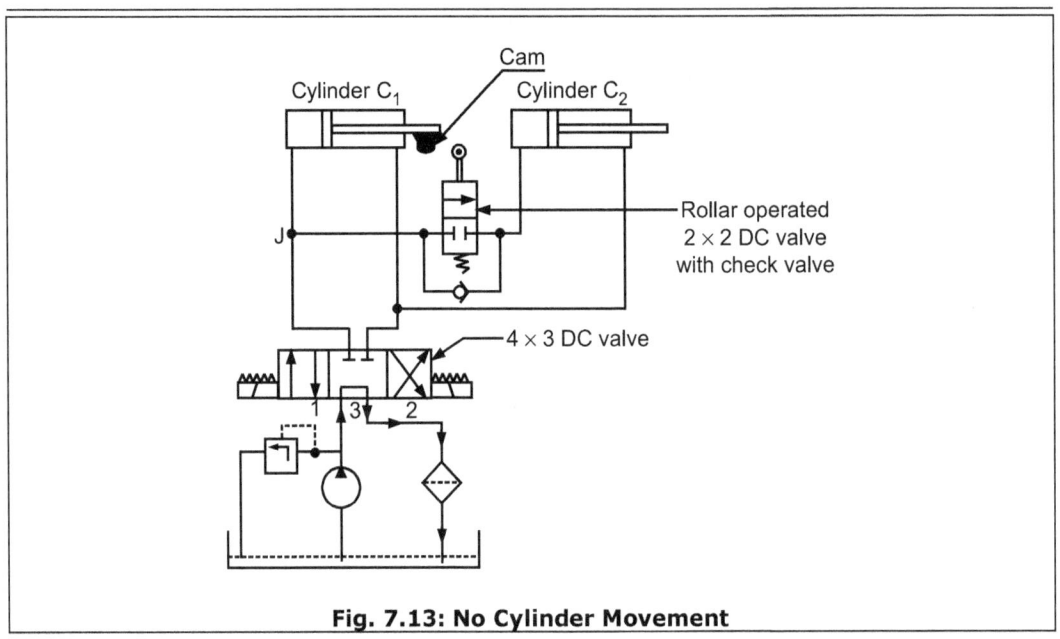

Fig. 7.13: No Cylinder Movement

- The circuit shown is Travel dependent sequencing circuit using roller and cam pair. In this circuit, cylinders C_1 and C_2 will be operated in sequence. But movement of piston of C_1 and C_2 will overlap for some distance. Position shown in circuit is no movement pistons.
- Now DC valve takes position 1 (Refer Fig. 7.14). Then oil flow starts towards junction 'J'. At this junction flow divides. Some oil enters into cylinder C_1 through port A_1, piston moves towards right. During this movement cam presses down rollar operated 2×2 DC valve. Then flow of port A_2 of cylinder C_2 starts and then the piston of this cylinder moves towards right. Thus movement of piston of C_2 will start only after cam operates 2×2 DC valve.

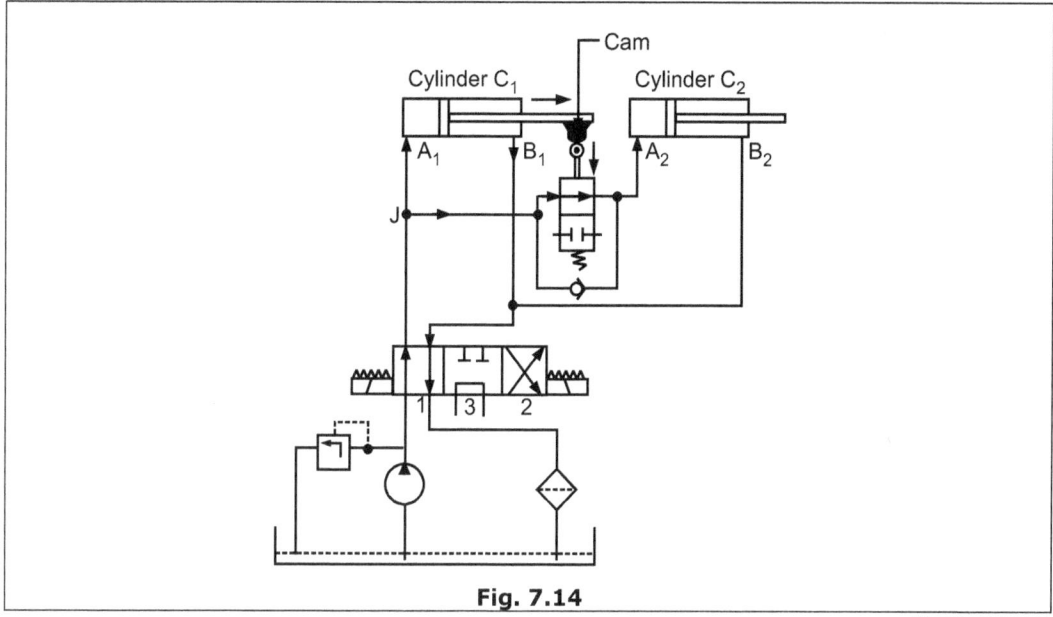

Fig. 7.14

7.2.6 Power Steering [W-14, S-15]

- The unledan weight of TATA 1613 Truck is not less than 6500 kg. When it is loaded then the gross weight becomes 16500 kg (16.5 T). The driver is steering this vehicle. To steer this vehicle with such a huge load, driver has to apply large amount of torque on steering wheel which, sometimes is not possible for a normal healthy person.
- To reduce the efforts of driver in such cases, power steering is used.
- **Power steering:** This system provides automatic hydraulic assistance to the turning efforts applied to manual steering system.
- **When power steering system operates?** The power steering system is designed to become operative or actuate when the efforts at the wheel exceed a predetermined value, say 10 N. That means when driver applies effort of 10 N at steering wheel then the system actuates.
- **Types of power steering based on operative system:**
  (i) Electrically operated power steering.
  (ii) Pneumatically operated power steering.
  (iii) Hydraulically operated power steering.

  Out of above types, hydraulically operated power steering system is most widely used in medium and heavy Duty Trucks/dumpers/Vehicles. Modern sophisticated cars use electrically operated power steering system.
- We will study hydraulically operated power steering system which is also called **Reaction Piston Type Power Steering.**

Hydraulically Operated Power Steering (Reaction Piston Type Steering)

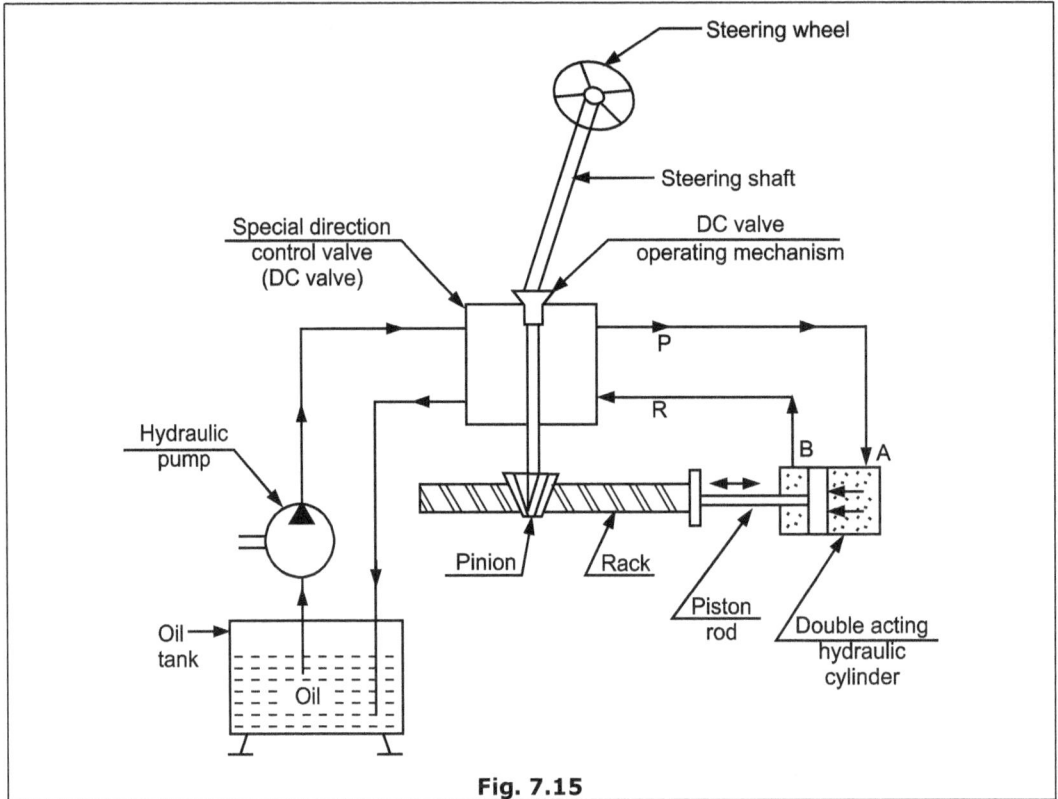

Fig. 7.15

Construction:

It consists of following assemblies / components:
(a) Oil Tank / Oil Reservoir
(b) Hydraulic Pump (Engine Driven)
(c) Direction Control Valve (made special in design)
(d) Rack and pinion pair to which piston rod is attached.
(e) Double Acting Hydraulic Cylinder.
(f) DC Valve Operating Mechanism.

Working:

- Pump is driven by engine of vehicle.
- Pump supplies hydraulic oil under pressure to specially designed direction control valve. This valve senses the input pressure at steering wheel and directs the pressurised oil to double acting cylinder.
- When steering wheel is almost steady and there are very low manual efforts at steering wheel the hydraulic oil enters into double acting cylinder through port A and B in equal amount and applies equal and opposite pressures on piston, hence piston is steady i.e. not moving.

- As soon as the driver applies more efforts than predetermined value (during turns on road), the steering arm actuates the direct control valve. This valve senses the input pressure at steering wheel and directs the pressurised oil to double acting cylinder say through port (A). Naturally piston will move towards left. The piston rod will move the rack towards left and pinion will rotate to help the driver these suppying additional efforts created by Rack and Pinion mechanism. Due to additional efforts, driver can easily turn the steering wheel.
- The oil from DA cylinder will return via port (B) and direction control valve to oil reservoir.
- If oil is supplied through port (B) then piston will move towards right and oil will return to oil tank through port (A).

Advantages of Hydraulic Power Steering

(a) The driver's efforts are substantially reduced. He can drive comfortably on 'hair pin' turns in Ghat section. His fatigue reduces.

(b) When vehicle suddenly meets a bump or if unfortunately front tyre bursts, there is no 'coming back' of steering wheel as in the case of conventional steering (i.e. steering without additional power). In this case, driver can easily control the vehicle.

(c) Even if the hydraulic power system fails due to oil leakage or failure of pump then driver can manoeuvere the vehicle easily with the help of manual steering.

Layout of Hydraulic Steering System in Vehicle

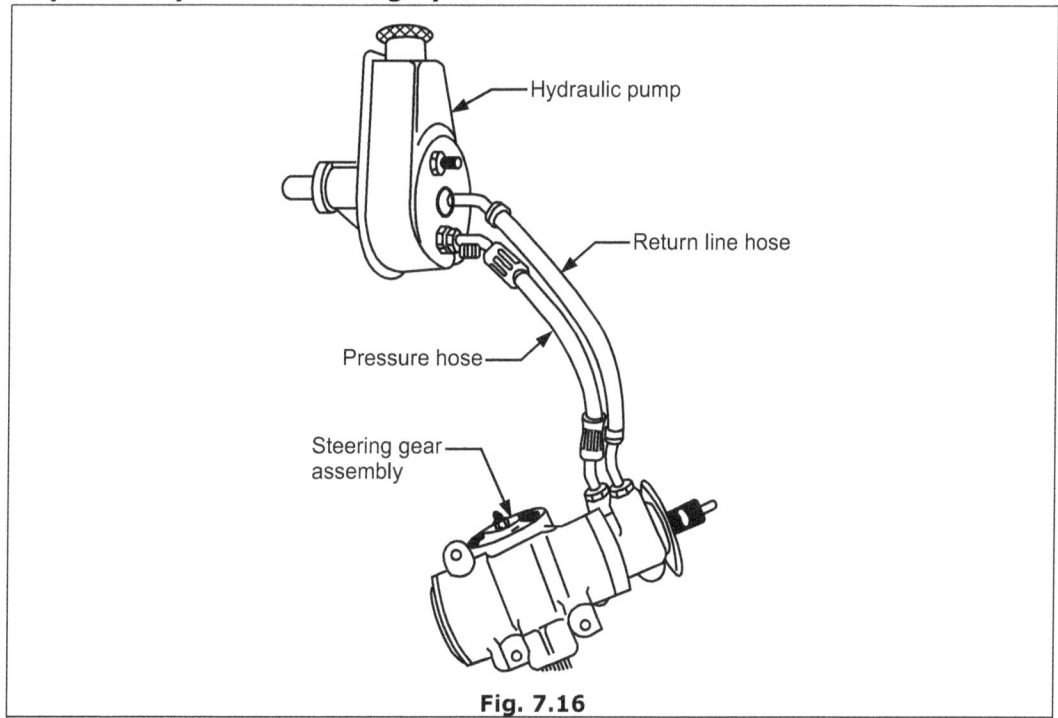

Fig. 7.16

7.2.7 Mobile Hydraulic System and Earthmovers

- Earthmoving equipments and machinery is unavoidable in infrastructure development.
- Infrastructure Development means:
    (a) Construction of Dock yards / Ports.
    (b) Development of Airports.
    (c) Development of Roads / Railroads / Highways.
    (d) Construction of Dams – Power sector.
    (e) Real Estate Development.
- Following earthmoving machinery / equipments are used in development of infrastructures stated above.
    (a) Back-hoe loader (popular name JCB)
    (b) Hydraulic Excavator (popular name Poclain)
    (c) Vibratory Rollars (Vibrator Compactor)
    (d) Hydraulic – Telescopic cranes
    (e) Bulldozers
- Back-hoe loader/Hydraulic Excavator/Bulldozers are used in land levelling/filling.
- Vibratory rollers are used for road levelling.
- Hydraulic – Telescopic cranes (10 T to 80 T) are used in material handling on site.
- Back-hoe loader can be transported on roads because it runs on tyres. This loader is having RTO registration number.
- Similar to Back-hoe loader, Hydraulic cranes can be transported on roads. These are also having registration number.
- Hydraulic excavator / Bulldozers are having scrawlar chain (similar to war tanks) for moving, hence are transported through heavy trucks/trailers.

Hydraulic Power (Mobile Hydraulic System) Systems

- All above equipments use hydraulic power, because hydraulic oil can create huge forces.
- The basic hydraulic system used in all the equipments is depicted in Fig. 7.17.

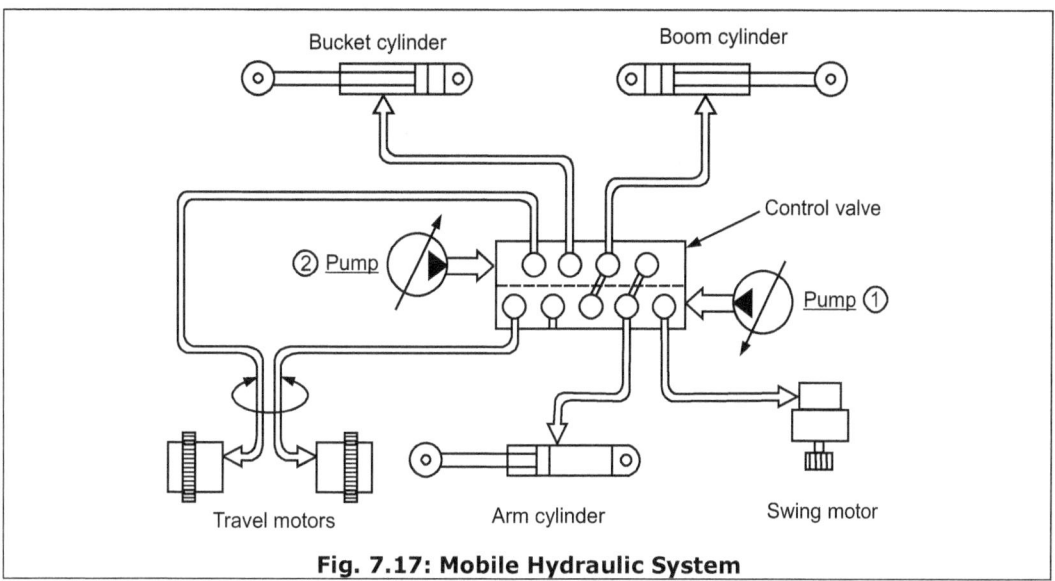

Fig. 7.17: Mobile Hydraulic System

Fig. 7.17 shows typical Hydraulic system of Hydraulic Excavator controlled on two hydraulic pumps. These two pumps supply pressurized hydraulic oil to bucket cylinder, boom cylinder and arm cylinder (these are linear actuators) and three hydraulic motors i.e. swing motor and travel motors (these are rotary actuators).

7.2.8 Hydraulic Excavator

Hydraulic excavator cannot be transported on road. It is carried in heavy trucks to excavation/levelling sites.

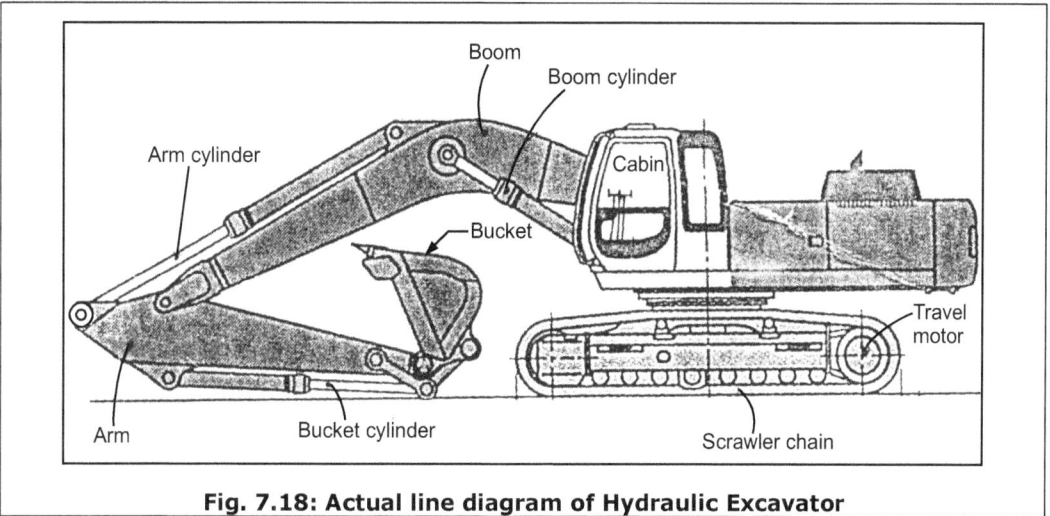

Fig. 7.18: Actual line diagram of Hydraulic Excavator

7.2.9 Back-hoe Loader

This is similar to excavator but it has 4 rubber tyres and it can travel on road. So its transportation cost is low. It has bucket on one side and back hoe (big bucket) on other side. Entire control of two buckets is on hydraulic power.

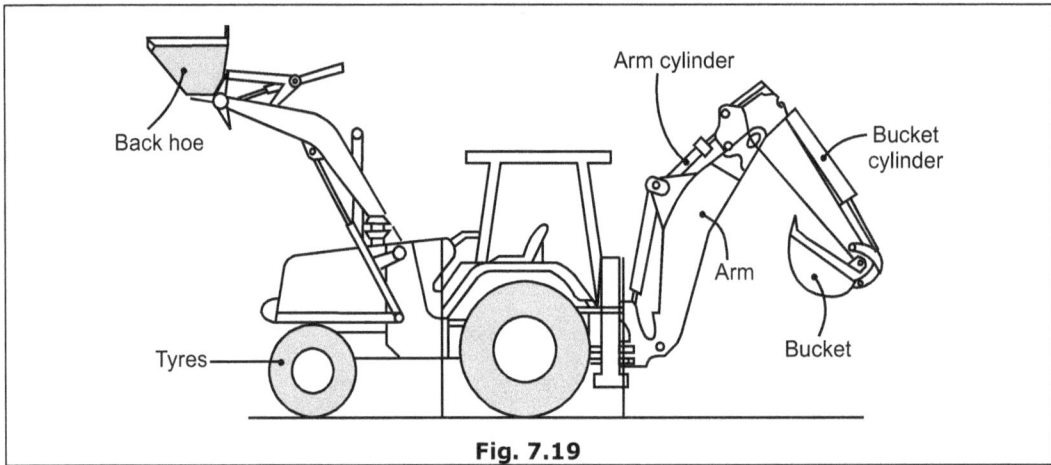

Fig. 7.19

7.2.10 Back-hoe Loader

These are sophisticated modern Road Rollars. They creates heavy pressures on road to compact Hot Tar metal on road to strengthen the road, while road asphalting. These machines have increased the speed of road making. Vibrator compactor uses hydraulic power to create high compacting pressures.

Fig. 7.20

7.3 SIMPLE PNEUMATIC CIRCUITS

- Any circuit diagram is symbolic representation of system which operates on push buttons or pilot signals and the actuator operates so that we can obtain useful work.
- Pneumatic circuit is a combination of various pneumatic elements arranged in a systematic manner to perform certain task.

- **Elements of Pneumatic Circuits**
  (a) Source of compressed air – Compressor working on Electrical power/Diesel Engine/Steam turbine.
  (b) Air storage element – Air tank.
  (c) Air Servicing unit – FRL unit.
  (d) Flow control and Direction control valves and other valves.
  (e) Actuators.

We will study following Pneumatic Circuits:
1. Speed Control of Pneumatic Motor
2. Speed Control of Double Acting Cylinder.
3. Speed Control of Bidirectional Air Motor.
4. Sequencing Circuit of 2 Double Acting Cylinders.
5. Sequencing Circuit with DA cylinder, SA cylinder and rollor operated DC valve.
6. Air Brakes
7. Low Cost Automation
8. Pneumatic Power Tools.

7.3.1 Circuit No. 1 Actuation of Pneumatic Motor (Air Motor)

Now we will see rotation of (or Actuation) unidirectional pneumatic motor using push button operated 3 × 2 DC valve.

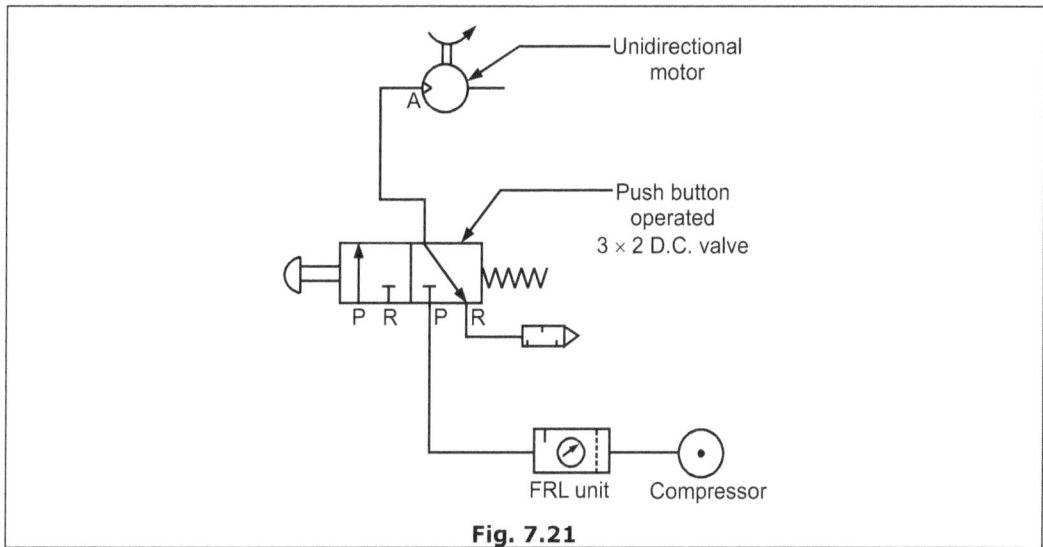

Fig. 7.21

Unidirectional motor: This motor rotates in one direction only i.e. clockwise or anticlockwise.

The push button is not operated. Pressure port P (compressed air) is not connected to port 'A' of motor. Hence motor is not rotating.

How push button of DC valve is operated:

Due to operation of push button of DC valve, the pressure port P will be connected to port 'A' of motor and motor starts rotating.

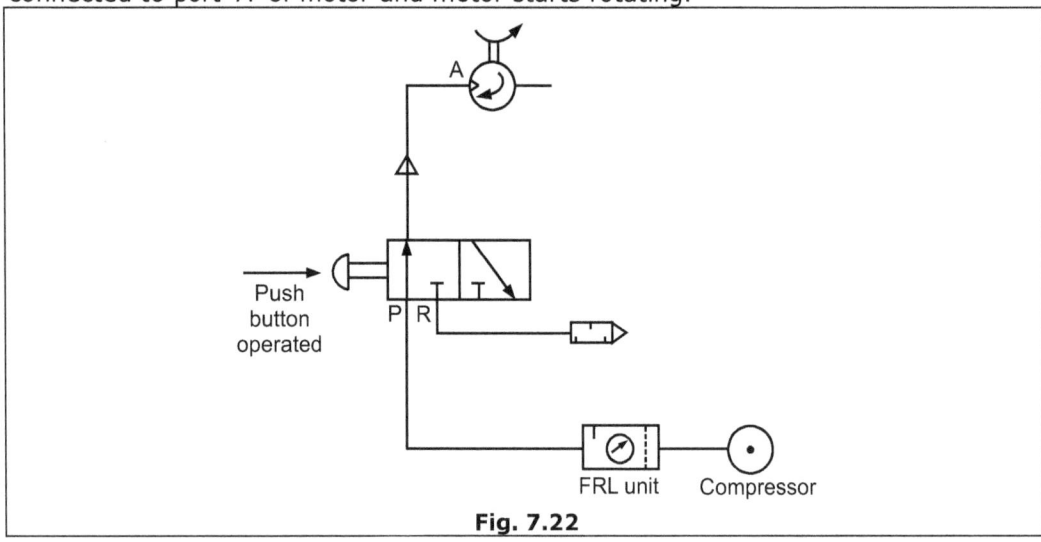

Fig. 7.22

Remember: See the symbol of unidirectional motor. The triangle apex is inside.

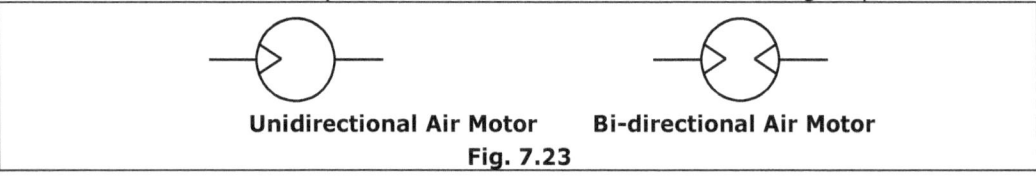

Fig. 7.23

7.3.2 Circuit No. 2 Speed Control of DA Cylinder [W-14]

Speed control circuits are adopted to control speed of actuators. This speed control is achieved by adopting flow control valve in circuit.

Remember:
- **SA cylinder or DA cylinder:** The movement of piston of these two actuators is reciprocating. i.e. piston slides in a cylinder. This clearly means that the piston is having linear motion and hence naturally having linear speed. The linear speed can be expressed in meter/sec. (m/s).
- **Air motor:** These are rotary actuators. When air is admitted in the inlet port of unidirectional or bi-directional motor, then the shaft of motor starts rotating. Hence these actuators are having circular motion i.e. rotary speed. This speed can be expressed in RPM.

Following circuit shows speed control of a Double Acting Cylinder (DA Cylinder)

In this circuit we are using:
(a) 4 × 2 DC valve – 1.
(b) Variable flow control valve with built-in check valve – 2 Nos.

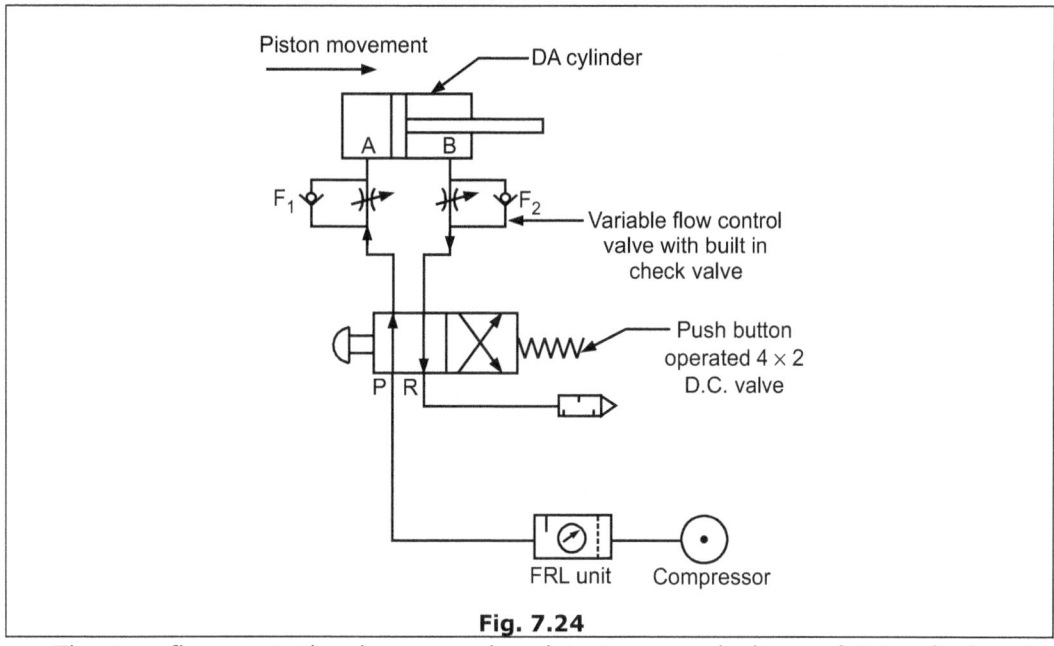

Fig. 7.24

The two flow control valves are placed in two supply lines of DA cylinder. As position shown in the circuit (Fig. 7.24), pressure port 'P' is connected to inlet port 'A' of DA cylinder. Now we can control the flow of air admitting in DA cylinder, through port A, by using variable flow control valve 'F_1'. If more flow will be allowed, then more air will enter in cylinder and piston will move towards right with more linear speed. If less air is allowed to flow, the linear speed of piston will be low.

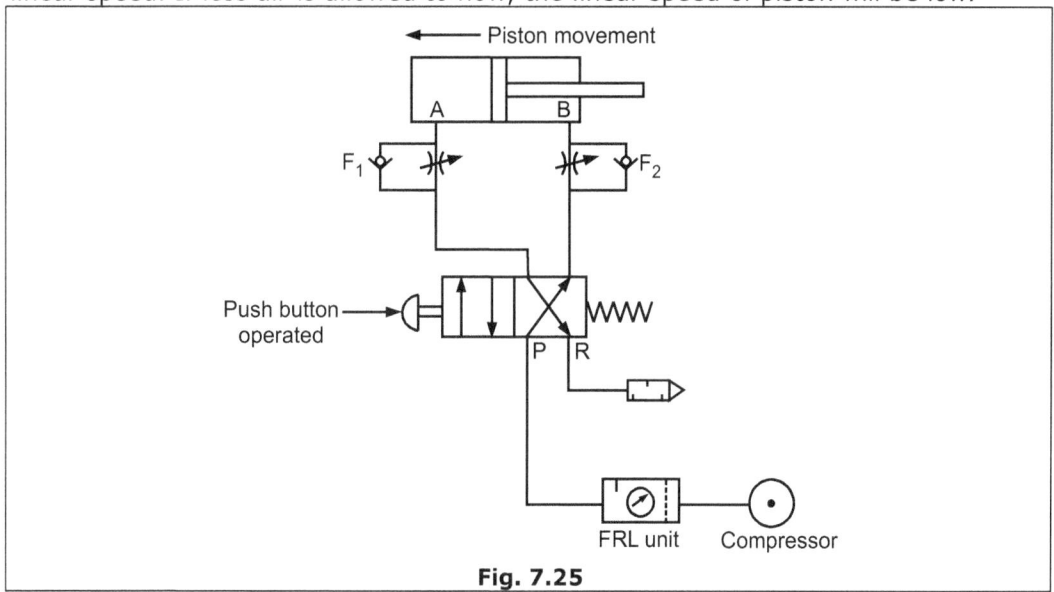

Fig. 7.25

When push button is pressed (Fig. 7.25), then pressure port 'P' will be connected to port 'B' of DA cylinder and exhaust port R will be connected to port A of DA cylinder. Here also by controlling flow control valve F_2 we can control the speed of piston. During this stroke, the air from earlier stroke in the other side of piston will be exhausted through flow control valve F_1 via DC valve.

During this return, the air flows to DC valve through throttled chamber of flow control valve. Air will not flow through check valve because, it is unidirectional valve.

This arrangement of circuit design with non-return flow control valve is called 'exhaust throttling' or 'Throttle out'.

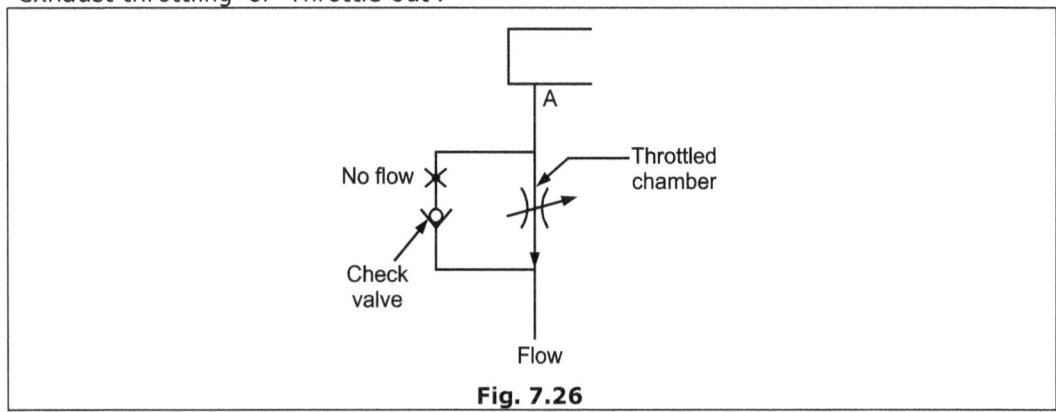

Fig. 7.26

7.3.3 Circuit No. 3 Speed Control of Bidirectional Air Motor

Bi-directional air motor rotates in clockwise as well as anti-clockwise direction. It is rotary actuator, the speed of which is measured in rpm. The speed of bi-directional motor is controlled as under.

The following circuit shows speed control of motor by using variable flow control valves (2 Nos) having built-in check valve; and 4 × 3 DC valve having zero position or central hold position.

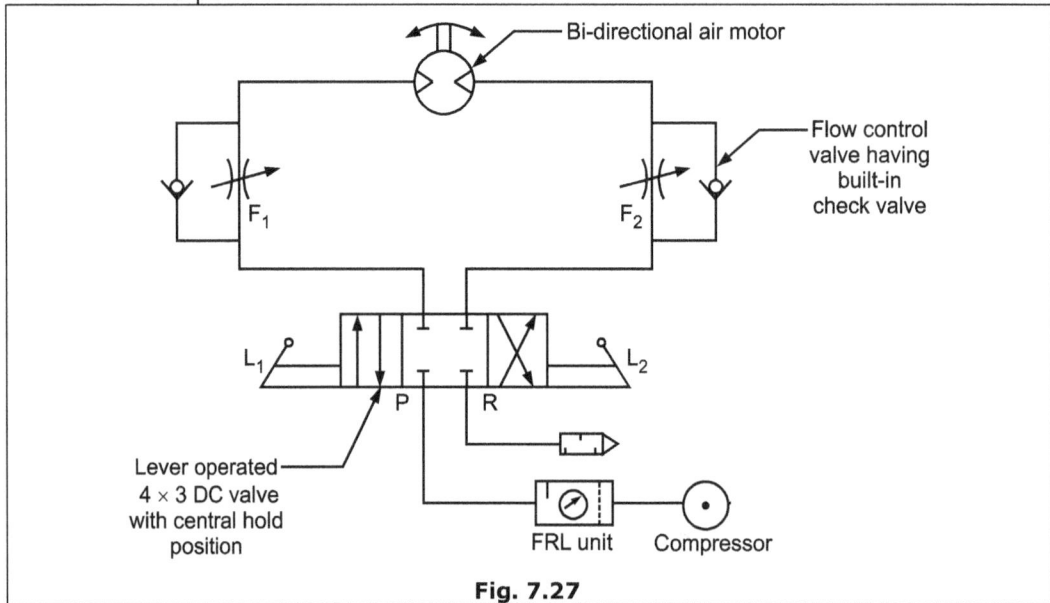

Fig. 7.27

In this circuit, 4 × 3 DC valve is used. The circuit shown is in central hold position. This clearly means that motor is not rotating. It is stand still.

Now lever L1 is operated.

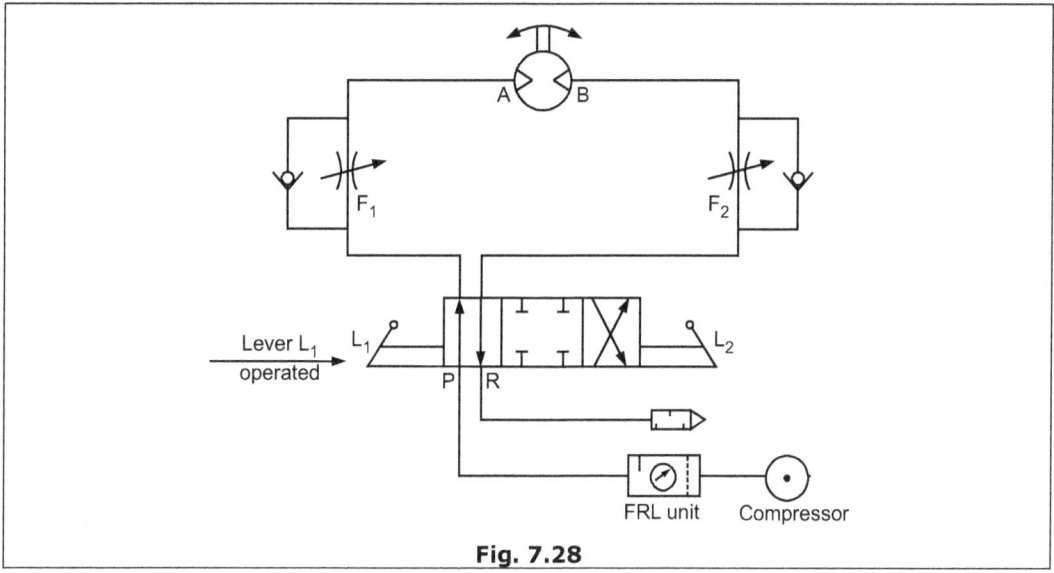

Fig. 7.28

When lever L_1 is operated (Fig. 7.28), port P will be connected to port A of air motor and motor will start rotating in say clockwise direction. Its speed can be controlled by using variable flow control valve F_1. Port B of motor will be connected to exhaust R. And the air in the motor will be exhausted through port R via DC valve.

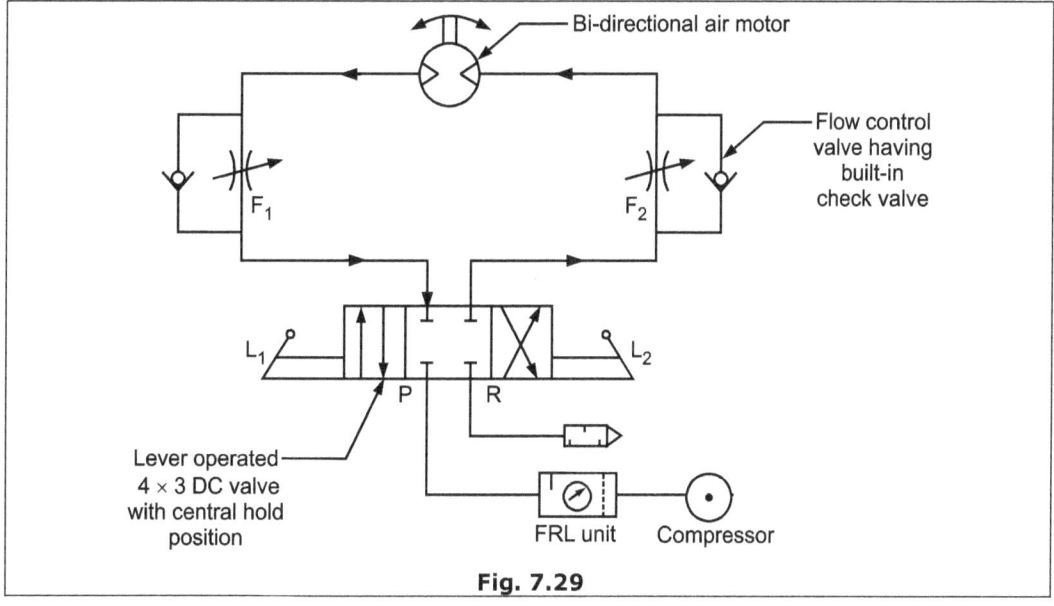

Fig. 7.29

When lever L_2 is operated (Fig. 7.29), pressure port 'P' will be connected to port B of motor and naturally motor will start rotating in anticlockwise direction. Port A will be connected to port R and air in the motor will be exhausted through port R via DC valve.

7.3.4 Circuit No. 4 Sequencing Circuit of 2 DA Cylinders [W-14]

The word 'sequence' indicates that, the operations one after the another. In bottling plants (Pepsi/Coca Cola), the liquid with CO_2 gas is filled in bottles and bottles are packed with crown cap. These plants are fully automatic and automization is done obviously with pneumatic power. In these plants, the movement of bottles needs 'sequence'. Many sequencing circuits are used in these plants. The actuators especially linear actuators are used to push the bottles for next operation in automation line.

Now, let us study a sequencing circuit using 2 DA cylinders. This circuit is having following units:

(a) DA cylinders with cam – 1 No.
(b) DA cylinder without cam – 1 No.
(c) 4 × 2, pilot (Air Impulse) operated DC valves – 2 Nos.
(d) Push button operated 2 × 2 start valves – 2 Nos.
(e) FRL unit.
(f) Compressor.

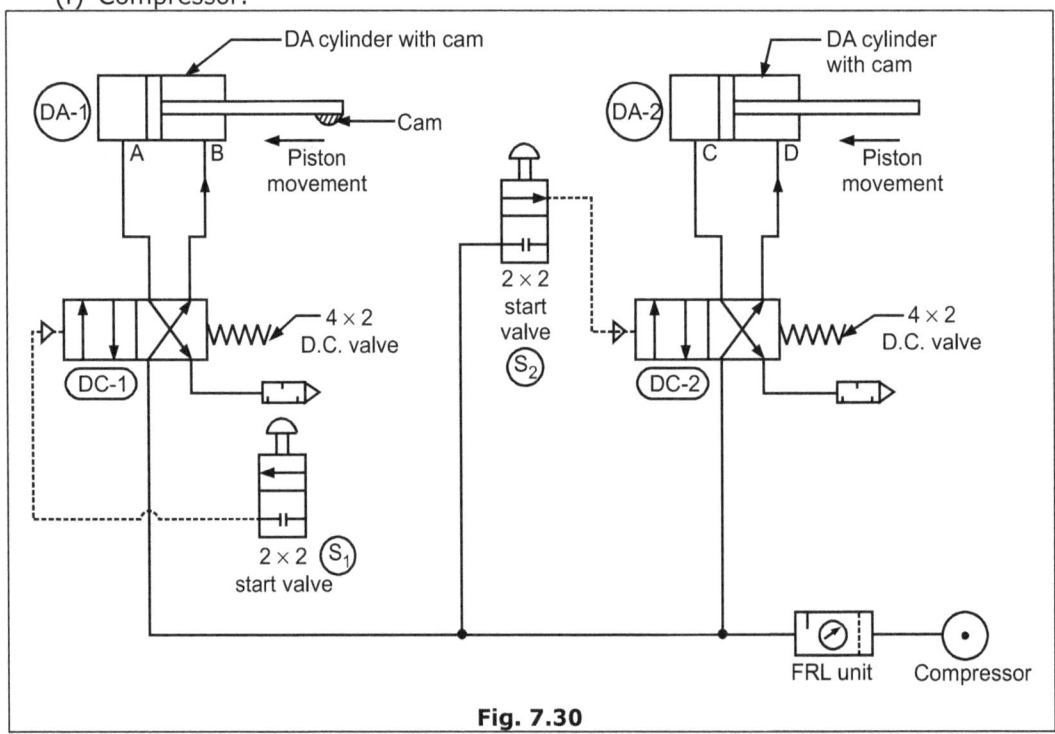

Fig. 7.30

As shown in circuit, air is admitted at port B of **'DA-1'** cylinder and port D of **'DA-2'** cylinder. Hence both pistons are moving from right to left in both actuators.

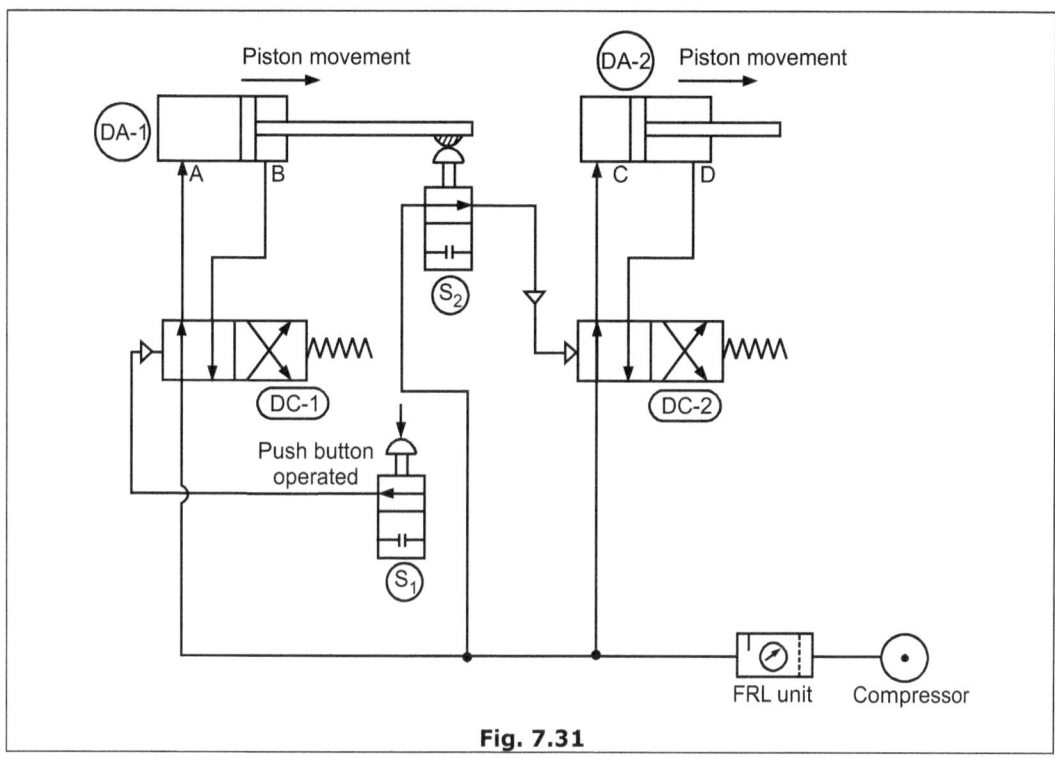

Fig. 7.31

When push button of start valve **(S₁)** is operated (shown in Fig. 7.31), the air signal (Impulse) will be supplied to DC valve **(DC–1)**. The air will be admitted through port 'A' of **DA-1** and piston will move towards right. The cam is attached to end of piston rod. This cam will push the push button of start valve **(S₂)**. Due to this air signal (Impulse) will be supplied to direction control valve **(DC-2)** and it will operate. Now air will be admitted through port 'C' of **(DA-2)** and the piston will now move from left to right.

The sequence is achieved by cam of **(DA-1)**. Unless and until **(S₂)** will not be operated with the help of cam, the piston of **(DA-2)** cannot move from left to right.

7.3.5 Circuit No. 5 Sequencing of SA Cylinder DA Cylinder using Roller Operated DC Value

Now, let us study the circuit in which SA cylinder and DA cylinder are in sequence. The circuit uses rollar operated 3 × 2 DC valve.

As shown in circuit there is no supply of air in any line because 2 × 2 valve No. (4) is not actuated i.e. it is in normal position (2 × 2 DC valve is normally closed).

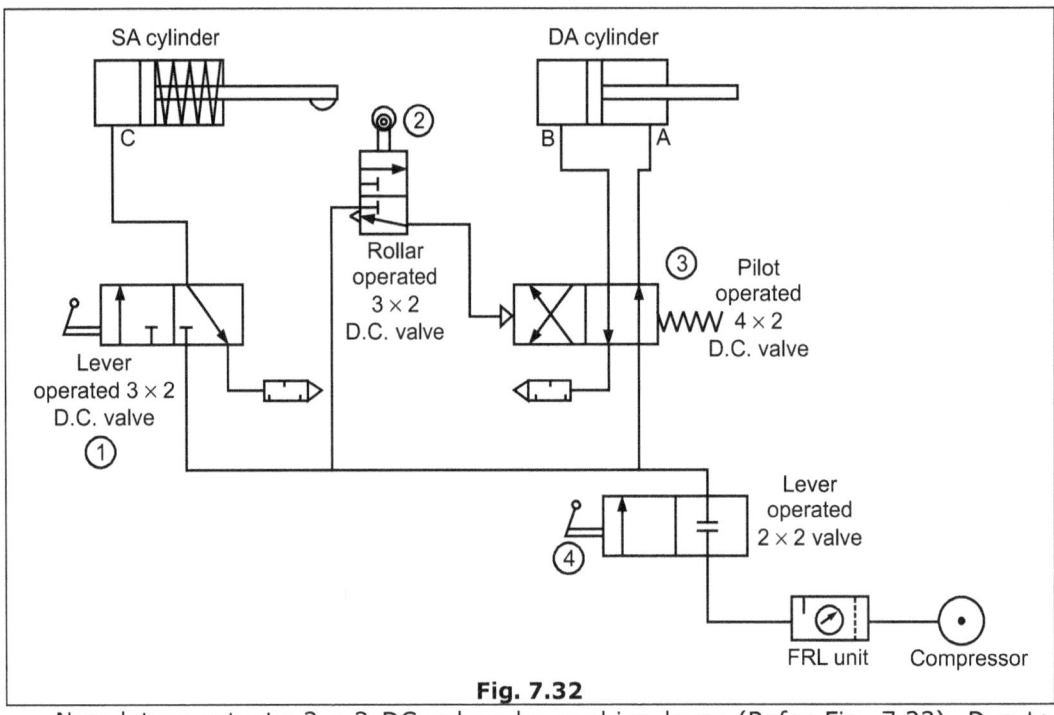

Fig. 7.32

Now let us actuate 2 × 2 DC valve; by pushing lever (Refer Fig. 7.33). Due to this, the compressed air will be supplied to all lines in circuit and the actuated position will be as under.

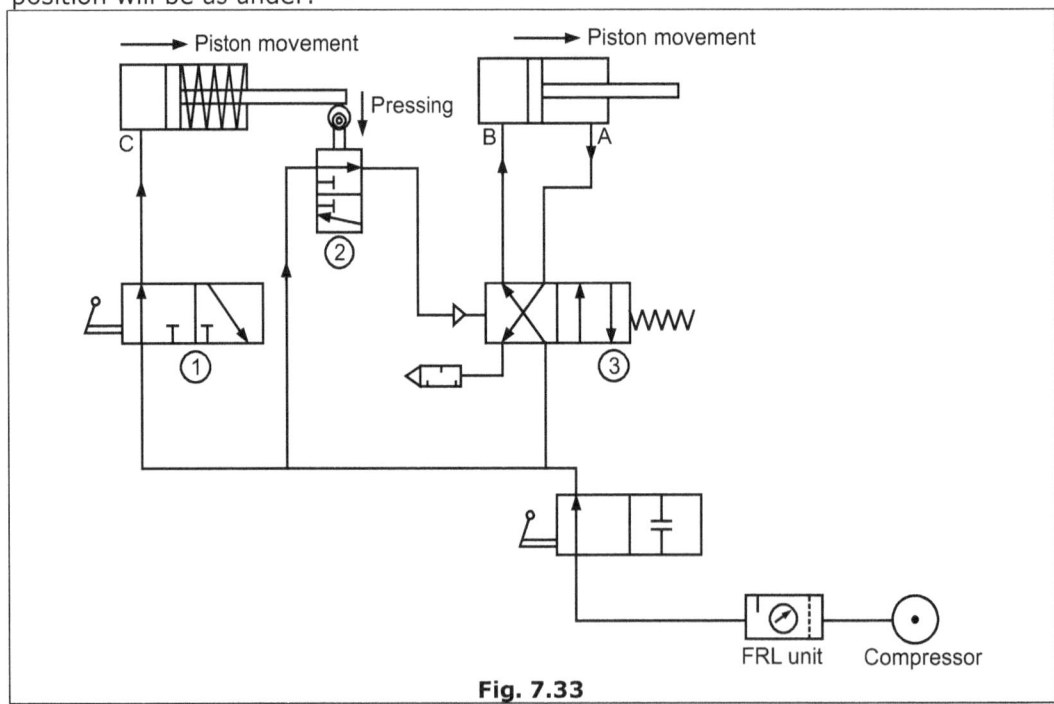

Fig. 7.33

Due to air supply, the compressed air will be admitted through port 'C' in SA cylinder and piston of it will move from left to right. During this movement the piston rod of SA cylinder will foul with roller of valve (2) and the rod will press the rollar lever down. This will operate valve (2) and air signal (impulse) will be supplied to valve (3). This valve will then actuate and compressed air will be supplied through port B. Due to this the piston of DA cylinder will also move to right.

7.3.6 Air Brakes (Pneumatic Brakes / Power Brakes)

- Brakes are one of the most important components on vehicle. The brake assembly is required to stop the vehicle within smallest possible distance.
- In braking the vehicle we are converting kinetic energy of the running wheels into heat energy which is then dissipated to atmosphere.
- One of the classification criteria of brakes is its method of actuation. The various types under this criteria are:

    (a) **Mechanical brakes:** Used on two and three wheelers.

    (b) **Hydraulic brakes:** Used on LCV, LMV, heavy vehicles.

    (c) **Vacuum brakes:** Used on heavy vehicles.

    (d) **Air brakes:** Used on heavy vehicles.

- In this topic we will study Air Brakes (Pneumatic Brakes) because this system uses compressed air.
- **General Layout of Air Brake System**

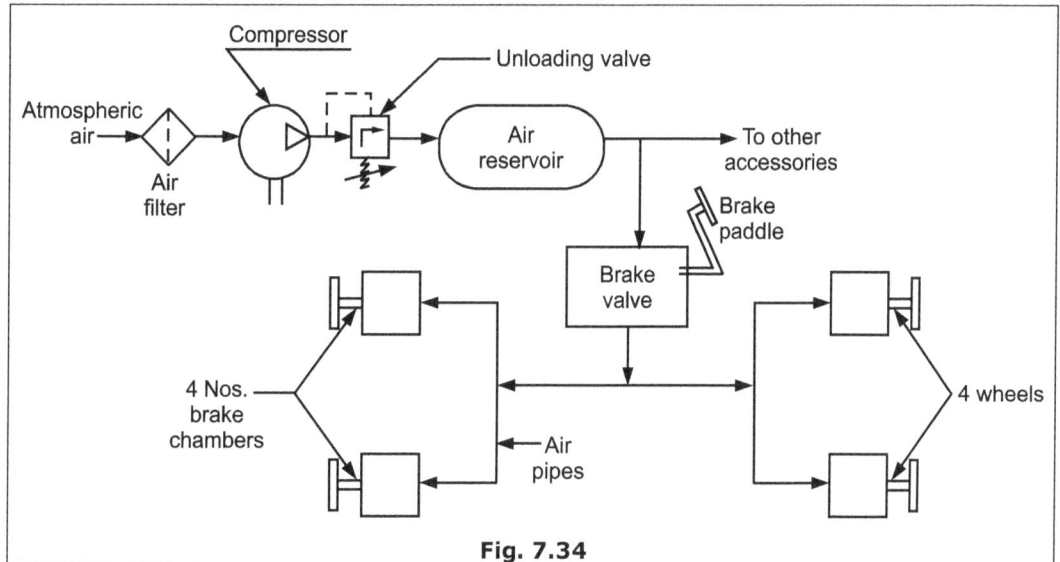

Fig. 7.34

- Fig. 7.34 shows complete layout of Air Brake system.
- It consists of Air filter, Unloading valve, Air compressor, Air reservoir (Tank), Brake valve and 4 Nos. brake chambers.

- **Working:** The compressor takes atmospheric air through air filter, and compresses the air. This air is stored under pressure in Air Reservoir. From this reservoir air goes to various accessories of vehicle which operates on compressed air. Part of air goes to brake valve. The control of brake valve is done by driver who can control the intensity of braking according to emergency.
- **Function of unloading valve:** This valve serves to regulate the line pressure. When specific air pressure has been attained, the unloader valve relieves the compressor. Similarly, when line pressure decreases below the required limit, it re-establishes the compressor.
- **Air Brake is Pneumatic Circuit** comprising of source of air i.e. compressor, pneumatic pipelines, air controlling valve (brake valve) and actuators (brake chamber) to obtain mechanical advantage.
- In this circuit of air brakes, we have to study brake valve and brake chamber in detail to understand the working of entire brake system.

Brake valve:
- This valve is actuated by driver through brake paddle. When driver presses the brake paddle down, more compresed air will be supplied to actuator i.e. Brake chamber and stopping of vehicle will be quick. We will see the construction and working of Brake valve and Brake chamber.

Following is the schematic diagram of Brake valve.

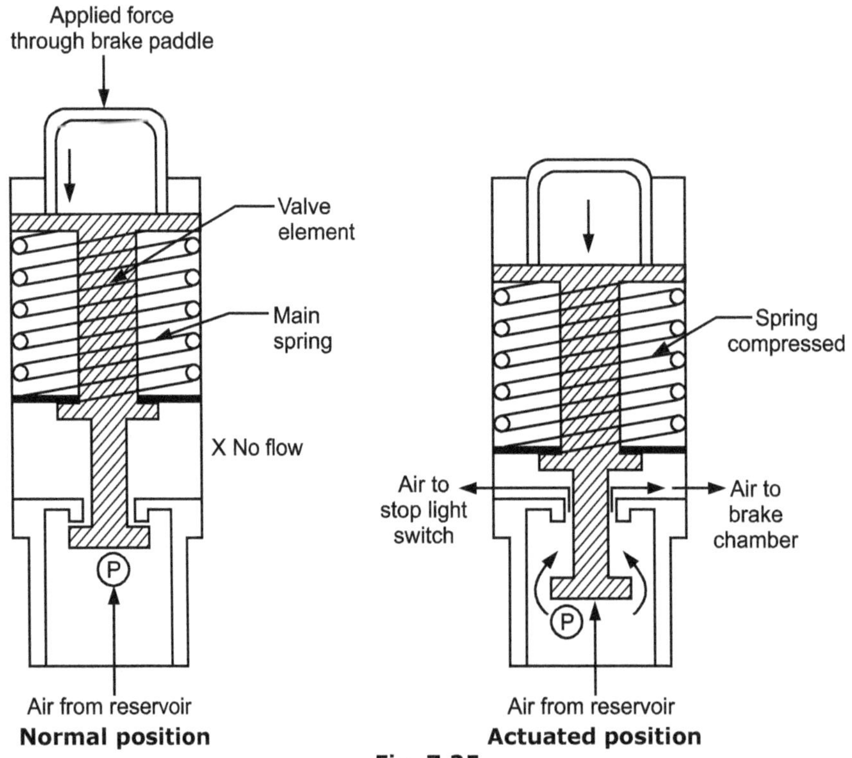

Fig. 7.35

Construction: This valve consists of body and special shaped valve element. A spring surrounds the valve element. There is pressure port (P) through which compressed air from reservoir comes in.

Working: When driver presses the brake paddle to apply brakes, this force will be transmitted to valve element. The valve element moves down by compressing the spring (see actuated position). When valve element moves down, the compressed air through port (P) will enter through open passages and main part of it will travel to brake chamber and some part will travel to stop light switch. In brake chamber, air will rotate the cam and brake shoes will expand to apply brake.

When driver reduces the force on paddle and stop braking action, the spring will expand and valve element will attain its original position and air flow to brake chamber will cut-off.

Brake chamber: One brake chamber is installed on each wheel. Its function is to convert the pressure energy of compressed air into useful mechanical energy for application of brake. Fig. 7.36 shows the schematic view of brake chamber.

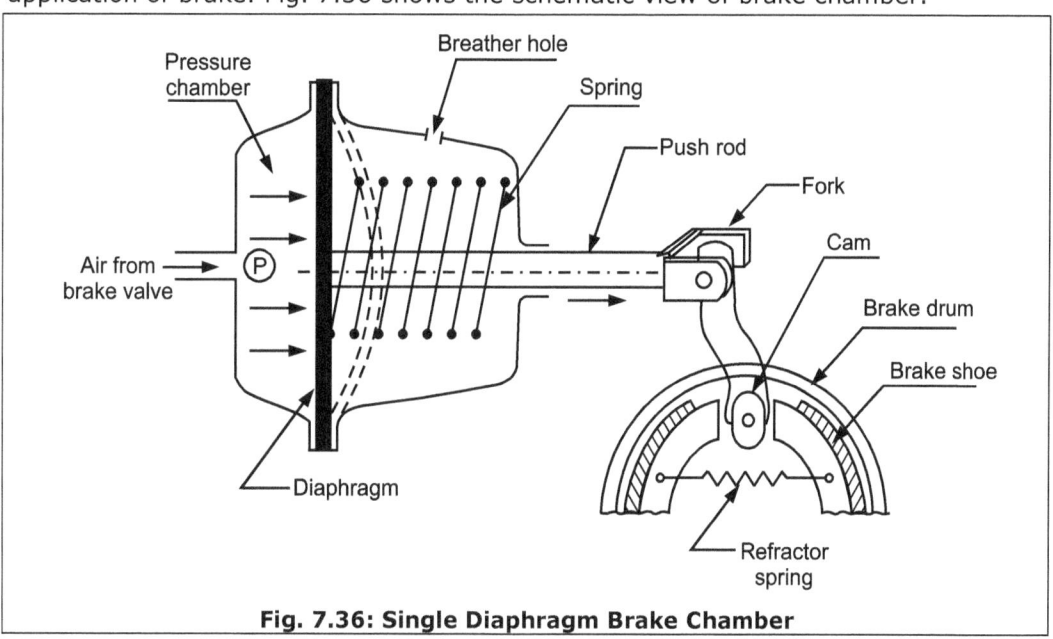

Fig. 7.36: Single Diaphragm Brake Chamber

Construction: Brake chamber consists of a single diaphragm. This diaphragm divides the chamber into two parts. On left is pressure chamber while right chamber is connected to atmosphere through breather hole. The push rod moves towards right because it is connected to diaphragm. Push rod is further connected to cam of brake cylinder as shown.

Working: When driver pushes the brake paddle in order to apply brakes, then brake valve operates and pressurised compressed air from reservoir passes through brake valve to port (P) shown in Fig. 7.36. The air applies its force on diaphragm and diaphragm gets deflected as shown by dotted lines. The deflected diaphragm pushes the push rod to right. The push rod is connected to cam actuating mechanism through fork. Now, cam rotates and brake shoes foul with internal surface of brake drum to stop its motion.

When braking paddle is released by driver air supply in pressure chamber stops and diaphragm regains its original shape. The push rod now moves towards left, cam attains its original position. The brake shoes return back due to Retractor spring.

- There are other types of brake chambers:

  (a) Double diaphragm brake chamber.

  (b) Triple diaphragm brake chamber

  (c) Diaphragm – Piston brake chamber.

7.3.7 Electro-Hydraulics

- The word Electro-Hydraulics has meanings for highly different operations. It can stand for an electrical control device that makes precise adjustments in a hydraulic system.
- Electro-hydraulic devices were first developed for weapon-control systems and missile launch platforms during World War II. Because the heavy weapons needed to be aimed precisely and because hydraulics are inherently unsuited for precision movements, a new kind of actuator was developed to give the weapon handlers improved control over the hydraulic systems. After the war, development on these hydroelectric devices continued, with a new two-stage mechanical feedback (MFB) servo valve being manufactured during the early 1950s. The MFB valve, which first saw service in the aerospace industry before moving into the industrial sectors, offered greater control and precision in hydraulic devices, and would be the standard of the industry for several decades.
- Perhaps the most well-known electro-hydraulic device is an automobile's power steering unit — also called an electro-hydraulic actuator. The unit combines high power with a high degree of accuracy to adjust for the minute movements of the steering wheel in a vehicle. This type of technology, where electrical components are used to increase the accuracy of hydraulic movements, can be applied to almost any situation where hydraulics is used.
- Position sensing and feedback devices (Electrical Part) enhance the functionality and productivity of a hydraulic system. At its simplest, cylinder extends and retracts until it meets a physical obstacle or reaches the end of its stroke. The addition of controlling electronics allows the system designer to regulate velocity and acceleration, and to link associated processes to points in the cylinder's cycle. The resulting system combines the flexibility of electronic control with the unmatched power density of hydraulics, benefiting both the designer and end user.

- **Electro-Hydraulic Manual Transmission** is a type of semi-automatic transmission system, which uses an automated clutch unlike conventional manual transmissions where the driver operates the clutch. The clutch is controlled by electronic computers and hydraulics. To change gears, the driver selects the desired gear with the transmission shift lever, and the system automatically operates the clutch and throttle to match revs and engage the clutch again. Also, many such transmissions operate in sequential mode where the driver can only up shift or downshift by one gear at a time.
- Depending on the implementation, some computer-controlled electro-hydraulic manual transmissions will automatically shift gears at the right points.

Electro-Hydraulic Power Steering Systems

Electro-hydraulic power steering systems, sometimes abbreviated EHPS, and also sometimes called "hybrid" systems, use the same hydraulic assist technology as standard systems, but the hydraulic pressure comes from a pump driven by an electric motor instead of a drive belt at the engine.

In 1990, Toyota introduced its second-generation MR2 with electro-hydraulic power steering. This avoided running hydraulic lines from the engine (which was behind the driver) upto the steering rack.

In 1994 Volkswagen produced the Mark 3 Golf Ecomatic, with an electric pump. This meant that the power steering would still operate while the engine was stopped by the computer to save fuel. Electro-hydraulic systems can be found in some cars by Ford, Volkswagen, Audi, Peugeot, Citroen, SEAT, Skoda, Suzuki, Opel, MINI, Toyota, Honda, and Mazda.

Hydraulic actuators are characterized by their ability to impart large forces at high speeds and are used in many industrial motion systems. In applications where good dynamic performance is important it is common to contain the actuator in a servo loop comprising a feedback transducer and electronic controller.

The majority of electronic servo-controllers used in these systems are analogue based implementations of the well-known PID type.

Applications of Electro-Hydraulic Servo Systems

The range of applications for electro-hydraulic servo systems are:
1. Manufacturing Systems,
2. Materials Test Machines,
3. Active Suspension Systems,
4. Mining Machinery,
5. Fatigue Testing,
6. Flight Simulation,
7. Paper Machines,
8. Ships and Electromagnetic Marine Engineering,
9. Infection Moulding Machines, Robotics
10. Steel and Aluminium Mill Equipment.

Hydraulic systems are also common in aircraft, where their high power-to-weight ratio and precise control makes them an ideal choice for actuation of flight surfaces.

A Position Controlled Hydraulic System

A typical position controlled hydraulic system consists of a power supply, flow control valve, linear actuator, displacement transducer, and electronic servo-controller. The servo controller compares the signal from the feedback displacement transducer with an input demand to determine the position error, and produces a command signal to drive the flow control valve. The control valve adjusts the flow of pressurized oil to move the actuator until the desired position is attained: a condition indicated by the error signal falling to zero. A force controlled hydraulic system operates in a similar way, except that the oil flow is adjusted to achieve an output force, measured by a suitable transducer.

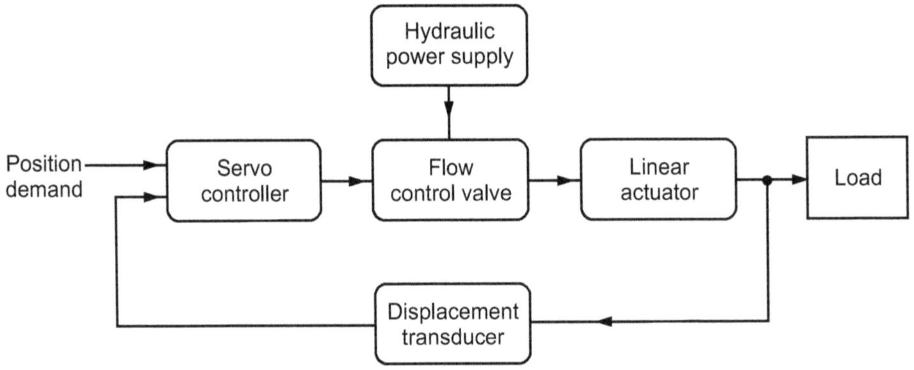

Fig. 7.37

Electro Hydraulic Stacker

The capacity of Electro Hydraulic Stacker is upto 2000 kgs. The stacker can lift load of 2000 kg upto 4000 mm height. This stacker is hydraulically operated. The lifting is through electric motor, gear pump and hydraulic actuator. Electro hydraulic lifting and lowering through gravity, hence electrical power is required only while lifting whereas while lowering electrical power is not required.

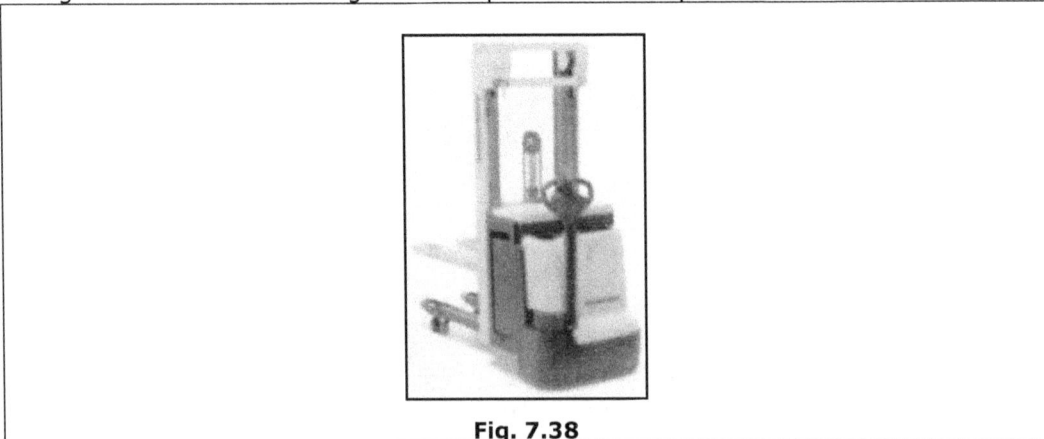

Fig. 7.38

7.3.8 Pneumatic Power Tools

- Pneumatic Power Tools are the tools which use pneumatic power i.e. Pressurised Air.
- These tools are used for grinding, chipping, rivetting, drilling etc.
- Various types of tools are used in industry. Some of them are:
  1. Pneumatic Grinders (Straight Grinders and Angle Grinders), 2. Pneumatic Drills (Pistol Drills), 3. Pneumatic Screw Drivers, 4. Pneumatic Chain Saw, 5. Pneumatic Borer, 6. Pneumatic Riveter, 7. Pneumatic Scrapper, 8. Pneumatic Wrenches, 9. Pneumatic Wood Cutters / Planners, 10. Pneumatic Hammers, 11. Die Grinders.
- Pneumatic Tools are Rotary Tools (Grinders / Drills etc.) and Reciprocating (Hammers / Scrapers / Rivetters).
- Rotary tools work with very high RPM. For example, 1.4" capacity heavy duty die grinders rotate at 25000 rpm.
- Wood borers (drilling a hole of square / triangular, round cross-section in wood) work on relatively low speeds.
- Pneumatic Rotary tools work with the help of vane type air motor and a gear train. Power developed by the pressurised air via air motor (vane type) is transmitted with the help of gear train.
- Pneumatic hand tools are generally operated at 4 to 6 bar pressure. Operation at higher pressure shortens the life of the tools.
- Pneumatic tools such as hammers, scrapers, rivetters use double acting pneumatic cylinders because we need reciprocating action in case of such tools.

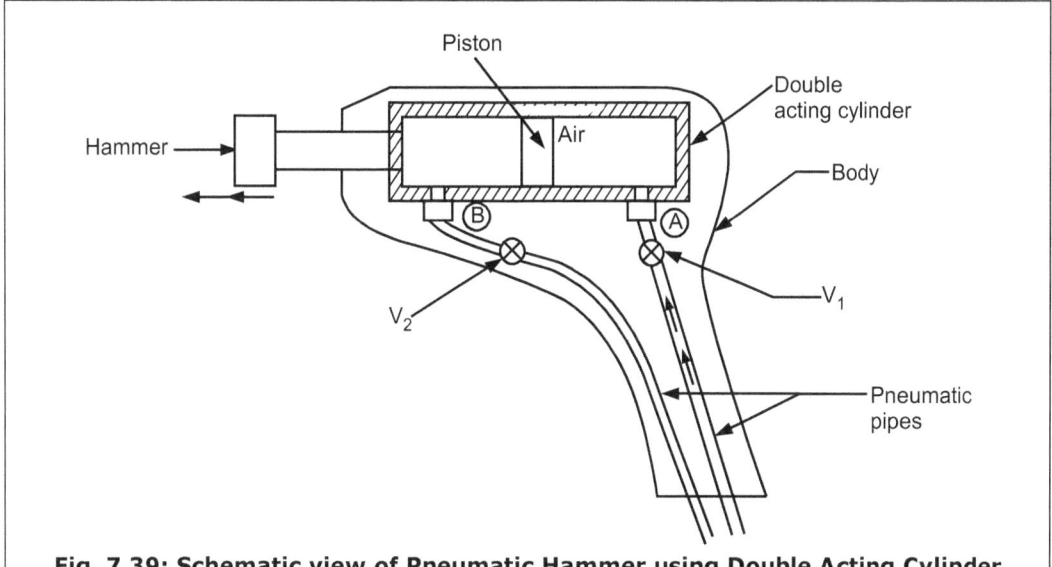

Fig. 7.39: Schematic view of Pneumatic Hammer using Double Acting Cylinder

Fig. 7.39 gives a general idea of how pneumatic hammer operates. Pressurized air enters intermittently in DA cylinder through port (A) when valve (V_1) is opened. Due to pressure of air piston moves intermittently towards left giving hammering action. When valve (V_1) is closed and (V_2) is open the piston of DA cylinder will move towards right and will return to the original position. Instead of two valves we can use combined direction control valve.

7.3.9 Pneumatic Drill (Using Vane Motor)

(Pistol Drill) This drill or Grinder is having almost same construction. All rotary pneumatic tools use Rotary Vane Motor.

Construction: Refer schematic diagram of Pneumatic drill. It is having CI body in which Air Motor (vane type) enhouses. The motor shaft is attached to 3 gear train and gear housing (This arrangement is somewhat similar to epicyclic gear train used in Automobiles). Drill chuck is attached to spindle of gear train which transfers power developed by air to drill. There is air supply pipe and flow of air is controlled by air flow control valve.

Working: When flow control valve (similar to trigger of pistol) is pressed, the pressurised air will pass over the vanes of air motor, as shown by arrows near each vane and the rotor will rotate in clockwise direction. This rotary motion will transfer to 3 gear train and thus drill will rotate.

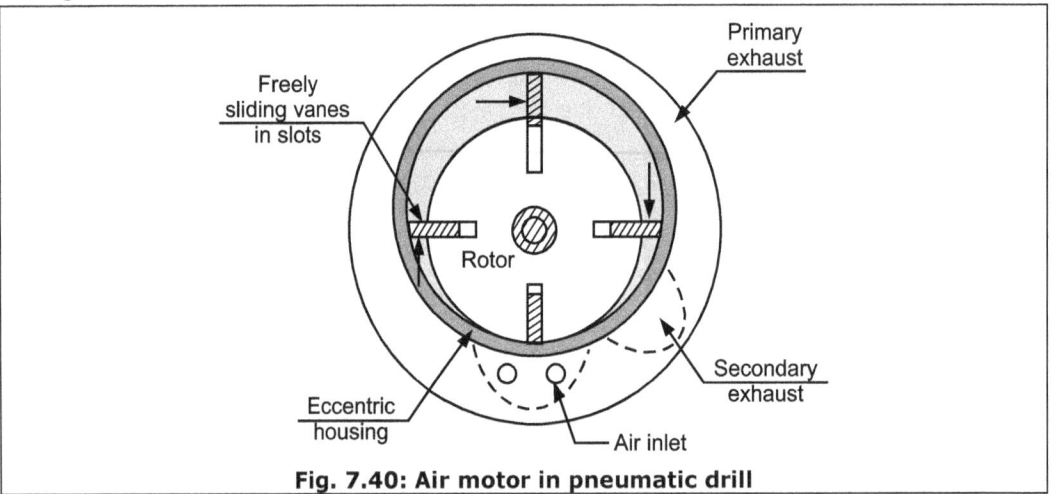

Fig. 7.40: Air motor in pneumatic drill

Maintenance of Pneumatic Tools:

Following are some maintenance hints noted in order to keep the tool for a long life.

(a) Always ensure clean and dry air supply to the tool.

(b) To avoid undesirable pressure drops, use short length hoses to tools.

(c) Use proper joints.

(d) Do not increase air pressure under any circumstances.

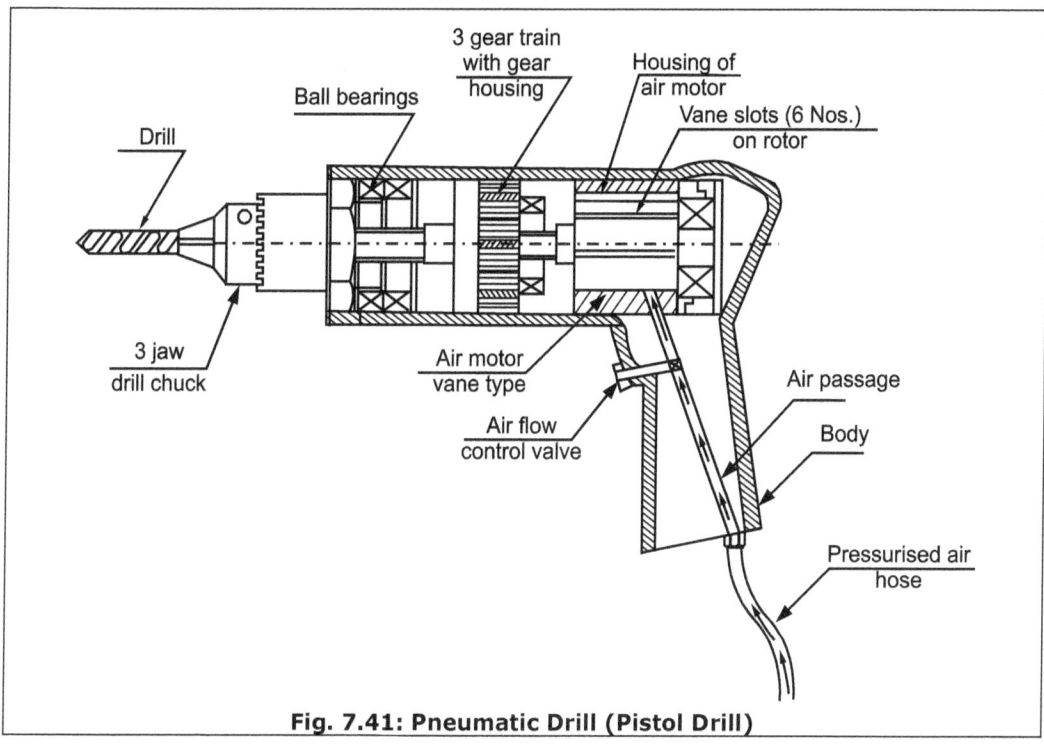

Fig. 7.41: Pneumatic Drill (Pistol Drill)

Advantages of Pneumatic Tools:
1. Pneumatic tools are compact.
2. They are having low operating cost.
3. As compared to electrically driven power tools, the maintenance cost of these tools is less.
4. For chipping of roads/stones in mines, pneumatic tool (chipper) is the only solution because it does not require electricity. The compressed air can be created with the help of engine driven air compressor.
5. Electrical power tools are hazardous in view of short circuit. No fire hazard with pneumatic tools.

Important Points

- **Sequencing circuit** is extensively used in Industrial Hydraulic Systems used especially in Mass Production.
- **Sequence valve** is 'close relative' of pressure relief valve; but sequence valve is used in hydraulic systems to cause various operations in sequential order i.e. one after another.
- **Power steering:** This system provides automatic hydraulic assistance to the turning efforts applied to manual steering system.
- **Hydraulic excavator:** It cannot be transported on road. It is carried in heavy trucks to excavation/levelling sites.
- **Back-hoe Loader:** This is similar to excavator but it has 4 rubber tyres and it can travel on road. So its transportation cost is low. It has bucket on one side and back hoe (big bucket) on other side.

- **Back-hoe Loader:** These are sophisticated modern Road Rollars. They create pressures on road to compact Hot Tar metal on road to strengthen the road, while road asphalting. These machines have increased the speed of road making.
- **Pneumatic circuit** is a combination of various pneumatic elements arranged in a systematic manner to perform certain task.
- **Bi-directional air motor rotates** in clockwise as well as anti-clockwise direction. It is rotary actuator, the speed of which is measured in rpm.
- **Brakes** are one of the most important components on vehicle. The brake assembly is required to stop the vehicle within smallest possible distance.
- **Pneumatic Power Tools** are the tools which use pneumatic power i.e. Pressurised Air.

Practice Questions

1. Draw general layout of Hydraulic System.
2. What is the function of:
   (i) Air receiver
   (ii) Air filter
   (iii) Moisture separator
   (iv) Air conducting elements
3. Compare Hydraulic and Pneumatic System on the basis of:
   (i) Pressure achievement
   (ii) Operational cost
   (iii) Working medium
   (iv) Weight to pressure ratio
4. Draw meter-in circuit. Explain its working.
5. What are the advantages of Bleed-off valve?
6. Why power steering is used on heavy vehicle? Explain.
7. Draw schematic diagram of hydraulically operated power steering and label the parts.
8. Write advantages of power steering system.
9. Write names of any four earthmoving equipments.
10. Draw simple circuit of control of bi-directional air motor.
11. How two double acting pneumatic cylinders can be sequenced? Explain with circuit diagram.
12. What is the function of Brake Valve in Air Braking System? Explain with neat sketch.
13. Draw neat sketch of Brake Chamber and explain how Brake Chamber works.
14. What is Low Cost Automation? Explain.
15. How we can obtain pushing/puling action by using Single Acting Pneumatic Cylinder.
16. Write any four advantages of Low Cost Automation.
17. Write any four pneumatic tools.
18. How Pneumatic Drill Works? Write its working principle.
19. Write four advantages of Pneumatic Tools.

■■■

APPENDIX A : COMPARISONS

1. Compare Hydraulic and Pneumatic System

Hydraulic System	Pneumatic System
(a) Energy carrying medium is oil.	(a) Energy carrying medium is air.
(b) Pump pressurises the fluid.	(b) Compressor compresses the air.
(c) Oil after pressurising needs to be used immediately. Storage of pressurised oil is not possible.	(c) Pressurised air can be stored in pressure vessel called Air Receiver.
(d) Can be used upto 700 bar pressures.	(d) Can be used upto 10 bar pressure.
(e) Return lines are essential to transport the used oil back to oil tank.	(e) Return lines are not required. Used air can be vented to atmosphere.
(f) These systems are having high costs.	(f) These systems are having much low costs.
(g) Motion accuracy is great. Hence used in CNC/VMC machine for tool movements.	(g) Due to uncontrolled expansion of air, motion accuracy is not good. Hence used in clamping like operations.
(h) Since hydraulic oil heats during the operations there is possibility of fire hazards.	(h) No fire hazards. Air is fire proof.
(i) Maintenance cost is high.	(i) Maintenance cost is low.
(j) Due to leakage of oil the overall system and space near by is not clean.	(j) Clean system.

2. Compare Single Acting and Double Acting Compressors

Single Acting Compressors	Double Acting Compressors
(a) Used for small capacities only.	(a) Used for large capacities.
(b) Compressed air delivery is in one stroke only.	(b) For same speed and cylinder volume air delivery is double.
(c) More compact and less costly.	(c) Cost is more.
(d) They are normally air cooled.	(d) For big size they are water cooled.
(e) Use for light duty work.	(e) Used for heavy duty work.
(f) Limited applications.	(f) Most widely used compressor.

3. Compare Gear Pump and Vane Pump used in Hydraulic Systems [S-15]

Gear Pump	Vane Pump
(a) Types are: → External Gear Pump → Internal Gear Pump	(a) Types are: → Unbalanced Vane Pump → Balanced Vane Pump
(b) Gears are used for pressurising the oil.	(b) Sliding vanes are used in this pump and due to centrifugal force they fly away from centre and create space for pressuring the oil.
(c) Gear pumps are used when pressure requirement is between 350 to 300 bar.	(c) Vane pumps are adopted when pressure requirement is between 125 to 175 bar.
(d) Noisy operation	(d) Less noise
(e) Less expensive	(e) Cost is slightly higher

4. Compare Seat type and Spool type DC valves

Seat type	Spool type
(a) Valve element rests on specially machined finished seat. This element is ball/cone.	(a) The valve element is a spool similar to piston and piston rod. It reciprocates in finely finished bore of the valve body.
(b) The construction is complicated.	(b) The construction is simple.
(c) Valve finishing is difficult and costly.	(c) Valve spool and bore finishing is simple and less costly.
(d) Wear and tear of valve is not uniform.	(d) Wear and tear is uniform.
(e) Valve actuation possibility is limited.	(e) Actuation is easily adaptable.
(f) Rearly used valve.	(f) Most valves are spool type.

5. Compare Linear Actuators and Rotary Actuators

Linear Actuators	Rotary Actuators
(a) Linear actuators reciprocate in a cylinder.	(a) These actuators rotate about the centre.
(b) These are having linear speed measured in m/sec.	(b) These are having rotary speed measured in RPM.
(c) Used for pushing, pulling type of tasks.	(c) Used where rotary motions are required e.g. straight grinders, pistol drills.
(d) Single Acting Cylinders, Double Acting Cylinders, Tandem Cylinders are its examples.	(d) Vane motors, Gear motors, Piston motors, Air motors are some of the examples.

6. Compare Meter In Circuit and Meter Out Circuit

Meter In Circuit	Meter Out Circuit
(a) 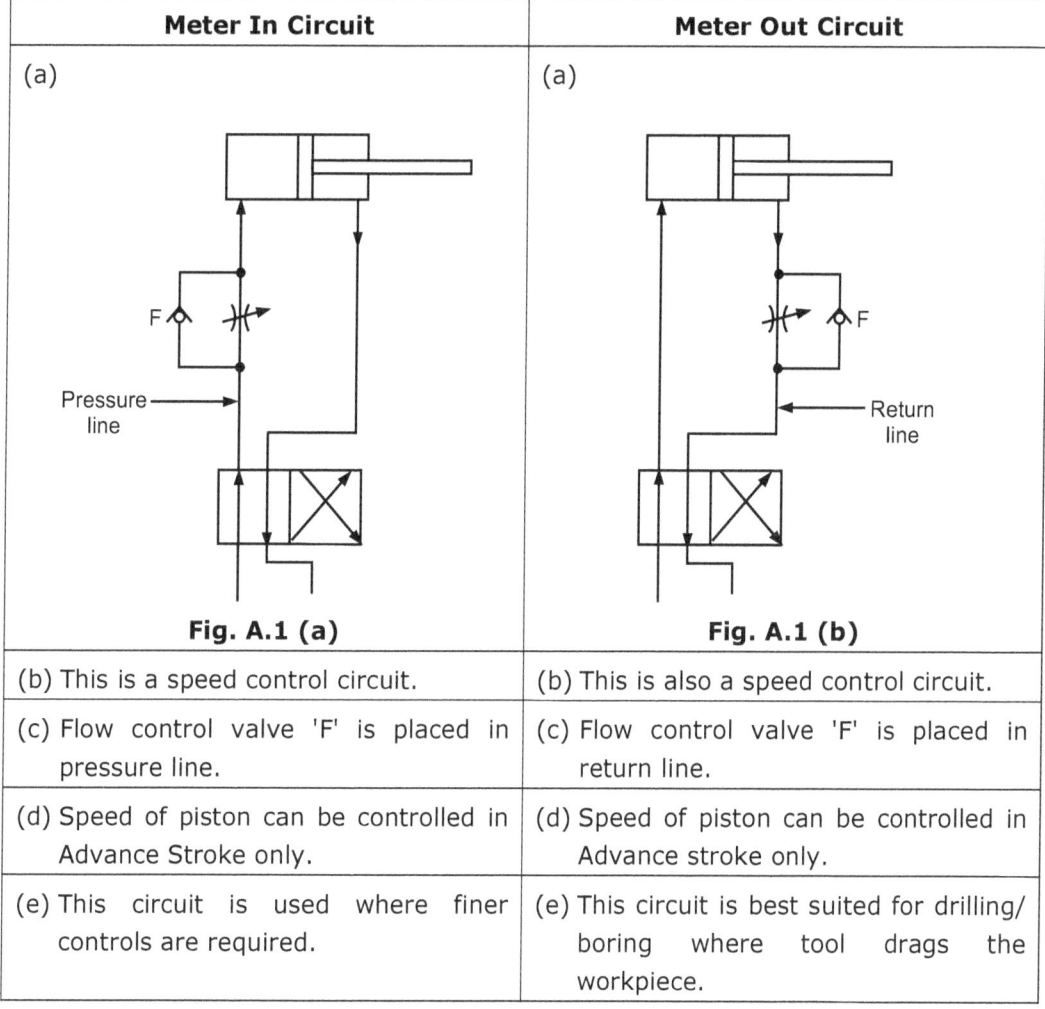 Fig. A.1 (a)	(a) Fig. A.1 (b)
(b) This is a speed control circuit.	(b) This is also a speed control circuit.
(c) Flow control valve 'F' is placed in pressure line.	(c) Flow control valve 'F' is placed in return line.
(d) Speed of piston can be controlled in Advance Stroke only.	(d) Speed of piston can be controlled in Advance stroke only.
(e) This circuit is used where finer controls are required.	(e) This circuit is best suited for drilling/ boring where tool drags the workpiece.

7. Compare Air Receiver and Oil Receiver

Air Receiver	Oil Receiver
(a) Used to store compressed air.	(a) Used to store oil which is at atmospheric pressure.
(b) Its pressure vessel is closed from both ends.	(b) It is MS fabricated box. It is not pressure vessel.
(c) Air compressor is fitted above the air receiver.	(c) Hydraulic power pack comprising of shut-off valve, pump, pressure relief valve is fitted above oil tank.
(d) It is vertical or horizontal vessel.	(d) No question of vertical or horizontal orientation.

■■■

APPENDIX B: CAUSES AND REMEDIES OF A HYDRAULIC SYSTEM AND ITS COMPONENTS

Sr. No.	Signs	Probable causes	Remedy
1.	(a) (i) Excessive noise in pump	• Cavitation in pump.	(i) Clean filters in the inlet line. (ii) Replace defective filters. (iii) Adjust drive motor to correct rpm if pump speed is too high. (iv) Check fluid temperature. If oil is too cold, warm up. (v) Suction filter too small or filter blocked corrected.
		• Air in oil	(i) Check for leakage in inlet pipe to pump-joint to be tightened to stop leakage. (ii) Pump shaft seal may be damaged. To be replaced. (iii) Bleed air from system. (iv) Oil level in reservoir may be down-top upto the specified level. (v) All return lines to be checked upto see if they are below the fluid level or not.
	(ii) Oil	• Poor suction	(i) Fluid level too low-needs topping up. (ii) Oil viscosity to high-use correct viscosity. (iii) Dirty fluid-improper filtration. (iv) Clogged filter-clean filter. (v) Foam in oil-use proper oil.

	(iii) Noisy Motor	• Coupling misaligned	(i) Correct alignment.
			(ii) Motor or coupling may be damaged and should be replaced or overhauled.
			(iii) Faulty seal-replace it.
	(iv) Noise in pressure relief valve	• Incorrect pressure	(i) Install pressure gauge and adjust valve setting.
		• Valve vibrates due to worn out seat or dirt on valve seat.	(i) Replace valve/clean valve.
			(ii) Valve setting to be checked and corrected.
	(b) (i) Excessive heat in pump	• Pump may generate heat due to cavitation	Check inlet pipe and oil level in tank.
		• Excessive air in fluid medium or improper fluid used.	Maintain the oil level.
		• Too high setting of relief valve.	Set relief valve to desired value or pressure.
		• Damaged pump.	Replace damaged pump.
		• Heat in pressure relief valve generated due to incorrect valve setting.	Set the valve correctly.
		• Valve seat may be worn out or dirt on valve seat.	Check up the physical condition of the valve and replace if needed.
		• The electric motor of the pump may get heated due to too high pressure relief valve setting.	Set the Pressure relief valve correctly.
		• Damaged motor	Replace damaged motor or repair.

	(ii) Excessive heat in oil.	• Reservoir may get heated due to system operates at higher pressure for which the system is not designed.	Check up system pressure and correct it to designed value.
		• Incompatible oil used.	Check up oil viscosity and replace oil is needed.
		• Inadequate or faulty cooling system used.	Inspect the cooling system and set right if found faulty.
		• Defective hydraulic components like pump, cylinder etc.	Replace defective components or repair.
		• Wrong pipe layout	Use proper pipe layout.
		• Wrong setting of pressure relief or unloading valves.	Set the valve to appropriate value.
		• Faulty choice of oil viscosity.	Check the oil viscosity and replace oil if required.
		• High ambient temperature.	Arrange proper protection from ambient atmosphere.
	(c) Faulty System operation	• Faulty system operation may create problem in the hydraulic system due to:	
		• No flow or pressure	Check-up pump
		• Inoperative sequencing device and valves	Check limit switches and their locations.
		• Worn-out or damaged motor, cylinder etc.	Check-up motor and replace.
		• Mechanical fault like shock	Take appropriate action for remedy.

	(d) Incorrect pressure	• No pressure	(i) Check-up pump and drive motor rotation and correct the same. (ii) Check relief valve setting. (iii) Check filter for clogging.
		• Low pressure due to:	
		• Operating pressure set to low	Set the desired pressure.
		• Pressure relief valve (PRV) seat may be dirty or damaged.	Check-up and clean the valve.
		• Mechanical damage to PRV	Replace PRV if damaged or replace spring of same specification.
		• Too much internal leakage in valve	Inspect the system and identify the cause of leakage e.g. seal failure etc. and take corrective action.
		• Excessive Pressure due to wrong setting of pressure relief or unloading valve.	Set the valves correctly.
		• Fluctuating pressure.	
		• Air trapped in oil.	Air to be bled-off from system.
		• Oil is contaminated.	Source of contamination to be detected and stopped.
		• Defective or damaged accumulator.	To be replaced or corrected.
		• Old or damaged PRV	Needs change.
		• Piston gets sticky.	Release piston, check cylinder for easy of movement.

	(e) Incorrect flow	• Excessive flow due to	
		• Too high setting of flow control valve.	Correct the flow control valve setting.
		• Pump/motor rpm too high	Check the motor rpm and correct it.
		• Wrong selection of pump flow rate and size	Check up-pump.
		• Insufficient flow.	
		• Low rpm of pump/motor	Correct the motor rpm
		• Pressure relief and unloading value set wrongly	Correctly
		• No flow	
		• No flow to pump due to wrong direction of rotation motor.	Set the motor for correct rotation
		• Direction control valve set in wrong position	Check the DC valve correct if found wrong.
		• Full flow passing through PRV	Set PRV correctly
		• Pump suction and delivery port wrongly connected	Connect the pump correctly.
		• Excessive leakage in the system.	Check the leakage points and set right.
	(f) Aeration of hydraulic system	• Foaming of fluid	
		• Pump inlet line permits entry of air.	Stop entry of air either through suction line or due to other reasons.
		• Fluid level in tank is insufficient.	Check the fluid level.
		• Defective shaft seal	Change the shaft seal.

		• Wrong oil.	Check for correct oil and replace.
		• Cooling system insufficient or inoperative.	Improve cooling efficiency.
		• Coolant temperature too high.	Check the coolant and take appropriate measure.
		• Ambient temperature too high.	Protect the system from poor ambient condition.
		• Thermostat set too high.	Set the thermo set correctly.
	(g) Slow movement	• Low flow	Check-up pump.
		• Damaged drive units	Repair/replace cylinder/motors.
	(h) Excessive fast motion	• Higher flow control valve due to wrong setting.	Set it right.
	(i) Erratic movement	• Pressure fluctuates erratically.	Check PRV, accumulator or oil condition.
		• Worn out or damaged driving unit.	Repair/replace cylinder or motor.
		• Air entrains hydraulic oil.	Top up oil.
	(j) No pump delivery	• Pump rotation may be wrong.	Should be corrected.
		• Oil may be of higher viscosity.	Use correct viscosity oil.
		• Pressure relief valve stuck open.	PRV may be cleaned and assembled.
		• Oil level in hydraulic reservoir may be too low.	Top up oil.
		• Air leak in inlet pipe.	Stop leakage by tightening all connections.
		• Mechanical trouble in coupling.	Coupling to be adjusted.

	(k) Pump wear too high	• In case of vane pumps, vanes stuck in vane slots.	Vanes/slots may be cleaned of dirt, metal silvers or debris etc.
		• Excessive pressure	Check relief valve setting.
		• Coupling misaligned.	Correct alignment.
		• Abrasive material present in oil.	Filter to be checked.
		• Improper oil viscosity.	Oil condition to be inspected. Use correct viscosity oil.
		• Excessive pressure	Check pressure relief valve setting and sets if correct
	(l) Pump pressure build up is low	• Internal leakage in pump	Identify the source of leakage and stop leakage.
		• Complete loss of flow.	May be PRV stuck open pipeline inlet and return line damaged.
2.	(a) Pressure control valve not functioning correctly	• Sequence valve develops back pressure.	Clean and flush valve.
		• Drain line blocked	
		• Valve spool sticky.	Check for oil cleanliness.
		• Valve spring damaged.	Remove/replace spring.
		• Sticky spool	Clean spool/check oil.
		• Valve Orifice blocked.	Clear blockage in orifice and maintain contamination level.
		• In seat type of valve, seat and valve cone does not match.	Check and replace.

(b) Flow control affected	• Broken spring.	Replace
	• Throttle blocked inside valve body.	Clear bore, throttle screw.
	• Mismatch between valve and valve seating.	Correct it.
	• Broken/damaged check valve.	Replace.
	• Excessive internal leakage.	Look for source of leakage, rise in temperature and oil condition.
	• Throttle drain blocked.	Clear it for correct.
	• Differential spool sticky.	Clean spool and spool bore.
(c) Accumulator leaks	• Leakage through bladder.	Replace bladder.
	• Gas valve or oil valve leaks.	Tighten condition, replace faulty valve.
	• Bladder charged, brittle or porous.	High pressure ratio resulting in high temperature and failure of material.
(d) DC valves do not properly functioning	• Valve vibrates	Solenoid may be defective.
	• Defective valve	Valve worn out, correct pilot pressure and check-up flow rate.
	• Improper flow rate through valve.	Incorrect port size selected or ports got blocked.
	• Spool sticky	Spool to be cleaned.
	• Solenoid fails to response	First check if indicating light works or not. Check then manually pushing the spool whether it moves or not ...
	• Presence of excessive back pressure in the valve lines.	Clear any restriction to the return line.
	• Mechanical failure of valve	Check-up if actuating spring, push button/pin etc. are broken or damaged and replace, if found faulty.

	(e) Cylinder malfunctions		
	(i) Noise Cylinder	• Faulty alignment, losse or inadequate mounting, piping vibrations etc.	Re-align, tighten mounting bolts, use adequate pipe clamps.
		• Load fluctuations too much.	Check loading patterns and take corrective action.
	(ii) Cylinder produces jerky irregular and motion during movement.	• Heavy load and slow speed, misaligned mechanical slides, wrong assembly of piston packing, air in system etc.	Take appropriate action like appropriate slide lubrication, proper alignment, proper and adequate tightening of packings etc.
	(iii) Mechanical failure of cylinder	• Seized piston rod, excessive rod wear broken linkages, misalignment etc.	Cylinder bore and piston clearances may be checked.
	(iv) Incorrect speed of cylinder	• Incorrect flow control setting	Reset flow control valve.
		• Low pump capacity	Replace with proper pump. Use correct motor rpm.
	(f) Pipes, hoses and fittings		
	(i) Leakage through the line fittings	• Faulty fittings	Check-up each fitting and replace faulty one.
		• Mismatch of threads	Straight male thread put into female tapered thread.
		• Threads damaged due to over tightening.	Use appropriate tightening only.
		• Pipe fittings loosened due to vibration.	Use adequate clamps and clamp tightening.
		• Damaged seals	Replace it
	(ii) Excessive pressure drop in hose	• Wrong size of hose	Check and replace.
	(iii) Hose tube cracked	• Excessive heat	Protect the hose and check fluid temperature.
	(iv) Hose bursts	• High frequency pressure surge	Use correct hose with spiral reinforced hose.

	(v) Tube of hose badly deteriorated	• Tube or hose material may be incompatible with oil or environment.	Check compatibility of oil with tube/hose materials.
	(g) Seal failure	• Excessive heat	Check operating and surrounding temperature.
	(i) Seal cracked	• Age hardening of seal • Seal exposed to heat • Abrasion of seal	Avoid long idle periods of system. Check operating temperature. Mating surfaces rough.
	(ii) Scoring of seals	• Poor machining of bore, Axial displacement of seal undersize bore.	Avoid sharp edges and use recommend finish.
	(h) Filter		
	(i) Excessive pressure drop takes place across filter.	• Filter element is clogged.	Replace the filter element.

■■■

APPENDIX C : CAUSES AND REMEDIES OF A PNEUMATIC SYSTEM AND ITS COMPONENTS

Sr. No.	Signs	Probable causes	Remedy
1.	**Air Receiver (Air Tank)**		
	(a) Pressure not Building in Air Receiver	• Leakage in Air Receiver body.	Check whether there is puncture in the body of Air Receiver. Repair it.
		• Leakage in the pipe going from compressor to Air Receiver.	Check the pipe and replace the pipe if the leakage is serious.
		• Problem with Air Compressor	Check various causes of not supplying pressurised air to Air Receiver and rectify it.
		• Leakages in the fitment of Pressure Gauge or other fittings.	Tight the fittings.
	Air Compressor		
	Compressor not starting	• Check electrical connections with the motor.	1. Repair it. 2. Electric Motor not working : Find our whether it is burned. Replace the winding or replace the motor. 3. Check bearing of motor : If faulty replace it. 4. Check whether 'V' belts over pullies are loose – Tighten. 5. Voltage may be very high or very low, check it.

	Compressor started but not delivery compressed air.	• Suction filter may be clogged. • Defective sealing. • Broken piston rings. • Valve leakage. • Intercooler leakage	1. Check whether suction filter are clogged – clean it or replace the filter element. 2. Defective sealing of cylinder head – Mount fresh sealing on cylinder head. 3. Broken piston rings – Replace it. 4. Valves of compressor leaking – Check whether spring of valve is broken – replace it. 5. Leakage in intercoolers – Check it and repair it.
FRL Unit			
	Filter not working	• Clogged filter.	Check filter, Replace filter element.
	Regulator not showing correct pressure	• Setting may be disturbed or faulty pressure gauge.	Set the pressure once again. If pressure gauge faulty replace it.
		• Main spring or dampening spring trouble.	Check the springs, if broken replace it.
	Lubricator not working.	• No oil in lubricator.	Maintain correct level of lubricator.
		• Lubricator plastic bowl may be leaking.	Check bowl is cracked. Replace it.
		• Oil compatibility	Check the viscosity of the oil and find whether the oil is compatible.
		• Jet problem	Clean the jet of lubricator.

Pipe Lines and Connections

High leakage of air through pipes	• Pipe broken/Loose joints.	Check pipes. Remove broken pieces and replace it. Tight the joints.
	• Blockage of pipes.	Remove blockage.
	• Wrong connection of hoses.	Properly connect the hoses.
Resistance to air flow	• Problem with pipe diameters/fittings.	Keep the pipes of pilot valves small in diameter but use higher diameter main pipes.
		Keep the pipes as short and as straight as possible.
		Reduce number of fittings to the pipe.

Valves

DC valve not working.	• Problem with operating system/ blockage/construction of DC valve.	Solenoid system for valve operation is working on electrical signal, check the signal and repair.
		Clear the blockages in ports of DC valve.
		Spring on spool might be broken, replace it.
		Spool may be broken – replace it.
		If DC valve is seat type, seat may be wearied off – repair the seat.

Flow control valve giving resistance to flow. Hence no proper speed control.	• Problem with operating system/ blockage/ construction of flow control valve	Flow adjustment knob is unnecessarily tightened – Set it correctly.
		Blockage is in the passage of air through valve.
		Built-in check valve is not properly in working – Check it and repair it.

■■■

MSBTE Question Paper Solutions

Winter 2014

1.(A) Attempt any THREE: [12]
  (a) Define the following terms and state their S.I. unit.
  (i) Specific weight.
Ans. Refer Section 1.1.4.
  (ii) Viscosity.
Ans. Refer Section 1.1.6.
  (b) Write the classification of control valves.
Ans. Refer Section 5.4.
  (c) Explain construction and working of sliding spool type 4/3 direction control valve.
Ans. Refer Section 5.4.5.
  (d) State the functions of flexible hoses and gaskets.
Ans. Refer Section 6.2.2.

(B) Attempt any ONE: [6]
  (a) Define all hydraulic coefficients. Derive relation between the hydraulic coefficients.
Ans. Refer Section 2.3.2.
  (b) State the types of hydraulic actuators. Describe construction and working of single acting cylinder with neat sketch.
Ans. Refer Section 7.1.5.

2. Attempt any FOUR: [16]
  (a) Define laminar and turbulent type fluid flow. State one example of each.
Ans. Refer Section 1.1.18.3.
  (b) What factors will you consider while selecting a centrifugal pump?
Ans. Refer Section 3.1.14.
  (c) State the possible causes and remedies for following faults in centrifugal pumps.
  (i) Failure to deliver water.
Ans. Refer Section 3.1.15.
  (ii) Produces noise.
Ans. Refer Section 3.1.15.
  (d) Draw a labelled diagram of swash plate type pump.
Ans. Refer Section 4.2.13.
  (e) Describe with neat sketch working of hydraulic ram.
Ans. Refer Section 4.1.2.

3. Attempt any FOUR: [16]
  (a) Compare gear pump and vane pump on the basis of:
  (i) Construction.
Ans. Refer – Appendix 3, Page A-2.
  (ii) Pressure.
Ans. Refer - Appendix 3, Page A-2.

Hydraulics and Pneumatics   P.2   MSBTE Question Paper Solutions

  (iii) Speed.

Ans. Refer - Appendix 3, Page A-2.

  (iv) Applications.

Ans. Refer - Appendix 3, Page A-2.

  (b) Write the construction and working of piston type air motor with neat sketch.

Ans. Refer Section 5.2.4.

  (c) Draw labelled sketch of sequence valve and describe its working.

Ans. Refer Section 5.4.16.

  (d) State two applications and two materials of seals used in hydraulic systems.

Ans. Refer Section 6.3.

  (e) Why FRL unit is used in pneumatic system? State the functions of each component of FRL unit.

Ans. Refer Section 6.1.7

4.(A) Attempt any THREE: **[12]**

  (a) Describe the working of hydraulic lift with neat sketch.

Ans. Refer Section 4.1.3.

  (b) Explain working of gear type hydraulic motor with neat sketch.

Ans. Refer Section 5.3.1.

  (c) Draw a neat sketch of proportional flow type filter and describe its working.

Ans. Refer Section 6.1.3.

  (d) Draw a neat sketch of meter-in hydraulic circuit.

Ans. Refer Section 7.2.1 (Circuit No. 1).

(B) Attempt any ONE: **[6]**

  (a) Draw and explain pneumatic circuit to control the speed of double acting cylinder.

Ans. Refer Section 7.3.2.

(b) (i) identify the following circuit in Fig. 1.

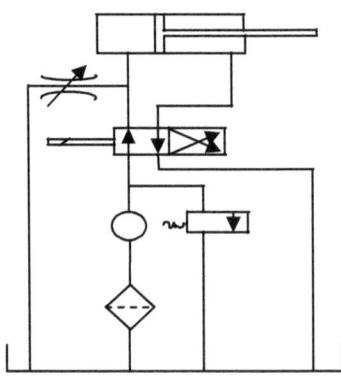

Fig. 1

Ans. Refer Section 7.2.3.

(ii) Label it and explain its working.
Ans. Refer Section 7.2.3.
(iii) State its applications.
Ans. Refer Section 7.2.3.

5. Attempt any TWO: [16]
(a) State Bernoulli's theorem. Explain orifice meter with neat sketch.
Ans. Refer Sections 2.2 and 2.2.3.
(c) Explain hydraulic power steering with neat labelled sketch.
Ans. Refer Sections 7.2.6.

6. Attempt any TWO: [16]
(a) Explain Bourden tube pressure gauge with figure and state its applications.
Ans. Refer Section 1.2.16.
(b) Draw a labelled sketch of double acting reciprocating pump and describe its construction and working.
Ans. Refer Section 3.2.3.
(c) Construct the pneumatic circuit using sequence valve to control two operations performed in a proper sequence and describe its working.
Ans. Refer Section 7.3.4 (Circuit No. 4).

■■■

Summer 2015

1.(A) Attempt any THREE of the following: [12]
(a) Define viscosity and specific gravity alongwith their unit.
Ans. Refer Sections 1.1.3 and 1.1.6.
(b) State two locations each, where seals and gaskets are used in hydraulic system.
Ans. Refer Section 6.3.
(c) Give classification of hydraulic actuators.
Ans. Refer Section 7.2.
(d) Write the function of flexible hoses, filters, lubricators and gaskets.
Ans. Refer Sections 6.2.2 / 6.1.1 / 6.1.10.

B) Attempt any ONE of the following: [6]
(a) Describe meaning and relation between atmospheric gauge and vacuum pressure.
Ans. Refer Sections 1.2.1 and 1.2.2.
(b) Write construction and working of non-return valve with neat sketch.
Ans. Refer Section 5.4.10.

2. Attempt any FOUR of the following: [16]
(a) Define Bernoulli's theorem and give its applications.
Ans. Refer Sections 2.2 and 2.2.1.
(b) The two faults in centrifugal pumps are; fails to start pumping and low efficiency; write two causes and two remedies of each.
Ans. Refer Section 3.1.15.

(c) How priming in centrifugal pump is done? Why it is done?
Ans. Refer Section 3.1.12.
(d) Compare the characteristics of vane and swash plate type pump and give one application for each pump.
Ans. Refer Sections 4.2.13, 4.2.5, 4.2.16.
(e) Explain construction and working of Hydraulic Ram.
Ans. Refer Section 4.1.2.

3. Attempt any FOUR of the following: [16]
(a) Draw labelled sketch of swash plate pump.
Ans. Refer Section 4.2.13.
(b) Explain construction and working of 4/2 DC valve which is used in hydraulic system.
Ans. Refer Section 5.4.4.
(c) Give classification of valves.
Ans. Refer Section 5.4.
(d) Explain full flow hydraulic filter with neat sketch.
Ans. Refer Section 6.1.2.
(e) Explain working of the FRL unit with neat sketch.
Ans. Refer Section 6.1.7.

4.(A) Attempt any THREE of the following: [12]
(a) What is Pascal's law? State its applications.
Ans. Refer Section 1.1.19.
(b) Explain construction and working of piston type air motor.
Ans. Refer Section 5.2.4.
(c) Draw neat sketch of proportional type of filter and write its construction and working with principle.
Ans. Refer Section 6.1.3.
(d) Draw general layout of pneumatic system and label the components.
Ans. Refer Sections 7.1.9 and 7.1.10.

(B) Attempt any ONE of the following: [6]
(a) Draw layout of hydraulic steering system. Explain its working.
Ans. Refer Section 7.2.6.
(b) Compare hydraulic and pneumatic circuit on the basis of – fluid used, ease of operation, noise, speed, cost, application.
Ans. Refer Section 7.1.11.

5. Attempt any TWO of the following: [16]
(a) Derive an expression of discharge through orifice meter.
Ans. Refer Section 2.2.3.
(b) What is negative slip in reciprocating pump and why air vessel is used in the pump?
Ans. Refer Section 3.2.5.
(c) Draw meter-in circuit and explain its working.
Ans. Refer Section 7.2.1 (Circuit No. 1).

6. Attempt any TWO of the following: [16]

(a) A oil of specific gravity 0.8 is flowing through horizontal venturimeter having inlet diameter 30 cm and throat diameter is 15 cm. The differential manometer shows reading of 30 cm of mercury. Calculate discharge of oil through venturimeter if $C_d = 0.98$.

Ans. Refer Solved Problem No. 1 (Chapter 2).

(b) Explain construction and working of centrifugal pump with neat sketch. Give its two applications.

Ans. Refer Section 3.1.1.

(c) Draw neat labelled layout of hydraulic braking system and explain its working.

Ans. Refer Section 7.3.6.

■■■

www.ingramcontent.com/pod-product-compliance
Lightning Source LLC
Chambersburg PA
CBHW080424230426
43662CB00015B/2211